The Dark Shadows Event Diary: Memories of Festivals, Film Screenings, and Fan Gatherings

Amanda Desiree

Published by Amanda Desiree, 2024.

THE DARK SHADOWS EVENT DIARY: MEMORIES OF FESTIVALS, FILM SCREENINGS, AND FAN GATHERINGS

First edition. August 19, 2024.

Copyright © 2024 Amanda Desiree.

ISBN: 979-8227408938

Written by Amanda Desiree.

Please be advised that the following reports contain plot details about the *Dark Shadows* series in its entirety, which could generally be perceived as "spoilers."

Table of Contents

*

Introduction

I attended my first Dark Shadows Festival[1] in July 2000, and for weeks afterward, I could not shut up about it.

I had started watching the show two years earlier, in my Freshman year of high school, during one of its runs on the Sci-Fi Channel. I tuned in just after Barnabas had dispatched Jason McGuire and Maggie had escaped from Windcliff. Gradually, I became more and more fascinated until, by the time the show shifted to 1795, I was hooked. However, I didn't personally know anyone else who liked *Dark Shadows,* so I couldn't discuss the series or share my enthusiasm with people who would be receptive to it.

Hence, when my mother told me in early spring of 2000 that there would be a convention at the LAX Marriott near to where we lived, I was elated. I'd finally get to meet other fans face-to-face! I would also get to meet the actors I'd been watching for so long. The three-day event moved like a dream. I was starstruck by glimpsing familiar people like John Karlen and David Selby, and even people like Chris Pennock, whom I hadn't yet seen on *Dark Shadows,* but whom I recognized from behind-the-scenes video interviews. Marie Wallace and John Karlen were particularly friendly when I finally spoke with them after reaching the front of the lengthy autograph line. My mother and I had stood for several hours awaiting our turn. I read *Catcher in the Rye,* assigned summer reading, while we slowly edged toward the tables where the actors were seated. I couldn't stand that book, yet I've always had fond memories of it because I've associated it with that first Festival.

Even better than meeting the actors was the chance to be around real, live DS fans. Though I was too shy to engage anyone in conversation—after all, why would anyone want to chat with a dumb kid like me?—I eavesdropped on questions over particular storylines, complaints about certain performances, and jokes about favorite bloopers. These people were saying the same things I had been thinking while watching the show. Our shared culture was also evident in the ballroom, where fan-made videos setting scenes from the show to relevant pop music or filmed skits of fans acting out their own interpretations of the show played, and on stage where the Collinsport Players, the amateur acting troupe, presented "The Spy Who Bit Me, featuring Austin Powers, Jeb, Carolyn, Julia, Adam, and many, many inside jokes. When Louis Edmonds took the stage during Saturday's cast reunion (in what turned out to be his final Festival appearance, I felt compelled to stand and applaud—and saw everyone around me doing the same thing. We were in tune with one another!

When my father came to pick us up from the hotel each night, I would repeat back to him all the stories the actors had told during their question and answer sessions. Over the following weeks, when relatives would ask how my summer was going, I'd rehash for them what my experience at the Festival had been like. Even when I tried out for a game show the week after the Festival, when each potential contestant had to say something interesting about themselves, I proudly announced that I had just attended my first Dark Shadows Festival. What could be more exciting than that?

I'd had so much fun that I begged my parents to take me to New York for the 2001 Festival; I couldn't wait two more years for my next fix.[2] They finally agreed. It became a family vacation with trips to Rockefeller Center, Little Italy, and Chinatown, as well as the 2 1/2 days spent parked in the ballroom of the World Trade Center Marriott. It was a vacation that would take on sepia tones the following month after the World Trade Center and the adjacent hotel were destroyed.

This time, when I came back from the Festival, I didn't want to just talk about the convention. I wanted to do something else to preserve it. So, shortly upon returning home, I started typing up my memories of everything that had happened: what the actors had said and done, what videos we had watched, what performances have been in the fan Costume Gala. I shared my report on the various Internet mailing lists and message boards to which I belonged. Back then, Yahoo had a number of very active lists, including Dark Shadows and Barnabas_Quentin. Hotmail had themed message boards, including several for Dark Shadows. Sci-Fi Channel had its own dedicated message boards where people discussed the daily episodes and shared fan fiction. Some individual fans also ran their own message boards from private sites. To my surprise, people from these various forums responded favorably to my report. Those who had also attended the convention thanked me for jogging their own memories or for filling in blanks where they had missed an event, and those who were unable to go at all said that my writing made them feel as if they were actually there. It was very rewarding feedback.

And that's how the tradition of the "Fest Report" was born. For years afterward, within a few days of my return home, I would write a recap from memory of what I had experienced at each Festival. After a couple of years, I started to bring a handheld tape recorder with me to get my memories down while they were as fresh as possible.

I attended the Dark Shadows Festival in 2001, 2002, 2003, 2004, 2005, 2006, 2008, 2009, 2010, 2011, and 2016, and the more truncated gatherings in 2012 and 2014. I also attended other special events, some sponsored by the Dark Shadows Festival and some not, including the COLLINS Association's Halloweenanthon in 2002, the Dark Shadows Halloween at the Vista Theatre in 2006, the Dark Shadows Island Weekend in San Diego in 2013, and the Friends of the 1991 Dark Shadows Cast Reunion in 2013. Because I lived in the LA area, I was also positioned to sometimes see DS cast members in other venues. Christopher Pennock and David Selby regularly performed live theater within the greater Los Angeles area. Lara Parker, who developed a subsequent career as an author, occasionally held book signings in local stores, libraries, and even at the Los Angeles Times Festival of Books. Whenever I attended an event, I wrote something about it.

As time passed and I transitioned from being a student with summers free to being an adult in the workforce full-time, I had less opportunity to write the detailed reports for which I had originally been known. Also, as the Festivals introduced more video programming in place of live appearances, I had less to say about the conventions. Finally, as other attendees began to share their own event reports, my write-ups felt redundant. I went into semi-retirement, writing shorter and more general summaries of the events. (When reviewing my reports for this book, I was greatly surprised to find that I didn't write a report of the 2010 Festival in Burbank at all).[3]

The last time a traditional, multiday gathering with *Dark Shadows* cast and crew in attendance and fan participation took place was in 2016. But we fans hold out constant hope for another Festival someday. That hope grows fainter as time passes. Just within the past four years, several stalwart attendees have passed away: Diana Millay, Robert Rodan, Chris Pennock, Robert Cobert, John Karlen, and most recently, Lara Parker. We also lost two of our most dedicated Festival volunteers: Ann Wilson and Marcy Robin.

From time to time, I'll reminisce with my long-term friends about the old days—the anticipation that would build throughout the year until the summer, and the exciting times (and occasional side trips we took) when we were able to get together at the Festival again. I also talk with my newer friends, who either only recently discovered DS and didn't know about the Festivals or couldn't travel to them when they were still regularly ongoing. They lament all that they missed, including the favorite actors they didn't get to meet. To fill the nostalgia for what once was and the void for what never was, I have decided to collect and share all of my Dark Shadows event reports from over a 20-year period.

Unfortunately, many of the sites where I used to post no longer exist. Sci-Fi Channel eventually took down its boards after discontinuing *Dark Shadows* in late 2003. The Yahoo lists completely folded in 2019. Other fan-run boards disappeared as the host sites went out of business. (They say that whatever you put on the Internet will be there forever, but somehow that doesn't seem to apply to things you actually want to save). Luckily, one site has withstood the test of time. The Dark Shadows Forums (www.dsboards.com[1]) has existed in its current form since February 2002. This is an incomparable treasure trove of information and fan discussion, a time capsule of what was happening in DS fandom at any particular point in time. I was able to retrieve nearly all of my original reports from the Dark Shadows Forums site. I offer my deepest gratitude to Midnite and Mysterious Benefactor for keeping the flame burning all these years.

I also thank Walter Ian Kaye for helping me rescue my 2001 Fest Report from the void of Facebook where I had reposted it after the Yahoo lists shut down.

1.　　http://www.dsboards.com

Allow me to stress that these reports were written from my memory, sometimes several days after the fact. Memory is fallible. If you were to watch a video of one of the conventions and compare it to my report, the dialogue wouldn't match exactly. Questions wouldn't necessarily follow one another in the precise order that I listed. A question that I reported was asked at the cast reunion panel might actually have come up during an actor's one-on-one Q&A at a different time during that weekend. I never intended my reports to be a complete, historic record of everything that was actually said, word for word, and done, gesture for gesture, and I have never pretended that this was the case. When posting online, I always prefaced each report with a disclaimer that my account might not be entirely correct and I invited other fans to redress any errors or add their own details. Nevertheless, I made a sincere effort to capture the substance and cadence of what was said and to evoke the atmosphere that I experienced. These reports were created for entertainment and should be treated as such.

The book is organized in chronological order. However, it's possible to read the reports in any order and jump around from event to event. Wherever I discuss a pertinent incident that relates to a different event occurring at another point of time, I include a footnote so the reader can locate the additional material.

For me, the creativity of the fans has always been a highlight of the Festival experience. In the Appendices of the book, I've included both the song lyrics I wrote for the fan Costume Gala events and the available videos of the Collinsport Players skits.

Within my Fest reports, I primarily refer to other fans by the handles they used on the Internet sites where I was posting. In cases where I cite an actual name, that person was either mentioned in the Fest program (*e.g.*, the cast members of the Collinsport Players) or someone publicly introduced them (*e.g.*, Marcy Robin announced a performer's name during the Costume Gala, or a fan introduced himself during a Q&A panel).

I chose not to edit my original Fest reports, except to remove references specific to internal discussion on the Dark Shadows Forums and to correct spelling or typographical errors. I wanted to preserve the original style to show how my writing evolved from my first report, written at age 17, to the present. Where pertinent, I've added footnotes to correct or expand on certain details and to cross-reference other reports.

Revisiting the various *Dark Shadows* events by rereading my old reports has been very fulfilling. It's allowed me to vicariously revisit old friends and to hear again from the actors and personnel who are no longer with us. I hope that readers will also find my reports to be entertaining and informative. I hope they will come away with a sense of what the conventions used to be like.

Who knows? Perhaps these memoirs can also serve as a guide to launch a new event in the future.

2001 Dark Shadows Festival (New York City, NY)

Day 1: Friday, August 17, 2001

Richard Halpern (a member of the Collinsport Players thespian group that does skits every year, and the grown-up in the 'Baby Dark Shadows' fan videos) was the emcee this year, a very funny and lively man whom I think did a wonderful job throughout the weekend. After making the greetings, repeating that Donna McKechnie and Nancy Barrett couldn't attend, and announcing that James Storm had an emergency at home in California and Lisa Richards was doing a play so neither of them would be attending, the videos started playing.

We saw a taped interview with Alexandra Moltke. She mentioned that she had never been especially fond of her Victoria Winters character. Her reasoning was something to the effect of, "She wasn't 'stupid', but she seemed to have something missing upstairs, because these terrible things kept happening to her and she never seemed to learn her lesson. She continued to go off by herself , and of course someone would get her." Alexandra shared memories of her co-stars, mentioning that she and Nancy Barrett had been best friends. ("She was a bridesmaid at my wedding. She's a lovely person with a lovely sense of humor, and we were very close. In fact, one of the most difficult things about doing the show was when Carolyn was mean to Vicki, because then she would have to yell at me, and even though we were only acting, it still hurt.") She went on to say that Clarice Blackburn was the actress that she admired most because she was so professional and took her role so seriously. ("She would never break up during a scene; the rest of us could be rolling on the floor laughing, but she would remain calm.") She mentioned how she felt it was a shame that, talented as they were, neither Clarice nor Thayer David ever had the recognition they deserved.

When asked about her favorite blooper, she related an anecdote about filming a scene in 1795. Vicki was in prison waiting to be hanged, and Roger Davis's Peter Bradford had just received a message as to whether or not she had gotten a reprieve. Her line was, "What does it (the message) say?" He handed her the message and said, "It doesn't say anything." Alexandra admitted that she had been a little fuzzy on her lines and the message was no help because the prop woman had only scribbled on it instead of writing an actual decree. "So, he was right, it didn't say anything, and for some reason, that struck me as incredibly funny." This was after several long days of rehearsal, and the stress had finally gotten to her. "I burst out laughing and I couldn't stop. We had to stop filming and do the scene over again, which was a big no-no because it was so expensive to do. I got in trouble for that one." She also mentioned that she was good at memorizing her lines for a 24-hour period, long enough to film her scenes and move on to the next script, but "the trouble came when they made changes or deleted lines. Whenever that happened, everything would go right out of my head and I'd be lost."

After watching the interview, we saw part of "The Resurrection of Barnabas Collins" tape—the portion that had clips from and an announcer's summary of the 1966-'67 pre-Barnabas episodes. Then, we watched a tape of some of Louis Edmonds's work outside of DS. We saw an interview he had taped from the year before for Sci-Fi Channel, (it was for a documentary that never aired[4]), a clip of him from a spy movie (dubbed in Spanish) that he had made just before taking on the role of Roger Collins, an interview he had done in his Langley days on "All My Children" along with a clip of him in that role, and clips of him performing two songs (one, a blues song he had written himself, the other, "Nobody Cares About Langley") and a dance. (He had such a marvelous voice! I never realized how many talents the late Mr. Edmonds had outside of his work on DS. It was clear from the various interviews that he was a very warm, charming, and fun man—quite unlike Roger or Joshua!)

After the video segments, Kathryn Leigh Scott came out and shared her memory of the time Louis had started to change out of his costume before taping of an episode ended, not realizing that he had one more scene to do. He had to rush back downstairs and film Roger's last lines at the mantel from the waist up with nothing more than a blazer coat, shorts, socks, and a glass of 'brandy'.

Then, we had a mini-reunion. Lara Parker, John Karlen, Christopher Pennock, Marie Wallace, and Denise Nickerson came on-stage to answer questions and share their memories of Louis Edmonds. Lara Parker said that his favorite scene on the show was when he got turned into a cat (1795; Joshua.) Marie Wallace talked about how close she and Louis had grown while attending all of the Festivals and how delighted she was when he invited her to his estate, The Rookery. It was this first visit that inspired her to become a photographer (she took pictures of the flowers in his garden.) She also spoke about how much she loved his voice, even doing an imitation of it. Then, John Karlen started to talk, and he ended up changing the subject. That session got very wild. John and Christopher are really very hyper guys.

At one point, John Karlen got in a debate with a fan from the audience about which was the highest point of elevation in New York. Someone had asked about when John lived in New York during the time the show was on, and when John proudly boasted that he had been born in the area of New York's highest elevation, (I can't remember where he said it was) another fan sitting near the stage, Charles Ellis, jumped up and corrected him, claiming that the highest point of elevation was actually in Staten Island—where he had been born. John even called him up to the stage and they went back and forth about it. Charles promised to bring back proof the next day. (Incidentally, Charles was right. John told him jokingly, "I never considered Staten Island a part of New York anyway.")

One fan asked Lara if she would write a sequel to *Angelique's Descent*. She answered that she was currently working on the new book, and had a deal with Tor Books rather than with Harper Collins. Another fan asked her whether the rumors that she would either join the cast of "Passions" or "Port Charles" were true. Lara said no, they weren't true, but she had submitted a script to James Reilly for "Passions," and she would like to guest on one of the soaps if they should ask her. (Later in the weekend she said she had submitted a script to "Port Charles"; I don't know if this was a mistake on her part or if she sent scripts to both shows).

An elderly man came up to the microphone with a question for John Karlen. "I've noticed that you've gotten much bigger since your days on "Dark Shadows," not only in your career but in size too. Are you on any kind of special diet?" I was stunned and the people around me in the audience were visibly horrified, too. John handled himself very well. "No, I'm getting ready for my next role; have you ever heard of Santa Claus?" "If you're going to be Santa Claus," the man replied, "I'll be one of your elves." That was the most unkind question I've ever heard a fan ask at one of these events, and I thought it was in very bad taste. To his credit, John Karlen didn't seem to take it too badly. He spoke politely to the man, but I'm sure the comment must have stung. Later, another woman who came up to the microphone mentioned that when she was a young girl waiting outside the studio for autographs, Jonathan Frid once pointed Karlen out and said, "There goes one of our best actors!" I hope that was able to reverse some of the damage.

A little girl, about 8 years old I think, posed a very good question: "Were any of you ever jealous of the other person's part?" "You mean, jealous of all the fan mail?" Christopher Pennock asked jokingly. "Like David Selby's cart loads of letters? 'Oh, here's your fan mail, Chris,' and it's only one letter, one fan." Lara said that she wanted to be Josette and play the ingenue. "People kept coming up to me saying, 'Stop crying. You're the heavy; you're the villain.'"

Toward the end of the Q&A, a man in a hat stepped up to the mike and said, "I have a comment to make to Denise Nickerson. Do you remember a couple of years ago when one of Michael Stroka's hats was up for auction, and you were upset because I beat you to it? You asked me if you could wear the hat the next time I came to the Fest. Well, (takes off the hat) it's right here and anytime you want this weekend..." She jumped out of her seat, smiling and looking so excited. "Can I wear it right now?" The man brought the hat up to her and she mentioned that there was a scarf that had gone with it. The man's wife was also in the audience and she brought Denise the scarf. She looked so happy in that scarf and hat, and wore them for the rest of the Q&A session.

When that panel ended and people began lining up for autographs, a clip ran from "A Darkness at Blaisedon" featuring the portrait of Louis that was up for auction, followed by a montage of Louis Edmonds's DS scenes: Joshua and Barnabas, Daniel and Gabriel, Brutus, Catherine, and Bramwell, etc. Then there were a few 'media highlights.' One was some coverage of the *House of Dark Shadows* screening at the Vista Theatre last October, the other was an interview with David Selby about his book of poetry. (I'd never heard of the network that did the interview, Oasis TV.) The night closed with a screening of "horror classics." I stayed though the first transformation scene of *The Wolfman* and then called it a night and went up to my room.

Day 2: Saturday, August 18, 2001

I went down early so I could be sure to get a good seat and perhaps meet some people that I knew on-line face-to-face. Marcy Robin (Shadowgram editor) was supposed to open the day with an information panel, but she was running late because of a long-distance phone call she received just as she was on her way out, so the Fest organizers showed fan videos to pass the time until she arrived. (Unfortunately, they didn't show mine.) Two were music videos (Cyndi Lauper's "Girls Just Wanna Have Fun" featuring Carolyn Stoddard, and The Beatles' "And I Love Her" focusing on Barnabas and Josette in 1795) and one was a Baby Dark Shadows skit of Richard Halpern and the children acting out scenes from 1897. (Hilarious!)

Finally, Marcy arrived and filled everyone in on some of the more recent DS events (the Museum of Television and Radio's Paley Festival salute to DS in March[5], the *House of Dark Shadows* screening at the Vista Theatre in October) and took questions from the audience (mostly "where are they now's" about some of the more reclusive actors—*e.g.*, David Henesy, Don Briscoe, Humbert Allen Astredo.) According to her current info., Sci-Fi does plan to run "DS" into 2002, so let's all keep our fingers crossed for the best.

When her panel concluded, it was announced that we would see part of "A Darkness at Blaisedon," (to promote the portrait) but as it happened, we ended up watching the whole thing. It wasn't a bad show. Though it certainly resembled "Dark Shadows" in certain plot elements, I thought it was eerier and contained more action and thrills.

We then watched an episode of "The Dating Game." In the first round, Madeline Sherwood ("The Flying Nun") was up to select a date, and in the second round, Michael Stroka was on as one of the bachelors. He was up against singer Lou Christie ("Lightnin' Strikes") and an aspiring actor whose name I didn't catch (and who I thought was somewhat on the obnoxious side.) The girl picked Lou. I think they were to go skiing in Austria. There was also a "Dating Game" episode with Joan Bennett that we were scheduled to see, but Richard told us they didn't have it available (they did eventually show it later on.) So, we watched "What's My Line?" with Alex Stevens instead.

Soupy Sales, Carole Shelley, and Arlene Francis were among the celebrities trying to guess the various contestants' jobs. The first subject was a woman who put cherries on cupcakes as they came down the conveyor belt. (Like Lucy and the chocolates?) After her line was revealed, everyone on the celebrity panel actually got the experience of icing and cherry-ing cupcakes, as there was a special table set up just for the occasion. At this point, Richard announced that they would simply fast-forward the episode to the proper part.

All the celebrities were blindfolded as Alex Stevens came out in full werewolf make-up. First, he slipped a 'paw' around the door frame, and then stuck his head in and looked around. He went to the blackboard and wrote down his name, "Wolfman" in squiggly print. Then, he sat down and proceeded to rasp 'yes' and 'no' to the panelists' questions. ("Are you known for your work in television or the movies?" "Yes." "Do you have your own TV show?" "No." "Were you also ever in a musical?" "No." "Are you in a costume of some sort?" "Yes." "Are you Santa Claus?" "No." "Is it a scary costume?" "Yes." "Are you one of the stars of the TV show?" Brief pause—"Yes." Here, the host interjected—"I don't want to disagree too strongly with our guest, but he isn't exactly one of the major stars.") Carole Shelley caught on first. "Oh! You're one of the people on 'Dark Shadows!'" "Which one?" "Oh, oh, that Frid character!" "No." The host finally told them to take off their blindfolds and introduced Alex Stevens. After he took off his make-

up, (it took about 3 hours to get it on, and 3 minutes to get it off) we saw clips of some of his stunts. (He jumped from the roof of a very tall building and rolled out the door of a moving car.) We never did get to see the "What's My Line?" with Jonathan Frid that was advertised on the schedule.

Roger Davis came out on-stage next, and I slipped out to the dealer room, so I don't know what he talked about. When I came back, KLS[6] was up sharing anecdotes from her latest book, *Dark Shadows Memories*. She mentioned a time she went to Italy to visit her boyfriend, Ben Martin. Joel Crothers came along, and caused a stir among people on the plane. ("They thought Maggie and Joe were eloping!") She spoke warmly of Joel, mentioning what a good and valued friend he was. She also spoke about her days as a bunny in the Playboy Club, and mentioned some of the other books available through Pomegranate Press.

The charity auction followed. I don't remember prices, but I do remember some of the items: a Marilyn Ross novelization of HoDS[7]; a postcard from Alexandra Moltke to John Karlen re: the Museum of TV & Radio ("For you, John, I'll be there!") complete with "distinctive signature" and stamp; a tie belonging to Michael Stroka; a framed copy of the "Edge of Night" logo signed by the cast (also one of Michael Stroka's former belongings); a set of tapes that Marie Wallace had recorded for the blind; (I don't remember what the name of the book was) a "rare" signature from Dan Curtis; a program from the Museum of TV & Radio's Paley Festival with one page devoted to "Dark Shadows" (it sold for $30, which I thought was rather high since it didn't even have any signatures;) a copy of KLS's *My Scrapbook Memories of Dark Shadows* (now out of print); and a poster replica of the NoDS[8] portrait of Angelique. The main item, the portrait of Louis Edmonds as Nicholas Blaise, sold for $3,100. The man who bought it had also purchased the 1795 portrait of Angelique a few years before.

James Storm wasn't present as scheduled, so David Selby came up to read his poetry. The poem called "Head Shot" about the tribulations of an actor trying to get that perfect shot that doesn't exist was very amusing. During the short Q&A session that followed the reading, a young girl of about 10 years came to the microphone and confessed that she had a crush on David. He was so touched that he invited her on-stage so he could give her a kiss. When the girl came up he asked her, "Did your mother watch the show?" She replied, "Yes, when she was about my age." David laughed, spinning around the stage. "Did your *grandmother* watch the show?" Another 'Yes' and more laughter. When he had calmed down David picked the girl up and gave her a kiss on the cheek before sending her back to her seat. Then it was time for the big cast reunion.

Each star introduced the one who followed. David announced Lara Parker's arrival, she announced John Karlen, and he announced KLS. When she came up to take the mike from him, she told everyone, "I'm going to show you all how to kiss Willie Loomis!" They shared a long on-stage kiss, and then Roger Davis took the mike. He complimented the ladies on how well they looked, then it was Donna Wandrey's turn to take the stage. She called attention to John Karlen's wardrobe. "Doesn't he look nice in long pants? It's taken me years to get him out of shorts and a T-shirt. Now if only I could convince him to wear a tie..." Marie Wallace and Denise Nickerson came on-stage. (They played the Oompa loompa song from *Willy Wonka* in the background when Denise walked in.) Christopher Pennock slipped in a little later, and Diana Millay didn't show up until Sunday evening.

People started lining up at the mike for the Q&A almost immediately. I can only remember a few of the questions and comments. Someone asked Lara Parker about her new book, and she shared some of the plot points. (It picks up where *Angelique's Descent* left off with a flashback to the Salem witch trials, Miranda, and Judah Zachary. Also, David Collins will have a major role to play, and will become involved in his first romance.) She also addressed the "Passions" rumors again.

Someone else asked why the show had to end after only five years when it was so much better than other soaps that ran for twenty or thirty years. "Well," John began, "the show was all about Barnabas, and—actually it was about David Selby too—and because Barnabas was so important—and Lara, it was about Lara too. My point is that Jonathan Frid wanted—all right, the show was about Kathryn too—but he wanted to do other things—OK, Roger Davis was important too." Roger added that the writers had run out of things for Barnabas to bite and seemed to be repeating the same plot lines. Kathryn took the mike and explained that Dan Curtis had wanted to branch into other things, and that was why the show had ended when it did. While KLS was talking, John Karlen inexplicably started kissing her hand and her arm. She didn't seem to mind.

Another fan asked the panel which time period was their favorite. Lara said 1795. Marie said that she never knew what time it was. Denise answered, "Anytime I didn't have to wear those darn old clothes!"

One woman told John that she thought he was one of the most talented actors she had ever seen, and politely added that he looked well and seemed to have slimmed down since the last Fest. "No, sweetheart, it's just a longer shirt," he answered drolly.

Someone asked what a Leviathan was supposed to look like. "I didn't even know what they were," Marie said. "I just learned my lines and said them, but I never knew what was going on during the show." (She actually remembered more about the show than she pretended to, as it turned out later in the weekend.) Chris offered to draw the fan a picture if he came over to the dealer's table later on.

A fan asked David if there would be a "Falcon Crest" reunion movie in the near future. He said he wasn't aware of one. The fan then asked John if we would see a "Cagney and Lacey" reunion movie. John said we wouldn't because "Tyne Daly, Sharon Gless, and I won't fit on the screen."

A question came up about whether the cast had played tricks on one another during rehearsals or taping. Lara admitted that people would sometimes find rude notes stuffed in drawers. KLS told us that someone had once short-sheeted Maggie's bed. Roger Davis confided that Addison Powell had a hard time learning his lines so he scribbled them on little notes and posted them around the set. "I used to cover them up with my hand," he shared gleefully. John mentioned a large doll that used to find its way into various dressing rooms and every so often into one of the coffins. Roger also made an obscure reference to David Selby. "He had his pockets stuffed with Vienna sausages and cans of Spam. Every time one of us tried to ask him a question, he'd hand us some Spam or some sausages." (I'm not sure what that was all about. David didn't respond and Roger said later that he'd been kidding.) A young boy asked David Selby about his characterization of 1995 Quentin.

Finally, Richard announced that they would have to end the session. Several people were still lined up at the mike, and Roger Davis generously pointed out that one of the main reasons the fans came to the Fests was to talk to the actors and ask questions, and that they would gladly stay until everyone in line had the chance to ask their questions. "We'll stay up here all night if we have to. Would you like that?" Loud applause. Richard did some quick conferring with Jim Pierson and with the actors, and unfortunately, Roger was vetoed. I thought it was a very nice gesture on his part, though.

My family and I left to eat dinner, and when we returned, a series of clips from the 1991 DS revival series, which I never saw, was playing. (I am generally inherently opposed to remakes and sequels of any kind, but I must admit that what I saw from the clips was very impressive!) This was followed by a series of highlights (by date) from the original show: Vicki's arrival at Collinwood, Josette's ghost's first appearance, Laura and David in a climactic scene from later in the current storyline[9], Willie opening the coffin, Barnabas's arrival at Collinwood, the first color episode, and the final episode (1841 PT.) We also got to see part of the "Sci-Luv" fan documentary that the Sci-Fi Channel had prepared on DS (never yet been aired.) The portion we saw focused on a fan named Lynn who wanted her boyfriend to get a pair of fangs. This was intercut with some Freudian speculation about the allure of "the bite." Then, as we waited for the Collinsport Players to prepare for their skit, we finally were able to see Joan Bennett's "Dating Game" episode. She was very lovely and elegant as always, and I enjoyed watching the show, but it felt strange to me nevertheless. I just cannot imagine Elizabeth Collins Stoddard saying to three strange bachelors such things as, "I collect hands; describe yours to me." and "If you and I were to star in a movie together, what would it be called?" There was a little rivalry between Bachelors #1 and #3, and Bachelor #3 kept "plugging" Bachelor #1. This amused Joan for some reason, and she chose Bachelor #3. Their date was at the racetrack.

Finally, the Collinsport Players performed their skit with the aid of John Karlen, Chris Pennock, and Lara Parker. (The men both had their scripts with them, so I assume they weren't given time to rehearse, which isn't really fair.) It was a DS/Austin Powers cross-over called "The Spy Who Bit Me." You really had to be there in order to fully appreciate it. They'd performed the same skit last year, and I think it went more smoothly then, but it was still very funny and enjoyable to watch. Austin Powers (emcee Richard Halpern) was transported through time and space to a locked coffin in the Collins mausoleum, courtesy of Dr. Evil, only to be released by Willie Loomis (John Karlen.) During the course of the skit, he also encountered Carolyn, Jeb, (Christopher Pennock) Roger, Adam, Mrs. Johnson, Julia, Mrs. Evil, (Lara Parker) her daughter, (Lara's real daughter, Caitlin Hawkins) and Peter Bradford/Jeff Clark.

The skit led into the Costume Gala/talent show. There were a couple of performing Pansy Fayes, a little girl as Angelique, a Countess Nathalie DuPres, a Lady Kitty Hampshire, an Adam, a man in 1840 dress, a little boy dressed as Barnabas who gave us his best "Willie!" shout, an adult dressed as Barnabas, a man who performed the 1840 scene between Gabriel and Daniel where Gabriel reveals that he can walk (he portrayed both parts), an actor[10] from the Collinsport Players in drag as Liza Minnelli who did a stand-up about the potential DS musical and sang "Shadows of the Night" and "I Wanna Dance for You," a man who sang a song about the 1970 playroom storyline to the tune of the Mamas and the Papas' "Creeque Alley," ("And 1995 is becoming a reality") and a man in Wolfman make-up who sang a song from Chris Jennings's perspective called "Slave to the Moon" based on REM's "Man on the Moon" ("Julia have you heard about this one, a man named Charles Delaware Tate? Do you think he could paint my portrait, before it's too late? Can you believe I'm still a slave to the moon?") both of which were wonderfully clever and creative! (I'm such a sucker for song parodies!) There were original compositions, too: a song about Angelique's 1840 death and how she and Barnabas really belonged together, and another song about Angelique's days as a servant in Martinique where she summoned people to the fire to join her coven. The Gala closed with another song parody, "When You're Josette, You're Josette" to the tune of *West Side Story*'s "When You're a Jet, You're a Jet" by a woman[11] portraying Maggie Evans in her days as Barnabas's prisoner. She did a clever little monologue prior to the song during which she wrestled back and forth between her warring identities. ("I'm Maggie Evans. I like strong black coffee. I serve it to everyone I meet. In fact, I force it on them!" Then in a light French accent, "*Non*! I am Josette. I like tea and crepe suzettes!") Then, all the participants came back on stage to take a bow. I decided to call it a night and returned to my room before the screening of *House of Dark Shadows*. That was the end of Day 2.

Day 3: Sunday, August 19, 2001

I got in line bright and early again. When we were allowed inside the ballroom, we discovered that the air conditioner wasn't working. I hadn't noticed at first, but soon I saw people fanning themselves with their programs. We were told that the hotel was working on the problem and it should be fixed shortly, but alas, that wasn't to happen while I was there. Marcy Robin started the day off with another fan information panel. This time, there were more questions about story lines than about actors. Poor Marcy admitted that her cable company didn't carry Sci-Fi, but she did her best—with the help of some of the other fans—to clear up some of the famous inconsistencies.

After her panel ended, we watched the entire "Sci-Luv" program. In addition to Lynn's story, there was a feature on a blind fan named David Block (who had performed the Gabriel/Daniel one-man show the night before) who had participated in the NY Marathon with Christopher Pennock as his guide. He had been able to identify with Gabriel as a child, David explained, because children at school often picked on him just as Daniel had been cruel to Gabriel. He said he had admired Gabriel because he stood up for himself, not realizing until much later that the character had been a villain. Also featured was a woman named Vicki who had been inspired by the character Angelique to take up witchcraft. She mentioned that one of the things she appreciated about Angelique was that she described her spells in detail as she carried them out, unlike Samantha of "Bewitched," who simply twitched her nose and caused things to happen with no explanation to the audience. Between stories, fans presented memorabilia items to an appraiser on the show. A woman named Bettie had a Dark Shadows Cookbook that she had found at a church rummage sale and had autographed by members of the cast. The autographs raised the value of the book, which was not in mint condition. I don't remember what price was quoted, though I'm tempted to say $40. Another woman name Jocelyn had a Barnabas Collins game (sans plastic skull) that was appraised at around $35-50. The last person to come in for an appraisal was KLS! She had something rather unique: locks of Jonathan Frid's hair. She explained that one day, he was getting a haircut and she had collected the bits of hair that fell on the floor, joking that they would someday be a collector's item. She was hoping to someday auction the hair for charity. It was appraised at between $400-600. There was also a feature called "famous name-ous" where several men—Barnabas Collins, Barnie Collins, and one whose first name was simply Barnabas—talked about how their names had impacted their lives. Barnie Collins shared that when his daughter was growing up, she told her friends at school that her father was Barnabas Collins. "I imagine it made her popular with her classmates. They came over to the house frequently, probably to make sure I was awake during the day."

We then saw a program from the "United States Steel Hour" featuring Diana Millay and written by Sam Hall (filmed live). It was called "The Secrets of Stella Crozier." Diana portrayed Stella, a conniving boy-crazy, rich girl who manipulates everyone around her. A selection of clips featuring the dearly departed DS actors was shown next. The memorial also included a tribute to Dave Brown, a videographer and Festival regular who passed away earlier this year.

Christopher Pennock read from his latest comic book next. The topic this year was his adventures in training for and participating in the NY Marathon. I won't go into details because I don't want to spoil the plot for anyone who plans to get the comic.

Denise Nickerson came up on stage afterward, dancing to the Oompa loompa music. As no one immediately lined up for the microphone, she began sharing anecdotes from her "DS" days. Yes, she and David Henesy used to smoke in Joan Bennett's dressing room. Her Jungle Gardenia perfume was more than enough to mask the smell of the smoke, but since Joan was a smoker anyway, nobody ever guessed what the kids had been up to. She also mentioned the little restaurant that she and David H. had set up. They used to sell lunches to the cast and crew members for $5, which was a fairly high price, but their customers gladly lined up to pay it. This went on for a couple of weeks until the novelty wore off.

Soon, the questions started coming. A woman asked Denise about her website and whether she had been prepared for all the e-mail she received. Denise said that she loved getting the e-mail and thought the fan response to her website was wonderful. Another fan asked Denise if anything funny had happened to her lately. Denise grinned and said that would take too long to answer. Someone asked her to share some of her memories of working with Gene Wilder. She told us that the upcoming 30th anniversary DVD of *Willy Wonka* included interviews with the "kids" where she shared just such stories. She also mentioned that there would be a reunion of the "kids" at the Warner Bros. Store in Times Square on Monday the 27. There was a question about whether DS had already gone off the air when she started making the *Willy Wonka* movie. She answered 'no.' Someone else asked how Denise had gotten her parts (Amy, Nora, and Violet) "A lot of luck," she replied. She had been up for DS against three other girls, and had been very glad to get the part of Amy. She said she had been too busy in the past to watch the show, but her friends were fans, and were very excited. "My parents had to change our phone number every week because somebody leaked it out—" she scanned the audience with mock suspicion, "maybe it was even one of you—and people kept calling me to ask if I knew Jonathan Frid's number or David Henesy's or David Selby's." As for the part of Violet, "They didn't have anybody else in mind for the part, and as soon as I walked in, it was mine." A man asked her what it was like to be on the set of the chocolate factory. "It was amazing! It was so huge and so beautiful—you really can't get the feel of what it was like to be on the set in Germany just from watching the movie. It's a shame that the camera couldn't capture just how amazing it was."

Because of time constraints, Richard tried to get Denise off the stage, but there were still five people at the mike. "These people have been waiting patiently to ask questions. That's what they came to the Fest to do. Now, last night, Roger Davis said that we would stay up here until the last questions were asked, and that's what I'm going to do." "Yes, and the other cast members beat him up afterward for saying it," Richard joked. "Notice he's not here today." Still, Denise persisted and won out. "You'll have to ask your questions quickly though," she warned. "They're about to drag me off the stage." The questions were taken and answered, and Denise left peacefully.

Next, Darren Gross treated us to some of the lost & found NoDS footage. We saw extended scenes of the trampling of Rev. Strack, Angelique and Charles necking in the art studio, Angelique's hanging, Quentin's bedroom attack on Tracy, and footage of a seance that I don't think was originally included in the movie. There was no sound for the seance, and no color either, but it was very impressive and eerie to watch. The camera moved slowly over the faces of the characters (Quentin, Tracy, Claire, and Alex) before moving to the face of Angelique, which materialized super-imposed over the ceiling. At that point, Carlotta burst in, interrupting the seance, and ending the scene. We didn't get to see the rest of the clips that he had brought for us because by that time, the Festivities were almost an hour behind schedule.

The Collinsport Players performed another skit. This one was called, "I've Got A Secret," and it focused on Julia's attempts to discover the truth about Barnabas while trying to hide a secret of her own. There were many little jokes pertaining to the early episodes. Again, you had to be there in order to truly appreciate the skit. The charity auction followed. Among the items up for grabs this time were: a replica of Josette's music box that played music (it went for at least $170 by my recollections, despite a small loose screw at the bottom); a necktie of Louis Edmonds's from his days as Langley Wallingford; a tie clip of Michael Stroka's; another set of tapes recorded by Marie Wallace; a Christmas card from Jonathan Frid to Louis Edmonds; a set of DS viewfinder cards; an autographed photo of Alexandra Moltke; an un-used ticket from the HoDS Vista Theatre screening; a hard-back copy of *Dark Shadows Resurrected* autographed by Dan Curtis; a kinescope print of a DS episode dubbed *en espanol*, "*Sombres Tenebrosas*, the adventures of Barnabas and Julia (HOO-lia) at Collinswood."; a HoDS video; a videocassette of the John Karlen film *Daughters of Darkness*; an original DS prop, Angelique's Book of Spells, (was this from 1970PT?) in actuality a paperback version of Satan's bible with the new cover glued on; another copy of Josette's music box, though this one was only a shell and played no music.

Following the auction, Marie Wallace and Donna Wandrey took the stage ("It's the Donna and Marie Show!" joked Richard.) Marie said that though she and Donna had never worked together on DS, they had become friends through the Festivals and the other things they had in common. "We have the same agent, and we go to many of the same auditions." One of the fans brought up another similarity. "You both portrayed vampires on the show. Can you tell us a little bit about what that was like?" Donna mentioned that it was hard for her to lie still in the closed coffin. ("I kept wondering how long I could last before I kicked the lid off.) Marie answered that she wasn't a vampire for very long, and spoke about how the fangs made it impossible to speak and so the actors had to pop them in while the camera was focusing away from them.

Another fan asked Marie what her favorite role on the show was, and she answered Jenny, because that character was complex and sympathetic. ("What did she always used to say? 'My babies! My babies!'") Here, Marie demonstrated that she remembered more about the show than she claimed to. "Why was it," she asked, "that Jenny and Magda were sisters, and Magda and Sandor had thick Gypsy accents (she said this in her own version of a thick Gypsy accent) but Jenny spoke in a normal voice?" A couple of the fans reminded her that Jenny had tried to divorce herself from her Gypsy roots, but that still didn't completely explain the voice discrepancy. ("Maybe they had different mothers?" she suggested.) She also shared one of her favorite lines as Eve. "I was standing at the window watching Peter Bradford down below because I was so in love with him, and Adam said, 'Eve, get away from that window!' I told him, 'You may tell me what to do, but you may not tell me how I am to look.' Poor, Adam," she added. "All he wanted was a bride—do you remember?" Here, she stood up and stomped in place, imitating Adam's stiff walk. "'I want my mate, I want my mate'—and then when I finally showed up, I hated him on sight." Marie was really very good at her impersonations, and very funny.

One man asked Donna, "How did you feel when you were standing in the doorway to parallel time and the flames were surrounding you and cutting you off from Barnabas?" "I felt like I had better start looking for a new job," Donna answered. "Everybody told me, 'Don't worry, you'll be flitting around soon as a ghost. You'll come back somehow.' but we were talking about coming back from another time, not just coming back from the dead." Somebody asked whether the actresses had earned less money for episodes where they were simply seen and not heard. They said that they earned the same amount no matter how many lines they had, but refused to say how much they were paid.

Then, John Karlen came on-stage to do a dramatic reading, but the author of the piece he was supposed to read had left it in her room, and while she went to get it, John was left to entertain us. "How many of you are from New York?" he asked. Hands went up. "How many of you are from somewhere else? Come on, don't just raise your hand, say something." More hands went up and people shouted. "I bet you can't wait to get out of here," he joked "to get back on a plane, a boat, a train, or a car and go home." He really did have a fondness for New York though. "People in California are dead. They don't realize it, but they're dead. New York is the only place in the world where you can really feel alive. Everybody is always in such a hurry though. When you walk around New York, walk slowly." He talked about his own experiences being back in New York. "They put me in a really nice hotel room. It has a great view of the city." He talked about some of the changes made to the city. "Do you know that they have tours now that take you to places where famous mobsters were killed? Can you believe that?" He told us about one man who'd been murdered in a hotel bathroom. "Shot in the back while he was shaving...there was blood everywhere—but no Barnabas! Can you imagine it? He would have had a feast. It was in the daytime though, so he couldn't be there—but Willie was!" He also mentioned that there were many great places to eat in New York and recommended an Italian restaurant. (I think it was called Patsy's.) He went on for several minutes about his career as an opera singer (with an outrageously long name) in Italy in 1933. He kept a straight face throughout, but finally confessed that he was just joking.

John also took questions from the audience. "When are you going to take Roger Davis on the road with you?" one fan asked. "You two are hilarious together." "Honey, I'd like to take him out right now and give him a punch in the eye," he kidded. Another fan asked him if he remembered all the dream sequences on DS ("I do, I do, I do") and if he enjoyed playing Carl and Willie. That set him off another hilarious spiel about how as Willie he had to round up steers for Barnabas to feed on in the early days. ("Hundreds and hundreds of steers, thousands of steers, and he wanted more!") By this time, the woman had returned with the fan fiction, but Jim

Pierson told John that he was doing such a good job on his own that they were going to let him continue until David and Lara arrived to perform "Love Letters." He was really funny, and it was amazing to see him come up with all of that material off the top of his head! I didn't stay for the play, the autograph session, or the banquet. John Karlen's impromptu stand-up act was the last thing I saw, and it was a wonderful note on which to end the Festival.

2002 Dark Shadows Festival (Anaheim, CA)

Day 1: Friday, June 28, 2002

On Friday afternoon, before the Festival officially began, my friend mordecaigrimes and I were lucky enough to meet up with several fans both on the way to the ballroom and then in line: Teresalita, CraigSlocum, casper collins, the Ghost of Sarah Collins, VAM, JamesLady, Minja, Bobubas, Vlad, Scarlett, and others. We spent the time talking and taking pictures until the ballroom doors opened.

Friday night's Festivities opened with emcee Richard Halpern showing the famous Baby Dark Shadows videos (1897 and 1795). He also gave an update on where the young 'stars' are today: the eldest boy trades stocks, the girl recently graduated from UCLA, and the young boy recently graduated from high school. In addition, Halpern explained why some of the cast members would not be present at the Fest. Lara Parker was preparing for her son's wedding on Sunday, and Diana Millay's plane had been caught in a storm. She'd decided against catching a later flight because she had business in NY on Sunday and it made no sense to her to fly to CA for only one day.

Then, the Collinsport Players presented their first of three Disneyland-themed skits, for which Bobubas took on the role of one of the absent cast members. He acted the part of DC, who'd built a new theme park and wanted Julia Hofman (Richard Halpern) to test the attractions. The skits involved numerous sound effects from the haunted mansion and various hysterics from Julia/Halpern. Bob did a great job, as did the rest of the cast.

I stepped out while the "Sci-Luv" documentary segment was screened since I'd seen it the year before[12]. My intent was to visit the display room, but it was locked, so I instead spent some time chatting with one of the volunteers about the show and some of the other television programs of the era. (One that he mentioned, *The Prisoner*, sounded very imaginative.)[13]

I went back inside to hear Kathryn Leigh Scott present her favorite bloopers. It really wasn't as unique as the Fest schedule would lead one to believe. The "favorite bloopers" were merely excerpts from the blooper tape interspersed between KLS's reading of some humorous letters that fans had sent to her (while on the stage, she occasionally wore Minnie Mouse ears.) One letter was addressed "Dear Sirs," in which the writer complained bitterly of how he had mistakenly been sent a second copy of the *Dark Shadows Movie Book* instead of the two other books he had ordered. KLS said, "I sent him the other books and told him to keep the extra movie book." It was during this segment that some trouble began with an unsupervised fan[14]. However, Kathryn handled the situation very well, making a light joke ("I don't think he was the one I sent the wrong book to.") and continuing with her presentation. I do applaud her for successfully getting everything back on track.

The other letters involved the show's bloopers. One fan listed all of the episodes, with numbers, where cast members' underwear showed. KLS's panties appear in ep# 931, "and you're all going to watch for that one, right?" she teased. She explained that some of the underwear bloopers were due to the popular mini-skirts of the day, and demonstrated the method for measuring the skirts. "We put our hands at our sides, and wherever our fingertips began was where the hem went." KLS answered a few questions: Q:"Did all of the clothes come from Ohrbach's?" A:"Yes, except when we went back in time; then we had to rent the costumes." and Q:"Why was Josette wearing a white robe at the beginning of one episode when the robe at the end of the last episode was purple?" A:"The actors weren't the only ones who made bloopers; apparently wardrobe made some mistakes too."

John Karlen crept on-stage next, crouching behind the podium while his first scene as Willie Loomis was shown on the big screen. He then took the microphone and asked the audience for some "deep questions. We're going to solve the riddle of the sphinx here." When he didn't receive many questions, he launched into his own spiel of jokes, quoting Shakespeare and reciting lines from his favorite role in "Prometheus Bound." Somebody asked him how he got the role of Willie Loomis, and Karlen provided a rather interesting little story. He was available to take on the part because he'd just been fired from his current play. "It was the first time I'd ever been fired—except for the seven or eight other times—and I was furious because

I knew I was good in the role. The director fired me and I chased him down the street; I never caught him though." I'm sure it must have been disappointing to have lost his job, but I'll bet Johnny was as glad as we are that he was able to join "Dark Shadows" instead. I enjoyed John Karlen's talk. He wasn't as manic as in previous years because he admitted that his voice wasn't what it should have been, but he made up for that later in the weekend.

Friday night concluded with scenes from the 1991 revival series and a screening of *House of Dark Shadow*s, neither of which I stayed for. On leaving the ballroom, I met up with several Grayson Hall/Julia fans both from the Julia list on Yahoo and from dsboards: among them were Bette, Dawn, Julia99 and her friend Scott. We went to the hotel bar/cafe for a bite to eat and stayed there talking until well past one in the morning! At last, I sleepily stumbled back up to my room, little guessing what was to follow later in the weekend.

Day 2: Saturday, June 29, 2002

The first event on Saturday was a Q&A panel with Marcy Robin as to what was new with DS the show, the actors, and Dan Curtis's future plans. I missed it because I was out in the lobby chatting with friends and trying to connect people who were looking for fellow fans. I made it back to the ballroom shortly after the tribute to Louis Edmonds began. It was a lovely series of clips (the same ones that were shown last year[15]) featuring an interview with him (from Festival 2000?,) his work on "All My Children" as Langley Wallingford, and Edmonds singing an original "blues" composition and "Nobody Cares About Langley." As I've said before, it's very hard to believe that the warm, energetic, and witty man in the clips was the same one who portrayed the cold and distant Joshua and Roger Collins.

Roger Davis took the stage next and predictably began meandering from one topic to another. At least he not only realized what he was doing, but admitted his guilt. "My mother tells me I'm like one of those practice golf balls, always full of holes. She says, 'Roger, I never know what the hell you're talking about.'" Finally, he got back to his point and presented a documentary/advertisement for his oft-mentioned housing project. (Narrated, directed, and produced by himself.) When the lights dimmed, I slipped out of the room and spent the next 45 minutes talking to Midnite and casper collins in the lobby. When we determined that it was safe to go back inside, we found seats for Jeanne Avery's (aka David Henesy's mom's) discussion.

Throughout her talk, Jeanne Avery constantly denied that she'd ever pushed David into acting or that she was a "stage mom." According to her, David came home one day from the private school where his baby-sitter had unilaterally enrolled him while his mother was working out of town ("And who do you suppose got stuck paying for the tuition?") and informed his mother that, "He was going to be on Broadway and that I had to call the stage manager. I said, 'That's nice, dear.' Of course I had no intention of calling any stage manager." She thought that young David was merely imagining himself on Broadway, until the stage manager actually called (on the day of Kennedy's assassination) to say that he was holding a role for David in one of Mary Martin's plays (I believe it was called *Jenny*.) This was the first step. Avery indicated that as a single, working mother, she had little time to spend with her children and felt guilty about this. Since she was also an actress, she thought that David's acting would give them a chance to further bond. In fact, she stressed that David was the one who chose to be an actor of his own volition by mentioning how his decision complicated the family's life. They had to struggle with personal schedules and travel arrangements while he was on Broadway. After working with Martin, David was inspired to continue acting by a performance of *Oliver* at his sister's graduation and would practice singing the songs while taking a bath. ("I guess he thought that we wouldn't hear him with the water running.") Eventually, he did earn a role in the musical as "the laughing boy."

Avery also told stories of David on "Dark Shadows," of course. Apparently, he felt very confident after auditioning for the show, and told his mother that he was sure he'd gotten the part. As with his Broadway debut, Henesy's mother initially didn't place much importance on the issue until David mentioned that he'd be working with "some old actress named Joan Bennett." It seems that Avery was a major Joan Bennett fan at the time. She mentioned that nobody on the DS set felt that they needed to discipline David and that he always felt the need to be professional. "He knew he had to be better than any of the other actors if he was going to stand out. He was a very quick study. He'd read through the script once or twice at home and was able to absorb all of his lines. There were times when he would feed the other actors their lines." Avery mentioned a friend of David's who used to visit the set and would earn tips by running errands for the cast and crew (picking up lunches, etc.) David felt that he was entitled to a portion of those tips, "So he was on his way to being a businessman already." The reason that he was absent from the show for much of its final run was because he was temporarily living with his father and stepmother. "I knew that if David decided he wanted to come back and live with me, he couldn't very well tell his father that, but if he had to come back to work on the show, he would have a valid excuse," Avery explained. "So, I asked Dan to keep David in the cast but only have him do a couple of episodes a month." She also stated that David didn't leave acting because he wanted a normal childhood. It seems he wanted to relocate to California to meet girls.

Jeanne Avery also spoke about her friendship with Don Briscoe. Both she and David were close to him. Avery even allowed Briscoe to stay in her apartment while his own lodgings were either being remodeled or repainted. She also revealed that he had suffered a breakdown while on the show, and that she had tried but failed to get through to him. He's recovered now and living with his parents in Tennessee.

Avery went on to mention her grandchildren, focusing on her latest granddaughter, a toddler given to theatrics. According to her anecdote, the little girl one day dropped a stuffed toy on the floor, then cried bitterly as she cuddled and tried to tend to it. Avery and the child's other grandmother comforted her, but a few moments later, the girl did the exact same thing, repeating the whole process several times (including her tears) in the hopes of getting attention. Apparently, acting runs in the family, for Henesy's oldest son also demonstrates an interest in the profession. Henesy himself currently owns and operates a successful restaurant in Cartagena, Columbia, which is frequented by major politicians and celebrities of the entertainment world. Avery does past life regression therapy for these same clients.

At this point, mordecaigrimes and I left for lunch, so I missed the charity auction and Darren Gross's presentation of lost *Night of Dark Shadows* film clips. (Fortunately, I'd been able to see the presentation at the Vista Theatre in October.) We caught the last portion of David Selby's cartoon, "The Griffin and the Minor Canon." The main theme, Selby stressed, was that "Nothing loved dies."

By now, it was almost time for the cast reunion to begin, but there were people lining up at the microphone for questions and answers. One woman asked Selby how he'd enjoyed his appearance on "Ally McBeal." According to Selby, his son is friends with Calista Flockhart and that was how he was able to get the role. "I wanted to come in and do the part where she spins me in the air," he said. It sounded as though he'd had a lot of fun making that episode. Another woman went to the microphone and asked him, "What are you doing tonight?" "Oh? What do you want me to do tonight?" he replied. A man asked him about the 1995 episodes where Quentin was insane. "Where did you get your inspiration for that role?" he inquired. "I bet a lot of my friends didn't think I needed any inspiration," David said. A woman who was a teacher wanted to know about "The Griffin and the Minor Canon:" was there a copy available and where could she get the educational packet that went with it? Selby remembered that there was a website for the packet but couldn't remember the address immediately. He arranged to give her the video that was shown at the Festival, which I thought was very generous of him. They popped it out of the VCR on the spot. Someone asked David if he'd brought any supernatural content from DS to any of his other shows. David mentioned one series, "Flamingo Road," that was a sort of prototype to "Miami Vice" in the late 70's/early 80's and wasn't quite as popular as it could have been. He suggested that the writers start to bring in supernatural elements (thus ripping off DS) and so David's character began to get involved with voodoo shortly before the series ended.

Richard Halpern then brought on all the cast members who were present for the reunion—John Karlen, Chris Pennock, Marie Wallace, Roger Davis, Kathryn Leigh Scott, Jeanne Avery, and David Selby—and as usual, they gave an update on what was new in their lives. Roger Davis politely took the microphone and declared that he'd already spoken and would "pass the baton" to Kathryn, but he held on to it for a while longer, rambling. Three more times, he offered to pass the baton, but it was at least five minutes before he finally did.

It seemed to me that there weren't as many questions this time as in previous years. (Maybe because the Fest attendance was so low?) David Selby did tell an amusing story of how John Karlen's exploits once landed him in jail. Johnny was casually eating a vanilla ice cream cone and a hot dog when he saw a young woman walking toward him dressed in full Western attire. ("She looked like Dale Evans.") Karlen asked her if she was working that night and the girl replied, yes, what did he have in mind? At that moment, police officers leapt out of their hiding places and seized Karlen, knocking his food to the ground. They arrested him for soliciting (the young Western woman was an undercover officer.) When Karlen went before the judge, the judge claimed to recognize him for his crime, but the crime with which he charged Johnny was not the crime he had committed. The judge "knew him" for something he didn't do! Karlen admitted to it anyway. ("He didn't want to go through the hassle of correcting the judge.") I thought that was pretty funny. Both Karlen and Selby were very lively during this year's reunion, getting up from their seats to re-enact various parts of the story.

The next question again dealt with why the final scene of one episode was performed slightly differently the following day. (It was similar to what had been asked of KLS the previous night.) This time, John Karlen acknowledged the blooper. "I was watching the show the other day," he said, "and I saw that Willie was wearing three different shirts—in the same episode!" Another person asked if the scenes in the show were shot out of order. ("Nope, they were shot straight through, just like in a play.")

Jeanne Avery was again asked to share her memories of Don Briscoe, and this time Roger Davis got into the act. He shared that he and Briscoe had both gone to Columbia together, and it was Davis who'd helped him get the role on DS. "I knew he was the better actor. He had a natural way about him, very talented. He lives in Tennessee now, practically never leaves the house. He has a car and he'll drive around, but I doubt we'll ever see him at a Festival."

Davis also poked fun at both Jonathan Frid and Grayson Hall. "Jonathan barely knew his lines and there were days when it looked like Grayson could have used a little more practice. Put them together, and they were a disaster. I remember one day when they went up on their lines. They both stared at each other for a moment, turned to face the teleprompter, and read the same line at the same time." He even gave an example of Frid's acting, using KLS as a model. "Jonathan would be sitting, talking to you," he put his hand on Kathryn's shoulder and looked her in the eye as he spoke, "and suddenly he'd look over at the camera," Roger shifted his gaze to the audience, "to read his lines. It made no sense because you were sitting next to him and yet he was talking into space."

To my delight, Davis also mentioned Thayer David during his little speech. "Whenever Thayer gave you a compliment, it was something to be proud of. I remember one time when we'd just finished filming a scene and as we were leaving the set, he said to me, 'That was very good.' It meant a lot to me. Then of course, there were other days when he would look at me and ask, 'What happened?' " It sounded as though Roger had a high opinion of him, and KLS looked as though she'd like to add something, but Roger rushed on to other topics.

That's really all that I can remember of the Q&A session off the top of my head. The autographs came next, along with a video interview of Alexandra Moltke and a vampire musical Evensong, neither of which I saw because I had to prepare for the Costume Gala. I had no costume, but I had decided to perform my parody song about the Dream Curse.[16] I'd brought my karaoke CD that I had practiced with for the past week, but I still felt uncertain about performing. Even though I'd already submitted my entry form, I was still wondering if there was a way to back out at the last minute. I am not a singer. I can barely carry "Happy Birthday" at a party. In fact, one time when I was rehearsing my song at home, my dog, who was curled up by the back door, began to whine and whimper as thought tormented. It was quite embarrassing. However, I'd already told several friends that I would be in the Gala, and so I decided to go ahead with my plans and do what I could. I hoped that the audience would be polite and not expect anything too professional.

I went downstairs shortly before 7:00 because we were told to meet "in the room behind the display room at 7:00 prompt. No exceptions." I checked at the information desk just to be sure of where the room was. Only three people were there when I arrived: one woman dressed as Maggie Evans/Josette and a brother-sister team playing Barnabas and Countess Natalie Du Pres from 1795. Feeling a little awkward because of my lack of a costume, I took a seat. We were all a little confused at first because hardly anybody was with us and there were no Festival supervisors to give instructions (it was well past 7:00 by now.) Little by little, they began to filter in. Eventually, Fest coordinators also arrived to collect entry papers (from those who had already filled them out and turned them in at the desk) and make newcomers fill theirs out. I had thought that we would rehearse our skits/songs/spiels, but all we really did was sit and wait until it was time to go out. I was a little disappointed because I would have preferred to be in the ballroom where the Festivities were occurring. The highly-touted DS documentary premiere was supposed to be shown at 7:15 (I later learned it hadn't been screened because of technical difficulties) and the Collinsport Players were performing another skit. I did catch the last part of the skit, which featured David and Hallie trapped in the Haunted Mansion. Julia rescued them and then made out with the ghost of Gerard.

There was a pretty good turnout by the time we were all numbered and in line. Several stragglers had joined the line at the last minute. There were about three Josettes, a man who'd written a song for Angelique, another man who'd written a song praising DS to the tune of "We Didn't Start the Fire," (I'd heard wonderful things about the song from someone who'd gone to the 1999 Fest, so I was delighted to be able to hear it for myself) Barnabas and Natalie, a mother-daughter team wearing costumes based on *House of DS*, a woman dressed as Angelique from *Night of DS*, a woman dressed as the vampire Carmilla, ("a friend of Barnabas from the Old World") Monique and Veronique (two cousins of Josette from France, dressed in period costumes of the French court,) two generic gothic characters, and a pair of ladies who gave us "The Many Faces of Julia Hoffman." This last act was a skit illustrating all of Grayson Hall's characters and their common mannerisms. (Example—Rev. Trask: "There is a witch in this house, Countess, and I'm going to find her!"

Natalie:*clutches throat and puts hand to forehead.* Count Petofi: "A curse on you, gypsy, for stealing my hand!" Magda: *clutches throat and puts hand to forehead.* Adam: "Make me woman now!" Julia: *hands to throat and forehead.*)

I was sixth in line, (although I'd indicated that I would have liked to be near the front so I could get my song over with,) just far enough back to have time for worries. There was a scary moment when I wasn't sure if I was going to have a microphone for my act, but thankfully the staff took care of that. At last, Marcy Robin called my lucky number, and I scaled the stage. I checked to be sure that the microphone was on, then waited for the music to begin. I wasn't used to holding the microphone or singing with it, so I know I lost some of the words at the beginning. I'd only gotten through the first few lyrics when the members of the audience began to chuckle and laugh out loud. Something told me they were laughing at my words, not at my singing, and I was immensely relieved! *Just keep going, just keep going*, I thought. *They seem to really like it; they don't care if I sound horrible.* The wonderful audience laughed all through the song. It was amazing! I was really starting to enjoy myself. None of the terrible things that I'd anticipated happened: my voice didn't crack, the microphone didn't squeak, I didn't run out of breath in the middle of a word. Indeed, everyone seemed to be having a great time; perhaps I was having the most fun because it was all so unexpected.

I finished my song, grateful for the applause, and as I returned to my place in line, Richard Halpern, in full Julia drag, ran over to pull me back on the stage for more applause! I was so stunned and so thrilled! I had never, never expected anything like the response that I received. It was a real Sally Field moment. As I left the stage for real, Marcy patted my shoulder and told me, "Good job." I was ecstatic! I was so overwhelmed that I couldn't focus on the next couple of acts. Friends rushed out of the audience to give me hugs, and the Josettes with whom I was in line complimented my song. (While in the "green room" they'd tried to assure me that everything would be all right, and apparently they were correct.) The other participants in the Gala were wonderful to watch and I really admire the creativity that went into their songs and skits.

After our last "curtain call," Jonathan Harrison of the Collinsport Players approached me and asked if I would like to join. At first, I thought that he was joking, but I've always enjoyed watching the skits at the previous Festivals that I've attended and had wondered what it took to be a Collinsport Player, so I said, "Yes." I was very surprised when he actually asked for my information. I was also astonished by the number of people who requested the lyrics to my song. I was in a beautiful daze as I left the ballroom and met Bobubas to seek out Midnite. (We had heard that Ben was going to play the piano.) Along the way, several people stopped me and told me how much they enjoyed my song. They were all so incredibly nice—and it went on that way for the rest of the weekend. (Some people even asked what I'm going to do next year to top this year's performance! I have never received that sort of reaction from anybody for anything that I've ever done. It was such a new experience for me. I felt like I was in the *Twilight Zone*. If anybody from my high school had been present, they wouldn't have recognized me; they wouldn't have believed it. I almost didn't believe it. In fact, when I awoke the next morning I had to wonder if it had all really happened (but I have the videotape as proof!)

A small group of posters from the dsboards forum gathered around the piano outside the ballroom. Bob swiped a table and some chairs and Midnite brought out the wine, the sodas, and the water (for me.) Ben proceeded to give us a wonderful concert, including various songs from Bob Cobert, Billy Joel, the Beatles, Barry Manilow, and even some show tunes. Some members of our little party even convinced me to give an encore of "The Dream Curse." (I fear I wasn't very good; without the microphone my voice didn't carry and I was more accustomed to the music of my CD than to live piano playing.) Bravo to Ben for his excellent, entertaining repertoire! He played for hours, rightfully deserving the jar of tips that he earned. As time went by, more and more people began to gather around the piano. At one point, guests from a wedding party also being held at the hotel marched past, clapping, shouting, and waving their arms. It was a wonderful time for socializing and picture taking (we must have taken about eight versions of the group photo.) I truly enjoyed becoming acquainted with new friends and catching up with old ones. I finally left at about 1:30, though I understand the party went on for another hour. It was one of the best evenings I've ever spent.

Saturday night surpassed my expectations by so much. It was better than anything I could have dreamed. This was the first time I've ever tried to write a song parody, and fortunately I was successful. I've always looked up to those people who have the gift of humor, and I'd so admired the song parodies from previous costume Galas. For once at least, on that night, I finally had my chance to make people laugh, and I am extremely glad and grateful! I had the time of my life, but the weekend was only going to get better!

Day 3: Sunday, June 30, 2002

I was especially eager to get to the Sunday Festival early. Not only was I supposed to meet a couple of friends from one of the other message boards that I frequent, but that morning was going to open with one of my favorite attractions at the Festival: the fan videos. Since Festival 2000, I've looked forward to the wit and creativity of the fans displayed in either music videos or skits. Both are wonderful. I had a particular reason for looking forward to these videos: I had made one of my own the previous summer and submitted it prior to the August Festival. When it hadn't played, I'd felt very disappointed, so I was keeping my fingers crossed that this might be my year.

Luckily, I found a seat just a couple of rows back from the front. Richard Halpern opened the show by saluting fans in the audience who wore DS T-shirts. The first woman who went up on the stage displayed a "Got Willie?" T-shirt with John Karlen's picture on it, the next fellow wore a shirt with the DS logo, and then CraigSlocum went up in a shirt featuring Craig Slocum's picture. Behind them, a large screen had been pulled down and the first scene of the first video had already flashed on; I was elated when I recognized it as the opening clip from my video! I could hardly believe that they were really going to play it.

At last, Halpern gave the signal to "Roll that beautiful bean footage," and my video (clips of Julia and Barnabas set to The Pretenders' "I'll Stand

By You") began to play. During the past year, I'd tried to picture what it would look like on "the big screen". I was so grateful when the audience seemed to like it. They laughed more often than I would have expected, but I guess that means they were having fun. I'm glad that my video was shown first because as the half-hour progressed, members of the audience became antsy and were no longer paying attention, which I thought was a shame because the other videos were very good.

Following my video were two Baby DS videos that I hadn't seen before, spoofing the Dream Curse and the Ghost of Sarah storylines. Then came two Josette retrospectives featuring clips of Josette in her many forms from both the original series and the 1991 series set to her music box theme. Among the other videos were a Barnabas and Josette tribute (set to the Beatles' "And I Love Her"), a video featuring Vicki ("Sitting at the Wheel" by the Moody Blues), an extended video covering clips from the entire show ("Home By the Sea" by Genesis), a Carolyn and Jeb montage (I couldn't identify the song), Adam's arrival at Collinwood and first meeting with Carolyn and Elizabeth (set to "Da Do Do Do, Da Da Da" by The Police) and Gregory and Jamison ("Losing My Religion" by REM').

Afterward, I stepped out to eat lunch, so I missed the tape of the Paley Festival tribute to DS and Donna McKechnie's video. I also missed the video vault, which was unfortunate because I understand that CraigSlocum had submitted a video of Craig Slocum's early work. I was back in time for the second half of the charity auction, however. VAM won an Angelique trading card. Jim Pierson also auctioned off an original pressing of "I Wanna Dance With You," a promotional Quentin trading card signed by David Selby, a couple of Josette's music boxes, a "Barnabuck," (a dollar bill with Barnabas's picture on it) and a portrait of Alexandra Moltke as Vicki in front of Collinwood drawn by two fans. They had given it to her at the Paley Festival in March of 2001, and she was now donating it to the Festival. It was a beautiful colored pencil drawing, and it brought a good price at auction.

We watched the final skit in the Collinsport Players' series, then Chris Pennock read his latest comic, *Fear of Losing Dark Shadows*. This issue dealt with his marriage to Marilyn Joseph, DS's Lorna Bell of 1840. (I realize that

Chris's comics are highly exaggerated representations, but I always wonder just how much of them are based on truth.)

After Pennock, Robert Rodan took the stage and inevitably, fans began to snap photos. Each time a guest had taken the stage, the audience had taken pictures, but this time, Rodan turned the tables on us. He whipped out a camera of his own to take pictures of *us*. He aimed the camera into the audience and snapped away several times, then turned it on himself, "just to prove to myself that I was here." After this, he showed clips from a porn movie that he had made called *The Minx*. (I was surprised that some of the clips were shown because of their content and the fact that younger fans were in the audience.) The backstory he told revealed that the film hadn't had an actual director in charge, but a professional photographer who hadn't been able to sell the film to a major studio. A producer of adult movies did agree to buy it, and called the cast back to film some additional scenes, making the film more explicit than it already was. Unfortunately, one of the scenes among the clips shown was the death scene of Rodan's character. "Why does something always happen to me?" he lamented. He discussed the death scene, mentioning that his dog had also had a role in the film. Just after being "shot", Robert had smeared chicken grease over his face so the dog would come over to lick his face for a last poignant clip. He said that he'd had a lot of fun making *The Minx* and told us some stories from those days. During the Q&A session, a couple of Rodan's female admirers stepped forward. One woman told him, "You're a very good-looking man." And another confessed, "It's hard for me to watch the show now because I don't like to see what happens to you."

Dennis Patrick succeeded Rodan. I was delighted to see him because I'd heard rumors that he wasn't going to show up after all. Though Patrick needed assistance climbing the stage and joked about his advanced age, he was in good spirits and offered some witty replies during his Q&A session. He shared a couple of limericks with us: one that he'd written about Lela Swift and another about John Karlen as Willie Loomis. Patrick also spoke in an Irish brogue for us, imitating the style of the town of Cork. He revealed that he'd spoken with an accent as a child, right until he went into acting.

Patrick showed some clips from a film called *Joe* in which he'd starred with Peter Boyle. In response to a question about the movie, he shared an anecdote involving Boyle, who was apparently tough to work with. During one scene, Boyle altered a line of dialogue to make a cruel comment about Jackie Kennedy. The director promised that the scene would be cut, but Dennis didn't trust him, so he pulled the film out of the camera and left it strewn on the floor. Patrick was also asked about his role as the golden man on "Lost in Space." "I was worried about playing the part," he confessed, "because I knew that you could suffocate if your skin was completely covered. I'd forgotten they were only going to put the gold make-up on my face. I had to get there early in the morning before anybody else arrived and I left after everybody else was gone because I had to struggle to clean the 'gold' off my face."

Somebody asked Dennis if he thought it was strange that the writers had the Jason Maguire blackmail storyline, which was pretty mundane and typical of soap operas, playing at the same time as the more exciting Barnabas the vampire storyline. Dennis replied, "I never knew what the hell the writers were thinking. I never knew what was in their minds." Another person asked if Dennis thought it was strange that he played Jason, a friend of Paul Stoddard, and later came back to play Stoddard himself. Again, Dennis claimed he never knew what was going on behind the scenes. He even volunteered the information as to why he had left the show the first time. "I offered to punch out the producer when he wouldn't let me out to go to my daughter's graduation. She still won't speak to me about that and she's 52 now." He did seem to have enjoyed his stint on DS though. "Whenever I was working with John Karlen, he always looked like he was going to burst out laughing. I guess he thought I was joking. I don't know what he thought was so funny." (Earlier, Karlen had mentioned how difficult it was to do scenes with Dennis Patrick because Patrick's eyes were constantly rolling back and forth. This made Karlen want to laugh, and "I had to bite the insides of my cheeks until they bled to keep from cracking up.")

Marie Wallace and Richard Halpern stepped up after Patrick had left and acted a scene from Neil Simon's *Plaza Suite*. They played parents on their daughter's wedding day who were trying to coax the bride out of the bathroom where she'd locked herself. It was a humorous skit and well-played. Marie put on a New York accent, and one of the people who stepped up to the microphone later said that it was the best New York accent she'd ever heard. A Q&A followed the skit. One man asked Marie if she'd ever taken home any of the show's props, for instance her babies. "No, but I do wish that I'd brought home my fangs. I think those would have been fun to have at parties," she replied. Marie also informed us that she'd never worn wigs on the show. "I had my own hair, even when I was Jenny. I would set it in little curls around my face the night before and tease it up before I went to work. It was my own idea, and it was my real hair." Another man thanked Marie for giving him one of his favorite lines, "that I always use on my bosses when they want me to do something I don't like to do: "You may tell me where I am to stand, but you may not tell me where I am to look." Marie recognized the line from a scene between Adam and Eve, and re-enacted it for us. Somebody else stepped up to inquire about a scene between Eve and Jeff Clark when Roger Davis had unceremoniously shoved Marie. ("We could hear your heels scraping over the ground. Were you mad when he did that?") Marie remembered that too, and explained that during rehearsals, Roger had only shouted at her, keeping his distance. Once the cameras were rolling however, and unable to be stopped, Davis had marched over and given her a healthy push. When she'd confronted him about it later, he'd apologized, claiming that he'd simply been caught up on the emotion of the scene. "I think he did it on purpose though," she confided.

The next event was a scene from the play *Love* (I didn't catch the author's name) featuring John Karlen (wearing mouse ears and riding a scooter) and Kathryn Leigh Scott. I really enjoyed that show, and the story sounded very interesting (I'm not familiar with this play.) The skit involved two divorced people who wished to get back together, but to do so, they had to dispose of their respective spouses. I would have liked to see them act the entire play; they did such a great job.

When the skit concluded, Roger Davis took the stage to close the Festival. "How many of you are here for the first time?" he asked. Many hands went up. "And how many of you are going to the banquet tonight?" Practically every hand went up, which surprised me. (This was to be my first banquet, and I was very excited about it.) After his survey of the audience, Davis began to share anecdotes from his days on "Alias, Smith and Jones," the first of which dealt with Cesar Romero's hair. Romero had been a guest star in an episode where the characters were supposed to have been riding in the desert for a time. Everybody looked pretty windblown with the exception of Romero who "always looked so shiny and perfect like he'd just popped out of a hatbox. So, the director went up to him and said, 'Well, what if we ruffle him just a little bit?' He put his hand out, and Cesar grabbed him by the wrist."

While Davis's stories were interesting, I was becoming impatient for him to finish up and "dismiss" us so that I could get into the line for banquet tickets. At last, he bid us good night, and I dashed out. The banquet line was nearly as long as the autograph line, but it moved much faster. There were no stars at our table, but I was lucky enough to sit with friends. Robert Rodan and Marie Wallace gave out door prizes (unfortunately, nobody from our table won.) After the chicken dinner, commercials in which Robert Rodan, Marie Wallace, and Humbert Allan Astredo had acted were screened, and those were a lot of fun to watch.

At last, it was time for the now-infamous 'DS Documentary[17]' (aka the DS episode of "Sciography") that was supposed to have been screened the night before. I know that a number of people were upset by the episode and by the reactions that the cast had toward it. Though it wasn't a popular program, I was still glad of the chance to see it; anything related to DS interests me. It's unfortunate though that this "documentary" was unable to capture the true magic of the series.

From the banquet, it was back to the bar/cafe to socialize with members of this forum. I didn't stay as long as usual because Midnite had graciously invited me to the Disneyland California Adventure park the following day (and that did turn out to be quite the adventure) and I didn't want to oversleep. All in all, I think that Festival 2002 was the best DS event of any that I've attended, and I know that I will always cherish the beautiful memories of that time.

2002 Dark Shadows Halloweenathon (Tarrytown, NY)

Day 1: Friday, October 18, 2002

Friday evening got off to a slow start due to technical difficulties. We were all gathered in the hallway outside the grand ballroom in the semblance of a line for about two hours, during which time I became fairly well-acquainted with the people standing around me. Originally, the doors were supposed to open at 7:00 p.m. Time passed, and we were told to wait until 7:45 p.m. then 8:00...then 8:30...

Sometime after 9:00 p.m., we were finally permitted inside the dimly lit, fog-filled ballroom. An ornate coffin lay in the center of the room while the humming of the fog machine and the recorded sounds of wolves howling played in the background. Diana Millay, Terry Crawford, and Marie Wallace took seats in the front row while Ed Lambese, the organizer, welcomed us to the eighth annual Halloween weekend. After introductions were made, we sat quietly for a few minutes while the wolves continued to howl and the fog in the room grew even thicker. Slowly, the coffin began to open and a white-haired woman in a long black dress climbed out. The figure gazed darkly over the audience, then turned and attacked Ed Lambese. Lights came on and the woman removed her wig, revealing herself to be Lara Parker, who had been waiting in the coffin all this time for a delayed cue.

For the first few minutes, Lara was on-stage alone, speaking about her son's recent wedding, which sounded very hectic[18]. Lara had been in charge of all the arrangements—the bride's family did zip. She had made the bridal gown herself and ordered wedding pictures (which the newlyweds hadn't even done.) Then, there were some difficulties with the "valet girls," who were nervous about driving guests' cars up and down the winding road to Lara's house and simply parked the cars wherever they pleased without informing anybody else. Nevertheless, it was still a happy event. Lara was also asked about her next book, and she admitted that she hadn't been able to write much lately because of the recent excitement. She's had two extensions so far, and hopes to have the manuscript prepared by January.

Soon, the other actresses—Marie Wallace, Terry Crawford, and Diana Millay—joined Lara for the evening panel. Since there were no chairs immediately on-stage, the four ladies made themselves comfortable on the coffin lid. At this point, we discovered that the Q&A panel was going to be a Ladies' Night as none of the male stars had shown up. Christopher Pennock had a part in "Who's Afraid of Virginia Wolf?" and I didn't hear what Jim Storm's excuse was. Nobody seemed to know where Roger Davis was, though they expected him to turn up later in the weekend.

First, the stars updated us on their current projects. Terry spoke about her ministry and how every summer she participates in a workshop in Europe, mentoring children. Diana discussed the trip to Romania that she will be hosting this May. "Before long, the United States will be pouring money into this country, and all of the historic buildings will be torn down, so this will be our last chance to see the real Romania." Marie is still a photographer, mainly at public events. Lara shared that she is working towards her Master's degree at Antioch College. Before being accepted into the program, she'd had to submit a sample of writing, and had presented a chapter from her book. "They turned me down, saying that they didn't accept genre writing. So, I wrote another story about making my daughter in-law's wedding dress, and they approved me."

The audience was then invited to ask questions, and one of the first that came up was, "Who was your favorite leading man—and who was your least favorite?" Marie glanced to the ladies on either side of her. "Well, I think we all know who our least favorite was," she remarked drily. Together: "Roger Davis!" "He used to sit on my hair all the time," Diana complained. "In our scenes, I was usually lying down, and he would just walk over, sit down and start saying his lines." Marie repeated her Festival 2002 anecdote about how Roger (as Jeff Clark) unexpectedly and violently shoved her (as Eve) out of the camera's range when he hadn't dared any such thing during rehearsal.[19] Lara spoke up for Roger, mentioning how much everybody liked him, in spite of how difficult he could be. "Roger is very brilliant, and he used to like to re-write the scripts. He did that on "Smith and Jones" all the time. He would change the dialogue and make it better—but he would do it at the last minute." "I think he had it planned in advance," Marie argued, "but he didn't pull anything during rehearsal because he knew he wouldn't be able to get away with it." Lara also admitted that she didn't really like to work opposite Jonathan Frid. "He would forget his lines, and it would make you look bad. When you watched the show, the confusion on Jonathan's face made him seem like a tortured, guilt-ridden vampire, and it was wonderful, but the pauses in between made it seem that you were the one who had forgotten the lines." Marie slyly confided that her trick for avoiding such a problem, even if she had been the one to flub the lines, was to immediately glare at the other actor as though it were his fault.

As for favorite leading men, Marie named Humbert Allen Astredo. Terry expressed how much she enjoyed working with both David Selby and James Storm. Lara stated that the actor she best liked to work with was John Karlen. "He was such a marvelous actor; he had so much talent, but he was frustrated because he was working on a soap opera instead of in films. He could make changes in the way he delivered his lines that were so subtle. If you watched him carefully, you could see how he added new layers to the scenes with each rehearsal, and he gave some really marvelous performances."

Lara then shared a story of how Johnny had recently come to stay with her family while he was between apartments. The weekend before, her meticulous mother-in-law had been a guest, and she had taken it upon herself to remove the sheets and blankets and fold them up before leaving. "I saw all of the sheets folded on top of the washing machine, and I assumed that I must have already put new sheets on the bed." When his visit ended, Johnny went to Lara and thanked her profusely for being so gracious. "I went into the guest room to change the sheets—and the only things on the bed were a pillow with no pillow case and a quilt. I was so embarrassed, I sat down and cried for half an hour. Also, that weekend, we had had an invasion of ants, and there had been ants all over his sink…But he was so nice and hadn't complained at all the entire time."

A woman in the audience noted that most of the female characters on the show were villains and asked how the actresses thought their characters might be written today as heroes. "I don't think Beth was ever a villain,"

Terry remarked. "You mean Edith? Why? Because I was a little mean to my husband who was in a wheelchair and only pretending he couldn't walk?" "I thought I was a hero," Diana protested. "If my character were on TV today, I would probably be a hero by setting fires." Marie pointed out that villains never see themselves as villains. "Part of the job of playing the heavy is to find the motivation for what you're doing, and play the scenes to justify that," Lara explained.

Terry was asked how she had enjoyed working with Robert De Niro in *The Swap*, and she softly admitted, "I didn't." When pressed as to why, she confessed, "I was a 'method actor,' and with method acting, you have to center yourself on your character and find something to inspire you in every scene." She'd had to draw upon such inspiration while playing a romantic scene with De Niro. "I didn't find him attractive, but I had to play the scene as if I did, and it worked—too well. He thought I was serious."

Lara had had a similar experience—with Robert Blake! While guest starring on "Baretta," she'd had to play a love scene with Blake, and he'd thought she was honestly interested in him. "If he didn't like you, he'd have you fired right away so I had to stay on his good side. He'd ask me if I was attracted to him, and I'd say, 'Oh, sure, I'm attracted to you, but, ah, I'm...busy tonight...'" Diana had worked with Blake on "Baretta" too, for a short time. "He kept trying to tell me how to play the scene. He said 'You're going to do it this way,' and I finally said, 'No, I'm not; I'm going home.' Dead silence in the studio. One of the producers said to me, 'You've said the wrong thing. Why don't you go to the ladies' room for a moment?' 'OK!' I left to call my agent to tell him what had happened, and he assured me that these things happen all the time and I wasn't going to be kicked out of the Screen Actors' Guild because of it."

Lara was asked about her guest appearance on "Kolchak, the Night Stalker." Apparently, it wasn't a very good experience. Darren McGavin wasn't very courteous and complained that, 'Nobody knows how a show like this is supposed to be played.' Lara asked him if he'd ever heard of *Dark Shadows*. 'Dark what?' During her death scene as the ancient, disfigured crone, Lara had more difficulties with him. "Normally," she explained, "when the camera isn't on you, you're supposed to help the other actor out by prompting him with his lines. He (McGavin) didn't want me to do that. He yelled at me that I was distracting him."

Another person requested that the ladies share their memories of Grayson Hall. "Grayson was the center of camp," Lara recalled. "Her acting was always so stiff and unconvincing but it was really interesting to watch." Marie conceded that it was mainly Grayson's own personality and presence coming through the characters that made them stand out.

Terry shared a cute story. "When I played Beth, I often had to cry. Beth was always worried about Quentin, and after taping one episode where she had run crying to Magda, Grayson asked me, 'How do you cry those real tears? You were really crying in that scene.' When she cried, she just dabbed her eyes with a handkerchief, and so she was very curious. I explained how I would prepare by trying to remember times from my childhood that had made me sad so that by the time I had to do my crying scenes, I was ready. Sometime after that, later in the story line, Magda had a crying scene and Grayson cried a single real tear. She was so excited. 'Did you see it? Did you see it?' she kept asking. 'I did it!'"

Diana had worked with Sam Hall before DS when he had written the teleplay for *The Secrets of Stella Crozier* and had visited the Halls' apartment one day. While there, she'd met Grayson, and been impressed by her. "I didn't even know she was an actress, but I thought she was a fascinating person." Everybody seemed to hold a high opinion of her.

Lara told of how Grayson had gathered all of the actors around her during the filming of the movie and given them tips on acting for the screen. "'You can't emote the way you do on television,' she said. 'When your face is on the big screen, every little thing you do is magnified.' We had to stop what we'd been doing up to then and re-train ourselves. Grayson helped us because she'd had the experience of being in *Night of the Iguana*. She would find movies for us to watch, and give us tips based on them. We were watching a scene with Deborah Kerr and Grayson told us, 'Look at her face. See how she's always moving, even though she's standing still.' She was wonderful. Even though her style was so over-the-top on the show, she was able to tone it down for the movie. It's just that she was trained differently. She was from another age, like Joan Bennett." This prompted the ladies to recall their memories of Joan.

Each took turns imitating her distinct, rich voice and manner of speaking. "When I was in my first play on Broadway, she was the only one from the (DS) cast who sent me a telegram of congratulations," Lara said. "It read, 'I wish you great personal success.' Of course, she had doubts about the professional success of the play—everybody did, and for good reason." Diana told how Joan Bennett had been a mentor to her. When she was a young girl just getting started in acting, her agent had dropped her off at one of Joan Bennett's parties. Intimidated by all of the (famous) adults, Diana had meekly gone to sit in the corner. Soon, Joan approached her to find out what was wrong and to encourage her to mingle. "I don't know how to mingle," Diana had explained. "Dear," Joan had informed her, "I'm going to send somebody over to you, and you're going to learn how to mingle." Before long a woman (Greer Garson) did emerge to walk Diana around the party and introduce her to everybody. From that point on, she and Joan had remained good friends.

When asked about favorite writers and directors, none of the ladies could really remember any particular writer, but both Terry and Lara named Henry Kaplan as their favorite director. "Lela Swift would just tell me, 'I need this from you and I don't care how you do it,'" Terry recalled, "but Henry was very good about coaching me through scenes. He would always remind me, 'Shoulder to shoulder'—which meant that when my shoulders were aligned with his, he could get the best shots." "He used to come into our dressing rooms at the end of taping and give us grades for the day," Lara remembered. "He would open the door and yell, 'B minus!'"

When the Q&A session came to an end, the actresses dispersed and the DS *Scariest Moments* video was shown (instead of the scheduled *House of Dark Shadows*.) Terry Crawford remained outside the ballroom for some time after the Q&A ended and I was able to have my photo with her. Then, VAM, MsHoffman and I went across the way to the local diner for a late bite to eat. Thus ended the first day of events.

Day 2: Saturday, October 19, 2002

Saturday opened with breakfast in the Hudson ballroom, after which we spent two more hours crowded outside the grand ballroom and in the dealers' area until the doors opened. The first guest of the morning was Roger Davis, who had finally arrived in Tarrytown.

I was surprised that he didn't show us the infomercial for his housing development that he had presented at the Festival. Instead, he very cheerfully greeted us and began to share a few of his memories from DS. One of the first things Roger mentioned was working with Addison Powell as Jeff Clark and Dr. Lang. "He could never remember his lines, so he used to tape them around the set and on me. He'd say, 'Stand right there and don't cross your arms.' (If he did it, it would cover the cheat sheet.) So, of course, I would purposely cover the line and put him on the spot. 'Now, as you know, Dr. Lang...and as you were saying...Explain it to me again, Dr. Lang.' All the while, he was pulling at my hand, trying to move it so he could see his lines. I was a real cut-up on the set. I remember the scene where I played Charles Delaware Tate and my head fell off. I couldn't stop laughing, and they had to stop the tape."

Roger told how he'd never been able to keep a straight face even in his early days of acting. "At Columbia, we performed *Edward II* with Don Briscoe playing Edward." Roger played a knight who was to present Edward (Briscoe) with a severed head. "In the middle of my line, I burst out laughing because I knew it was really just a cabbage in a sack that I was offering him." Roger also brought up the DS *Sciography* that was screened at the last Festival, stating that "it was all in fun" and implying that everybody had taken it too seriously. Soon, Roger appealed to the audience for questions.

One of the ladies in the audience begged him to do the voice over for the L'eggs stockings commercial, claiming that it was what she had lived to hear during its original run. Roger attempted the voice over several times but none of the microphones would cooperate with him. However, this did give him an opportunity to discuss how he'd become involved in voice overs in the first place. Roger had been in a play called *MacBird* in which he'd played Bobby Kennedy. Later, he was invited to do a voice over for Anacin using the Bobby Kennedy voice, but the effect didn't work very well, as Roger demonstrated for us. "The guy in charge finally said, 'Just forget it. Why don't you read in your own voice?' They had already fired me—this was just for the heck of it. So, I read the lines…and the guys in the studio all huddled together and whispered for a little while. Then, one of them said to me, 'Did anybody ever tell you that you sound like Henry Fonda? Can you try to make it sound more like Henry Fonda?'" Since then, he's made a fortune with voice overs. Another fan in the audience asked Roger to share a memory of Gloria Swanson, with whom he'd worked in the film *Killer Bees*. He spoke highly of her and said that she'd once told him, "If you had been around a few years earlier, you would be a famous movie star by now instead of a television actor."

This brought Roger around to speaking of "Alias, Smith and Jones" and its rotten luck with scheduling. One day after filming the show, he was riding in the elevator with the president of Universal Studios. "To break the ice I said to him, 'Look, Sid, I got a new hat!' He looked at me and said, 'Roger, you don't need a new hat. You need a new time slot.' Roger's current pet project is a film called *The War Magician*, which his studio is co-producing and in which Tom Cruise is supposed to star. "There was a major bidding war for this film some years back," Roger explained, "and my little studio managed to get a hold of it. Now I can't wait to have lunch with Dan Curtis. I can just imagine what he'll say." In a gruff voice, Roger imitated Curtis, giving us a sample conversation. "He'll tell me about all of his projects and then ask, 'So what's new for you, kid?' 'Well, I'm co-producing Tom Cruise's next movie, *The War Magician*.' 'Bull****!'"

Terry Crawford replaced Roger for the next Q&A session. She greeted us warmly and expressed how happy she was to see so many familiar faces again. She spent some time discussing her Inner Light Ministry, which fights for human rights and encourages young people around the world to make a difference through the media. Her work sometimes takes her to dangerous spots in the world, but she feels secure and protected by her faith. Terry told us a bittersweet story with a humorous twist that came about in part because of her work. A dear friend of hers, whom she referred to as her little brother, was recently involved in an ugly, international custody dispute. His Russian wife was determined to keep the couple's daughter with her in her native country and never let her ex see the child again. To effect her purpose, she had told vicious lies about how the girl's father was abusive and unfit. Because of her work with human rights abroad and because she knew the defendant so well, Terry was called to give testimony. To prepare for how to give testimony, she'd watched *Law and Order*. On the day of her deposition, the female prosecutor approached Terry with an odd little smile on her face. "She started to ask me questions about where I was born and who my parents were...Then she started to ask me other questions, like what was my favorite color. Even the defense lawyer thought that was a little strange. Finally, she asked me what sort of work I had been doing in the 1960's. I said that I had been a television actress. Then she took out a huge folder of information that she had collected about me and opened it. The first thing she pulled out was a picture of Barnabas and Beth as vampires!" This woman had been a fan of DS growing up, and she'd recognized Terry. After that, Terry no longer felt uncomfortable answering questions. She happily told us that her 'brother' now has child custody that she has learned valuable information about international law and life in Russia from the experience.

Somebody asked Terry what her favorite scene from the show was, and she named two. One was the death of Jenny. "I was sick that day, but the show had to go on. During rehearsals, I said my lines but I didn't use as much emotion as I could have because I didn't want to exhaust myself. The director noticed that I wasn't putting all my energy into the performance and he asked me what was wrong. I told him not to worry, that when the real thing came, I would be ready. It really was an intense scene, to have Jenny (Marie) rushing at me with the scissors. You all remember how wild she looked. I was a little scared during the scene because she was really getting into it and I thought she might actually overpower me." Her other favorite scene was when Beth kills Quentin. Terry smiled mischievously and told us another story. One day, while visiting family, she had tried to persuade a relative who kept loaded guns in the home that such precautions were unnecessary and dangerous. After finishing her lecture, Terry had played a video that a fan had compiled for her featuring Beth's scenes from the show. "As luck would have it, the very first clip was of me, Beth, with the gun, shooting Quentin. And I had just finished my speech against guns."

When people no longer had questions for Terry, she went into the audience and encouraged them to share stories with her about their memories of DS or how it had affected their lives. A woman named Mary talked about her father, who had been a cameraman on the show, and how she had been able to go to the studio and meet the actors because of him. VAM told a story about the 2000 Festival when she had dressed as a werewolf for the Costume Gala and surprised John Karlen in the autograph line by slamming her hands down on the table. "He let out a scream and jumped out of his chair. He was really scared." A man named Louis (or Lewis) mentioned how, as a child, he used to watch DS in secret until his mother assured his father that it was "a very slow-moving show, and not very scary." The day that his father chose to watch the show with the children turned out to be the day that Chris Jennings became a werewolf and attacked a jailer. After that, he was forbidden to ever watch the show again, and his father would constantly call home to make sure that the kids were obeying. Terry also asked the fans for updates on their own lives, mentioning how she enjoys getting to know them better each year and learning what new things have occurred since the previous year. I was impressed by how personable and genuine she was.

Next, Ed Lambese popped the video of *The Best of Dark Shadows* into the VCR and Terry Crawford sat down to watch it with us. She doesn't see the show very often, and enjoyed viewing the clips. Throughout the video, she made humorous comments. For instance, in the scene where Beth watches Quentin transform and pushes him into the pentagram (and temporarily off-camera) she remarked, "Get out of the way; I want the camera on me." During the scene where Nicholas Blair performs the black mass over Maggie Evans, Terry remarked to Louis, "Your daddy would have loved this." By the time the video ended, it was time for a lunch break, and I walked over to the diner with a friend. Because there was such a crowd, we were given a booth with another party of two, a couple that was also attending the Halloween party. I was glad to sit with other DS fans since it gave us some common ground to discuss.

After lunch, Marie Wallace arrived for a Q&A session. Somebody wanted to know which of her DS characters was her favorite. "They were all so much fun. I liked Jenny because she was so vulnerable, but I liked

Megan Todd too, and Eve." In response to the question of what her favorite memory away from DS was, she named the day that she'd gotten married. One fan asked her if she thought that Adam was annoying. "I didn't, but my character Eve certainly did. Adam was so bumbling and stupid and she thought she was above him." Marie went on to talk about how important it is to differentiate between actors and their roles. "I once read an article by a fan who wrote that he 'hated Robert Rodan (Adam).' The character's name was in the parentheses instead of the actor's, so it sounded as though he hated Robert Rodan, not that he hated Adam. I advised him to change it—'hated Adam (Robert Rodan).'" One man asked Marie if she knew how to speak French because she had once used the language as Eve/Danielle Roget. "No, I've recently learned to speak Italian, but I never cared much for French." She imitated the nasal vowels to demonstrate unintelligible French.

Marie also answered a question pertaining to her photography: whether she preferred black and white film or color. "In the beginning, I only used black and white film," she answered, "until one time I took a trip to Florida. I was staying on the beach and I decided to get up early the next morning to photograph the sunrise." Her first attempt was thwarted by a false alarm. "I woke up when I saw a red light outside my window and raced down to the water with my camera, trying to avoid the various people who were sleeping on the beach. Then I stopped and looked around. It was pitch black; there was no sun. I realized that what I'd really seen was the light from a passing ship. The second day I overslept, but the third day I went down to the beach and took several pictures. It was a beautiful sunrise, but when I developed the pictures, they looked a little ridiculous because they were in black and white and you couldn't see anything of the colors." The moral of the story was that B&W was better for capturing form but color was better for image. Upon request, Marie talked about a particular photo that she had taken of the World Trade Center about six years before Sept. 11. "It was taken from the ground looking straight up at the building. After I got home and developed the film, I thought it was an interesting picture and I decide to use it in a collage. It was very abstract, but I had it in a show and it did well. I sold a couple of copies, so I decided to make one for myself. This time, I used the image of the building to make the shape of a cross and I put it on a blue background. It looked a little like the sky. After the terrorist attacks, I went back to look at the photo and it was almost like a tribute to the Trade Center, but I had made it years before."

Lara's turn came after Marie's. One of the first questions that came up was about her mother's book for children, *Bugs and Other Critters I Have Known*, which Lara publishes through her own company. "When I do readings in public libraries or bookstores, I ask the kids, 'What's your favorite bug?' and there's usually a poem in the book to go with whatever they choose." She also stated that she's looking for a larger company to take over the book because it's difficult to handle all of the packing and shipping of orders herself. Somebody else asked Lara about her own book and she shared some of the plot details with us. The sequel to *Angelique's Descent* will focus on Miranda DuVal's story and the Salem witchcraft trials. It will also treat David Collins's coming of age and Barnabas's desire to become a vampire again. "I already have the story planned," Lara revealed, "but I haven't written all of it yet."

Lara was also asked about her experiences as a high school English teacher. She grimaced as she recalled her difficulties. "The boys all sit in the back of the room and the girls brush their hair and put on their make-up. When you stand at the front of the classroom, they just stare at you. They're so hostile, and when you give them assignments, they complain: 'Why do we have to read this? Why do we have to write about this? What's the point?' It took me months to learn not to shout at them. When I spoke in a normal voice one day and said, 'Today, we're going to read a poem. I hope you enjoy it,' they were so shocked that I wasn't yelling. The only time they ever really paid attention to me was when I lied and said I was at Woodstock. That's not to say there weren't any good students. I met some really wonderful kids, but it was such a demanding job."

Somebody else asked Lara whether any of the fans had ever done anything terrible to her because they'd confused her with her character Angelique. "My sons were embarrassed that their mom was a witch on TV. Whenever their friends came over, they were a little bit afraid of me. When I picked my sons up from school, I had to wait for them a couple of blocks away because they didn't want anybody to see me." She also recalled the crowds of kids who used to swarm around her as she walked from the studio to the subway after work. "There was a school near the station and I was always passing it just as classes were letting out. The kids would see me and come running after me. Now, imagine how dozens of screaming kids must sound when their voices are echoing through a subway tunnel."

Another fan asked Lara to share memories of Thayer David. "He was a speed-reader. He could read a book in about 20 minutes. He was amazingly brilliant, very intelligent, a marvelous character actor. If you look at his characters on the show, you realize that you're seeing somebody who could change. When he was Ben, he was the oaf, and then to be able to turn around and play Professor Stokes and Petofi was just terrific. He really dug acting, and he was a great friend."

Before Lara could take any more questions, Ed Lambese called her attention to the doors of the ballroom where a waiter, followed by Marie, Terry, and Diana, was wheeling in a cake with candles. Ed announced that it was Lara's birthday and we all sang for her while Marie took pictures. After Ed helped Lara blow out the candles, she began to cut the cake (which featured a picture of her from *Night of Dark Shadows*) and the fans lined up to get a piece. Lara seemed very pleased with the surprise party and happily chatted away with the fans while passing out slices of cake.

After the party wound down, Diana Millay took the stage to talk about her work teaching troubled children as well as the upcoming trip to Romania. She was very excited about the trip, which costs the same amount as the trip to Egypt years before. Though listed as lasting seven days on the fliers, it's actually been extended to nine days since the price remains the same. There are about 30 spots open on the tour. Diana plans to start at the top of the list and take the first 30 people, so if this tour sounds like something that would interest you, I advise you to register as quickly as you can.

When Diana had finished talking, we were allowed a break of about 45 minutes until the auction began. Diana played the auctioneer at that event since Ed could not be found and nobody really felt like waiting for him. Terry played the Carol Merrill/Vanna White role, showing off each item with a flourish and walking them around the tables for everybody to see. When the time came for Diana to auction the famous glittery blouse she had worn to the *Night of Dark Shadows* screening in Hollywood last

October, Terry put on the blouse and flitted around the room, showing it off. There was a pretty good selection of items (such as a record album, several CD's and cassettes of the of the DS music, two Marilyn Ross books, several comics based on the 1991 series, a signed copy of *Angelique's Descent*, a book of David Selby's poetry and a book-on-tape of him reading it) as well as a couple of suspect ones (e.g., copies of the pilot episode script signed by nobody affiliated with DS; even Diana couldn't read the autographs). But unfortunately, not many people were bidding, and when they did, the prices never climbed very high. I can only recall two items that passed the $20 mark, a signed copy of A *View of Collinsport* and Diana's blouse. At times, Diana would ask for an opening bid ("Do I hear $5.00?") and then go down. (Do I hear $4.95? How about $3.50?") Considering what some of these things can go for at the Festivals, the prices were ridiculously low. Near the end, Diana began combining items, giving away two comics for the price of one, or a soundtrack with a Marilyn Ross paperback. I probably should have bid on as many items as I could at those favorable prices, then turned around and put them on E-bay, but it didn't seem right.

When the auction concluded, the 'cocktail hour' began. Because of all the technical difficulties and delays, the Hilton was providing all of the party guests with free drinks. By this time, a number of people had changed into their costumes for the evening. I was a standard Collinsport time-traveling afghan blanket (yet many people asked if I was a hippie.) I saw and snapped pictures of a number of very impressive outfits while everybody was standing around. One of the most striking costumes was surely VAM's. As Angelique the crone, (after her portrait was made-over by Sam Evans) she posed with 'Tony Peterson' and a cigarette lighter so that several fans could take pictures. We fans mingled for quite a while.

During this time, the highly-touted haunted parallel time room (which by now had been postponed by about three hours) was allegedly being set up at last. When we heard the news that it was finally ready, we hastily lined up and rushed downstairs to the Sunnyside ballroom. Unfortunately, the call must have been premature because once we were queued up against the wall, we got to wait for what must have been at least another half-hour. The extra time afforded more photo opportunities. It also gave one of the volunteers (whose name I didn't catch) the opportunity to move up and down the line and try to rally us. From time to time, she yelled out questions requesting our opinion about Barnabas and Julia as a couple or the possibility of Johnny Depp playing Barnabas in a future movie. [20]Once she even exhorted us to howl like wolves! I realize that she was trying to distract us from the boredom of waiting, but I can't help wondering what the guests in that section of the hotel were thinking of us.

At long last, the doors to the secret parallel time room opened—but only to groups of 40 at a time. I happened to be lucky number 13 in the line, so I made it through. After navigating a short flight of stairs in the dark, we grouped to one side around a coffin lying in the middle of the floor. Ed Lambese, dressed as Quentin, paced back and forth in front of the coffin while the recorded voice-over in the background warned of how Barnabas Collins's hopes for a cure from his curse were soon to be thwarted. Soon, one of the party staff members emerged from the coffin in Barnabas's 1795 attire and quickly conferred with Quentin about whether or not he would ever be free. Suddenly, Lara Parker appeared from the shadows to re-invoke Angelique's curse. The scene culminated in Barnabas attacking the vengeful witch.

The next scene consisted of Eagle Hill Cemetery and its tombstones for the victims of 1795: JEREMIAH COLLINS, ABAGAIL (sic) COLLINS, SARAH COLLINS, MILLICENT COLLINS, and JOSETTE COLLINS. Nearby, the bodyless head of Judah Zachary reposed in a glass case. Passing this, we were herded into a rectangular pentagram and told to remain there for safety. We remained for many minutes (more technical difficulties) before Quentin (Ed) and Beth (Terry) appeared from the next room. It was the night of the full moon, and Quentin was beginning to feel the pangs of the transformation. While Beth rushed about in a panic, begging the audience for help, Quentin fell to the floor as though dead. A rubber mask tossed through the door of the next room turned Quentin into the werewolf, and he leapt to his feet to attack Beth. She was forced to shoot him in self-defense (that gun again!)

After that scene from 1897, Diana Millay stepped into the room clothed in a long black vampire's cape. She summoned flame from an urn and then told us the story of the Phoenix. The strobe lights that flashed in the room sent eerie shadows over her face. At the end of the story, Diana dropped the cape and took flight as the Phoenix in shorts. (I believe this scene was improvised; the day before, she had complained about Roger Davis's absence because she was supposed to do a scene with him over the weekend. Perhaps the original skit was supposed to involve Dirk and Laura.) By this time, more people were beginning to filter into the room, and since not all of them had seen the last performance, we were encouraged to remain behind and watch it a second time for their benefit. However, since most of us were starving, we went on to the banquet room instead.

The banquet/costume party was really the highest point of the day. There were many wonderful costumes in the evening's contest: a bloody-mouthed vampire, a spider from the West Wing (a lady in a cape with a sparkling cobweb design,) Josette's ghost, Mrs. Johnson, Victoria Winters, Hallie Stokes, Carolyn (as seen in *House of Dark Shadows*,) Tony Peterson, aged Cassandra, and a trio in stunning 19th Century-style clothing. The female winner of the event was, by unanimous approval, Mrs. Johnson. The men's contest ended in a tie between PatrickM (1840) and JVjr (1897.) A number of people were out on the dance floor. Even Terry and Lara participated. At one point, everybody formed a large circle (actresses included) and danced in a ring. Later, a man who was dancing with Lara Parker lifted her off the floor and spun her around. I couldn't resist joining in the fun either and danced to nearly every song (probably making a fool out of myself in the process, but it was a lot of fun, and I had some very nice dance partners.) The party went on past midnight. However, I didn't stay for the entire thing, but went to the bar (which was open to all ages) with a few friends until a little while after one. Even though it was late, I still felt refreshed and excited about the events for the next day.

Day 3: Sunday, October 20, 2002

Notified in advance by Teresalita, I went down to the lobby at 9:45 a.m. and was able to get my ticket and walk in a group over to Lyndhurst at 10:00 a.m., the time stated on the program. For once, it looked as though things were going to run on time, but I was too optimistic. Since there had been no formal announcement at the banquet the night before, not everybody who was attending the party knew when or where we were supposed to meet, and so didn't have the tickets they needed for entrance to the estate grounds. Since the Hilton staff failed to give any wake-up calls, the stars were also running a little late, so it was a little over an hour before the Q&A session began in the carriage house. That left time for some casual sightseeing.

Teresalita and Ren981 had made the trip previously, and they were kind enough to lead the way. One of the first things I noticed as we passed through the gates was the number of geese comfortably scattered over the lawns. I was told that these are Canadian geese that apparently simply come to camp out at Lyndhurst. They were very sedate creatures. Cars drove to within a foot past them and they never budged; I know pigeons and sparrows that would have panicked at just the sound of the vehicles. One of the things that I appreciated most about the Lyndhurst estate was how close to nature it was. Seeing the trees as their leaves were just beginning to change color was a big deal. Seeing the trees, period, was a big deal to me. There were so many that it felt like being in a forest, something I had never done before (with the exception of a trip to the redwood forest of Northern California, but that's rather unique). For a good percentage of the day's visit, I pointed to various sights and asked, "What's that? What's that?" In addition to the Canadian geese, Lyndhurst is also home to squirrels, chipmunks, a groundhog that lives under the greenhouse, and a pale blue bird of which I only caught a glimpse that I was told was a blue jay.

I snapped pictures of the first glimpse of the house through the trees when only its tower was visible, as well as the greenhouse, and "Rose Cottage," a miniature playhouse. The carriage house where Gerard Stiles saddled the horses in *Night of Dark Shadows* has since been transformed into a restaurant. Located in the same area are a gift shop and a viewing room where a video tour of the mansion plays. There was a bit of trouble when we realized that none of us had been given silver stickers when we'd arrived at Lyndhurst; without these stickers, guests are not allowed to enter the mansion. We went into the gift shop to beg stickers (and maps) from the sales clerk, but she seemed suspicious, and was reluctant to help out since she didn't know anything about our convention group's visit.

In time, the stars and the rest of the party guests arrived, and we gathered in the carriage house to listen to them. Marie Wallace had left the night before, so the day's guests consisted of Roger Davis, Lara Parker, Diana Millay, and Terry Crawford. Roger was up first for his independent Q&A session. He finally explained why he'd run out on us the day before. He had gone to see a play because he was considering one of the actors for his studio's upcoming movie, and as it happened, the particular actor he'd gone to see was the one he'd liked the least. Then, Roger spent some time discussing his houses. He referred the audience to his website, Viewmont.Com. Somebody in the audience asked him about whether he had actually surfed in the movie *Ride the Wild Surf*. "It's interesting that you bring that up," he remarked. "That film's been a cult classic for a while, but now after *Blue Crush*, it's been showing up on some of the classic film channels. I was curious to see *Blue Crush* because of all the computerized special effects. Of course, we didn't have any of that in *Ride the Wild Surf*." Roger and the rest of the cast had gone on location to practice surfing, but weren't very successful. "The only person who really learned how to surf was Tab Hunter. The rest of us—" he mimed surfing "—were in a studio while they threw water at us." Roger had to wrap up his Q&A session because his cell phone kept ringing and he finally couldn't ignore it anymore. He stayed long enough to introduce the ladies, who were waiting in the wings, and spent a few minutes with them before making his exit.

Roger asked Diana, Lara, and Terry about their memories of making the movies. "I remember my one line as the nurse, 'Here is the blood, doctor,'" Terry recalled. Diana mentioned that something frightening had happened to her when she was staying the night in the tower room. She didn't give away too many details, but said that the story would be included in an anthology that Craig Hamrick is soon to release. Lara recalled doing her own stunts for the hanging sequence. "They put a harness around my waist and told me to jump off the platform and start kicking. I had to twist my head a little so that it looked like my neck was broken." There was also a disagreement between Lara and Roger over what time of the year the movie had been filmed. Lara distinctly remembered the trees being in blossom, but Roger claimed that there were dead leaves on the ground. (He wasn't in *Night of Dark Shadows*, so I'm not sure how he would know this.) Lara also mentioned that this was her first time visiting Lyndhurst since making the movie. "My taxi driver said to me, 'Wow, you must be so excited!' I don't know. Maybe there's something wrong with me. Are you excited?" she asked Diana and Terry. "Oh, yes," they insisted. "Very excited!" The actresses also talked about how they had gotten involved in the film. "When Dan made the first movie, he left me back at the studio to hold down the fort," Lara explained, "but he promised that when he made the second movie, I could star in it. Well, he eventually decided that it would be better to let the film star David Selby and Kate Jackson. That young couple hadn't been a part of the original vision."

Diana mentioned that Dan Curtis had convinced her to be in the movie because of a great scene he had written for her and Charles in the tower. Unfortunately, that fabulous scene was one that ended on the cutting room floor, and Diana didn't seem too happy about it. Both she and Lara had worked in the tower room and they agreed that it had been difficult because the area was so cramped. "Quentin and Angelique had a love scene, and we practically had the cameramen breathing down our necks. Dan Curtis, the crew, the lights and cameras were all in the room with us," Lara remembered. Another difficult scene was for Diana in the pool house. "Quentin was supposed to drown Tracy and flash back to Charles drowning Laura. So, Dan wanted me to get in the water, but there were sparking wires all around the pool. I had a young son at home. I wasn't going to risk my life for a movie, and I told him no. Then, Kate Jackson jumped right in and started swimming around the pool. She even dived underwater and stayed there until she almost ran out of air. Dan expected me to dive in too, but I wouldn't do it. Finally, they brought me back to the studio and filmed me in a tub while somebody poured water over my head. It looked ridiculous, and most of it ended up being cut anyway."

Somebody asked if the ladies had understood the film's ending. Neither did. "It's whatever you imagine happened, how you would want the film to end," Diana said. Another person inquired whether the scenes of Angelique's corpse dangling from the tree had really been Lara Parker or a dummy. "I think it was me," she said. A similar question came up regarding Carlotta and whether Grayson Hall had had a stunt double jump from the tower. The actresses believed that a dummy had simply been tossed off the roof. Lara also remembered how Kate Jackson would warm-up for rehearsal by "cursing like a sailor." It was part of a new acting technique that she was studying that was meant to help her loosen up and feel more comfortable in her roles. Needless to say, the tactic left her co-stars disconcerted.

Lara thought that Kate had been working under Sandy Meisner's guidance at the time. Terry and Diana also remembered this particular coach. "He was like a Svengali," Terry said. "He held me after class one day and told me, 'You have potential. You can be a great actress." He then began to outline the course she would have to follow under his direction, but his controlling demeanor put her off. "I never went back." Diana had gone through the same thing. "He told me, 'I shall create a new identity for you. You will not be yourself anymore, but you will be my own creation, somebody completely different. What do you think of that?' I said, 'I think I want my mother.'"

When the Q&A came to an end, we filtered outside and waited until everybody had obtained a sticker from the gift shop before continuing to the mansion. There were so many of us that only groups of 20 were going to be allowed through the house at a time. The three actresses were among us, and I could hear them whispering to each other from time to time, pointing out areas of the house that had changed, or discussing their scenes. I made it into the first group, and our particular 'tour guide,' the man who had played Barnabas in the Haunted Room and was still wearing his costume, was very informative. He told us exactly which scenes had been shot in which rooms and even knew the precise blocking. When leading us through the front entrance, he'd stated, "Mrs. Johnson stood right here and Carolyn collapsed right in that corner." It had been a couple of years since I'd seen the movies and I don't think I would have recognized the locations without his help.

Our guide told us that occasionally, Curtis & crew set up partitions to cover doorways and disguise the way that the rooms were arranged in order to make the movie house seem larger or more elaborate. This was done in

'Maggie's bedroom' for instance, in order to create the 'secret panel.' Also, the sequence in which some scenes were shot made second floor rooms appear to be on the first floor, etc.

The house itself is beautiful, but for such an immense building, the rooms within are surprisingly tiny. It was hard to believe that Dan Curtis managed to get all of his equipment, crew, and cast into the various locations. I think I would have been able to appreciate the mansion much more if there hadn't been so many other people. It was difficult to see what was in each of the rooms since most of them were roped off at the doorway and we were only allowed a glimpse of a few seconds before moving on to let the next person have a look. Sometimes it was difficult to simply turn around, let alone walk. Even though we'd been broken into groups before entering, the additional tour parties were filtering in close behind us and at times, our respective groups meshed, making the hallways and rooms even more packed.

I felt guilty because I had brought along my video camera (which I didn't even use) and so was carrying around the large camera bag and my purse. It must have been rather annoying to the people around me who were trying to squeeze past. There were renovations in progress in the mansion that day, complicating our tour just a bit because certain sections were roped off. Mainly what I remember being able to see were the ceilings in the rooms. They were elaborately and brilliantly painted and some even had carvings. There were some impressive statues scattered throughout too, and I was tense about not bumping into anything. Fortunately, we received the special privilege of being able to go down the 'back stairs' that Todd Jennings had taken in order to meet vampire Carolyn in *House of Dark Shadows*; this area had earlier been roped off, but was opened for us. From there, we went through the kitchen (which served as Julia's laboratory in *House*) and outside. Unfortunately, we were not allowed into the infamous tower room (now, that would have been a squeeze, but if they could fit cameramen and equipment inside...) Later, I learned that the reason for this is a NY code that prohibits people from being in any area without

Once outside, we were taken to Angelique's hanging tree[21] where Lara posed for several photos. The tree looks much different in person than on film. For one thing, the ground slopes, almost like a hill, and the tree doesn't look quite so tall. One of the guests told the story of how he had visited Lyndhurst one day since it was near his home, and had been shocked to find Dan Curtis with his film crew and Angelique dangling from the tree. The signs advertising the filming of *Night of Dark Shadows* that were posted around the grounds took him aback as well because by this point the show had already gone off the air.

The tour group continued in one direction, but I remained behind with a few friends to take pictures of the mansion and the tree. Gradually, we made our way to the greenhouse, from which all the glass had long since been removed. The ground inside was made up of engraved bricks and it was fun to read some of the inscriptions. A fountain was running beneath the greenhouse dome, and it added beauty to what was otherwise a fairly stark building.

The rose garden was nearby, and it was absolutely lovely. Surrounded by a fence and closed gates, it took a moment before we were able to find our way in. As soon as I stepped inside though, I could feel a difference in the air. It seemed fresher and more moist. The grass in this area was almost impossibly green. Rows of various colored flowers surrounded a white gazebo in the center of the garden. I think that was probably my favorite place on the grounds.

From the greenhouse, VAM and I returned to the carriage house for lunch where we were soon joined by our friends Dolores and Walter. Our booth was in what had once been a horse's stall, and we joked that it might have been the one where James Storm had saddled Quentin's horse. After lunch we went our separate ways. VAM was intent on trying to see the tower room, and I believe Dolores was on her way to the pool house, which was open for a charity auction. Although I hadn't yet seen that, I preferred to return to the hotel. It was already past two, the time that our group's tour was supposed to end. Walter and I tried to find our way out of the massive maze-like estate, trying all the while to keep out of the way of the many cars that had a habit of sneaking up on the road behind us. At one point, we became so turned around that we ended up in the area for private houses. A jogger was kind enough to point out the proper exit.

Upon returning to the hotel, I headed for the grand ballroom to see if there were any activities immediately lined up and was astonished to find that the room had been rearranged and now rows of desks had taken the place of the rows of chairs. I learned from a couple of fans gathered in the lobby that the evening's activities had been moved to the Sunnyside ballroom (where the haunted room had been,) and that the movie screening of *Night of DS* wasn't going to be for a couple of hours yet.

At a quarter to seven, I went down to the ballroom. Not too many people were present yet, but the actresses were there. Terry was walking around, playing with some of the attendees' babies. She and Lara made an announcement expressing how much they had enjoyed the weekend and wishing us well before leaving. While Ed and his associates worked out technical difficulties with the VCR, I had the good fortune to meet elizabeth from the dsforums. We talked for a bit before the movie began. Even though I prefer *Night* to *House,* I hadn't planned to stay and watch the entire film, but I did anyway (there were flowers on the trees—Lara was right,) and it was a good thing, I did because afterward the Cheep Productions videos, which had been advertised all weekend (and postponed) were finally played.

These videos, made by JVjr, his brother Daryl, and their friends, are hilarious full-length episodes (20-30 mins.) in the tradition of DS. We were treated to three episodes: "Save Our Cemetery," (my favorite) "Barnabas vs. the Bed," and "Heifer Hi-jinx." "Cemetery" even featured a guest appearance by Sharon Smyth, reprising her role as the ghost of Barnabas's little sister Sarah. The plot of that episode involved an evil developer who was planning to bulldoze the cemetery while Barnabas and Julia tried valiantly to stop the destruction by protesting, hypnotizing, and finally calling upon Collinsport's dearly departed (Jeremiah Collins, Dr. Woodard, and Sam "Pop" Evans) for aid. Cured of his vampirism in "Barnabas vs. the Bed," Barnabas struggled to adapt to a mattress instead of a coffin. "Heifer Hi jinx" was set earlier in the series when Barnabas was still feeding on cattle, and used actual clips from the show to set up a scenario where Julia disguised herself as a cow in order to get Barnabas to bite her.

For a so-called 'cheap production,' these videos were very sophisticated and well-done. Daryl played the dual roles of Julia and Barnabas to perfection. If I closed my eyes, he sounded exactly like the real actors, not only by the sound of the voice but by the delivery of the lines. The last syllables of Barnabas's words were drawn out just as Frid always spoke, and Julia's hysterical sobbing was spot-on. The costumes were impressive, too. During some of the close-ups, I almost believed that I was really looking at Jonathan Frid as Barnabas. In "Save Our Cemetery," the actors portraying the ghosts were dead ringers for Sam Evans and Dr. Woodard III right down to Woodard's glasses and Sam's white cane. The sets for the episodes could have passed for those from the show. I understand that Eagle Hill Cemetery was completely fabricated, yet it looked real enough to me, and the Old House was arranged just as Barnabas himself would have wanted it. Even classic bloopers were reconstructed, (an ABC TV camera stealing a scene, falling tombstones, line flubs, etc.), and some of the actual bloopers that occurred during Cheep Production's filming added even more authenticity to the films. I was in awe of the attention to every detail and the effort and creativity that went into these videos. I understand that this was the last time that those tapes will be shown at a Halloween event, and while I'm thrilled that I was able to catch them, I do wish there was a way they could be shown at future Halloween parties or Festivals.[22] I honestly feel that these are quality productions, and I know the fans would love to see them.

Following the last video, I said good-bye to a few of the people I had befriended who remained in the ballroom, then went upstairs to the bar to meet some friends. When the bar closed, we moved our party to the hotel lobby. Walter loaded his photos into his laptop and showed us the images he'd captured from the weekend. He also provided a wonderful little concert for us by playing his guitar and taking special requests. My evening wrapped up at about 2:30 a.m. because of a morning flight home. I would have liked to stay longer.

I truly enjoyed the weekend in Tarrytown. It was somewhat different from what I had expected, but I have a feeling I'll be coming back next year and for years after that.[23] The scheduling changes and postponed events were offset by the wonderful new friends I made and the existing friends I was able to get to know better. I am very grateful to everybody who helped to make my time in Tarrytown memorable!

2003 Dark Shadows Festival: Brooklyn, NY

Day 1: Friday, August 29, 2003

Friday was an exciting day for me. While my roommate victoriawinters walked across the Brooklyn Bridge and into Little Italy with our mutual friend Tina, I spent the afternoon lounging in the hotel's upstairs lobby and greeting all of my dear DS friends as they arrived to check in. I hadn't seen some of these people in over a year so it was quite the 'family reunion'.

Though registration wasn't scheduled to begin until 4:00 pm, people began queuing up shortly before 3:00 and soon, a serpentine line curved through the hallway, tripling on itself and spilling into the main lobby (these lines would present a problem throughout the weekend. Since the Brooklyn Marriott's lobby is rather small, the overflowing crowd filled it quickly and more than once, security had to redistribute fans in order to avoid a fire hazard.) By around 3:30, several fans were sitting on the floor, camping out. The line finally began to move at around 4:15. This year, none of the badges had names written on them in advance, which saved time for the Fest volunteers who would normally have to label the badges and then search out the correct ones for each fan; unfortunately, it was problematic for people like me because some fans (unlike me) never bothered to fill in their names themselves. This made it a bit awkward to seek the real names of my online friends, or talk to people in line when I didn't know whom I was addressing.

Since the first event wasn't scheduled until 6:00, I left to eat dinner. While calling my friends on my cell phone in the lobby, surprise guest Terrayne Crawford walked by and asked to take a look at my Fest program. Ordinarily, she would be overseas doing ministry work, but due to recent political upheavals, Crawford was unable to go to Morocco and came to Brooklyn instead. She's a very pleasant person, kind to the fans, and so it was a delight to have her with us.

I missed the opening ceremonies because I was impulse buying in the dealers' rooms. However, I made it back just in time to watch an original episode from the 1897 storyline. Episode#873 featured Count Petofi briefly traveling to 1969 in Quentin's body, only to be jerked back to the past when Beth discovers his portrait is missing. After first accusing Pansy Faye of the theft, Count Quentin threatens Barnabas, but discovers his hand no longer has power. The real Quentin uses Petofi's hand to make Kitty realize that she is actually Josette. The episode was interspersed with original commercials advertising everything from sewing machines, to Chef Boyardee spaghetti, and peanut butter. A favorite ad for cologne featured Jerry Lacy as Humphrey Bogart and Marie Wallace as a femme fatale.

After the DS episode, we viewed a touching tribute video for the late Dennis Patrick.[24] It opened with a lovely musical photo montage of Patrick set to "When Irish Eyes Are Smiling" and segued into an interview from his *Dallas* days broken up by clips from his numerous TV appearances.[25] As Patrick expounded on his TV appearances, his unusual training at the hands of stage legends, and the joys of playing a charming villain, we watched his scenes from *Lost in Space, The Rockford Files, Kojak, Joe*, several live programs, and naturally, *Dark Shadows*. Delightful outtakes from the MPI "Behind the Scenes" video showed Dennis laughing over working with John Karlen and quoting naughty limericks about Lela Swift and David Thayer Hersey. "Nobody's going to see this, right?" he double-checked before reciting his infamous poetry. "It's off the record? Good." The video closed with another touching photo montage, this time to the tune of "Danny Boy."

Next, Terrayne Crawford, Lara Parker, Kathryn Leigh Scott, Marie Wallace, and Diana Millay took the stage and were invited to reminisce about Dennis. Lara mentioned that one of her mentors was Barbara Cason, Dennis's wife, and so she got to know him that way. Dennis was also praised for his humor. The ladies were invited to share their memories of Dennis's funniest moments, but at this point, John Karlen waltzed onstage. "They told me to be here at 8:00," he announced, "and here I am." (Indeed, the original scheduled that was mailed to Festgoers lists a 7:30 panel of John Karlen, Diana Millay, Kathryn Leigh Scott, and Roger Davis, but this was changed to a ladies-only Q&A in the official program.) Anyhow, Karlen was invited to sit down and to share his recollections of working with Dennis.

"Dennis Patrick is dead, gone. Dust! He was Irish, you know. At an Irish funeral, you would pick up the corpse and dance with it. We would all be dancing with him now." I admit I was a bit surprised by this rather morbid answer and wondered whether it was difficult for him to talk about his good friend and if the flippant response was meant to cover this. I've since learned that Mr. Karlen wasn't feeling well during the weekend; perhaps this was a factor.

Next, several clips of Dennis's scenes as Paul Stoddard and Jason McGuire aired. During the scenes between Willie and Jason, Karlen comically pantomimed the activities being discussed. For instance, when Jason remarked that Willie left town without money, he turned his pockets inside out. When Burke wondered whether Willie had hit his head during a bar fight, he rubbed his forehead as though nursing a wound.

By this time, a number of fans had lined up at the microphone with their questions. The first woman commented that while Lara and Kathryn had played bitter enemies on the show, they seemed to get along well in real life. "Are you friends, or do you argue?" "Yes," Lara answered. "We are friends in real life, but we do argue. If we go to see a movie, I'll love it and she'll hate it. We're at different ends of the political spectrum. I'm a liberal Democrat and she's Republican. Well, actually, you're more in the middle now, aren't you, Kathryn? You used to be a Republican but then you shifted. (Emcee Richard Halpern joked, "So you're voting for Arnold [Schwarzenegger],[26] Kathryn?") For example, I think the recall is a circus but she thinks it's democracy in action. So, we disagree, but, yes, we're friends." "You mean you used to be before this," kidded the woman who had asked the question, upon catching a glimpse of Kathryn's startled face throughout Lara's explanation.

A man next stepped up to thank all of the stars for their work on the show and their continued attendance at Festivals. He has long been in ill health (cancer maybe?) but having the Festivals to look forward to and the stars to speak to kept him motivated to stay healthy. In particular, he cited the generosity of Louis Edmonds and requested that the audience give a standing ovation in his memory, which was done.

Another man wanted to know if Kathryn remembered the riddle that Sarah had recited to Maggie in order to help her escape from Barnabas. "Do *you* remember it?" Richard Halpern challenged. Indeed, the fan did: "One, two, away they flew. Three, four, near the door. Five, six, count the bricks. Seven, eight, the clue is great/grate. Nine, ten, home again!" "I remember the line, 'Somebody's been tampering with the bleeder valve in Roger's master brake cylinder,'" Kathryn laughed.

A woman wondered if Lara would feature the 1692 Salem witch trials in her upcoming novel, but Lara was coy about sharing details. Someone asked whether anyone kept in touch with Jonathan Frid. "I just got a letter from him," Diana shared. "He's in Canada, living the life of a country squire. He asked me, 'Do you still have your apartment in New York? Let me know if you ever intend to sell it. That's the one thing that might get me to come back.'" One enterprising woman requested a hug from John Karlen and he invited her onstage to collect it. Erfette from the Sci-Fi board asked the actors if any of them ever visited the various fan sites and message boards to read what people had to say about their characters. None of them did. Another fan asked whether Kathryn had enjoyed her appearance on *Star Trek: The Next Generation*. She had. One woman had a technical question: How did cameramen who taped kinescopes keep the film from recording a black band due to time lapse photography and proximity to the screen? Nobody on the panel, which by now included James Storm, knew the answer. Caroleena from the Sci-Fi board stepped up shortly afterward. "I know Joe Haskell was taken away to Windcliff, but what happened to Joel Crothers in reality? Why did he leave the show?" Kathryn answered this: "He moved on to other things. He found another job on *Secret Storm*." Diana Millay also recalled working with him on this soap.

Following the short Q&A session, Roger Davis took the stage. However, by this time, I was to meet with the Collinsport Players for our first rehearsal of "House of Dark Shadows" (I was playing Maggie) and so I have no idea what happened in the ballroom for the rest of the night. I first went across the lobby to the lounge/bar where I met my fellow actors. One by one, everyone assembled, and then we set off in search of a place to practice. First, we considered rehearsing the play in the hallway since we couldn't immediately locate a spare ballroom. This wasn't really an appropriate spot, however, and we found ourselves moving on to the kitchen, which was a teensy bit cramped. Eventually, we settled in Siberia—actually Salon I, a remote room far in the back with a powerful air conditioner, through several sets of doors and just off the kitchen. I made a special note of how to get to Salon I, since we would be rehearsing in this room again the following morning.[27]

The rehearsals were tremendous fun! My fellow castmates were a highly talented bunch, and I caught myself cracking up over their gestures and ad libs, many of which were later added to the script. We ran through the play twice before dispersing for the night. I made my way to the bar to join my friends, who had called to inquire where I was after the evening Festivities had ended. When the bar closed, we gathered to watch videos of past events in the room of some of our friends. I didn't get back to my own room until after 1:30 a.m. It was a full day, just the way I like them.

Day 2: Saturday, August 30, 2003

Saturday opened with a traditional fan panel hosted by Marcy Robin during which time, fans are invited to ask 'Where are they now?' questions about the actors, address plot inconsistencies, or inquire about the future of the show and what plans Dan Curtis may have for DS. It was here that Marcy announced there *will* be a 2-day event in the summer of 2004.[28] I wasn't in the room at the time, but victoriawinters swears she has Marcy on tape claiming the event will take place in California (despite recent information on the net indicating the venue will be in Tarrytown. We'll have to see what happens next.) After Marcy spoke, we were treated to a screening of Guy Haines's fan videos. However, I wasn't able to stay to see all of them because I had to split for a dress rehearsal at 11:30.

We were on the third floor in the Fulton Ferry conference room since our other rehearsal room had been absorbed into parallel time. The new room was smaller than Salon I, but we made the best of it, took our places, and spread our props on the tables: a giant strand of plastic Fisher Price beads to represent Naomi Collins's necklace, a plastic crossbow and arrow, a flashlight, a tennis ball, etc. Unfortunately, we were missing a Barnabas cane. I had seen one in the dealers' room the previous night, but when a couple of the players went downstair to ask to borrow it, they found it had already been sold. We were able to make do without it though and as far as I know, no one complained.

Richard Halpern (Julia) held up a paper bag. "We don't have a mask, so this is what Barnabas gets to wear when he ages. What do you think?" He put the blank paper bag over his head and began to stumble around. So that no one would have to be attacked by the Unknown Vampire, innovative Stuart quickly sketched a realistically grotesque, aged face with a couple of markers and even tore ears from the sides to give the makeshift 'mask' more dimension. The end result was quite convincing, but in the meantime, people got a lot of laughs trying it on and bantering back and forth: "Julia, I knew you were an old bag." "Dan Curtis, you cheapskate!" (This one actually made it into the play.)

We were only able to rehearse once all the way through before going downstairs. During the last twenty minutes of David Selby's film *The Flatboatman*, I milled around at either corner of the stage, seeing where we would place our props and where Eileen Lynch-Farrar (Carolyn) and I would be changing our costumes. (We ended up in the kitchen. Fortunately, I was wearing a bathing suit under my costume so nobody would get a free show.) Once the Selby film ended, I expected that we would go onstage, but instead, a video of Jonathan Frid interviews began to play. "Why are they playing a video?" I asked my fellow players. "I thought we were supposed to be onstage at 1:00." Kathryn Leigh Scott was to narrate our skit, and 1:00 was her designated free time. If the event ran late, we wouldn't be able to have her participate. I was told it was common for the skits to be delayed, and eventually the video, which was in reality only about 10-15 minutes long, ended and the lights went up. It was showtime!

Kathryn Leigh Scott gamely read her self-referential lines, poking gentle fun at her Pomegranate Press sales and career as an author and publisher. Peter Mac had Barnabas's voice inflections down precisely, right to the last drawn-out syllable. Eileen Lynch-Farrar sang a hilarious parody of the Crystals' "Then He Kissed Me" ("Then He Bit Me") backed by Jay Keaveny (Roger) and Richard Halpern (Julia). Halpern drew enormous laughs from the audience with his portrayal of the investigative, jealous

Julia. Jonathan Harrison, a man over six feet tall who portrayed little David, devised an ingenious way to play the part by strapping sneakers on his knees and crawling on his knees over the floor. Stuart Manning played a popular Willie, adopting a bit of Karlen's accent for the role. Walter Down represented Jeff Clark, a noble hero right up to the bitter end. Overall, the show was quite a success! The audience loved it, applauding and laughing all the way. There were one or two bloopers—at one point, I lost one of my shoes and had to quickly turn and step back into it while trying not to miss my line—but the Players were highly professional and covered up the rare dropped line or missed cue quite smoothly. I was concerned that I might not be facing the audience as often as I should or that I might not be projecting my voice as loudly as I ought, but my fellow cast members seemed pleased with my work. Even Kathryn Leigh Scott tapped me on the back as she was passing through the lobby and told me that I did a good job.

After the show, we took pictures in the lobby and a number of fans complimented us, saying that this was the funniest show they'd seen in years. One man asked if we were going to play it again later in the weekend. A couple of our actors had previous engagements though, so Saturday afternoon was the only opportunity for a Collinsport Players show. I understand that next year is the 20th anniversary of the Collinsport Players' founding, so I'm sure there will be something grand to commemorate that. I hope I get to be involved again because I had a marvelous time. I'd first seen the Players perform at Festival 2000 and I laughed myself silly. I had told my mother, "I wish I could do that. I'd love to be in one of these plays!" Three years later, I had achieved that wish.

After taking photos and visiting with friends, I slipped back into the ballroom toward the end of James Storm's Country Western concert. The next event was a Behind the Scenes panel, which was actually very intriguing. Two of the show's cameramen, Stuart Goodman and John Woods, participated in a Q&A session, sharing the unusual perspective of DS backstage. The pair talked about working in the cramped studio with the unwieldy cameras. "When you hear all the clanking and clattering going on in the background," joked John, "that was us crashing into each other."

They also discussed putting Vaseline on the edges of the camera lenses to give the picture a blurry, dreamlike quality.

The pair also swapped some gossip about the actors. One day, Thayer David fell asleep on the set (according to them, he had been drunk.) Another time, Mitchell Ryan came to work drunk and burst out laughing while saying his lines. It became infectious, and soon everyone in the studio was laughing so hard that they had to stop taping for the day. John shared his favorite funny moment from the show. "We had a stuntwoman who was supposed to fall from the top of the stairs and roll all the way down. (She was a stand in for Cavada Humphrey, who played Mme. Findley during Quentin's haunting of Collinwood.) It was a pretty dramatic fall, and she was too scared to do it, so we got Alex, the wolfman, stuck him in a dress and slapped a wig on his head. It was the most hilarious thing!" He burst into chuckles at the memory. "Alex wasn't the best person to play a woman," Stuart explained. "I mean, he was short and his build was small, but he was a real *grrrrr*! (here, Stuart flexed his muscles) kind of guy."

Next, we had a short Q&A session, during which time the Great Kinescope Controversy began. The woman who had asked the previous day about why there was no black band in the kinescopes repeated her question for the cameramen, who would be most likely to know. "We never had kinescopes," they claimed. "Some of the other studios made them, but we never did." The woman expressed disbelief and several people in the audience whispered, too. After all, some DS episodes survive only in kinescope form; where did they come from if there were no kinescopes? Later in the session, someone else addressed this issue. "You must have had kinescopes because some of the DS episodes were lost and all we have left are the black and white kinescopes." The panelists didn't seem to understand the point she was trying to make though. "At the end of the day, any kinescopes would be destroyed," Stuart explained. "The studios didn't save them. Nobody ever expected to be rerunning soaps 30 years in the future. A few of the soaps in New York made kinescopes, but they didn't save them." At last, a third person stepped up toward the end of the Q&A session and actually quoted the pages and page numbers from KLS's almanac that mentioned kinescopes and the surviving kinescope prints. Finally, the cameramen compromised. "What that book calls 'kinescopes' wasn't really kinescoping. Some people in the industry use terms differently. *Dark Shadows* never made actual kinescopes, but we did another type of taping."

In between kinescope questions, one member of the audience asked Stuart if he was working on any other projects for A&E. ("Not at the moment.") Someone else mentioned just having recently seen the cameramen listed in the closing credits. "At what point in the show was that done? I don't remember seeing them before." "We never got credits," Stuart Goodman objected. "Well, only at Christmas. Then Dan gave us credit." Another fan commented on the current trend in film and television to use overblown computerized special effects. "Do you think that the people of your generation were more imaginative and used greater creativity with their effects?" "Wow, that's a tough question," John remarked. "When we did the show, it was so long ago. It was right at the beginning of the special effects era and we were on the cutting edge...I suppose it was more creative."

The Behind the Scenes panel was running about fifteen minutes overtime when Roger Davis took the stage. After talking for about ten minutes, asking the usual questions about who had been present on Friday night and how many fans were attending for the first time, he opened the stage to his co-stars. First, Richard Halpern asked the stars what was new in their lives. James Storm has gone back to surfing and is helping Chris Pennock with his production of *Who's Afraid of Virginia Woolf?* Pennock was very excited about the play; evidently, he'd been trying to get permission to do the show for a while, but was unsuccessful. Another actor in the LA area had secured the rights, and it wasn't until the 'George' in that production had to drop out that Pennock finally got his chance to take on the part. He enthusiastically invited everyone in the audience to come and see the show.[29] Diana Millay has written a new book called *The Power of Halloween*. Marie Wallace discussed her role in cancer charities. Kathryn Leigh Scott told us that she had just sold the *Charlie's Angels Casebook* to be made into another TV special. David Selby quietly spoke about how glad he was to be back in New York after the World Trade Center tragedy of two years ago. He requested five seconds of silence from the audience to remember the victims. Terrayne Crawford again mentioned her ministry, as well as a recent brief appearance in General Hospital. Donna Wandrey has made a couple of commercials that should air soon. Lastly, Roger Davis talked about the movie that he is making with Tom Cruise. "The Los Angeles journalist who wrote a story about our production described me as 'mild-mannered producer Roger Davis'. The crew asked me, 'What were you on when he interviewed you that day that would make him think you were 'mild-mannered?'"

At this point, the introductions were over, so Kathryn stood up and addressed the audience on a very important topic. "As you know, there's been a lot of talk that this is the final Festival. Please know that none of us had any part in that decision. We were just as surprised as you are about the news. We're all interested in continuing the conventions and we'd love to come back next year, but that all depends on Jim Pierson. He's in charge of organizing the Festivals. Where is Jim? Let's see him. You know none of this would be possible without him. He is the driving force behind the Festivals. Let's have a standing ovation for Jim!"

Kathryn cajoled Pierson onstage and persuaded him to sit down with the actors, where she promptly put him on the spot. "Now, Jim, how can fans contact you to let you know that they support another Festival?" He shifted in his chair, gazing down at the stage. "Well, you can e-mail Ann Wilson from the Festival website." "No, Jim," KLS cut him off, "how can they contact *you*?" "I've got his cell phone number," Roger Davis volunteered. "Auction it!" shouted someone in the audience. "She'll pass the e-mail on to me," Pierson assured. After guaranteeing that there will indeed be another event next year, Jim Pierson wasted no time in scurrying offstage.

After that, the Q&A session began in earnest, interrupted only by the arrivals of John Karlen and Lisa Richards, who had just stepped off the train. (Lara Parker was absent, for she was taking her daughter to Pennsylvania to register for college.) The first person to take the microphone began his question with a disclaimer. "I would never advocate violence against children. I'm not a violent person, but when you were working with those kids, did you ever want to just..." He mimicked a slap. "When we first started *Dark Shadows* in 1966, do you know who among us had the most acting experience besides Joan Bennett?" Kathryn questioned.

"It was David Henesy. He had been on Broadway for a couple of years when he just decided to audition for *Dark Shadows*." Reflecting on the child actors, Kathryn said ruefully, "They were so good. It seemed that they just had to blink and they would know their lines." The gentleman asked if anybody had heard from any of the younger cast members. "Sharon Smyth (Sarah) used to come to these events. And David Henesy e-mailed me not too long ago." (The interview is in the *DS Memories* book.)

Someone asked David Selby who was his favorite leading lady, but after taking a quick look up and down the stage, he declined to answer. A fan asked Marie Wallace if playing Jenny Collins had made her more sympathetic to the plight of the mentally ill. "Well, I was already a little bit crazy, so it wasn't much of a stretch to understand was she was going through," Marie kidded. Terry spoke up and shared that the storyline between Jenny and Beth had inspired her to study psychology and thus made her more understanding of the insane.

Another man had a question for Roger Davis. He pulled out a reference guide: "Did you know that, according to this book, Roger Davis acted in a number of silent movies and died in 1980 of cancer ?" Roger chuckled. "Did I really? Well, I feel pretty good for someone who's dead." He then went on to relate a funny story about his experiences at the hotel. "Did you all know there's another Roger Davis here this weekend? Is Roger Davis here? Raise your hand." A young man in the audience signaled. "When I tried to get my hotel room on Friday, the front desk told me that Roger Davis had already checked in. I kept telling them that *I* was Roger Davis but they kept telling me that I would have to pay for my room. Finally, I go to my room, get into bed and say, 'Wait a minute, there's someone else in here'—it's the other Roger Davis." I assume that the confusion was eventually resolved.

Someone wanted to know where John Karlen went when he wasn't on DS. "I went West," he explained, sharing that he was able to pursue stage and TV roles outside of DS because he didn't actually have a contract with Dan Curtis. "We just shook hands and he passed me a twenty every so often." He then asked if anybody was familiar with his film *Daughters of Darkness*. "That movie had about 20 different titles. I think in one country it was called Ruby Red Lips or something. Does anybody know any others?" Nobody volunteered any information.

Another fan asked about a play in which both Lisa Richards and John Karlen had acted together: *Marat/Sade*. They remembered the production vividly. "I played Charlotte Corday and John was Marat," Lisa explained. "He was supposed to stay in the bathtub but he would break out and start running around onstage. In fact, you got carried away and broke somebody's arm once. Do you remember that, John?" He remembered the incident and the name of the unfortunate guard who had tried to restrain him. "He was just a little guy and the nicest person there. It was an accident." "Yes, I remember you felt so bad," Lisa murmured sympathetically. "I think he was afraid of you after that." "I also played a guard in *Marat/Sade*," Chris Pennock shared, "and in one of the first shows, I somehow dislocated my shoulder. They had to take me to the hospital in an ambulance." "That's funny," Roger joked," because *I* was in *Marat/Sade* right around the same time and shortly after, *Jim* was in *Marat/Sade*..." It would appear that *Marat/Sade* is the DS actors' play of choice.

A man asked David Selby if *Lincoln and James* might become expanded into a screenplay. "That is going through quite a few re-writes at this point," David explained.

One other fan wanted to know from the actors, "Did you ever do something really out of the ordinary when auditioning if there was a role that you really wanted?" "You really want every role that you audition for," Marie explained. "I don't remember auditioning," David Selby said. "I just remember picking up golf balls in Dan's office." Terry repeated her story about her tearful, hysteric first audition for DS while Kathryn told the story of how she had been cast as Josette. (She'd volunteered to stand in for the dummy that Bob Costello was originally going to use as the Ghost of Josette in 1966.) "Sure, I went to extremes to get a role," Chris Pennock laughed. "At the time, gurus were very popular and everybody was going to see them for advice. I was getting ready to audition for a play and I *really* wanted the part, so I went to a popular guru in New York. He gave me a mantra: *Om mani shivaya*. I kept repeating it to myself all during the drive to the audition: *Om mani shivaya, Om mani shivaya*. Backstage: *Om mani shivaya, Om mani shivaya, Om mani shivaya*. I said it so often that eventually I became one with the words! *Om mani shivaya*! It all made sense and I just kept saying it until finally one of the producers said, 'Uh, sir, it's your turn.' 'Oh, right, right!' So, I gave them my best performance, I mean I really became the character, and I was good. The only problem was I had recited the wrong lines. But they were impressed with me anyway so they did cast me. Those gurus! They really work."

The actresses were questioned about the elaborate hairstyles they had to wear when the series went back in time. "We had to go in at least two hours early to have our hair and wigs styled," Kathryn remembered. "My hair at the time was very long, all the way to my waist," Terry recalled, "and even then, I had still more hair with the added wigs." "I was very happy with what my stylist was able to do, considering that my hair was very short at the time" Donna Wandrey said.

Julia99 asked for the cast to share any memories of Grayson Hall. "Her cooking!" Johnny blurted out. Terry Crawford repeated an anecdote that she had previously shared at the Halloweenathon about how she had taught Grayson to cry. "I learned method acting. You try to match your emotion to the scene. So, in the show, Beth might be crying because Quentin left her for Angelique, but in reality ,I might be crying because I'm remembering a favorite pet that died. Grayson was surprised that I could cry real tears, and so I explained to her how I did it. A few months later, we filmed another episode together and she came running over to me. 'Did you see it? Did you see? I cried a real tear!' She was like an excited child; it was so much fun to see how pleased she was."

The last woman approached the microphone. "This might be an appropriate final question: did you know that *Dark Shadows* was going to end, or were you surprised? What were your reactions when you found out?" Kathryn went first. "I was shocked. I was living in Europe at the time. It was just after finishing *House of Dark Shadows* and I picked up a magazine one day only to see that *Dark Shadows* was going off the air. I felt so disappointed. I had always believed that Maggie would come home from Windcliff one day, and now it would never happen." David Selby claimed he didn't remember anything about that time (probably because he was in the hospital with appendicitis during the show's last days.) "I was in the dressing room when I found out," James Storm explained. "They had brought me back as Gerard in another time, but I wasn't on for very long." "I experienced heart palpitations—in fact, I'm still having them," Chris joked. "It was a scary thing to hear. I'd just gotten married and now I was going to be out of a job." He did find work on another soap opera after DS, fortunately.

When the Q&A session finally ended and the ballroom cleared out, (everybody who wasn't trying for autographs had to filter out only one set of doors—the rear doors) Tina, victoriawinters, and I went back upstairs to eat dinner in our rooms (a nearby diner delivered to the hotel) before the Costume Gala, and to give victoriawinters a chance to put on her stage make-up.

This year's Costume Gala was one of the largest in years, with 32 participants! They were a very talented bunch this year, too, offering several clever song parodies and humorous sketches. We met in the Fulton Ferry ballroom around 8:00 to receive our order assignments and then go downstairs to the convention room. It took three packed elevators to get everyone on the ground, and then we were instructed to line up in the kitchen, of all places. Last year, we had been able to stand against the wall so we could still watch the action on stage. It was harder to see and hear this year unless you got out of line and crept up to the stage, which I eventually did (after all, we all had been numbered going into line and nobody was going to steal my place.)

Among the acts were several costumed Kittys, Magdas, Julias, and Angeliques (ranging from 1795 to 1970 PT) a Pansy Faye, a Daphne Harridge, and a young Barnabas who recited "When I am Dead, My Dearest." As a victim in thrall to the vampire Barnabas, victoriawinters danced and sang to Evanescence's "Haunted." David Block repeated the dual monologue between Daniel and Gabriel that he had performed in 2001. One man dressed up in elaborate creature make-up to demonstrate what Mary Shelley may have had in mind for her creation. (When I asked, he said it took two and a half hours to apply!) One young girl recited a cynical but funny monologue as Carolyn Stoddard.

Eileen Lynch-Farrar (Carolyn in our skit) sang two songs: one as Carolyn, ("Leader of the Pack" about Buzz Hackett) and the other a "Baby Face" parody about Barnabas as sung by Julia Hoffman. The audience loved her and joined in singing the chorus. ("What the heck? Come on and bite my neck! You're my hero, Barnabas"). VAM performed a song[30] and dance in her elaborate Count Petofi costume. Also, one man sang *a capella* as John Yeager, ("Still Cyrus" to the tune of REM's "The Apologist"), and David Short continued last year's brilliant "We Didn't Start the Fire" parody, picking up right where he left off in early 1968 and moving to the start of the Leviathan sequence. ("At this point, the ratings dip; Dan Curtis abandons ship!") I performed "Ode to Collinsport," set to the tune of the Beatles' "Octopus's Garden." During the performance, I was concerned that I might not have been holding the microphone properly or singing loudly enough, but the audience was laughing and clapping along so they must have been able to hear enough of the words. I was especially thrilled that some people even howled along with the lyric, "When you hear all the dogs howling, you know a vampire must be prowling." I was a bit disappointed with the lighting this year. The overhead lights in the ballroom had been turned off and bright stage lights blinded me from either end. I squinted a lot and wasn't able to make eye contact with the audience. Last year in Anaheim, the ballroom lights had remained on and I was able to pick out my friends' faces in the crowd, which made me feel a bit more comfortable about performing. (I do know that Diana Millay was in the front row of the audience this year.)

Toward the end, we were treated to some hilarious skits. Bobubas provided cue cards, narration, and sound effects for a brother and sister team who were re-enacting the scene where Barnabas shoots Angelique (with a spray gun—you see, the real thing was confiscated at JFK Airport) and in return, the witch inflicts on him a curse that will last "through time travel, through parallel time. Anyone who loves you will die, and if anyone loves you after they're dead, they'll die again!" I found it charming that several people made the issue of the "Final Festival" the focus of their skit. Providing his own sound effects, Michael Culhane as Nicholas Blair announced, "I hear this is a 'Farewell' Festival; I will not permit that! This is *your* Festival! Legions of the damned, I salute you! We will rise again—next year!" At this point, Marcy hastened to step in and assure him that the Fests really were continuing. In the final skit, two gypsies walk into a bar.

Magda asks Sandor, "What's with the loud shirt?" "Wardrobe department screwed up again," he laments. "Now I look like hippie instead of gypsy!" Upon looking into her crystal ball, Magda discovers doom for the Festival. To remedy this, she and Sandor set a gypsy curse: "Whoever tries to end the Festivals, when they turn on their radios, they'll hear only Britney Spears music!" After the last performer had stepped down, everyone crammed back on the stage for a final bow—and a surprise for Marcy. When Ms. Robin had finished thanking all of the volunteers who helped with the Gala, several of the Gala participants declared, "Let's hear it for Marcy!" Everyone in the ballroom started to chant, "Marcy! Marcy!" and one person even presented her with flowers. As one of the original founders of the Festival, she surely deserves the credit for twenty years of hard work.

After the Gala, I met up with some friends for group photos and more private video screenings. It was another late night, ending shortly before 2 am, but again, it was a ton of fun.

Day 3: Sunday, August 31, 2003

On Sunday morning, I went downstairs a little before 10:00 since, according to the original schedule, that was the time when events were supposed to begin. I was hoping that the advertised morning screening of fan videos would include the ones that I had submitted earlier in the month (a fight montage set to "Kung Fu Fighting", a Carolyn character video set to "Rich Girl", and an Angelique character video set to "Every Breath You Take.") Friends of mine later told me that my videos had been played the night before just prior to the Costume Gala; I was still upstairs at the time and missed them. Unfortunately, the schedule printed in the program proved correct and the doors didn't open until 11:00. By that time, I'd had plenty of opportunities to bond with the people standing around me in line.

The first event of the morning was a screening of *The Secrets of Stella Crozier,* a teleplay featuring Diana Millay and written by Sam Hall. Since I had seen this already in 2001, I went into the hall to visit with friends who were moving back and forth through the lobby and the dealer rooms.

We actually spent about three hours just standing around, taking pictures and getting to know one another better. At about 1:30, RobinV and I strolled down to the Wendy's at the corner to pick up lunch, and then walked back to the hotel. We had a lovely chat in the meantime and I was privileged to sit next to her through the DS charity auction, the Q&A with Terrayne Crawford, and the reading by Diana Millay. Putting Terry and Diana onstage was a last-minute change to the program. Originally, a video of Donna McKechnie and an interview with make-up artist Dick Smith were supposed to air, but instead we were treated to real live people.

Diana came onstage to read a true ghost story that had happened to her at Lyndhurst during the filming of *Night of DS*. Her story appears in Craig Hamrick's latest book.[31] Diana related how she had gone back to the mansion to retrieve a script that she had forgotten, only to be stranded there by a severe rainstorm. The night watchman, an unusually sober figure, had prevented her from going to the parking lot. 'Go back to the house, milady,' he repeatedly told her. So, Diana spent the night in the tower room, listening to strange noises all the while. In the morning, she learned that the house had no night watchman. "But if he was actually a prowler or a vagrant, why didn't he attack me or try to steal my purse?" she wondered. "And what about the flooding from the storm?" Had the 'nightwatchman' actually been a ghost? Could Diana somehow have slipped into another time dimension during the night and then fortunately slipped back?

Terrayne Crawford came onstage next and spoke ardently about her ministry, the World Foundation for Children, which aids young people who live in high-risk areas of the world and also sponsors budding journalists by taking them out into the field where they can meet those in need. "Kids always ask us, 'Why do you care?'" Terry related tearfully. "Why do you come here? Why do you want to help? These are very special people. They realize that they don't have to keep living the way they are. They want to make a difference in the world, and we want to help them do that." When asked how fans could support the charity, Terry explained that the organization's website was still in development.

Next followed a brief Q&A session. A fan praised Terry, saying how well she looked. "Thank you. When you tell us how we look just the same as when we were on the show and how much you enjoyed watching Dark Shadows, it really makes us feel so good. It's wonderful to see all of you here!" she gushed. Terry also spoke about her first audition for DS. It was a very dramatic scene: someone put a ring on her finger and she became possessed. When the ring was removed, she became hysterical, bursting into tears.[32] Terry won the role of whatever character this was supposed to be. However, at the same time she was also offered a television commercial and a part in a movie, and was undecided as to which job to take. She finally chose the commercial instead of DS, but luckily Dan Curtis invited her back to play Beth a few months later.

Next came the auction. Jim Pierson sold several CDs: the soundtrack to the DS movies, a soundtrack from the show, and Robert Cobert's "Night Stalker" album. Other items included a program from the Museum of TV & Radio's DS reunion, *a Dark Shadows Resurrected* book, a sound card of DS music cues, (which nobody will be able to play without studio equipment) trading cards, a *House of DS* video (out of print), an MPI marketing item the "Barnabust," (a small statue sculpted to look like Jonathan Frid; "makes a nice paperweight") and several articles of clothing. Among them were the jacket that Jim Fyfe wore as Willie in the 1991 series, a pair of shoes (size 11) and ascot that belonged to Michael Stroka, and a dress and shawl supposed to have been worn by Lara Parker during the 1970 season of the show. "We tried to find stills of her wearing the dress, and it seems that Lara didn't actually wear it for the show," Pierson confided, "but this *was* part of the *Dark Shadows* wardrobe, and if you bid on the dress, you can get the shawl for free." Finally the major item of interest, the portrait of Josette from the 1991 Revival series, went up for bid. "There were actually two portraits," we were told. "The first was used in the pilot and we auctioned that one off a few years ago. But this was the one seen in the next twelve episodes of the series." This portrait of Joanna Going as Josette eventually sold for $2,400.

Following the auction, the video tribute to Dan Curtis began to play, but since I wasn't especially interested in seeing this, I thought I might as well get in line for the "Return to Collinwood" show. Yes, get in line; we'd been warned all weekend that on Sunday afternoon, the ballroom would be cleared so that the organizers could perform a sound check of the microphones and other equipment. Thus, everyone who was already sitting in the front and had been there since the morning would lose their great seats.

It was only about 3:00, an hour before the show was scheduled to start, when RobinV and I walked out. As soon as we left the ballroom, I could see a long line near the entrance door, wending its way through the dealers' room. "Is this for autographs?" I asked. (Earlier that morning, people had been standing in the same spot to meet David Selby.) "No, this is the line to get in for 'Return to Collinwood,'" a woman told me. "What?! The line is already this long?" I stared out past the ballroom, past the dealers' room. As we walked, I could see the queue stretching along the length of the convention hallway and out the doors, into the main lobby, and around the hotel itself. In fact, people were lined up in front of the elevators, curving around the balcony, almost all the way across the lobby, and practically through the doors of the lounge/bar! I had never seen such a line! And these people had been waiting for several hours already to ensure that they got good seats!

My kind friends Sunsetter, eeriekitty, and eeriekitty, jr. generously allowed RobinV and I to join them in line; later, we were joined by Tina, JVjr, victoriawinters, mazing, and a few members of Grayson's Legion (AKA the yellowshirts.) Not long after we'd secured our places in line, security came over and split us right where RobinV, Sunsetter, the eeriekittys, and I were waiting. There were too many people in the lobby. We were taking up all the space and it was a hazard, so they were moving us. We feared that if they took us from our current spot, we'd be at the back of the line instead of somewhere in the middle, but they assured us that we would keep our place and only stand elsewhere for a little while. They split us from the larger line and led everyone back into the hallway where they made us stand against the wall. They turned our line around a few times, but eventually, we did get back into the ballroom.

There were so many people in the rows in front of me that I could barely see the stage, but that didn't turn out to be such a bad thing. We learned that instead of an actual play where the actors put on costumes and performed actions, the cast would be performing in the style of a radio play, reading scripts at the microphones. Therefore, all I had to do was relax and listen.

The play, scripted by Jamison Selby, was supposed to be about an hour long, but it ended up running for two. Alternately dramatic and comedic, it was entertaining, though the ending left me wanting resolution to some of the loose ends. I hear that this script was labelled 'Episode One,' so perhaps we'll have a follow-up performance in the future with additional actors.[33] Toward the story's end, the characters commented on how wonderful it would be if only David were with them or if they could just find Victoria. I turned to RobinV and asked, "Do you suppose David Henesy or Alexandra Moltke is backstage waiting to make a surprise appearance?" We watched to see if this was so, but it never happened. That's not to say it couldn't happen in the future, however. Nancy Barrett and Donna Wandrey turned in exceptional performances as Carolyn Stoddard Stuart and Mrs. Franklin (successor to beloved housekeeper Mrs. Johnson). Highlights of the show include the reading of Elizabeth's will and the revelation that Victoria Winters was Carolyn's half-sister, Maggie slapping Cassandra and calling her a bitch for trying to steal Quentin from her, and Willie taking ownership of the Old House and installing a Whirlpool. (Now he can finally soak away the pain from all of Barnabas's thrashings.) A standing ovation concluded the show, and the ballroom quickly emptied out for autograph lines and banquet lines.

A second line for banquet tickets developed, and I was lucky enough to get mine fairly quickly so that I could run up to my room and change for dinner. Unfortunately, going back downstairs, I encountered yet another banquet entry line that was almost even longer than the one for "Return to Collinwood." Because the autograph line was in the main hallway, everyone destined for the banquet was split up throughout the convention area. One group was lined up in a ballroom just behind the gift shop at one end of the hotel while others stretched around the lobby and all the way to the back near the kitchen. I estimate that we must have stood in line for a good two hours at least. The banquet was originally scheduled to begin at 8:00, but since the play had run over and the autograph session was lengthy, as usual, we weren't allowed into the ballroom to be seated until after 9:00. Roger

Davis walked the line, apologizing for the delay and promising us that we would be eating very soon. I know that several of my friends complained of hunger, the pain of standing, and the general disorganization.

Once inside, I was amazed to see that there were over sixty tables in the banquet hall, stretching all the way from the stage to the very rear of Salon I. Unfortunately, those of us sitting in the back (I was at Table 59 with Minja, Teresalita/Springsteena, and ReneeC/DSFan1970) weren't even able to hear Jim Pierson's announcements above the clatter of silverware and dishes as the waiters bustled around serving coffee and dessert. We shouted, "Louder! Speak LOUDER!" but even then, it was nearly impossible to understand what was going on. Dinner wasn't bad. The main course consisted of chicken, vegetables, and rice, preceded by a salad and rolls. (Vegetarians ate vegetable lasagna.) Sadly, our table ran out of rolls before the basket could circulate the entire table and we weren't able to get a refill on the breadbasket. Dessert was fruit in cream cheese, which I was unable to sample because of my allergies.

I can't say I was thrilled with the way the door prizes were given out. The process involves drawing two numbers: the first number stood for the table, the second number for the person at the table. (Each table selected one person to be "Number One" and all the other diners numbered themselves 2-12 clockwise.) So, if someone drew 12 and then 7, the seventh person at Table 12 won. This year, it seemed that all of the winning tables were in the teens and twenties. I heard one 30 and one 50,but that was it. I wondered if someone had bothered to put in enough numbers to represent all of the tables. Eventually, we gave up hope of winning any door prizes, though we were given complimentary sunglasses with the DS logo on the earpiece. Unfortunately, I forgot to pick mine up as we were being rushed out of the dining room. The Marriott staff wanted to clear the ballroom by midnight, so the banquet ended at 11:15, immediately after we had finished eating. We just had time to watch two of Guy Haines's music videos and no further programming.

Not ready to settle for an early night, my friends and I went to the bar for about an hour where Bobubas talked the Marriott into letting us watch Guy's recording of the Collinsport Players' skit on the big screen TV in the bar. Just as we were watching the curtain call, we were told that the bar was closing and we would have to leave. Oddly enough, several patrons remained in the bar even up to an hour after we were told to go. Since the Brooklyn Marriott doesn't have a 24-hour meeting area for guests, we simply stood around in the lobby, talking, taking pictures, and enjoying one another's company, knowing that we would all be leaving the next morning. When we grew tired of standing, we sat or sprawled on the floor. At one point, Jonathan Harrison and Richard Halpern of the Collinsport Players started dancing and singing "Puttin' on the Ritz" in the style of *Young Frankenstein*, drawing several laughs. A few times, security came around and asked us politely to go back to our rooms because we were too noisy, but we remained until nearly3:30 AM, making every moment last. This gathering was a thrilling end to a lovely weekend.

2004 Dark Shadows Weekend (Tarrytown, NY)

Day 1: Friday, August 13, 2004

Friday the 13th—not the best day to begin a Festival weekend. My bad luck actually began on Thursday when my flight to NY was delayed by an hour and our baggage was held up for half an hour upon landing at JFK. However, on Friday morning, I was awake fairly early and went downstairs to meet and greet my friends and fellow DS fans.

Friday was the day trip to Lyndhurst. I had expected a single bus to take people to and from the estate, but actually a series of shuttles left throughout the morning, so people could trickle out at their leisure. I thought that this system was very efficient. However, the shuttle drivers all went on their lunch breaks from 1:00-3:00 (not so efficient) leaving fans either stranded at Lyndhurst or at the hotel. I had visited the estate back in October of 2002 during Ed Lambese's Halloweenathon.[34] The grounds of Lyndhurst are beautiful, but I felt that the house was too small to accommodate the large DS tour groups, so I chose to stay behind at the hotel to avoid the crush this time. I was glad that I had remained behind, for it rained heavily on Friday afternoon (actually it rained off and on throughout the weekend), and I don't think it would have been pleasant to explore the grounds in the wet and the mud. The people that I spoke to all seemed to have enjoyed their trip, rain or no rain, although I know that some people who went searching for the remains of the Spratt House (used as the Old House on DS the series, which burned down in 1969) found only bug bites for their troubles.

The registration line was not as bad as it has been in previous years. The line actually split alphabetically; there was a window for people whose surnames began with A-G and another window for H-Z. In addition to our programs, we were all given free 1999 DS calendars. All of the pictures in the calendar were from one of the DS movies; I'm guessing they were given to us because this year's location was in the movie's territory.

Opening ceremonies were delayed until everyone in the registration line had been helped, but in spite of this I still missed them because my friends and I were in one of the hotel's two restaurants waiting for our food. However, I do know that the Collinsport Players did not open the Festival with a skit, despite what was listed in the program, so those of you who told me that you missed the first skit on Friday can relax. Both of the shows, "My Fair Julia" and "Scooby-Doo and Barnabas, Too" took place on Saturday. The Players holed up in a room in back of the main ballroom to conduct rehearsals after hours on Friday night and for much of Saturday. Because I was rehearsing with them and didn't see everything that went on, my coverage of this year's events is going to be brief.

By the time I finally made it to the ballroom, I was able to catch the tail-end of the Q&A with Marie Wallace and Denise Nickerson. Someone asked how far in advance of taping did they get the scripts. Denise thought they'd only been given the scripts the day before, but Marie disagreed. "I can remember carrying my script around with me for about a week before we taped." "But," Denise pointed out, "they always made changes in the scripts right at the last minute, so we didn't know what we were really supposed to do until the night before." The actors and actresses would also come to the studio the day before the taping to do a read through of the script.

webby asked for memories of Joel Crothers. Both ladies praised his talent and mentioned how nice he was. Marie had actually known Joel before acting on DS with him. "It was a little TV production about two girls who were roommates and their boyfriends. Joel didn't play my boyfriend, but he was the boyfriend of the other girl. So that was where we met for the first time. I don't think anybody knew about it except the two of us. And then he was on *Somerset* later at the same time that I was."

The actresses were also asked if they had been approached to participate in the new DS that the WB was planning.[35] "In my case, that's a big no," said Denise. Marie's response was more in-depth, and it seemed to me that she was a bit hostile to the idea of a new DS. "I don't see why they have to remake and recast DS at all. I don't think the executives get it. Part of the reason why DS was so successful was because of the people who were involved, people like Jonathan Frid, and the stories they told. I know they made a new DS in the early 90's, and it may have been pretty slick—in fact it was too slick. That was one of the problems. What they made was nice, but it wasn't *Dark Shadows*." Emcee Richard Halpern added to this topic by asking the audience how many would like to see a next generation continuation of the show versus a revival of DS.[36] There was enthusiasm for both (personally, I vote for a continuation) as well as for a feature film.

Marie and Denise left then and we were treated to what I call the KLS and Karlen Comedy Half-Hour. Kathryn Leigh and John took their places amidst applause. Then, she turned to Johnny, who was wearing a T-shirt and shorts, and asked, "What happened to the rest of your pants?" "They're in your room, sweetheart," he replied. The rest of the Q&A session was like that—friendly joking and bantering back and forth. John addressed the line of people that was already forming at the microphone. "This year, I want you to ask us personal questions, real deep, dark questions. Instead of asking about some dumb music box like we hear every year, why don't you ask about the good stuff?" I knew he was waiting for a specific question. Earlier in the dealer's room, Johnny had pointed to the MPI vendor's table where the five DS bobbleheads (Josette, the werewolf, Barnabas, Quentin, Angelique) were on display. "Where is the Willie Loomis bobblehead? That's what I want to know. When I go onstage, I want you all to ask, 'Where is Willie Loomis's bobblehead?'" Now that he was onstage, he ordered the audience to shout the question at the count of three. After we'd finished demanding a Willie bobblehead, the personal questions began.

The first question, addressed to John Karlen, was, "What's your dress size?" "I don't know," he replied, "but whatever it is, I'm growing out of it." Next, Gothick asked several in-depth questions about the *Daughters of Darkness* film. Karlen mentioned that the movie will be screened at the Egyptian Theater in Los Angeles (I believe he said it would be on August 27.) They discussed a scene in the film where John and the two lead actresses recall the crimes of Countess Elizabeth Bathory. "That movie really did have some great dialogue," Johnny said. "I'm glad you noticed it." Johnny seemed to have had a lot of fun making the film and traveling to and from Paris with the lead actress, Delphine Seyrig. "Don't knock the French[37]," Karlen pleaded. "They have much better cooking than we do. *Much* better cooking!" Gothick also asked Karlen why he punched the director, Harry Kumel, an event that Karlen apparently discussed on the DVD of the film. "He started it," John asserted. "He slapped one of the actresses, Daniele. I thought that was awful and I ran down the stairs, yelling at him. Then, he turned around and hit me. I knew that was going to happen as soon as I got involved, but I went ahead anyway. So then I punched him. Man, now that I'm thinking about it, I'm starting to get really mad again. Now I don't think I want to go to the screening after all. I might want to hit Harry again; I hate that guy." "It could be a 34th Anniversary punch," Kathryn teased.[38]

Another question was, "Did any of the cast members have affairs with each other?" "No," Johnny answered, "I never had an affair with any of the actor-esses." However, he did joke about having a thing for Lela (Swift). "Since you want us to get personal, how much money did you make on the show?" asked a fan. "Nothing. Not a cent. Dan Curtis made all the money," Johnny replied.

Someone else wanted to know why Karlen was hired to replace the original Willie Loomis (James Hall). "I have no idea," he said. "They were in the middle of a story and they just put me to work."

"I can answer that," Kathryn said. (Meanwhile, Karlen pretended to snore.) "[James] was a former classmate of mine from acting school, a very nice guy. But he had a bit of a drinking problem. It was clear that he was pretty nervous while he was on the set. One day, we were in the middle of shooting an episode, and it became obvious that he just could not go on. It was a shame, but the producers were very nice to him. Then they hired John Karlen."

"There's no shame in being an alcoholic," Karlen insisted. "In fact, Lee Strasburg taught that, when you feel nervous, just take a drink and it will help you relax."

"Lee Strasburg said that?!" Kathryn asked incredulously.

"Yes, he did."

"That's silly," she scoffed. "We lost some wonderful actors (from the show) because they were too 'relaxed.'"

Johnny began a list. "John Barrymore, Spencer Tracy, Humphrey Bogart, Clark Gable—they were all alcoholics."

"And look what happened to them!" Kathryn shot back.

"Yeah, they had the greatest careers of anybody in Hollywood," Johnny returned. "It's OK to be an alcoholic."

Rolling her eyes, Kathryn addressed the audience. "Don't listen to him."

Johnny was asked whether he preferred working with Dennis Patrick or Jonathan Frid (while he answered, Kathryn pretended to snore.) "You want me to say I liked one more than the other? Well, how about if I say I liked them both equally?" John Karlen obviously has great respect for Jon Frid and stressed that they were good friends (I guess all the canings were forgiven.) He also spoke about his first meeting with Dennis Patrick. "We were taking a walk on my first day—we hadn't even shot our first scene together yet—but he started opening up to me about the divorce he was going through at the time. From then on, we became good friends."

Kathryn was asked to share her memories of Joel Crothers, and she told of a time she took a last-minute trip to Italy to visit her then-boyfriend, Ben Martin. She'd mentioned her plans to Joel, and he showed up at her apartment later that day with a packed suitcase and his own All'Italia ticket. "In the airport, all the stewardesses were watching us and whispering, wondering if Joe and Maggie were running away together."

A fan remarked that John Karlen's DS characters, in particular Willie Loomis and Carl Collins, had very nervous mannerisms. "Was that the way you played them, or were you really nervous in those scenes?" Johnny answered that the nervousness was how he interpreted the characters. "The characters on DS were so great! I had a chance to play such wonderful parts, and then they gave me the dumb Emmy for *Cagney and Lacey*! All I ever did on that show was make pasta." Kathryn remarked that she thought John Karlen was the most talented actor on DS. John himself went on to praise Jonathan Frid's work. "I just had to go on, do a silly scene and leave, but Jon (Frid) had to stay on camera the entire time and deliver these long speeches."

Karlen was asked what he had been doing while he was not on the show. "I was probably in plays," he explained. "I didn't have a contract. I just showed up here and there, and Dan would let me be on the show." Lastly, someone made a joke about one of Johnny's earlier comments. "I believe you when you say you didn't have affairs with any of the actresses, because I heard a rumor that you had an affair with Jonathan Frid." "Honey, I'm going to set the record straight on that—it's not a rumor," Karlen joked. "He's going to call me later tonight. He calls me all the time from Canada."

Next, Lara Parker came onstage. She shared recent news, such as the marriage of her youngest son and the fact that her daughter had recently started college. The usual questions—how did you audition for DS, what was your favorite blooper—were asked, and Lara told of how, during her audition, Jonathan Frid had whispered that the role was that of a witch. Learning this, Lara had glared into the camera with her best witchy look, and she believed that was what got her hired. But she wasn't entirely happy with the part at first, for she'd wanted to play a heroine. "Jonathan had to keep reminding me, 'You're the heavy, you've got the best part. Stop crying and be mean!'" As for a memorable blooper, she cited the time during the 1795 storyline when a prop man had doused her house of cards with too much lighter fluid, and it burned to ashes before she could finish her incantation.

Fans also wanted to know about Lara's books: what was the new book about, when would it be available, and would *Angelique's Descent* ever be back in print? "If the new book sells well, Tor may re-release *Angelique's Descent*. I recently got back the rights to the book, so we can do that now," Lara explained. The new book should be available in either summer or fall of 2005. In this novel,[39] Lara touches on the history between Judah Zachery and Miranda DuVal, the first Angelique, who really was a witch in Salem. Also, Barnabas is cured of his vampirism, but he's not entirely happy with his new life as an aging, powerless mortal—particularly when a new vampire comes to town and Barnabas has no way to fight it. Lastly, a group of hippies living on the Old House property play a part in the unfolding events.

LdyAnne also asked Lara about her recent online short story, "Her Robert Blake" and how much of it was inspired by Lara's actual guest stint on *Barretta*. At this, Lara laughed and laughed. Not her famous Angelique chuckle—she was asked to do that later—but bemused, embarrassed laughter. "Oh, boy. . .I didn't know anybody had read that! I made it up, none of it really happened. It's called 'fiction.'"

Lara was asked to share her memories of making the film *Race with the Devil*. Specifically, she recalled a scene where her character discovered a rattlesnake in her trailer. A live snake was used for this. "We had six-foot tall Teamsters who wouldn't come near it. Loretta Swit gave me all her lines from that scene." In fact, the rattler was harmless. "Before filming, a handler milked the snake. He put the fangs over the edge of a jar and squeezed down on the venom glands. All the poison came out and went into the jar. My character was supposed to find the snake, pick it up and start screaming. Meanwhile the director was calling to me, 'Hold it up. Let's get a shot of you showing both the fangs and the rattle.' He wanted me to throw the snake down, but I didn't want to hurt it, so I just—" she mimed placing the snake down carefully. "The director was getting frustrated with me. He said, 'Just throw the fucker down.'"

Another fan wanted Lara to share her memories of Humbert Allen Astredo. "He was a very nice man, and a method actor," she recalled. "He tried to teach me how to act. For example, if someone held up a cross and I screamed, he would ask me, "'What are you screaming at?' A cross isn't really scary, so I would have to think about something else that would make me scream." It was evident that Lara thought highly of Humbert. One man brought up the issue of religion. "I don't know what all of the actors' backgrounds in faith are, but in scenes where you had to perform black magic or call up the devil, did you ever feel guilty?" "Well," Lara admitted, "when I'd go home after taping a scene like that I'd think, 'Oh, please, don't let that really work!'"

Lara ended her Q&A by reading the first chapter of her new book, in which Barnabas and Willie visit the reconstructed Old House, now owned by an Angelique lookalike named Antoinette. In *Angelique's Descent*, the Old House burned to the ground (a point that evidently upset many fans and readers,) but Antoinette purchased the property and proceeded to rebuild the estate, presumably using old blueprints that she had discovered. However, the details of the new Old House are so similar to the original, right down to the furniture and the aged look of the paneling, that both

Barnabas and Willie are disturbed. Their fear increases when they descend into the basement and discover evidence that a vampire has been there!

From here, I left the ballroom for a night of skit rehearsals, but I understand that the night ended with a screening of both *House of DS* and *Night of DS*.

Day 2: Saturday, August 14, 2004

I woke up fairly early on Saturday morning (considering that I'd been up late visiting with friends the night before.) I quickly got ready and went downstairs to see who else I could find to chat with. While walking through the lobby, a man stopped me and asked if there was a *Dark Shadows* meeting going on at the hotel (he must have seen people walking around with their programs, badges, and T-shirts.) I told him a little bit about the Festival—how the actors were available for autographs and Q&A's—and he became very excited. He introduced himself as Orville and said he was from the Caribbean—and that he used to watch DS on TV in the 1980's. "I know it was on in the 70's—we get everything much later than you get it in the US—but I used to watch it all the time. It's very big in the Caribbean. Everyone watches *Dark Shadows*." Now, I've always heard that DS was broadcast internationally, but this was the first time I'd ever met anyone from abroad (other than England) who knew the show, and I was excited to learn just how internationally famous DS really is. Orville described some of the characters and I showed him my program. He recognized Barnabas and Angelique, and I told him that Lara Parker was at the Festival and that he could get a day's admission if he wanted to attend the events. He seemed very eager to do just that but I didn't see him for the rest of the day. I hope he got to check out some of the events.

Saturday's events kicked off with a screening of various videos—TV interviews with the DS cast, a *King of Queens* episode where one of the characters wanted to go to a DS Fest, fan videos such as Baby Dark Shadows and (for the first time in many years) the brilliant Cheep Productions (full length parody episodes of DS, complete with recreated sets and bloopers.)[40] While the videos played, the Collinsport Players rehearsed for the day's two skits.

This was only my second time working with the Players. I'd always admired their work from the audience, but observing them in rehearsals was a real blast, too. These are very talented and dedicated people, and I'm not sure why they recruited me because they are light-years ahead of me in terms of craft and ingenuity. I just wish I had the time and the room to detail all of the ad-libbing and brainstorming that went into shaping the skits. I've worked backstage on a couple of community theater productions before, and I enjoy watching the rehearsal process—the genesis of the play—more than I enjoy seeing the finished product. So it was with these skits. I had received my scripts about a month before the Fest, but I didn't know who was playing which parts, so to finally have everyone assembled and working together was great fun. We worked for about two hours, reading and blocking the first skit and then we were able to take a break when the "live" events began, so I got to see the last part of KLS's talk and the beginning of Jamison Selby's.

Kathryn Leigh Scott was discussing her *DS Memories* book-on-CD when I sat down. "I have a new CD out. It feels strange to say that. Pop stars say 'I just released a new CD.' This is my first, but here it is!" Next, someone inquired about her book *The Bunny Years*, so she told us what inspired her to undertake that project. Kathryn had worked alongside Gloria Steinem as a bunny at the Playboy Club. Later, in her feminist literature, Steinem said some disparaging things about the club and the women who worked there. "I felt offended by her remarks," Kathryn explained. "I felt like she was putting us all down—she didn't get what being a bunny was really all about. So, with fire in my belly, I sat down to write my own book as a rebuttal to her."

Kathryn also discussed her work on *Star Trek: The Next Generation* in the episode "Who Watches the Watchers." "I was walking around the set with all this green make-up on my face, but people recognized my voice. They remembered me from DS. The people on the set would ask, "Aren't you—Didn't you used to be—Were you ever on a show called *Dark Shadows*?"

Someone asked why Kathryn had originally worn a short blonde wig while playing Maggie. "I had first tried out for the part of Victoria Winters," she explained. "With my long, dark hair, the producers were afraid people might confuse me with Alexandra Moltke, who also had long, dark hair, so they made me wear the wig. I wore it for the first few weeks even during rehearsals, and then one day Dan Curtis saw me rehearsing without it. He wanted to know, "Why are you wearing a wig?' He thought my natural hair looked good, so he said I should leave it as it was. Lela Swift was in a panic. She said, "Dan, we can't let her go on camera with dark hair when she was blonde the day before.' Dan replied, 'Oh, the audience will never notice.'" We all had a good laugh about that.

Jamison Selby came onstage next to discuss the "Return to Collinwood" play that he wrote last year. (The CD is now available for $20. A limited number of bound scripts were also for sale at the Fest for $15, but I understand that those sold out.) The first question was, "How has DS affected your life and what are your earliest memories of the show?" "Well, obviously my name came from the show. My dad said he always liked the name "Jamie" so he chose the name Jamison. Teachers always asked me why I spelled Jamison with an 'I' instead of an 'E' I didn't want to have to go through the whole explanation of how my dad used to work on this show about vampires. Now, my earliest memories. . .I can remember people from the show coming over to our apartment. I didn't know who they were at the time. I didn't know that they were from DS. I guess my earliest memory is of John Karlen walking around shouting."

The next fan wanted to know what Dan Curtis's reaction was to the radio drama. "I don't know. We sent him a copy of the CD, but I don't think he's heard it yet. Jim (Pierson) and I have listened to it over and over, making sure it sounds all." Another fan asked if the recording on the CD was the same production that was seen at the Fest last year and the same as the text in the script or if any additional scenes had been included. "There might be some small adjustments—we combined a couple of lines and deleted a couple of other lines to make it flow more smoothly, but essentially it's the same as the script and what was performed onstage." Jamison was asked if there would be a sequel to the play. "That depends on all of you. If this CD sells well, there may be a sequel.[41] How many people want a sequel?" I think every hand went up.

Someone asked whether future radio dramas would include voice artists playing Julia, Roger, or some of the other characters whose actors are no longer with us. "No," Jamison answered. "We wanted to do a play that would show where the characters would really be now and what they would actually be doing today. It wasn't possible to use the Mrs. Johnson character, for instance, but DS needed a creepy housekeeper, so we created a role for Donna Wandrey." He added that it had been Donna's own idea to play the part with a British accent. "We all loved it and thought it was great." Jamison started to answer another question about how much research he'd had to do prior to writing the radio play (watching the episodes, studying the characters, etc.) but at that point I left the room to get into costume for our first skit so I missed his full response. (I gather that Jim Pierson provided a lot of background information.)

According to the schedule in the program, the charity auction was supposed to start at 2:00 after Jamison Selby's Q&A, but instead the Collinsport Players presented their first skit, "My Fair Julia." In this play, Carolyn pretties up Julia to impress Barnabas and takes her to the Blue Whale for a wild girls' night out. Unfortunately, Julia drinks too much, gets too wild, and embarrasses herself in front of Barnabas. Touched that she went to such great lengths for him, Barnabas romances Julia and they go off to the Old House together for some "¦recreation;" also, Carolyn rides off with Buzz Hackett, and Roger and Mrs. Johnson pair up.

2004 marks the 20th Anniversary of the Collinsport Players. Commemorative programs featuring biographies of this year's cast were distributed prior to the performance. Jim Pierson and Richard Halpern even made announcements prior to the skit honoring the anniversary. Clearly, this show was a big deal as it continued the long tradition of skits. Unfortunately, it was marred by a series of technical difficulties.

The highlight of the skit was to be a musical number ("Popular" from *Wicked*) that Carolyn (Peter Mac) sings to Julia (John Schaefer) and Mrs. Johnson (Eileen Lynch-Farrar) while giving them make-overs. However, when it came time to play the music, nothing happened. We were told that the tape was blank! (A ridiculous statement, since we had been playing the tape during rehearsals.) I couldn't believe what was happening at the time and I felt awful for Peter and John, knowing how diligently they had rehearsed for the show over the last day and a half. It was a terribly tense few moments—silence onstage, restlessness in the audience—while we waited for the sound to come back. I know that if I had been the one onstage when all of these problems were occurring, I would have felt so awkward and tongue-tied, but they handled the whole business very professionally, joking and ad-libbing ("Carolyn, did my husband write this episode?" "I don't know, but I think Alexandra is running the sound booth.") while they waited for the music to start. When we all realized that the tape was not going to play (we later learned that it had jammed in the tape deck), I hoped that Peter would sing *a capella*, but instead he chose to skip the musical number, and the play resumed with a scene between Barnabas (Walter Down) and Roger (Jay Keaveny) at the Blue Whale. There was a lot of scrambling—some lines were dropped, entrances and exits rearranged—but we finished the show to the best of our ability. The audience seemed to like it and they were very understanding about the technical difficulties. (Now I know exactly what the DS actors had to deal with!) I think that the show we performed was good, but the show for which we rehearsed would have been better. I feel frustrated and disappointed that the audience was not able to see the skit in its entirety and as originally conceived.

Once the first skit was behind us, I decided to get something to eat. Because I went out for food, I missed the first of the charity auctions (hosted by Denise Nickerson. I had a salad-to-go in the lobby and talked with LorraineAAB and mscbryk before the *Night of DS* lost footage presentation began (I wanted to make sure to get a seat for that, since I missed it the last time it ran in Anaheim.)

Darren Gross first made the exciting announcement that a longer print of *House of DS* was released in Japan and that he was focusing his efforts on getting it. Everyone applauded to learn of this new development. Next, Darren explained that the footage he was about to show us was in black and white and had no sound, but that he would preface each piece of footage with a description of what was taking place and where in the movie the scene belonged. He had brought about 25 minutes of lost footage with him. A total of 40 minutes was deleted from the movie shortly before its release in an attempt to meet MGM's demands for a shorter film. This left the plot of *Night of DS* relatively incomprehensible and muddied the continuity. As an example, Darren cited a notorious blooper where Quentin falls asleep wearing one pair of pajamas, has a nightmare, and awakens in a different set of PJs. In fact, this happened because two separate scenes from two separate dreams on two separate nights were edited together in the final cut.

He began to play the lost footage with Bob Cobert's soundtrack playing in the background in lieu of dialogue. The scenes included some gorgeous, establishing shots of Quentin riding a horse on the Lyndhurst estate, Tracy comforting Quentin after one of his nightmares, Quentin discovering a sketch that Charles had made of Angelique, Quentin and Alex walking and talking about the recent bizarre events, Claire cowering in a corner after Gerard had harassed her and Tracy, and (one of the longest and most important blocks of footage) a flashback of Angelique and Charles flirting at the piano while Charles's wife Laura looks on. Some of these scenes were so integral to the meaning of the film that I have to wonder what the studio executives were smoking when they ordered the footage to be deleted.

To my chagrin, Jim Pierson popped in and informed Darren that Nancy Barrett was scheduled to perform at a certain time and that the *NoDS* presentation needed to be sped up. Darren suspended showing the extra footage and went directly into the Q&A with Diana Millay, Lara Parker, John Karlen, and David Selby. Johnny demanded to know where Nancy Barrett was and was told that she was still rehearsing for her cabaret.

The actors then briefly commented on their memories of Lyndhurst. Diana mentioned that she had spent a night in the tower room and had a frightening experience that she would discuss with us the next day.[42] Lara also commented on the small size of the tower room. "Can you imagine trying to cram David Selby, me, and a bunch of movie cameras into that little space?" She also joked about being hanged in the tree in back of the house. "I think that scene of you hanging was the best one in the whole movie," David said. Lara glared at him and he quickly elaborated. "I mean, cinematically, it was a great scene. It was filmed very well. It should have been made into a poster."

John remarked that he had visited Lyndhurst just a couple of days earlier and he didn't even recognize the place. "I didn't know where I was," he said. However, he did share his favorite memory of making the film. "I like to watch the movie so I can see myself riding a bicycle. I never knew how to ride a bicycle before. I had to learn for the movie, and if you watch real closely, you can tell that I'm not very good at it. I haven't ridden a bike since, but I just like to see myself riding in the movie. Then I know it really happened."

Next, people from the audience were invited to ask questions. Someone asked if an alternate ending had been filmed for the movie; the answer was no. Another fan commented on the language in the movie. "There's a scene where John Karlen's character Alex refers to Gerard Stiles as an SOB. That really shocked me. I think that was the first time I'd ever heard that phrase used in a movie. Is that how it was written in the script?" "I think so. They were just writing that script as they went along," Karlen confided. "I don't think they knew what they were doing. It was a really bad script." (Editorial: I've read the full script in KLS's *DS Movie Book*, and I don't think it's bad at all. As it reads in its entirety, *Night of DS* is very suspenseful and well-paced. It wouldn't have won an Oscar, but it's not Ed Wood or Roger Corman.[43]) "This movie was doomed from the start," Karlen claimed, "because it didn't have Jonathan Frid. He was supposed to be in the sequel. They'd written a script for the second movie, but then he didn't want to be in it, so they had to throw together this ghost story at the last minute.[44]"

Someone else wanted to know if Angelique in the film really had some sort of powers, or if she was just a ghost. "No, I played a totally different Angelique in the movie than the one on the show. I was not a witch, I was a ghost," Lara explained. She added that *Night of DS* was supposed to be her vehicle—Dan was going to make it up to her for not putting her in *House of DS* by making her the star of this movie—but her role was diminished, especially by the editing. Lara was asked if she could describe how the overlapping scenes of her ghost floating over the other cast members were filmed, but she couldn't remember.

Another person asked about the Carlotta character. "Grayson Hall's character in the present is the same as the little girl in the 1810 flashback, right? Wouldn't that make her over 100 years old?" Lara explained that Carlotta was a reincarnation of the child in the past. "Have you found someone yet to dub Grayson Hall's voice?" a fan asked. Darren admitted that nobody has been selected yet. "That's going to be so hard to do," Selby remarked. You just can't replace these people. You'll never be able to find another Thayer David (my thoughts exactly, David) or Grayson Hall."

Another fan mentioned how eager he was to see the (restored) movies on DVD. "I know that you've said Warner Bros. isn't interested in putting the movies on DVD anytime soon, but is it possible that we could pre-order them? Maybe if they see how much interest there is in these movies, it will motivate the studio to release them on DVD." Darren said he would inquire into this possibility. Another fan had a question about a picture in the movie calendars that we'd been given. "Did you have any mules in the movie in addition to the horses? There's a picture of Kate Jackson on a mule." (November) "There were no mules on the set," Lara said. "But this animal in the picture has long ears like a mule," the fan insisted. "They're too long to belong to a horse." "Well, our budget was so low when we made that film, maybe it really was a mule and they dressed it up as a horse," David joked. "I've never had very good luck riding horses," he admitted. While filming another production that required him to ride a horse, the horse had gotten away from him and stepped on his foot. "It smashed my big toe," Selby explained. "To this day, my toe is flat." John Karlen tried to persuade Selby to take off his shoe and show us, but he refused.

The actors mentioned various mishaps on the movie set. Diana Millay recalled the live electrical wires that jumped and crackled in the water at the pool house, and John Karlen remembered how perilous the greenhouse was. David Selby remembered the scene in which Gerard falls from a railroad trestle. "We had a stuntman to do the actual fall, but the rope holding him was the wrong length and when he fell off the trestle, he hit his head against the side." John Karlen told us how another of the movie's stuntmen, Alex Stevens, (who also played the werewolf on DS) actually crashed a car into a tree while Curtis was filming a car chase. "Alex broke both his legs in that crash, but Dan told the cameramen to keep rolling, to film everything. Finally, we got Alex to a hospital; he was in a lot of pain. I think it was right after that he started taking morphine. I saw him years later; he was a broken man, an addict. If you ever want to see some of his best work, see his movies before *Night of DS*."

The Q&A session concluded and the actors left the stage, but various clips of the film (including the famous and fantastic seance) continued to run while the stage crew set up the lighting and sound for Nancy's cabaret show. Then, the doors were closed; those who wanted to see the show had to come inside and stay inside. I had never seen her perform before, so I was very excited about it. Nancy started out talking about her childhood ambition to be an actress (singing "In My Little Corner" from Rodgers & Hammerstein's *Cinderella*), the glamorous but intimidating NYC, and the discouraging pattern of auditions and rejections she endured until finally striking gold with *Dark Shadows*. She performed a parody of Cyndi Lauper's "Girls Just Want to Have Fun" with lyrics that fit Carolyn Stoddard's life that was very funny. She also sang a medley of songs in character as Millicent Collins, Charity Trask, Pansy Faye, and her 1995 alter-ego Carolyn Fredericks. I didn't recognize all of the tunes, so I can't say which they were or what shows they came from. I know that Charity's song was "Follow the Fold" from *Guys and Dolls,* aged Carolyn's song was about vodka, and Millicent's was about getting married. Undoubtedly, the highlight of the act was when Nancy tapped and sang to "Razzle Dazzle" from *Chicago*. I thought she did a wonderful job of easing from character to character and I enjoyed her show very much.

Immediately after Nancy's cabaret act, the Collinsport Players rushed to the rehearsal room to practice for the night skit, "Scooby-Doo and Barnabas, Too," set to go on in just a couple of hours. This was the most elaborate of the skits in terms of dialogue, blocking, music cues, and costumes, so it needed a lot of preparation. As it happened, there wasn't enough time for several thorough rehearsals so we ended up doing a "staged reading" of the play, meaning that although we would be using costumes, props, and blocking, we would also be using our scripts.

In "Scooby-Doo and Barnabas, Too" the Mystery, Inc. van crashes outside of the great estate on the hill, and the gang gets Elizabeth's permission to stay at Collinwood for the night. It won't be a quiet stay though, for some recent mysterious happenings—the discovery of an empty coffin in the Collins mausoleum, attacks on several young girls after dark—indicate that the legendary Barnabas Collins, an alleged vampire, has returned from the grave to find his lost Josette and the Collins family jewels. Scooby and co. investigate, discover various clues, and ultimately reveal the vampire to be Jason Maguire. A former employee of the Collins cannery, Jason seeks revenge against the family for firing him, as well as the chance to rejuvenate his bankrupt brewery with the Collins fortune. This skit seemed to be particularly popular with the audience. Walter Down and Richard Halpern perfectly imitated the voices and mannerisms of Shaggy and Scooby. The only snag was that someone neglected to turn off the blue screen projector before we went onstage, so in the video footage of the skit, I'm afraid we look more like the Smurfs than the Scooby gang.

After we took a few cast photos, I had to make a quick costume change and get back into line for the Costume Gala. We had a small, but innovative group of participants this year. I was surprised not to see any Josettes or Pansy Fayes. A little girl playing Sarah recited her riddle about the hidden room; Angelique had an amusing exchange with the ghost of Jeremiah; David Block acted out a scene between Gabriel and Daniel Collins; Charles Ellis played Charnak the Great, a take-off of Johnny Carson's Great Karnak character, and psychically discerned various jokes about the DS characters; a man dressed as the Creature (Adam) sang a poignant song about the unfairness of the world; a woman portraying Angelique did a little dance; Quentin'sGal and deckert/adamsgirl acted out an original scene where Maggie confronts vampire Angelique about Joe; an e-mail buddy of mine shared her top 14 list of signs that you're a DS addict; I sang a song parody about Vicki to the tune of Toni Basil's "Mickey;" Michael Culhane's Nicholas Blair warned that first-time attendees would need to return again and again and that the Collinsport Players would need to play on for 20 more years in order to avoid his curse; Eileen Lynch-Farrar of the Collinsport Players performed a song parody of "Camelot" about life in Collinsport; several newcomers who had thought they were going to a costume party where everyone would be dressed up apologized for not having a skit prepared, and showed off their outfits; and finally, Peter Mac and John Schaefer of the Collinsport Players announced that they had discovered lost footage from the afternoon's skit and were able to perform the musical number "Popular" that had been skipped earlier. I was glad that the audience was finally able to see this act, knowing how hard the actors had prepared for it.

For the rest of the night, I socialized with various friends right through the early hours of the morning before finally retiring in preparation for the final day of events.

Day 3: Sunday, August 15, 2004

Sunday morning started with more videos, specifically "Save Our Cemetery" by Cheep Productions. In my opinion, this is the funniest and most elaborate of the CP videos. Barnabas and Julia (both played by Daryl Schaffer) summon the deceased Jeremiah Collins, Dave Woodard, and Sam Evans to defeat a ruthless construction company from demolishing Eagle Hill Cemetery. Ultimately, the ghost of Sarah, played by an adult Sharon Smyth-Lentz, saves the day—er, night.

At this time, I was also pleased to meet CastleBee, who was volunteering. I stepped out for a while to talk to some friends and when I came back, Marie Wallace was onstage.

Marie's big news is that she is writing her memoirs, *On Stage and in the Shadows*, to be released in 2005. A fan asked her to tell us the story of how she auditioned for DS. "There were three women—a blonde, a brunette, and me with my red hair. The other two both had long, straight hair; they looked like they could play vampires or ghosts. None of us had a very clear idea of what the show was looking for. I tried to think of a way to make myself stand out. When we all got called back, I decided to stand back and let the other two go first so I could watch them and decide how to play my audition. The blonde girl went up first. I think she was taken aback by the sort of directions she was given; she wasn't prepared. Then, the next girl was called forward. Meanwhile, I had stepped off to the side to tease up my hair—not like crazy Jenny, just enough to make it real big and full. By the time I had to go on camera, I had figured out exactly what to do." She described how she had put on her sexiest airs for the camera. "I've been told that Dan Curtis was in the sound booth, watching. When he saw me, he threw his script up in the air and yelled, "Hire her!""

Another fan asked her about working with Joel Crothers and she repeated the story she had told on Friday of working with him both before (in a teleplay) and after DS (on *Somerset*). Marie talked about her role on *Somerset*. "I played India Delaney—you can tell she was a bad girl just by the name. Nice, sweet girls, the ingenues, have names like Mary-Jane, but an India is a different story. I was so bad that I even testified against my own husband (on the show) at his murder trial. Later on, my character became a bit nicer. That's a bad sign. When the villains go soft, it means they're getting ready to replace you."

Someone requested that Marie tell us about working with Gwen Verdon on stage. "Gwen was very personable. She'd gotten her start as a chorus girl and so she took a personal interest in our lives and how we were doing." She went on to describe some of the elaborate musical numbers of the show. "There was one large number where all of the girls were supposed to form a Christmas tree. We wore strategically cut costumes so that when we were all assembled, we would look like ornaments on the tree. Money became tight, and several such scenes needed to be cut." Marie also did seamstress work behind the scenes. "One day, Gwen went into the city to find a dress for her costume. She didn't find anything she liked, and when she came back, she asked if I would design a dress for her. Gwen offered to pay me for making the dress but I told her not to bother, I was glad to do it. One of the producers took me aside and told me, "Gwen is a major shareholder in this production. If she wants to pay you, let her. So, I made the costume and later, when there was a revival of the production in London, I was pleased to see that they had copied *my* costume, not the original design." Marie also remarked on how warm it was in the ballroom. "Is anyone else hotter than I am?" she asked, cooling herself with a red fan. "Marie," Richard Halpern told the lovely actress, "nobody is hotter than you are."

Toward the conclusion of Marie's talk, John Karlen approached the stage and started pounding away at the piano. Marie laughed and pointed out that he had always liked to ad-lib. As he came onstage to replace her, he climbed onto a chair located at the back of the stage—and tumbled off the stage! I didn't actually see him fall; I was just aware that one moment he was onstage and the next minute he wasn't. At first, I thought he was just clowning around. After all, Marie had just reminded us all what a kidder he was. But this was serious. Everyone was stunned. Poor Marie sat frozen in a half-turned pose. Because Johnny had been behind her when he fell, I don't think she quite knew what had happened, even less so than we did. This was one of the most harrowing moments I'd ever experienced at a Festival, rivaled only by the time in 2002 when an angry (and under-the-influence) fan went up to KLS while she was onstage and started shouting at her.[45] I had no idea what had happened; I was sitting at the other end of the stage. I didn't know why Johnny had fallen or how badly he was hurt. Several fans gathered around him. Karlen's voice boomed out: "Who the *#$! put the *^$#%*! chair too close to the *^$#%*! edge?" I was told by someone close enough to see him that he picked himself up without any help, and when he began walking around the stage, we all applauded.

It appeared that he was OK. He did say that his leg hurt, but otherwise he seemed not to be injured. He even faintly joked about his fall. "There was one moment while I was falling when everything was OK. Then, I landed and it hurt." Pointing in the audience to webby, who had taken a nasty spill[46] the night before and was now in a splint and a wheelchair, John said, "See—I tried to join the club." He did want to know who had left the chair by the edge. "I'm not out to get anybody. I just want them to know what happened, so they don't let it happen again. Someone could get hurt." At this time, Marie, who must have been feeling pretty awkward after such a scene, made a break from the stage and left Johnny to do his Q&A.

Long-time Karlen fan MaineGirl was the first at the microphone. After some light bantering with Johnny, she asked him to talk about his experiences at the AADA (American Academy of Dramatic Arts.) That led to a lengthy and intriguing story. "I was eloping with this girl, Judy. She was Jewish, and her parents didn't want her marrying a *goyim* like me, so we ran off. Soon after we left, it occurred to me that I wasn't ready for marriage. I didn't have a job. Also, I wanted to study to become an actor." Judy was very understanding. "She gave me the money to attend the Academy of Dramatic Arts. Judy was a wonderful girl," he added warmly. "She was the best." "Did you ever pay her back?" joked someone in the audience. "No, the money was a gift," Karlen insisted. "That's the problem with the world today; everything is about money." This set him off on a semi-political tirade. "Greed! Everyone is so greedy. This war that's going on now—it's not about people dying in a third world country—it's about money, greed! That's the way it's always been. When people see a bum lying on the street, they don't help him. He's still lying in the street. They treat bums in India better than they do here in America. Here, they're professional bums."

Moving on, another fan asked Johnny to tell the story of the time he met Muhammad Ali. (Ah, so that's where Johnny learned to punch his director.) "I was walking down the street when I saw Muhammad Ali on the other side of the street with his body guards. He spotted me and pointed at me. This was about 1968, 1969, when DS was still on the air, so he must have recognized me as Willie Loomis. I came over to him, and his bodyguards made a little circle around us. Then Muhammad Ali shook my hand. You can't imagine what a wonderful thing it was to meet a young and handsome Muhammad Ali in 1969 when he was in his prime." Then Karlen started raving about how Ali had defeated Joe Frazier. He even got into a friendly dispute with another fan over who was a better boxer for defeating Frazier—George Foreman or Muhammad Ali. "Frazier was on his way down by the time George Foreman got to him," Johnny argued. "Muhammad Ali had a much harder time trying to beat him because Frazier was still pretty strong when they fought."

Another fan asked Johnny to tell us about working with Basil Rathbone in a Kraft Theater TV production. "Oh, man! That was the highlight of my career—just six months after starting at the acting academy, to have top billing over Basil Rathbone! Everything from then on was downhill. Basil was a great guy. He told me all about working with Errol Flynn. They were great friends and made six movies together."

"Tell us about your guest star appearance on *All in the Family*," one fan requested. "What was Carrol O'Connor like?" Karlen's memories were not happy ones. "It was just a small part at the beginning of an episode, but I was disgusted with myself for being on that show. After it was over, I took my lunch and went out to Long Beach where the oil rigs are. As for Carrol O'Connor—he wasn't a very nice man. He didn't have a whole lot to say to me. Later, when he knew who I was, after I'd won the Emmy, he was nice to me."

Karlen was also asked again about *Daughters of Darkness*, and reminisced about that. He praised his co-star Delphine Seyrig and shared a particularly interesting tidbit about the cast's accommodations: "We stayed at a fancy hotel in Germany that used to be Nazi headquarters." Karlen was also asked to describe his experiences with the new DS, for he had visited the set of the WBDS pilot while it was in production. "I met the people who were working on it. They were all so short! The kid playing Willie[47] was a real sweetheart. What can I say?" He trailed off. "They were all very nice, but. . .but they were—short." Like Marie, he seemed less than enthusiastic about the production.

Denise Nickerson was scheduled for a Q&A next, but she failed to show up, so we watched a video interview with Chris Pennock instead. He described how he came to be on DS. "I first auditioned for the Chris Bernau part, Philip Todd, but Dan Curtis saw me and said, "Let's save him for the thing in the box!' I didn't want to be a thing in a box; I wanted to *act*! But the thing in the box turned out to be a very hammy Jeb Hawkes." This was a part that Chris was able to have fun with, in spite of how nerve-wracking it was to make a show like DS. "When I started out, I was a cocky young actor. I'd look at Jonathan Frid and think, 'Ha ha, he doesn't know his lines.' But soon I realized just how difficult it really was. I was so nervous on the set. This was live taping. You couldn't make a mistake because if they had to stop the cameras, it would cost five billion dollars and you'd get fired. So even if you nearly sliced off Elizabeth Eis's head because the prop guy gave you the real sword instead of the fake one (referring to a near-mishap that occurred when he was playing John Yeager in 1970 parallel time), you had to keep going. Eventually, I got to be pretty good at using the teleprompters. Years later, when I was working on *Guiding Light*, everything was so different. I looked around and asked, "Where are the teleprompters?!' They told me, 'We don't use teleprompters anymore. If you make a mistake, we'll just tape the scene again.'"

Chris also talked about his deceased co-stars. "Michael Stroka was my best friend— " looking up "—Mike, I miss you so much. He taught me the ropes of acting. We'd go out to the Brittany [du Soir] for drinks after the show and he'd point out which girls were available." About Thayer David: "He was a brilliant actor, very talented, but he was so humble. After taping a scene, he'd look at the director and ask, 'Was that OK?' I got to work with him on the film *Savages*, with Sam Waterson. Thayer played Otto Nurder. He was great in that, but he wasn't in good health. He was diabetic, but everyday he'd bring two six-packs of soda to the set to drink." Pennock had a unique memory of Grayson Hall. "I was in make-up one day and she came up behind me and said, 'His eyes are too close together. They should be spread farther apart for the camera.' That really bothered me! I don't know why, I mean, there was nothing I could do about it. But I still remember that to this day." As for his living co-stars, Pennock said he had the most fun working with Nancy Barrett. "We were always giggling together about what was going on in the show."

Chris's video interview was followed by an interview with Geoffrey Scott (Sky Rumson) at which point I lost interest and stepped out. I didn't think I had been gone very long, but by the time I came back, Diana Millay was already well into her Q&A session. If she told her Lyndhurst ghost story, I missed it. A fan asked Diana what she had thought of all the kids who lurked outside the studio doors for autographs. "I was never a part of that," she replied. "During my time on the show, I was always either pregnant or I had young children to take care of, so I was given permission to slip out a different exit. I'd go out the side door and jump into a cab." Diana spoke glowingly about being a mother. "Raising children is more fulfilling than writing or acting. If I could have, I would have devoted all my time to my children instead of working." She also talked about her other passion: doing charity work in and around NYC. "It's the most gratifying thing to be able to help other people and to give something back to the community. Everybody should do it."

The charity auction began next and I left the room again. (I understand that some of Michael Stroka's belongings were auctioned. VAM acquired a bracelet of his.) However, I did return in time for the suspenseful showdown over this year's top prize—Josette's music box from the 1991 series. The bidding progressed at a normal rate until it reached about $500; then Nicky placed a bid. A fan on the other side of the ballroom quickly topped this. Nicky bid again and the other fan bid again. The price of the music box rose to $600, $620, $650, $700. "Let's see who loves Josette more," Jim teased. As if anyone needed an extra incentive, he added, "I'll give Joanna Going's phone number to whoever wins. I can't promise that it's her current number, but you can have it." The bidding climbed higher and higher. The final bid: $800. "Going once, going twice, sold!" Jim announced. The lucky buyer turned out to be Midnite (on whose behalf Nicky had been bidding.)

After the excitement of the auction, Jim prepared to screen clips of the 2004 WBDS pilot. I didn't care to see this, so I went outside and made some phone calls. When I came back, Jim was speaking about the pilot. According to him, this particular pilot is worthless. Pierson cited PJ Hogan's directing as well as some casting choices that didn't work out, "and were not featured on this clip reel." He also claimed that if the WBDS had been picked up, John Karlen would have played the recurring role of Sam Evans. There may still be a chance of getting a new DS on TV sometime within the next few years. Dan Curtis is still very interested in reviving DS in some form. Now that *Dracula* has been made into a musical, he wants to try to get DS on Broadway, too. Jim also acknowledged Johnny Depp's remark that he would like to play Barnabas on film. Jim wrapped up the pilot session and we prepared to watch the live dramatization of Art Wallace's *Goodyear Theater* teleplay "The House," which had been billed all weekend as a pilot for the original DS.

"The House" was a real treat. I thought it was well-written and well-acted. The plot is essentially a condensed version of the Jason-Liz blackmail storyline. Set in 1910, it begins with an aging sailor named Jeb Calloway (John Karlen) complaining to a former shipmate, Walt Cummings (Jamison Selby) that nobody will hire him to sail because they believe he's too old. Walt suggests that Jeb find someone to stake (sponsor) him, and Jeb recalls a wealthy woman in his hometown of Collinsville called Caroline.

The scene shifts to Caroline Barnes (Marie Wallace), who is teaching piano to young Jane Stoddard (Denise Nickerson) while Jane's mother Martha (Lara Parker) looks on. Caroline's daughter Elizabeth (KLS) is dating a nice young local boy, Larry, played by David Selby. Larry wants to marry Liz, but she always puts him off with an excuse. For one thing, she doesn't want to leave her reclusive mother alone in the big old house, and she knows that Caroline will never leave the house to move in with her and Larry. In truth, Liz is reluctant to commit after seeing what marriage did to her mother. (This is the same problem that Carolyn experienced according to Wallace's *Shadows on the Wall* story bible.) Caroline's husband stole her jewelry 25 years ago, shortly after Liz was born, and left town. Since then, Caroline has never left the house; she is waiting for her husband to return.

Jeb Calloway appears mysteriously, introducing himself as an old friend of Mr. Barnes. Caroline is shocked and distraught to see him, but reluctantly agrees that Jeb can stay in her house while he is in town. Liz suspects that Jeb is really her father, returned under an alias. Instead of feeling happy though, she is afraid. In truth, Jeb is Caroline's accomplice. We are told that 25 years ago, Caroline accidentally shot and killed her husband when she discovered that he was trying to run away with the family fortune. Jeb, who had been waiting outside the house for his friend, heard the shot, discovered the body, and offered to bury it in the basement. Caroline gave him the jewels as payment with the understanding that she would never see Jeb again. However, he has now returned.

With plenty of charm and sarcastic humor, Jeb intimidates Caroline, even disrupting her piano lessons, and hints that he would like to live in the house permanently as her husband. Caroline is anxious for Liz's sake. When Larry confronts her and accuses her of ruining Liz's life by living as a recluse and passing her own problems onto her commitment-shy daughter, (just as a drunken Joe did to Elizabeth on DS) Caroline makes a decision. She sends for the town constable (Jamison again) and tells him to dig in a particular area of the basement. She also tells Liz what really happened to her father. The constable informs Caroline that he found nothing in the basement. Jeb finally confesses that Caroline is no murderess; the bullet only grazed her husband and he soon regained consciousness. Jeb conned Caroline out of the jewels, the two men split the loot, and Barnes later died at sea. The constable is ready to press charges, but Caroline dissuades him. Though she is angry at Jeb for condemning her to 25 years of a private hell, she is relieved to learn of her innocence and happy to be able to leave the house at last.

I felt that Karlen stole the show with an Irish brogue patterned after Dennis Patrick's. Marie Wallace was also quite good as matriarch Caroline, and David Selby played Larry with an appealing boyishness. Jim Pierson had a small part as a bartender. Richard Halpern played the narrator and read stage directions. Details of "The House," from character names to plot points, are very similar to those found in *Shadows on the Wall* and those that eventually found their way onto DS. It was a fun show and I was glad to have seen the genesis of DS. However, I did find it difficult to remember that in this story, Elizabeth is the daughter while Caroline is the mother. On DS, the name roles were reversed.

After "The House," Jim Pierson gave us instructions for the evening's banquet: tickets would be distributed at 5:00 and the banquet would begin at 7:00. The actors would give autographs in the intervening hours. Jim stepped down and David Selby gave a Q&A session. He was asked about his audition process for the role of Quentin. "I didn't really audition. I went to Dan's office, picked up a few golf balls, and did a scene from Tennessee Williams's *Summer and Smoke*. He gave me the part." Another fan asked David whether he had felt frustrated waiting for his character to have a speaking part. "Actually we were all nervous about what would happen when Quentin finally did speak. It was like when Hollywood made the transition from silent pictures to talkies; some of the major actors couldn't cut it anymore." Obviously, Quentin's popularity suffered no harm from David's voice.

Another fan stepped up to the microphone. "On the series, you played four different characters named Quentin: which one was your favorite?" Unhesitatingly, Selby replied, "The first one. To me that character resembled Heathcliff very closely." Selby praised *Wuthering Heights* and shared an anecdote told by an actress (IIRC, Joanne Woodward) who had attended the premiere of *Gone With the Wind*. "Laurence Olivier had accompanied Vivien Leigh, and everyone else was calling to her, shouting, 'Scarlett! Scarlett!' But Joanne was calling, 'Heathcliff, Heathcliff!'"

David was asked about what it was like to work on an escapist soap like DS in the middle of the socio-politically turbulent 1960's. "The 60's were a strange and difficult time," David replied soberly. "Not everyone made it through. I can remember leaving the studio and seeing groups of protesters on the way home. I suppose that DS did provide an escape from all of that."

Like his co-stars before him, David was asked about the WBDS and whether or not he was supposed to have been involved. "At Dan Curtis's tribute,[48] I met Mark Verheiden. He told me, "We'd love to have you in a recurring role on our show!' I said, "That's nice. Thank you.' One of the first rules of the business is never to turn down a potential role." By the tone of his voice though, I didn't think that David was particularly excited about this potential role. Pansity asked Selby what roles, on film or TV, he would have liked to play but didn't have the chance. He cited the *Lord of the Rings* trilogy and the *Harry Potter* films. "I really liked the wizard. That would have been a fun part. I would have liked to play Gandalf. I prefer the *Lord of the Rings* to *Harry Potter*; I'm not sure why. Although, I did enjoy this latest *Harry Potter film* very much."

Selby was also asked about his recent commencement address to West Virginia University. He had been a little apprehensive about what to write. "I even researched some famous commencement addresses online before I started writing mine—but that only made me feel more self-conscious about it. I did find some quotations that I liked, and was able to incorporate those." The fan who had asked the question told Selby, "My sister read your speech when it was posted online and she loved it. She said it was exactly what she had wanted to tell her son when he graduated, but she just didn't have the words to phrase it." That cheered David.

Periodically, I glanced at my watch, remembering the brutal banquet ticket lines of years past. At 5:05, I ducked out of the ballroom and went to the ticket window. I didn't see a line of people waiting; in fact, I didn't see any kind of crowd, and my first thought was that the ticket distribution had been delayed. I asked one of the Fest volunteers, "Is this where we pick up our banquet tickets?" "Yes," he replied, "right here." I was amazed and impressed; no line, no wait. The entire process took about 30 seconds! Quickly, I returned to the ballroom and told my friends that the window was open and the way was clear. They went out and came back in about a minute! Selby finished his talk, and we all left the ballroom so that the hotel staff could clear it and set up the banquet tables.

The actual banquet line in no way resembled the nightmare queue of 2003. A small loop of people stood off to the side door of the ballroom, waiting to be admitted. We might have waited about half an hour, 40 minutes tops. When the room was opened, nobody stampeded in search of a table; nobody had trouble finding a seat. This year, I sat at table 26 instead of 59 (a much smaller crowd than last year attended this banquet). For the first time, I knew everyone at the table. Our souvenir was a silver bookmark with the DS logo stamped on it in blue (nice).

Dinner started with a salad and a roll. The main course was some form of breaded chicken (which I didn't finish,) rice, and vegetables. I think dessert was ice cream. Denise Nickerson raffled off door prizes (one of which was a DVD Set 13 of DS—wow, pricey!) From my table, CynD won a *DS Resurrected* book. After the food had been cleared, we watched trailers of the various movies and commercials in which Dan Curtis or the DS actors had been involved: *House of DS; Burnt Offerings; Come Spy with Me* (Louis Edmonds); *Tarzan and the Great River* (Diana Millay); *The Girl in Blue* (David Selby); *Father of the Bride* (Joan Bennett); *A Small Town in Texas* (John Karlen); *Night of DS; The Minx* (Robert Rodan); *Race with the Devil* (Lara Parker); *Daughters of Darkness* (John Karlen); *1776* (Virginia Vestoff and David Ford); *Zero to Sixty* (Denise Nickerson); *Up the Sandbox* (David Selby); *Up the Military*[49] (Chris Pennock); *Willy Wonka and the Chocolate Factory* (Denise Nickerson); *War and Remembrance*; *Joe* (Dennis Patrick). At my table, it became a kind of game to see who could spot the DS alum first and figure out whose movie we were watching. When the trailer clips ended, we were invited to pick up some old, surplus DS calendars on our way out.

From the banquet, we moved to one of the hotel bars where videographer Rich Blanco[50] hooked his video camera to the bar's television set and played back footage from the weekend's events. The first thing that everyone wanted to see was how John Karlen had fallen from the stage. Looking at the video, we saw that Johnny had sat in the unlucky chair and tipped backward, chair and all, finally landing on his back behind the stage. Seeing it once was enough to satisfy my curiosity, but a number of people in the bar (you know who you are) insisted on seeing it again and again and again and again. Failing to detect any amusement in repeatedly watching a 70-year-old man fall off a stage, I moved to another table out of sight of the TV and had a nice chat with LdyAnne[51] instead. Eventually, we were able to watch footage of the Costume Gala, the Collinsport Players' Scooby-Doo skit, and bits of Nancy Barrett's performance. Those were all very enjoyable to see; the clarity of the picture was spectacular. At last, at around 3:30AM when the last stragglers were leaving, I bid goodbye to Teresalita and DSFan1970, who were on their way to the airport for a red-eye flight, and retired for the night.

All in all, the Festival/Weekend was a blast, a great opportunity to unwind and spend time with old friends. I was also delighted to make some new friends and to finally meet face-to-face online friends like Gothick, dom, LdyAnne, CastleBee, Darren Gross, ClaudeNorth, Nancy, mscbryk, webby, deckert, Cassandra's mother, and CrazyJenny's fiance. Plans for next year are up in the air. At the banquet, KLS said that Jim is "open to doing something next year" and Jim himself invited us to give him suggestions for a location. (From my table in the back, I was calling for California, but I'm afraid the Miami people might have drowned me out.[52]) Festival 2006, which marks DS's 40th Anniversary, will be held in NY (meaning that I get to choose between going to this event or going to graduate school.[53]) Wherever they may be held, I'm thankful that the DS conventions are indeed continuing and I hope for many more years of Fests, friends, and fun.

August 27, 2004 - Daughters of Darkness Screening (Egyptian Theater, Hollywood, CA)

I attended the *Daughters of Darkness* screening with my friend Tina. After buying our tickets and soda, we spotted John Karlen in the lobby, but he was walking out. I lingered for a moment to see if he would return, but then we went to find seats. I was delighted to see Bette and Midnite, and we sat with them.

The good news is that nobody got punched.[54]

Tina and I saw Harry Kumel right away, shortly after we sat down. In fact, he sat right in front of Tina in the seat marked "Simone Simon." (The chair in front of me was labeled "Marlene Dietrich.") Remembering what John Karlen had said about him, we gave the director the evil eye at first. But when he spoke, he actually seemed like a very personable guy. He was able to laugh at himself and at the movie. When he was called forward just before the film started in order to say a few words, he mentioned that the movie was rather funny and chuckled to himself about it. In spite of my earlier prejudice, I found myself liking him. The moderator of the evening's discussion announced that, unfortunately, the full-length restored print of the film had not arrived from Belgium in time, so we would be watching the edited, American print from the UCLA archives. I was disappointed after reading all the hype on the message board, and I know Midnite was also very frustrated.

I had never seen *Daughters of Darkness* before. I enjoyed it. The print that we watched in the theater was, unfortunately, very scratched and faded. :However, the story itself was interesting. It begins with a honeymooning couple, Stefan (John Karlen) and Valerie, (Daniele Ouimet) traveling by train, ostensibly to meet Stefan's mother. The train breaks down and the couple ends up staying at a deserted Belgian hotel. They plan to stay for just one night, but when the Countess Elizabeth Bathory (Delphine Seyrig) and her companion, Ilona, (Andrea Rau) arrive, plans change. The countess is fascinated by Valerie, much to Ilona's annoyance, and she sets out to get to know the couple better. Meanwhile, a series of murders are occurring in nearby Bruges; young girls are being found with their throats torn open, and not a drop of blood in sight. Gradually, as Stefan's true, beastly nature is revealed, Elizabeth uses the opportunity to begin her seduction of Valerie.

Kumel was right; the film is rather humorous. There's a lot of ironic dialogue. Delphine Seyrig is probably the best thing about *Daughters of Darkness*; she relishes her part completely. I wasn't prepared for John Karlen's character to be such a creep. It was quite a shift to see Willie dealing out the beatings for a change. I felt that the isolation of the hotel added to the suspense and the apprehension about what the vampires would do next. Overall, it was a better movie than I expected.

After the film ended, Harry Kumel and John Karlen took their seats onstage with the moderator. Kumel said a few words about how his movie had been cut to satisfy "puritanical America" and advised us to see the DVD. He was asked where he had gotten the idea for *Daughters of Darkness*. Kumel explained that an earlier film of his had done well but that he'd been advised to make something "more commercial." (e.g., with more sex, violence, blood and gore.) "By chance, I had picked up a book about Countess Elizabeth Bathory. I was fascinated by the story and wanted to make a film based on it, but there was no money for something so elaborate. Then I suggested, 'What if this woman was still alive and out in the world?' Then we could set it in modern times." Hence, the premise for *Daughters of Darkness* was born. Next, Kumel needed to find a star. "Delphine Seyrig was the most chic actress in France. I showed her the script. She liked it. She wanted to get started right away."

The moderator addressed Karlen. "You've had a long career in television, most notably on the vampire soap *Dark Shadows*—there are a few fans of that in the audience. Were you chosen for this movie because of your work on that show?" John said that the movie casting was not related to his part on DS, and then went on to share some of his memories of making the movie.

"I remember getting off the plane and meeting Harry at the airport," Karlen reminisced. "We went out for drinks and then I fell asleep. Harry had to wake me up so that we could go and meet Delphine. We had dinner together. I can still remember her ordering the food: scallops, white wine. . . " He listed various dishes. "The next morning, we had a wonderful breakfast at the hotel. Then, on the way to Paris, we stopped and had a picnic lunch by the side of the road. We finally arrived at Paris, and Delphine went to Alexandre's to get her hair done. I jumped out of the car right away and stared at everything. I'd never been to Paris before."

The mention of the hairdresser inspired Kumel to tell a story. "Delphine had red hair, but I had envisioned Countess Bathory as a blonde. I wanted a 1930's style for her, to give her a modern but timeless look. So, we took her to Alexandre, who was the Michelangelo of hair styling. He had to agree to see you, and he agreed to work on Delphine. I told him I wanted her blonde, platinum blonde, and he set to work dying her hair. She started out as a redhead so to go to platinum blonde, she had to pass through green. Alexandre told me, 'Go to the Tuileries and look at the paintings until I'm done.' When I came back, Delphine was a blonde and he had styled her hair, but it wasn't exactly what I had in mind. Something must have shown on my face because Alexandre looked at me and said, 'No good, eh? Let me try again.' So, he put Delphine under the sink again to fix her hair. And this wasn't just *mise en place*, he had to use the hot iron. The things these actors have to endure for their art! It took about three tries, but finally her hair was perfect. I saw a lot of Monets that day."

As a contrast, Kumel talked about Paul Esser, the actor who played Pierre, the concierge who recognizes Countess Bathory from her stay at the hotel 40 years earlier. "I wanted him to put some gray in his hair to make him look older, but he didn't want to do it. 'No, no,' he said. 'I'll *act* gray.' And he did! He did a magnificent job in this film, and he didn't speak a word of English at the time."

Next, Kumel talked about the locations. "We actually used two locations for this. The exteriors were a hotel in Brussels and the interior was a hotel in Ostend (the actual setting of the movie)." They actually had gone to film during the hotel's off-season, so the deserted look to the hotel and streets was accurate. "There were just a few people on the streets when we filmed outside the hotel. But it worked. The audience doesn't care about what goes on the background; they focus on the main actors. Some directors try to make their films seem realistic. They try to get every detail down perfectly, but that doesn't really work. The famous director David Lee said that 'Film is like a fairy tale. Anyone who tries to incorporate too much reality sooner or later falls flat on his face.' So, I tried to make a film that was like a fantasy."

The moderator turned to John Karlen and asked him about a particular scene in the movie in which his character is almost buried alive, but Karlen remained fixated on food. "All I can remember are the ham sandwiches and all the delicious breads and rolls we got to eat," he claimed.

The moderator turned to the audience for questions, for which there was only time for one. A man in the audience asked Kumel to give us an idea of what the deleted footage showed. "You really should get the DVD to find out," the director encouraged. Some of the more overt lesbian-themed scenes were cut down. "When Ilona tries to leave the Countess and Elizabeth says to her, "You would never leave me. Without me, you'd have no life.' Ilona replies, "You call this a life?' But that last line was cut in this version. There's still enough left in the movie that you can get an idea of what's going on but it's very subtle." He laughed. "That's like saying Michael Moore is subtle. No, no, I'm not comparing myself to him." The scene where the medics are carrying a corpse out of the hotel was also longer and more violent. "Stefan sees the corpse and goes berserk. His wife tries to restrain him, but he hits her and throws her back against the side of the building. But in America, the rules are so strict. You can't even have a man wearing Speedos in a movie. They all have to wear those awful trunks."

Kumel also complained that the vivid and contrasting colors in his original print had been washed out in the American version. "Americans like to equalize their colors. You can't see how some colors are more subtle than others. It's a little thing but the little things are important. Look at the famous paintings of the world. What are the subjects? People writing letters. People pouring milk. There's nothing remarkable about that. But it's the little things that are so important! The unimportant things make all the difference. So, beware of 'really important documentaries' that claim to have a lot to say." (Zing!) He chuckled.

Kumel also made a reference to some of the comedy included in the movie. "The scene where the countess is in the car saying, 'Go faster. Faster!' was almost a joke because the film is paced so slowly. But we didn't want it to go any faster. We had to stretch it out as it was because it was such an awful script." Both he and Karlen snickered about that.

Karlen went on to say a few words about Kumel. "Harry was a great director. He always told us exactly what to do, where to go, and let us know what he expected from us. He was always on top of things."

The discussion had lasted longer than it should have, so the moderator rushed to clear the theater. Karlen posed for just a couple of pictures before leaving. I had hoped to see him in the lobby, but by the time we got there, he had already gone. Leaving the building, I saw a couple of my fellow Shadows in the Sun club members and talked with them for a bit before going next door to the Pig 'n' Whistle.[55] It was a very nice evening, all in all

2005 Dark Shadows Hollywood Weekend (Hollywood, CA)

Day 1: Friday, July 29, 2005

On Friday afternoon, the Festival officially began. Registration was at 4:00, but of course everyone lined up before then. In the corridor leading to the ballroom, Marie Wallace and Kathryn Leigh Scott were setting up their tables opposite each other. I very much wanted Marie's new book *On Stage and in the Shadows* so I queued up with the rest of the folks to get it. She autographed it to me and even made sure that I got my change when she ran out of single bills. A friend took my picture standing with Marie beside the poster for her book. We stood then in the registration line in the middle of the room; there was barely enough room as we were sandwiched between the people at Marie's table and the people at Kathryn's. Registration finally officially opened about 4:15 (so it was still pretty much on time.) Like last year, there were two lines separated alphabetically. I was a bit confused about which line to stand in because I was one of the people who took advantage of the two-for-one offer, and my friend's last name started with a different letter than mine. Everything was sorted out once I got to the front of the line and I was amused to see that the volunteers handing out name tags and programs were themselves wearing badges that read "Fashions from Ohrbach's." Once I received my program, I flipped to the back to check the location and dates for the 40th Anniversary. The next Fest will be in Brooklyn at the same hotel as in 2003 from August 25-27. Be sure to get your rooms right away. This hotel will sell out!

The evening's first event at 6:00 was a DS episode featuring original commercials. Although I'd seen presentations like this before and enjoyed them, I didn't really feel like sitting for half an hour and watching something just then, so I wandered into the dealers' room to check out the merchandise and visit with friends. The emcee for the Fests is usually Richard Halpern who is also the official Austin Powers impersonator, but this weekend he had another engagement to attend in Chicago. (He eventually returned to us on Sunday.) Instead we were graced with the presence of Jeff Thompson. Jeff was one of the co-founders of the Collinsport Players, and this was his first Festival in many years. I was waiting to hear him make an announcement about Kathy Cody; earlier in the weekend, a friend of mine with inside information told me that she would not be attending the Festival after all because she had to have gallbladder surgery. But Jeff made no such announcements. In fact nothing was said about Cody until Sunday afternoon, the very last day she was supposed to do a Q&A. I imagine many people were disappointed by her absence; I know I was. I had been planning to ask her about her work with Thayer David and Clarice Blackburn in "The Crucible." Oh, well.

After the video, we waited for the first panel with the women of DS: Marie Wallace, Lara Parker, and Diana Millay. To fill the void, we saw a couple of Guy Haines's classic fan videos. The Pet Shop Boys' "Always on My Mind" was about Barnabas and Julia's relationship, and "Dreamtime" by Daryl Hall underscored scenes of Maggie's torment as Barnabas's prisoner, the premise being that what happened to her was a terrible nightmare.

Once the actresses were seated, a line of questioners formed at the microphone. One of the first questions asked was about Lara's movie Race with the Devil, the DVD of which has recently been released with her commentary. "Is it true that the devil worshippers in the movie were devil worshippers in real life?" "I didn't hear about that," Lara said, "but they were scary. We stayed away from them during the filming." Someone else in the audience shouted out, "Was one of the devil worshippers A. Martinez?" (the actor from *Santa Barbara* and other shows.) Lara didn't know.

When asked what was going on that was new in their lives, Lara told us how she had recently gotten her Master's degree. "My thesis topic was about Gothic horror literature. I learned a lot about what made DS so popular and why you all like it so much. I read *Dracula* for the first time and Freud's book on *The Uncanny*." It gave her a lot of insight into good and evil. "The supernatural is so popular now," she explained, "because of the rise of Fundamentalism. I have nothing against Fundamental beliefs, but it's just that when God gets big, so does evil. It's a balance. That's why we're seeing such a resurgence of supernatural-themed shows." The fan then asked if we would ever be able to read Lara's thesis, if she would publish it. She hesitated. "It's very dry and dull reading—for me." After some prodding, she finally agreed to post her thesis on her website for us to read. Lara also told us that she had finished her sequel to *Angelique's Descent* called *The Salem Branch*. "It's about trees," she joked. "It's at the publisher's now. It's done; I'm just waiting for them to print it." This book deals with Angelique's long-ago origins in Salem as Miranda DuVal. It also introduces a present-day character, Antoinette. "Is Antoinette really Angelique?" a fan inquired. (At the end of *Angelique's Descent* and in Lara's preview of *The Salem Branch* that she read last year, it was implied that Antoinette might be a reincarnation of the witch because of her physical resemblance to her and because of her peculiar, intimate knowledge of the Collins family. "No, Antoinette is not Angelique; she only looks like her," Lara shared. "But Barnabas believes she is Angelique and he falls in love with her. I kept a similar name: Antoinette, Angelique."

Diana Millay has also written several books that she talked about at length. "*The Power of Halloween* is my bestseller," she told us. "Everyone is so fascinated by it." She explained to us that she is a descendant of witches with a line stretching back to Salem (though obviously Diana's ancestors survived.) Throughout the rest of the Q&A, Lara made what seemed to me to be several catty remarks about Diana's magic powers and the fact that she was a real witch. I'm sure it was all in good fun, but it seemed odd to me because she had never done that at other gatherings. Diana spoke at length about witches. "People didn't understand what these women did. They were healers. They took their craft seriously, but nobody could understand how they could do what they did. They thought these women must be using magic, so they burned or hanged them."

Lara chimed in to discuss the heritage of Salem, where she had done research for her novel. "There is a museum in Salem that features displays of three different types of witches. The first is a stereotyped witch with a pointy hat and broomstick, the Halloween witch. The second is a woman selling her soul to the devil, the Satanic witch. Last is a Wiccan witch, a woman in the woods celebrating nature. These are the three witch archetypes." "I thought it was very strange," one fan commented," that there was such an uproar in Salem over putting up a statue of Elizabeth Montgomery (as Samantha from *Bewitched*). The tourist trade is built on witches. That's how they make their money. It seems hypocritical for them to say they don't want the statue because it's offensive to the memory of those who died there. And when are we going to see a statue of Angelique in *Salem*?" People chuckled. "People there take their witches very seriously," Diana insisted. "There are many shops that sell crystals and herbs. People go there regularly to get what they need for their spells. It's not a joke to them."

DSBarnabasFan asked Lara whether the slap that Julia (Grayson) had given to Cassandra (Lara) had been real. Lara couldn't recall that scene (although it's a fan favorite.) "It probably wasn't," Lara explained. "When you slap someone, it's just a stage slap; it's faked. Somebody off-stage makes a slapping sound-effect. Do you want to know how someone gets shot on TV?" She demonstrated to us. "You yell, 'No, no, don't shoot me' and back away. Meanwhile, you've got a sponge with fake blood hidden in your hand and when the other person pulls the trigger, grab your chest and look down. It looks like you're bleeding."

The women were asked if they had been invited to do any cameos in the 1991 DS Revival. Marie said no. Next a fan asked Lara if she would be willing to do a cameo in the new *Night Stalker* series since she had played in an episode with Darren McGavin. Lara said she was open to it if asked. "I hope I don't embarrass you," one woman said to Lara, "but watching your love scenes with David Selby in *Night of DS* got me all hot." Lara chuckled. "Well, if you had been there, you might not have felt the same way. That entire room was smaller than one of the circles on the ceiling." (She gestured to a round panel overhead.) "Try to imagine cramming yourself, David Selby, a light crew, cameramen, and a director into that space. It was a very tight squeeze."

Another fan asked about the character voiceovers. "In scenes where your character is thinking, your actions and facial expressions match the voiceover for your thoughts. Could you hear yourself thinking while you filmed those scenes?" Lara told us that the actors always pre-recorded their "thoughts" prior to taping, and then the audio was played back during filming. "So we could hear our own thoughts."

"Did you enjoy being on such a popular show?" one girl asked. "Yes," Marie answered quickly. "Well, Marie did," Lara teased. She indicated that it had been an intimidating experience for her. As one of the leading ladies, I'm not surprised she was under so much pressure. "Of course, none of us had any idea when we started that it would be so big. Well, except for those of us who are psychic." Lara shot a pointed glance at Diana. Marie told us an anecdote about how people recognized her from her work on DS. People knew her as Crazy Jenny, even though she wore her hair teased high and had false eyelashes above and below her eyes as that character. She had another story that was even stranger. "I was walking down the street one day and I sneezed. Somebody in a nearby office building had a window open and yelled out, 'God bless you, Marie Wallace!' Now, how did they recognize me from my sneeze?"

The actresses were also asked who their favorite character to play was. "My favorite character is always the one I'm currently playing," Marie said. "I loved each of my roles while I was playing them. Eve was so delicious and evil. Jenny was vulnerable and passionate. Megan was the most difficult. She started out normal and then she got that box that belonged to the Leviathans. She became part of their conspiracy." "It's fun to play the bad guy," Diana agreed. "And to not know that you're evil." She had played Laura the Phoenix each time on DS. The role was very special to her. "I refused to play any other character. They asked me to come back as other people, but I told them, 'No, I only want to be Laura.' So, they said, 'OK.' My favorite scene is the monologue when Laura tells David the story of the Phoenix. It's because I meant it, every word of it." Lara's favorite character was Angelique, of course. "It took me a while to get used to it though. I wanted to be the ingenue and weep. I would be casting spells with voodoo dolls and Tarot cards and have big tears gushing out of my eyes the entire time. Everybody kept telling me, 'Don't cry. You're the *heavy*. You have to be *mean*.' It was so hard for me. Jonathan Frid finally took me aside and explained to me that it was such an important part. 'But I don't know how to do this,' I said. 'I've never been jealous of anybody.' 'Dig deep,' he advised." It worked.

The ladies then shared a delightful story about one of Joan Bennett's last Fest appearances. "A fan had asked us what was our favorite project to work on—of movies, TV, or stage. Joan had been in so many wonderful films. We were going down the line naming different roles that we enjoyed. Joan was at the end and when it was her turn, she said in her broad mid-Atlantic accent, 'Oh, *Dark Shadows* was my favorite!' Everyone applauded.'"

"You always died and then came back as different characters. Was that hard for you? Did you not know when you were going to return?" someone asked. "Oh, we loved dying! It's fun to die," Lara said cheerfully. "In fact, I remember a scene of Chris Pennock playing Jeb the green slime monster and he took forever to die. The director kept gesturing to him to hurry it up but he stretched it out and hammed it up as long as he could." (Actually this scene involved Dennis Patrick, not Chris Pennock; Lara was misremembering it.) "But we didn't know when we were going to come back, or if," Marie acknowledged. "Unless you had magic powers and could see the future," Lara added.

Jeff Thompson asked the ladies if they preferred modern or period clothes while on the show. Diana, Marie, and Lara all stated that they preferred the period costumes. "In the present day I had to wear a big thick coat to hide my pregnancy," Diana shared, "but in the past, I had beautiful gowns to wear." Marie joked that her present-day character Eve was one of the first lingerie models.

John Karlen came onstage to sit with the ladies but just as he was getting comfortable, Lara, Diana, and Marie had to leave. It was time for the DS movie panel with Karlen and KLS. First of all, Kathryn made an announcement. "I'd just like you all to know that I'm well and safe. Many of you know that I live in England. With the news about the recent bombings,[56] people have been contacting me to find out if I'm OK. I had actually been traveling. I returned to England just after the first bombing, and I left just before the second one, so I wasn't affected."

KLS doesn't live in the city of London proper; she lives in a country cottage and she told us some fascinating things about it. After describing the layout of the estate, she shared that the cottage was built over a route along which executioners often led prisoners to the gallows. "I don't know who it was that went through those tunnels, but they must have been in a good mood. They were probably good and drunk on their way to be hanged. The cottage is haunted, but it's a benevolent presence. It's really wonderful. Whenever you go there, if you've been feeling sick, you'll start to feel better. If you've been arguing with someone, once you set foot in the cottage, your anger subsides and you become friends again. It really has a restorative power. That cottage used to belong to Henry Kaplan, one of our DS directors. He owned it from 1956-1970 and then I moved in."

We then saw a clip of *House of DS* from the opening of the film when Maggie is searching for David and Willie tells her about the treasure map he's found. Jeff asked the pair what they remembered about making the movie. "That was a really good scene," Kathryn commented, "but I can't believe I wore such short skirts in that weather. Did you see how windy it was?" John Karlen remembered that he had brought home his curlers after the filming, but that Edith Tilles the hairdresser had ruined his hair. He also spoke about Lyndhurst, the estate where the movies were made. "I only went to that house twice. Once for the filming and the second time was only last year when we held the Fest in Tarrytown."

"Is it true," Thompson asked John, "that you filmed a scene for *HoDS* where Willie tells Prof. Stokes the truth about Barnabas but that scene didn't make it into the final cut?" "Professor Stokes? Who was he?" Karlen asked. When told Thayer David played the role, his eyes lit up. "Thayer David! What a champ! What a saint! No, we didn't have a scene like that. I would have remembered if I had done a scene with Thayer and it didn't make it into the movie.[57]"

Several questions unrelated to *HoDS* were also asked. One of the first questions was whether the actors received residuals for their work on DS, the videos, and DVDs. "Yes, we do get residuals," Kathryn confirmed. Sisters from our local fan club, Shadows in the Sun, went to the microphone and told Karlen how much they'd enjoyed seeing his movie *Daughters of Darkness* at the Egyptian Theater last August.[58] "It was so funny when they put that bowl over your face," Jane said. (In the movie, Karlen's character is suffocated and then cut when the women put a big glass salad bowl over his face and the bowl breaks.) "I was rooting for you to tear it away from them and throw it against the wall." Nancy reminisced about how she and her sister had become fans of the show. "We were swimming in our pool and our grandmother told us, "Girls, there's a new soap on TV called *Dark Shadows*. We jumped out of the pool and came inside to see it. We loved it from the first moment." "You had a pool?" Karlen sounded incredulous. "I didn't have a shower until I was 14." He thanked them for their comments, and then frank_b went to the microphone to tease Karlen about something that had happened earlier in the day. "I was walking toward Grauman's Chinese Theater. In front of the building, there are a bunch of people dressed as famous movie characters. I saw this guy—" he pointed to Karlen, "—hitting on a pretty lady dressed as Catwoman. I came over to help him out and said, "Hey, aren't you John Karlen the Emmy-winning actor?'" "You spoiled it for me," Johnny joked. "I told her I'd won multiple Emmys." "Where is she now?' frank_b asked. "Up in his room," Kathryn interjected. (She and Karlen have a great rapport.)

Karlen turned his attention to her next. "Look at this woman; isn't she beautiful? And what's that dress you're wearing? You showing off for the crowd?" "At least you're wearing pants this time," she retorted. "You know, I realize that you're both Polish, but in that clip we saw," she turned to the audience, "didn't you think he looked a lot like Roman Polanski?" "No, no!" Johnny denied the resemblance. "But I met Roman Polanski once, and poor Sharon Tate. Since then, I have never seen or smelled a woman as beautiful as Sharon Tate. What a tragedy!"

Again, Jeff Thompson asked if they preferred modern or period dress. KLS said she preferred modern clothes. Karlen didn't specify a clothing preference. When asked who was their favorite character to play, Kathryn immediately said Maggie and Johnny chose Carl Collins. "Carl was such a fop and so much fun to play!" He turned to Kathryn. "How do you define a fop? That's not a word people hear often anymore" "It's an English term," she began. "It means someone who is a dandy, who pretends to be rich—someone who's foppish."

Another person went to the microphone and commented on something a lot of my friends have also said. "Kathryn, I'm surprised that after you started playing Josette, Dan Curits didn't hire somebody to touch up that portrait and make it look more like you." "She was more beautiful than that portrait, wasn't she?" Johnny claimed. "And she's still beautiful!" Kathryn told us the story of how she had come to play Josette. The story is featured at length in *DS Memories,* but here it is again. "When the team first decided to introduce the ghost of Josette Collins, they planned to use a clothes dummy draped in white sheets with a fan behind it to make the clothing billow." After rehearsal one day, KLS had seen the team struggling with the dummy and trying to find the most realistic angle. "'How does this look?' asked the director. 'Like a ghost?' I said, 'No, it looks like a dummy wrapped in a sheet.' 'Well, do you want to double as the ghost?' he asked me. I said, 'Sure!' Everyone thought I was crazy to take on extra work, but I thought it was fun. They put white powder in my hair and on my face, then they turned on the fan. The powder got in my eyes and made my eyes water. Everyone thought it was a great effect—the weeping ghost."

Another fan told KLS how DS was never the same once Maggie left. "Why did you leave and where did you go?" "My contract had expired," she recalled. "I wanted to move to Paris and marry my fiancé,[59] so I told Dan that I was leaving the show. He didn't want me to go and tried to talk me into staying. He thought I was crazy for walking out. I think that's why he sent Maggie to Windcliff; it was his revenge. It was his commentary, his way of telling me he thought I was crazy. He told me, 'You'll be back!' but the show was cancelled before I got back to the States."

Lastly, Karlen was also asked to share his memories of Dennis Patrick. "Dennis was the greatest! Whenever we had scenes together, I had to bite the insides of my cheeks to keep from laughing. I bit them so hard they bled. He was so hilarious. When he talked, he got excited and his eyes would roll around in his head. He wasn't doing it on purpose, it just happened that way. It was so funny. Poor Dennis! There's another one who died tragically." (Patrick was killed in a house fire in October, 2002).

Following these panels was a video screening and the autograph session. I departed so that I could rehearse with the Collinsport Players for our skit the next day. In the middle of one of our run-throughs, the DS actors and actresses popped their heads in to take a look. Jim Pierson was with them; he must have been showing them the room where they would rehearse the radio play the next day. Naturally it was a shock to have them there. Here were the people that I'd watched perform for so long and now they were all watching me! I tried not to let myself be distracted or feel self-conscious and we all continued with our scene. Out of the corner of my eye, I could see Lara and Marie watching us. They seemed to like what they saw because they chuckled at all of the jokes. That was an unexpected treat.

When rehearsals concluded around midnight, I returned to the lobby where I was glad to find many of my friends still awake and visiting. I hung around with them until nearly 3:00 and then went upstairs to bed.

Day 2: Saturday, July 30, 2005

Saturday morning, I was downstairs early for a 10:30 rehearsal with the Collinsport Players (John Schafer as Julia, adamsgirl/deckert as Mrs. Johnson, Jay Keaveny as Roger, Peter Mac as Carolyn/Barnabas, and myself as Vicki/Carolyn). However, Nancy Barrett was rehearsing her cabaret act in the room we had used the previous evening, so we went up to one of the cast member's rooms to rehearse. I slipped away to catch the fan videos at 11:00. This is one of my favorite events each year, and I was pleased to see a new crop of videos this time around by DLA75. He used montages of various episodes set to classic rock music such as "Clap for the Wolfman" for Quentin and Chris, "Gypsy Woman" for Magda and Jenny, and "Frankenstein" for Adam. A video of *The King of Queens* episode about a DS convention followed at 11:30, but I didn't stay to watch it.

Of course, I did return at 12:00 for Guy Haines's video tribute to Dana Elcar, Anthony George, and Don Briscoe. The video was touching and beautifully done. It comprised still photos of each of the actors, clips from their DS episodes, (including Chris's first visit to Amy at Windcliff, and Burke and Barnabas comparing their adversarial relationship to a duel) and footage from other shows and movies they had been in (e.g. *Bonanza, I Dream of Jeannie, Checkmate, The Untouchables, 2010: The Year We Make Contact, Adam at 6 AM*). I was impressed that Guy had taken the trouble to find scenes where the deceased actors were performing alongside other DS alumni such as Dennis Patrick and Grayson Hall.

The charity auction followed the tribute video, but I left then to eat lunch with EmeraldRose, QueenKitty, mazinG, bananabry, and Philip from our Shadows in the Sun club. However, I understand that the original Blue Whale sign from the 1991 series sold for $1,100; I could not find information about the model of Greystone that was also supposed to have been auctioned. My friend Erfette did win the Ouija board used on the show (I told him he should bring it to our SITS club Halloween party.) When we returned from lunch, I was able to sit with QueenKitty, her husband, and EmeraldRose.

I came in after the start of Robert Cobert's Q&A panel, and I'm very glad that I did not miss the entire event. Cobert is a hilarious, peppy, friendly man, and he was a highlight of the Fest. I really enjoyed his session. Throughout the panel, whenever he was asked questions about specific songs, he would hum a few bars of his tunes.

He told us first of all that he was not a horror fan. "I don't like scary movies! I watched the original *Dracula* and *Frankenstein*, the old movies, when I was a kid, but that's as far as I'll go. DS was almost too much for me." He also told us how Dan Curtis had always believed Cobert was home watching the show. "In fact, I hadn't seen any of it. I only came down to the studio once or twice. Whenever Dan wanted me to write a new piece of music for whatever spook he was introducing next, I'd ask him for a brief description of the character and go from there."

One fan asked if there had ever been lyrics for the DS theme song. "No, it was too short. But there were lyrics for "Quentin's Theme." He was also asked about the distinctive Theremin used in the DS them and music cues. That's when Cobert dropped a bombshell. "I'll let you in on a little secret. That actually wasn't a Theremin. A buddy of mine, Dick Hyman, had a Yamaha with a loose string and that's what we used to make the weird noises."

Somebody asked Cobert how he'd gotten his start in music and where he studied. "I studied at Julliard (this drew a rousing applause, as Julliard is one of the most renowned music schools) but I didn't start out to be a composer. I started out in medicine. But music was always my first love, and after a while I realized that the world would be better off if I did not become a doctor." "What about the music in the Blue Whale?" somebody else asked. "Where did you get your inspiration for that?" Cobert hummed a bit of the Blue Whale theme for old time's sake. "Those were patterned after the popular music of the day like the Beatles, a light and cheery beat." One woman asked him, "What musicians do you admire today?" "Hmmm.

. ." Cobert mused for a moment. "Well, you finally got me to shut up. Who do I like in the world of music today? Well, I like Eminem." (I'm not sure if that was a joke or not.) Cobert finally confessed that he couldn't think of anybody else.

The final person who went up to the microphone told Cobert how much he enjoyed the song "Ode to Angelique" and that it was his favorite. "I don't think I know that one. I don't remember it," Cobert admitted. "Can we hear it?" Obligingly, the sound crew cued up the music. As it played, Cobert smiled. "Oh, yes, this is good. This is really good! I like this. I think this one is my favorite now. Who wrote it? I like this guy!" He sang along with the song until the end and then went off-stage. Cobert was great fun and I hope he decides to go to Brooklyn next year. He's someone you really ought to see as well as hear. It would have been fun to put him onstage opposite Johnny Karlen.

Next came Darren Gross's *Night of DS* restoration panel. He began by telling us the sad story of how Curtis had originally made the movie 131 minutes long. However, *House of DS* had only been 97 minutes long and MGM wanted the sequel to be the same length. So, the night before the movie was supposed to be released in theaters, Curtis and company had to do a quickie edit, what one producer nicknamed "The Night of the Long Knives." Bob Cobert began to chime in excitedly during this part of the story. He was one of the few people who had been able to watch the uncut film as it was meant to be seen and he deplored what MGM had done to it. "They didn't understand the movie; they cut all the good parts." The cuts backfired on MGM in the end; *NoDS* bombed at the box office.[60]

Ultimately, a number of vital scenes were chopped out, but Darren was lucky enough to have uncovered some scenes in a Kansas salt mine. Some of the reels didn't have sound and weren't in color, but he was working diligently to restore it. "We're almost done with the voicework," he reported proudly. "We've recorded all of John Karlen, Nancy Barrett, Lara Parker, and Diana Millay's dialogue, and we're half-way through with David Selby and Kate Jackson's dubbing. This is difficult work," he reminded us. "The actors have to match their words with their movements on film and they have to pitch their voices to sound as they did thirty years ago. Very few people sound like they did thirty years ago." He added that they were looking for a voice artist to imitate Grayson Hall since Carlotta is no longer with us, but he didn't name any prospects.

The clips he showed us were mostly violent extensions of scenes already in the movie: a scene of Rev. Strack (Thayer David) being trampled by a horse, Quentin roughing up Tracy in bed, Angelique's body swinging from the trees, Gerard's bloody face at the window with Claire and Tracy screaming, Gerard fondling his prisoner Tracy in the car, a scene of Gerard plummeting to his death on the train trestle and Alex making a snide comment about how the 9:30 will be running late tonight, and a silent scene of Angelique and Charles at the piano when Charles's wife Laura bursts in. This was an important scene for Cobert. "This scene was supposed to set the tone. The music she's playing at the piano is the same song we hear when Charles's ghost has possessed Quentin in the present. The music establishes that connection." The *piece de resistance* was a (silent B&W) seance held by Claire, Alex, Quentin, and Tracy to contact and hopefully put to rest Angelique's ghost when Carlotta bursts in and interrupts them.

Following the presentation of the fabulous footage, Darren had a brief Q&A session with Lara Parker, Chris Pennock, and Diana Millay. "Were you upset that you weren't involved in the first movie?" he asked. They responded no. "We had to stay behind at the theater and hold down the fort," Lara responded. (True enough; their characters were the focus of the 1970 PT storyline while the other actors were away filming.) Lara then reminisced about her role in the film. She was supposed to have been the leading lady, but Curtis cut down her part to just a few ghostly appearances and a couple of flashbacks. "My white dress was very stiff and I had trouble sitting down," she remembered. "I also had to wear a lot of very stiff, sparkly white make-up to look ghostly. Those first days on the set were interesting. Dan had just gotten started as a director, and we spent a lot of time standing around waiting for him to yell, 'Action.' He would forget."

Chris also spoke about his role. "I had just come from playing Gabriel in parallel time, a nervous, drunken wimp—just like I would become in real life a few years later. But at the time, I thought I had made it big as a film star."

"Did you know, Diana, that Virginia Vestoff was originally supposed to play Charles's wife?" Darren asked Millay. Diana claimed she did not know this. "She would have been Samantha Collins, but she got tied up doing *1776*" (Thank goodness! I adored Virginia's portrayal of Samantha on the series, but *1776* is my favorite musical and one of my favorite movies, so I much prefer having her as Abigail to having her in *NoDS*.) Diana claimed she had not known this. "Is it true that if DS had continued, you would have returned to the series?" he followed up. "Yes," Diana confirmed. "But only as Laura Collins," Lara added.

"How different was it to film the movies from filming the show?" Darren next asked. "It was intimidating at first," Lara admitted, "but we had several members of the cast who had experience at making movies: Grayson Hall and Thayer David. We all thought Grayson was a real pro. She said, 'Don't move. When the camera is on you, it can see everything you do. Your face will be huge on-screen.' On television, you're supposed to react. Harry Kaplan, one of the directors, always told us, 'If I don't see something happening on your face, you're not going to get your close-up!'"

"Is it true that Kaplan used to give you grades at the end of taping the day's episode?" Darren asked. Lara said that it was. "He used to scream at me: 'A-minus!'" "He never did that to me," Diana said stiffly. "But I have a photographic memory, so it wasn't a problem for me to learn lines."

"I learned to do whatever Grayson Hall told me to do," Chris said. "Do you remember," Lara said, turning to him, "your death scene as Jeb? You were dragging it out, crawling around the stage, rolling around and covered with green slime. They kept telling you to hurry up and cut it out because you were taking too long to die." Chris said that he did remember, and they laughed about it. (Actually, this is a false memory; it was really Dennis Patrick as Paul Stoddard who had the interminable death scene. The cameras finally had to tear away from him before he had finished dying. Jeb died by falling from Widows' Hill.) Then, Chris returned to talking about Grayson Hall. "As a matter of fact," he added, "I'm involved in a production of *Night of the Iguana* at the Actors' Studio for this fall." (This was the film for which Hall was nominated as Best Supporting Actress. Our local DS fan club is planning to see Chris's show when it begins its run.[61])

Then, Darren broke away from *NoDS* talk to give a shout-out to Julia99, the founding mother of Grayson's Legion and one of her greatest fans. She has made an admirable effort to keep Grayson's memory alive and to honor her legacy. "Rebecca Jamison is working on a biography of Grayson Hall.[62] She recently wrote an article on-line that she's planning to expand and she's also working to track down one of Grayson's early movies, *Run Across the River*. There's only one print of it left that we think survived, but it's been lost. It was given to the wife of the film's producer, but she's dropped off the face of the Earth. Nobody can find her, and it seems that this is now a lost film." Nevertheless, we wish Julia99 the best of luck tracking it down. Darren went on to talk about other lost films and lost footage and films that had ultimately been restored. As an example, he cited *The Big Red One*. Funny he should do that, because bananabry was the sound editor for that particular restoration and he happened to be visiting the Fest that day. I thought it was a neat coincidence.

Following this was a tribute to Joan Bennett with Brian Kellow, author of the new biography *The Bennetts*, Joan's daughter Diana (called Diddy) Anderson, and June Lockhart of "Lost in Space" fame. Lockhart, who also hails from a prominent acting family, had gone to school with Diddy and remembered Joan fondly, so that was her connection to the Bennett family. The tribute opened with a stellar DS scene of Joan as Judith Collins who taunts her brothers with the contents of their grandmother's will, lording her newly-elevated position over them. Kellow was up first and he told us some background information on the various family members. Richard Bennett was the father and the head of the clan. He was an irascible stage actor known for making snarky asides in the middle of a show if he didn't think the audience was responding well. Once when he didn't think they were applauding as much as they should, he turned to the audience and said, "I guess I'll have to tell a dirty joke in order to get you to pay attention." Barbara Bennett, who was briefly married to Morton Downey and who is the mother of Morton Downey, Jr., was the middle daughter. She was a successful dancer. Unfortunately, she went through a messy divorce, and Downey practically blackmailed her into giving up custody of the children (an unusual thing for a woman in those days to do.) Barbara regretted giving in to him for the rest of her life. Constance Bennett was the eldest and best known of the performing daughters and a wild child, much like Carolyn Stoddard. Kellow described her as "the quintessential flapper." She had no interest in acting but she only turned to it when she needed a job and couldn't (or wouldn't) settle for any other actual work. Fortunately, she was a natural at it and had a successful career in film. Joan was the youngest Bennett and the one from whom the least was expected. And yet, she was the one who had the lengthiest and most diverse career and the one who had the most interesting life.

Kellow claimed he felt a special connection to Joan when he started working on the book and was privileged to know her in her last years. Joan started making movies as a blonde and then dyed her hair dark so that she could get better roles as a femme fatale instead of the ingenue. She had four daughters, the eldest of whom, Diddy, had brought with her a video retrospective of Joan's work that had played at her mother's 70th birthday party. The film consisted of still photos of Miss Bennett and film clips, some of which dated back to the silent era. (She was absolutely gorgeous! I've always thought so since I started watching DS. I was 14 at the time and wishing I was Mrs. Stoddard. If only I could look as good as Joan Bennett when I'm 60.) The photos and films showed a range of Joan's styles with bobbed, curled hair and long, flowing tresses; blonde and brunette; from the 20s, 30s, 40s; innocent and vampish. We also saw a few film clips, including *Scarlet Street* with Edward G. Robinson, in which Joan's character Kitty is a conniving, manipulating tramp who rebuffs Chris's (Robinson's character's) overtures for marriage. In the story, Kitty has only been stringing along Chris, essentially using him as a sugar daddy, while maintaining a masochistic relationship with a hood called Johnny. When Chris realizes she's made a fool out of him, he murders Kitty with an ice pick.

Diddy also read from some letters that Joan had written to her while she was at boarding school. The letters were affectionate but filled with smirking asides. I had no idea Joan was such a smartass. The first letter was written after Easter break, and Joan was expressing her displeasure that Diddy had lost a cross necklace. "I was very saddened by the loss of your cross,' Joan wrote. "I noticed you didn't have it at Easter and I hoped that you had merely misplaced it. But now I know how foolish it is to be optimistic when total carelessness is concerned. I am sorry about it. I had hoped that you would pass that cross on to your own children—that is if you don't leave them in the park by mistake." It went on like this with Joan gently berating her daughter while at the same time letting Diddy know that she loved her. "I think of all the people in my family, I am the only one who truly found happiness," Joan wrote. "It took a long time and it was a difficult road but I have found it. While other girls my age were worried about boys, parties, and make-up, I was worried about you. I had you to take care of and think of. (Diddy was born when Joan was 16, IIRC.[63]) I am so proud to have such lovely daughters."

Finally, June Lockhart stepped up to read "a few pages" of *The Bennetts* that turned out to be an entire chapter. I didn't stay for all of this; I was feeling restless so I got up for a quick walk outside. The section that June read dealt with *Scarlet Street*, Joan's best and most controversial film, the clips of which we had just watched in the tribute video. The film was originally released in the mid-1940s and although film noir was popular back then, *Scarlet Street* was more shocking and immoral than the usual fare, and it provoked an outcry. First of all, Joan's character was supposed to be stabbed seven times by the icepick, but the censors were so perturbed by this that it was cut down to one stab. There's an amusing sing-song rhyme about this in the book. June also read a reprint of an angry letter from a California moviegoer who was outraged at the violence, the immorality of the characters, the fact that Robinson's character was never punished for the crimes he committed (though his guilt eventually did drive him insane) and the catcalls of the teens in the audience. "But I bet she stayed for the entire movie," June added.

There was a moment toward the end when the microphone emitted a terrible shriek. A fierce look came over June's face, and she fell silent, glowering at the crowd. For a moment, I thought she might storm off-stage, but she collected herself, back-tracked a sentence, and finished her reading. It was her pleasure and honor, she said, to be involved in this tribute and to see so many people in the audience. (At this time the ballroom had been partitioned in half, even though there were too many people in the front half and a lot of room in the sealed-off rear section. Numerous people had no choice but to stand along the sides of the room, crowding in front of the doors, left with nowhere to sit. It made for a nice fire hazard). "Joan would have loved this crowd," Lockhart said.

The Bennett panel was only scheduled to last for an hour, but it went on for more than an hour and a half. This pushed the Fest schedule, which until then had only been about 10 minutes behind, to a half hour and then 45 minutes behind as they set up and tested the microphones for the "Vengeance at Collinwood" play. Thankfully, they also opened up the rest of the ballroom for this event.

Finally, it was time for the radio play. Unfortunately, this portion of the Fest was not videotaped and I don't believe there are plans to put it on CD either. This was the only performance of the show. I didn't like it as well as "Return to Collinwood." I don't think it was as well-written. It contains many repetitious bits of dialog (e.g. Trask constantly prods Tony to "Kill them. Kill them now!" and Tony replies, "Shut up. I'll do it my way, when I'm ready.") In one of the opening scenes, Quentin and Maggie, who are now an official couple, have an exchange wherein Maggie wakes up to find Quentin out of bed.

Q: "I thought I heard a noise."

M: "I didn't hear anything."

Q: "Well, I didn't either. I only thought I heard a noise."

M: "Oh, you thought you heard a noise but you didn't really hear a noise?"

Q: "That's right, I only thought I heard something but I really didn't."

There was a wonderful scene between Lara Parker and Nancy Barrett when a lonely Cassandra makes an appearance at the Big House (Cassandra is now living in Rose Cottage) to make her presence felt (and to point out the absences of Donna Wandrey and Roger Davis.) In the story, it is explained that Ned is traveling on business and Mrs. Franklin has taken two weeks off. "Then you won't mind if I keep you company," Cassandra says. "Oh, it's heartwarming to see you," Carolyn replies in a tone that says anything but. The cattiness between these two leading ladies was delicious; I think their scene was my favorite to watch.

Thin dialogue aside, the plot was pretty straightforward and engaging. Tony Peterson returns to Collinsport to take vengeance against the family that ruined him (in 1968, Cassandra Collins used her witchcraft to make Tony her slave) and his family, for Tony is a descendant of the Trasks and he is possessed by the spirit of his witch-hunting ancestor, who urges him to destroy the evil Collinses. Posing as a representative of Trask Industries who is interested in buying land from the Collins family, Tony weasels his way in to see Quentin, who is suspicious of Peterson's intentions. Both Quentin and Willie recognize the name Trask and decide to research what they can about the Trask family and to shadow Tony wherever he goes so they can discover what his plans really entail. Carolyn is pleased to see her old beau return while Cassandra remains coy and seems to behave as though she does not remember him clearly. She is the real target of Tony and Trask's ire. Tony is unconcerned whom he has to hurt in order to get his target. He kidnaps and poisons Quentin's lover Maggie, using her as a hostage until Quentin can bring him Cassandra. Quentin agrees to go along with it, drugs Cassandra, and brings her to Tony, who then shoots Quentin. Fortunately, because of Quentin's magical portrait, he survives the attack and later confronts Tony. It is revealed that Quentin did not really drug Cassandra; she was only pretending to be Tony's prisoner and her witchcraft is still as strong as ever. "The enemy of my enemy is my friend," she explains as she and Quentin join forces to rescue Maggie, turn the tables on Tony, and entomb him in Barnabas's old coffin. It is implied that Tony is turned into a vampire and will have to spend the rest of eternity in that box with the ghost of his vicious, berating ancestor Trask. The performances were good all around. I especially enjoyed Lacy's Gollumesque turn in a dual role during which he would speak one line in his normal voice as Tony and then follow up it up with one of Trask's rasping orders. Even though I don't think "Vengeance" was as good as "Return" or "The House,[64]" I'm still happy that I saw it.

Following this was the autograph session. This was the first year since my first Fest in 2000 that I waited in the autograph line. I wanted to make sure I got Jerry Lacy's autograph. I had purchased some pictures of him as Gregory Trask at that first Fest and I wanted him to sign one.

I was also hoping to have my picture taken with him. Ultimately, I did. Everyone lined up inside the ballroom while they screened an episode of *Love, American Style* featuring Joan Bennett. Handicapped and special needs people went up first. The security guard would send 6-7 people from the ballroom door to the autograph table. Unless you only wanted KLS's autograph, you were unable to skip to a specific actor so those of us who only wanted Jerry Lacy had to wait. The bouncer at the door was a very nice man. He chatted with us at length about our interest in DS and the convention. He had watched the show too, but wasn't as devoted to it as we all were. We also talked about other TV shows on the air. He was very friendly and not at all intimidating. He talked about some of the other people he had worked for, including Michael Jackson, though he wouldn't say much about him. Finally, he sent us to the autograph table.

I was standing with EmeraldRose at this time and I took her picture with David Selby, John Karlen, and Jerry Lacy. Joan Bennett's daughter was also briefly at the autograph table, but she left before we could get to her. The line stopped for about 20 minutes in front of Selby's table and did not move at all. We couldn't figure out why this was so but we were growing restless. His publicist was angry, too; we overheard her complaining to Jim Pierson on her cell phone, asking him to get the line moving. A volunteer, Damian, came along reminding everybody that the actors could only give one autograph to each person in order to speed things along. It was still another 10-15 minutes before the line budged, but at last we reached Lacy. I got to talk briefly with him. He asked me how I had gotten involved in DS since obviously I wasn't around for the original broadcast. He signed my picture and I went around the table to get a picture taken with him. Then I was free to get into costume for the skit and the Gala.

By this time, the events were running about two hours behind schedule. The [2004] pilot was supposed to air at 7:00 with the Collinsport Players' first skit at 8:00 and the Costume Gala at 8:30. Ha! The pilot would have aired a lot sooner except that the fans insisted on watching the blooper tape (even though this is available for sale through MPI and will be on DVD next year.) At long last, the WB pilot aired for the first and perhaps last time.[65] I am staunchly opposed to remakes and I did not want to see this film so I walked out, but not before I heard a little bit about what the commentator Mark Dawidziak had to say about it. First of all, he commented that we would not have a discussion or Q&A after the screening because "we'll be here until 2 AM." He informed us that the WB fully acknowledged that not picking up DS was the biggest mistake it had ever made. What with the slew of popular supernatural-themed shows on the air today—*Lost, Medium, Ghost Whisperer, Invasion*, the new *Night Stalker*—"WB could have been there, too. They could have been there first, but they passed it up. Now they're kicking themselves. In fact, they went out and bought a machine that will kick them." He informed us that what we were about to watch was a rough cut with unpolished special effects and with just standard music laid down, instead of Cobert's soundtrack. He also warned us that some characterizations were very different than what we were used to (specifically Blair Brown as Elizabeth). Again, once the lights dimmed, I walked out so I don't what transpired in the pilot. Most of the people I later talked to who did watch it enjoyed it and lamented that it did not become a series. Only a couple of people said they hated it, and practically everyone denounced Blair Brown's portrayal. You'll have to read one of their reviews to get an idea of what the pilot was like.

As soon as the pilot wrapped, the Players went on. This was an encore of "My Fair Julia," the show we did last year in Tarrytown. This time, fortunately, we did not have any technical errors, though there were a couple of prop mishaps. Everyone was able to ad-lib and keep the show running smoothly, though. The audience seemed to really enjoy it. The plot of this show is that Julia is fed up with being overlooked by Barnabas, who would prefer to go out with Victoria "your name is so lovely I couldn't surrender a syllable of it" Winters. Carolyn decides to give Julia a make-over, and they head out for a night on the town. At the Blue Whale, Julia has too much to drink and makes a fool of herself. Barnabas finally realizes he's been an idiot for not giving her the time of day, and the two of them waltz off into the night together. There were minor modifications to this skit; the most noticeable was that two actors (myself and Peter Mac) played dual roles. I appeared as Vicki and Carolyn, and Peter played Carolyn and Barnabas. We did double duty to cover for Richard Halpern, who was unable to be in our skit that night. I had never played two roles in one play before, and it was quite an experience (especially those speedy costume changes), but we explained it away by saying that I was Diana Walker, the actress who filled in for Nancy Barrett in one episode of the series. There were even a couple of jokes about how different my Carolyn was from Peter's. We also had a couple of stalling jokes during which the characters chased around the infamous, intrusive fly with fly swatters; these comic chases bought us some time for our costume changes. It was brilliantly designed and it went off very well.

The Costume Gala came next. Surprisingly, a good number of people still remained to participate (nineteen in all), although many more people had been in costume earlier in the evening. Presumably, those folks had either had to leave to catch their trains and buses, or were just too tired to stick around. It was really only the die-hards left, and I think the audience must have been pretty worn-out too because they were a tough crowd this year (you could say they were pretty dead.) Usually, there is some kind of reaction during the performances—laughter, applause, participation—some kind of acknowledgment of what is happening on-stage and what people think of it. This time, there was only silence. I know I felt awkward during my performance (a parody of Disney's "Be Our Guest" called "He's Possessed" about David Collins and Quentin's ghost.) Other performers included victoriawinters and her parody of "God Bless America" ("Blair Curse My Collinwood"); a woman dressed as 1960s waitress Maggie Evans; a skit in which Vicki (QuentinsGal) tries to help Maggie (Maybellique/DJ/GracefulKittah) recover her memories of being held prisoner by Barnabas; Alice Faye Landis's monologue about a vengeful Polynesian spirit accompanied by a hula dance;[66] VAM as Rev. Gregory Trask performing "The Final Brick in the Wall" (Pink Floyd's "Another Brick in the Wall"); a skit in which Julia hypnotizes Maggie into giving her all of Maggie's jewelry; a top ten list about dating on DS by Massachusetts fan club co-president Janice; a hilarious parody of "Sittin' on the Dock of the Bay" about the various female characters on DS sung *a capella* by Irene B (I was very impressed; I know I could never sing without music); another *a capella* song by Lalinda about the fallout from Grandmama Edith's will (to the tune of "Red River Valley"); the Collinsport Players' John Schafer as

Julia/Julius singing "You Made Me Love You" and Peter Mac as Liza Minelli doing a short DS-themed cabaret routine. Costumed performers included a realistic vampire with sharp fangs and red contact lenses; a young girl who was a dead-ringer for Angelique in *NoDS*; Princess Margaret, an original character who is a Bavarian countess related to the Collinses; Amanda Harris and Tim Shaw; Jeremiah's ghost; Quentin Collins and vampire Angelique.

Generally, the acts are supposed to last only 2-3 minutes although some leeway is given to songs and skits. This year though, some performances lasted nearly 10 minutes! I could see Marcy chafing and I sensed the audience growing restless too, but I applaud her for not cutting anybody off. It was a very long show and a very long night, and I'm grateful to everybody who stayed long enough to watch it. I only wish the schedule had been on time so more people could have enjoyed what was going on on-stage.

When the Gala ended, I went down to the lobby to visit with friends and stayed there until about 2:30 AM.

Day 3: Sunday, July 31, 2005

Sunday morning began for me with a rehearsal of "Who's Afraid of the Big Werewolf?", the final Collinsport Players' skit in which Carolyn and Jeb celebrate their marriage with a party that includes zombies dancing to Michael Jackson's "Thriller" and concludes with a Twister game played by Jeb, Carolyn, Sabrina, and Chris Jennings as a werewolf, who frightens Jeb terribly. The cast members for this skit were Jonathan Harrison as Jeb, me as Carolyn, Laura Brodian-Freas as Elizabeth, Walter Down as Chris, Jaqui Baric as Sabrina and her sons Kyle and Nicki as David Collins and David's friend. Jeff Thompson and Richard Halpern had cameos as Barnabas and Julia, and victoriawinters played a zombie.

The first official event of the day was Marcy Robin's fan panel during which time fans are able to ask questions about the show or the stars or make comments. I took the opportunity to inquire about the survey Dan Curtis Productions circulated a couple of months ago inquiring whether fans would be interested in seeing a DS revival as a primetime series or in daytime format, and whether they would be willing to pay extra for cable/satellite. Marcy knew what I was talking about and admitted that this had been a feeler for DCP to learn which options held the most interest for the fans and would be most lucrative for Dan to pursue in the future. DCP did get its answers, but Marcy didn't say what the results were or what they planned to do with the data. She did explain that different answers might be worth a different number of points. For example, a 'Yes, I want a daytime show' would be worth one point, 'Yes, I'll pay for premium cable' would be worth 10 points, and so forth. She didn't say anything more than that but I was glad she acknowledged my question. Hopefully, something will come of Curtis's efforts.

After Marcy spoke, a video of the Museum of TV and Radio's tribute to Dan Curtis was screened. I had been present at this event when it was live so I wandered out into the lobby to visit with friends. Unfortunately, I had to be in costume and in rehearsals when Chris Pennock was reading his new comic book "Fear and Much Loathing: Beyond DS", part 5 in his on-going serial. We came in for the tail-end of it but I didn't catch what the overall plot was. One of the featured incidents was that Chris cheated on his then-wife Marilyn with an extra from *NoDS*. Another plot point dealt with parallel universes. Chris also detailed fan David Block's oft-performed scene between Gabriel Collins and his father Daniel in 1840. Chris's daughter Tara also performed a song from *Wicked* called "Loathing" (*a capella,* way to go!) that fit in with the theme of Chris's books. I sometimes wonder what his daughter thinks of the stories he tells about the wild things he did in his youth, about the drugs he took, about the bouts of depression he openly confesses to experiencing. I admire Chris for his willingness to be so candid with his audience, but I'm not sure how I would feel if it was my father on-stage saying and drawing such things.

Then it was time for our skit. victoriawinters was our lone zombie dancer. We'd originally had other dancers lined up but they had to attend a dance workshop that weekend, so we were very lucky to have victoriawinters on our side. Following the skit, we took some photos of the cast so I missed the opening of Marie Wallace's talk about her new memoirs.

Marie did tell us how people often mistook her for a model early in her career. She was an actress who did modeling on the side and she looked like a model—very tall, very glamorous. "But I didn't want to be a model who acted. I was an actress and I knew that deep down," Marie emphasized. "So, I eventually stopped modeling and I stopped carrying around my modeling portfolio."

Marie complimented Jonathan Frid on his directing her in *The Lion in Winter* and pointed out that he had written the Foreword for her new book. Marie also made a poignant comment about taking advantage of all of life's experiences when a fan asked her if she ever thought she had done all she could in her career. "No, I've never had that feeling of 'Been there, done that' and I've never understood people who take that attitude. There's always something to be gained. Can you imagine if someone offered you a trip to Rome? Would you say, 'Been there already, done that.' I can't." She urged us to remain open to life's experiences, and then it was time for Diana Millay to take the stage.

I learned a lot that was new about Diana Millay. She didn't start her Q&A by recounting her Lyndhurst ghost story, though the audience pressed her to do so. Apparently, she had promised some fans the previous day that she would tell it. "Tomorrow, after the dinner," she had promised (which I didn't think was fair since not everybody attends the banquet.) "And for those of you who are coming to the Festival next year, I'll have pamphlets made with the story printed on them so you can have it to read for yourselves."

We first saw a clip of her in the *Tarzan and the Great River* movie trailer, then Diana spoke of her experiences making this movie. "They really hired the right person to be in that movie when they got me. I was the only person in the cast or the crew who wasn't afraid of the animals. I guess whoever cast the movie forgot that so many big animals would be appearing in the scenes. Everybody in the camera crew and the other actors were terrified, but I loved them and they loved me. The two chimps, Elmer and Vicki were my friends. Asia the lion was my baby from 9 to 5 all week long. Sometimes I would lie on her back to take a nap. Everybody would be afraid because when she yawned—" here Diana bared her teeth in imitation "—they were afraid she was going to eat me. Once, Asia got sick and we had to take her to the animal clinic in town. We loaded her into the back of the truck and I rode with her. We actually caused a lot of car accidents on the way because people were stopping suddenly; they were so surprised and distracted to see a lion's head sticking out of the back of the truck." She also talked about how her mother came to visit her on location in Brazil. "My mother had never seen anything more exotic than our pet dog, but when Elmer the chimp saw my mother, he just leapt right into her arms. They were inseparable from then on."

Diana then talked about her human co-star who played Tarzan. "Frankly, I would have preferred Johnny Weissmuller. (The audience hooted) He was a real outdoor person, like I am. This guy was an executive at CBS studios. He refused to grow his hair long. He only made this one movie." Apparently, Tarzan's looks weren't the only thing detracting from the realism of the scenario. "The director would have put me in skirts in every scene. I had to push him to let me wear safari clothes. Nobody wears skirts in the jungle."

Diana was asked if she supported animal charities—no fur, big cats groups, etc. "No, I don't. If it's a question of donating money, I would rather give it to disadvantaged children. My son works with underprivileged children so I'm familiar with what their needs are. I did support wolf preservation for a while." She shared that she had once raised a wolf cub. "Its mother had abandoned it and they were afraid it wouldn't survive. But they gave it to me to care for, and it was a good thing they did because I kept him healthy. I love animals; I like them more than people sometimes."

We also saw clips of Diana's work in *Bonanza* (she played a character called Diana) and a movie with George Montgomery called *Street of Sinners*. Diana played a woman involved in some seedy deal with a pair of tough guys. She and her friend went to meet the ruffians, one of whom was played by Montgomery. "It's amazing that he was in a film like that—B-movies, they called them back then," Diana commented. "He did it for the money, if you can believe that. He didn't make much money, and neither did his wife, Dinah Shore, not until her last TV show. She was the one who got me the part. She didn't trust George around the other actresses and she had it in her mind that I was only eleven or so, just a kid—though I was a little older than that. She said, 'I trust you, Diana.' But I really had no business being in that movie. I had very little experience." She was able to get experience on the set though. "It was a wonderful, wonderful opportunity and George Montgomery was an amazing person. I enjoyed working with him so much."

When Millay left the stage, Sy Tomashoff the set designer stepped up. He'd been to a Fest before, but not in many years. He'd also attended the Paley event where DS had been honored in 2001 and Dan Curtis's tribute in 2004. Tomashoff talked about how he had gotten his start in the business and how the tactics for dressing a set had changed by the time he got to DS. "I used to work on movies, and on movies you need the real thing. You can't just have stenciled paper on the walls; you need real wallpaper." That was what inspired him to try for so much realism in the DS sets: real wallpaper, real stained-glass for the windows, real plaster, real antique furniture, etc. One of the first questions came from DLA75 as to whether Tomashoff had recycled the DS sets on his other shows like *Ryan's Hope*. He had read messages online that seemed to indicate this had happened. "I don't know about that," Tomashoff said. "You'd have to show me the sites where you read that had happened." Later in the Q&A though, he seemed to indicate that set pieces had ended up on *The Bold and the Beautiful*.

Someone else asked if he had had a favorite prop (this particular fan favored the grandfather clock.) "There was one candelabra. It had a human figure carved at the bottom. That one stuck in my hand," he said sheepishly. "It's at home on my mantel." Tomashoff was also asked why the interior of the clock had been wrapped in felt. "The clock didn't always work," he explained, "and the felt muted it so it wouldn't strike the wrong hour. It also kept you from seeing the inner workings of the clock." He also received questions about some of the color choices on the sets. "Why blue candles?" one fan wanted to know. (Anyone who has watched DS will recognize the omnipresent blue candles in the Old House, mausoleum, West Wing, and anywhere else.) But Sy didn't seem to remember the blue candles. "Blue candles? You mean in the Old House?" He couldn't say why he had chosen that particular color. He was also asked about the colors of the bed sheets. "There are times when you have blue blankets and acid green sheets. What was that all about? Just because it was the 60s?" the man asked. "When you film bedroom scenes, you don't want to use white sheets," Tomashoff stated (though he didn't detail why they were a bad idea, but I imagine they might not show on camera very well.) "We couldn't find any other colors but those." Apparently, the fact that the colors clashed so much was secondary.

"Where did you get all of those beautiful antiques? And what happened to them after the show? Do you know how much all of that stuff would be worth today?" one fan asked. Tomashoff chuckled. "If only we had held onto it a little longer, but we had no idea." He could not account for the props (well, except for the candelabra) but indicated that some of them may have landed on other soap operas.

"How many Emmys have you won for your set designs, and were they all for the same shows?" Tomashoff told us he had won seven Emmys (that's six more than John Karlen) though none were for DS. That show pre-dated the awards, but you can bet if the Emmys had been around then, Sy would have been honored (along with the likes of Joan Bennett, Thayer David, and Jonathan Frid, I'm sure.) Next came another question about a prop. "There was an afghan, a throw, that found its way onto every set in every timeline of the show," one woman pointed out. "What was that all about? Was it a private joke for you or did you not realize you were using it so much?" Again, Tomashoff couldn't recall that particular blanket (I know you know the one—the multi-colored blanket that looks like the one from *Rosanne*).

Inevitably, Tomashoff was asked about the famous 1995 sequence in which Collinwood was trashed. "How did you accomplish that? And was it easier to mess the place up or to clean it up afterward?" "Some things were pretty easy to do," Tomashoff explained, "turning over the furniture, breaking the furniture. I also had the idea that I wanted to show some of the plaster had crumbled off the walls to reveal bricks underneath. So, I stuck paper that resembled bricks on the walls to simulate the bricks peeking through. I also had a lot of plants growing up around the building. We strung up cobwebs too. It was the Friday night before we were supposed to start filming that sequence, and the set crew and I were working late to get the set ready. It was almost midnight and the foreman said to me, 'Sy, we're going home. You can stay and work if you want, but it's late and we're leaving.' They certainly were dedicated. Then, about a week after shooting, we had to clean up the whole mess. Cleaning up wasn't as bad making the mess in the first place."

Someone else asked him if he would ever consider working on another type of show besides soap operas, like a talk show or a game show. Tomashoff reiterated that he had worked in other formats—other soap operas, movies, and stage—but the woman kept pressing him about whether he would consider one of the types of shows she had mentioned. "You mean something like *The Price is Right*? I don't really want to do a game show. Most game shows have panels that you have to lift up; that gets complicated."

Robert Rodan took the stage after Sy Tomashoff. Kathy Cody and Geoffrey Scott had originally been scheduled to join him, but Kathy was out with gallbladder surgery and we were informed that Geoffrey Scott's wife had just had an operation so it was uncertain if he would join us. (He never did; weird how both of the touted first-timers were deterred by medical emergencies.) This was the first time I had heard an announcement of Kathy's absence. Usually, they will state at the start of the Fest if someone won't be able to attend.

The first thing Rodan told us was that he had just come from seeing a great movie, *Must Love Dogs*, about internet dating. This was something he could relate to as he had been on an online dating service for three years. "Until I finally met my lovely fiancée." Here, he gestured to a woman in the front row of the audience. Congratulations to him on finding love at last! The first person at the mic asked whatever became of Adam. "What did happen to Adam?" he puzzled aloud. "He was at Prof. Stokes's house, there was a knock at the door, and Stokes said, 'Adam, (here, Rodan imitated Thayer's gravelly voice) go hide in the closet.' And I went into the closet and I never came out. Was there ever any mention later in the show about a resolution to that storyline?" he asked the audience. We said no. "Then he must still be in the closet. That's what I get for talking so much. Prof. Stokes taught me how to speak and I spoke too much. That's how I ended up in the closet." (From what I understand, in real life Rodan had asked Dan Curtis for a raise and was immediately sacked for his audacity.)

DwightFry went to the mic and asked, "How many green sweaters did Adam have?" "Only one, and it stank to high heaven!" Rodan said.

Then, I went up to the microphone. I had never asked any of the stars a question before, but this time I had two. First, I complimented Rodan on his performance as Adam in the early part of the storyline when he was unable to speak and had to behave like a newborn child conveying everything with gestures. "It was very believable. Was it difficult for you? Did you have any special training? Pantomime?" "No," he replied, "but I was born. I played it like someone who was very innocent. Everything was new. The light was new, the chair was new, Jim Pierson was new." I also asked him to share his memories of Thayer David (I was glad to hear some applause from the audience when I asked this. It goes to show how Thayer still has his loyal fans.) "Thayer, Thayer," Rodan recalled fondly. "He was wonderful; it was a joy to work with him and to listen to his marvelous voice."

Adamsgirl/deckert asked him a question about Adam's relationship with Carolyn. "When you played it, did you intend for your love for her to be innocent, or was it more of an obsession?" "It was very innocent," he explained. "She was like my puppy dog. I was in love with my puppy dog." Jane from our SITS club asked if he had read Mary Shelley's *Frankenstein*. He said that he had. "Oh, that explains it!" she said excitedly. "Your portrayal of the monster was so faithful to the book, how he started out so innocent and was corrupted by the people around him." Someone else asked him what it was like to work with Marie Wallace. "Marie was wonderful but Eve gave me so much trouble..." We chuckled.

There were a couple of very odd fans about that day. One particularly weird woman, who was wearing an open blouse and practically flashing the actors, went up to the microphone and demanded to know why Rodan hadn't contacted her when he was on the dating service. "Where are you from?" she asked. Rodan is a local boy from California. "Why weren't you at the last two Fests? Are you going next year to the 40th Anniversary?" "That depends. Where is it next year, New York? Jim, are you paying for transportation?" he called out. I didn't hear Pierson's answer, but it would be nice to see as many of the actors there as possible.

Someone else asked Rodan if he had been classically trained. "No, I was a method actor." He was also asked which format he preferred: stage, TV, or film. "They're all very different." In the end, he seemed to be leaning toward stage and TV as his preferences. "How long did it take you to put on your make-up and all those stitches?" asked another fan. "It took about one to two hours," Rodan revealed.

Nancy Barrett's cabaret act followed Rodan's Q&A, but first of all, Pierson kicked us all out to do a sound check (and I had a good seat too!) This was the same thing that had happened before "Return to Collinwood," although they didn't do it before Nancy's cabaret last year. It took about 30-40 minutes for everyone to leave the ballroom, line up outside, then filter back in once the microphones had been tested. Fortunately, neither the line nor the wait was as long as before "RTC," and as chance would have it, I was able to get my original seat back.

Nancy's show this year differed from the one last year. That act was more autobiographical; this one dealt with Hollywood. It included a couple of staples like "I Wanna Dance with You" and a version of "Girls Just Wanna Have Fun" but it also contained other songs about the glamour of Hollywood and the dream of being rich and famous: "Hooray for Hollywood," "Just Go to the Movies," "Oh to be a Movie Star," "The Bus from Amarillo" (this was Selby's favorite, he later said[67]) "Razzle Dazzle," "Look What Happened to Mabel," "Capped Teeth and Caesar Salad," "Poor Little Hollywood Star," "So Beyond," "Film Cliché," "Movies Were Movies," and "As if We Never Said Goodbye." My favorites were "Look What Happened to Mabel," "Bus from Amarillo," and "Capped Teeth and Caesar Salad." The first few songs emphasized the glamour of Hollywood, the stars who'd made it big, people who dreamed of visiting Hollywood. Nancy wove the second set of songs into a story about a hypothetical secretary who dreams of making it big, finds an agent, submits her photos, auditions, squeaks past the casting director (who happens to be from her hometown and gives her a break) and reaches stardom only to find that it's not all it's cracked up to be. Nancy closed her show with a thank you to the fans, to people involved in her show, and wrapped with the song "I'm Tired" from *Blazing Saddles*. I really enjoyed this performance and was sorry that it wasn't videotaped. I would have enjoyed a record of it. Nancy hasn't lost her ability to slip from character to character in the wink of an eye—to be a shy woman, a lusty femme fatale, a cynical director, a gruff agent, Pansy

Faye, Carolyn Stoddard, and even herself. She's as versatile as she was on DS.

The final event that day was a Q&A with the stars. The program only listed a handful of people to be on stage—David Selby, John Karlen, KLS, Lara Parker, and Jerry Lacy—but in fact all of the present cast members appeared including Diana Millay, Marie Wallace, Robert Rodan, Chris Pennock and Nancy Barrett. (Jim Storm never materialized although he was listed in the program; no reason was given as to why.) I had stepped out at the beginning of the panel to get something to eat (knowing that I couldn't hold out another three hours until the banquet) so I missed what initially went on. Unfortunately, although we had a number of people on the stage, we didn't really learn much from them. Few people got to ask questions, mainly because of one woman who made to the microphone early and didn't seem to want to give it up.

Jerry Lacy got most of the questions. The first person asked him to grace us with one of his famous Humphrey Bogart impersonations. "I'm out of practice," he protested. "I haven't done that in so long." However, he finally gave in and spoke the line, "Of all the gin joints in all the world, she had to walk into mine" (this one made it on AFI's recent top 100 movie quotes list.)

Next, somebody asked a fairly unusual question of John Karlen: "What is your favorite cereal?" "My favorite cereal? You mean for breakfast?" John seemed taken aback. "Rice Krispies. When I was a child, it was Rice Krispies and now it's still Rice Krispies." (So next year when we see Johnny in Brooklyn, let's all invite him to breakfast for Rice Krispies.)

The same woman who had practically propositioned Robert Rodan also had questions for Jerry Lacy. She seemed to be very well-informed about his career and said she had been in his fan club. "Why didn't we see more of you after DS?" she demanded. "You were so good! Why didn't you make other movies and TV shows? We were so disappointed not to see you." "How do you think I felt?" Jerry replied glumly. He discussed some of his other ventures. "I wrote scripts for some sitcoms, including *Newhart*, but I hated it. I also wrote some screenplays but nobody bought them.[68] I did stage work." "Tell them the story you told me about your auditions," Nancy Barrett encouraged. "When I would go in to audition for something, people would recognize me as Humphrey Bogart," Lacy explained, (he had played Bogart in Woody Allen's *Play it Again, Sam* and a variety of commercials) "and they would ask me to read for the part as Bogart. That killed me. If I refused, they would get angry and wouldn't hire me, but if I went along with it, I knew I wouldn't get the part because I was typecasting myself. Either way, I was sunk." Another fan praised the actors for their work on "Vengeance at Collinwood." "Did you like that?" Selby asked. "Would you like to see more radio plays?" We all yelled, "Yeeess!" Hopefully, Jamison will have something for us by the 40th Anniversary.

Then, a woman went up to the mic and took nearly fifteen minutes telling her life story. First, she thanked the actors for coming. "If it wasn't for you attending every year, none of us would show up." (Well, maybe she wouldn't. It's fun to see the actors, but my main interest now is seeing and making friends.) Then, she started going on and on about how she'd gotten interested in DS late in its run ("All my friends at school stared at me and said, 'You mean you've never heard of DS?') and how it was such an important part of her life. "It spoke to my inner child! All of you really helped to awaken my inner child!" She kept stressing this point throughout her lengthy statement until one fan in the audience yelled out, "Tell your inner child to go back to sleep!" That didn't deter her though. "Thank you all for coming, you all mean so much to me. It's great to see you! Jerry Lacy—where have you been all my life? Where have I been all this time? You've had twenty Festivals already and I got a late start. But this really means so much to me and to my inner child. . ." Both the fans and the actors were growing visibly weary of this spiel. People from the sidelines called for her to hurry up or shut up. I can't remember what her final point was, but once she finally finished, everyone applauded.

"How much did you get paid?" the next fan asked. "It varied," Kathryn explained. "Dan paid us on what was called a sliding scale. The way it worked out was that the more often you were on during the week, the less you made. If you were on Monday you might get $20 an hour—I'm just using a sum as an example—then on Tuesday, you'd only receive $15 and by Friday you'd be down to $5." That system seems unfair to me: the hardest workers get stiffed.

Someone praised John Karlen's acting abilities and asked whether he was a method actor. Johnny admitted to studying with Lee Strasberg, "But I never finished. Strasberg always talked about technique. I hate that word. You don't use technique when you act." Nancy Barrett chimed in. "I know what Johnny is talking about. I heard a quotation once that "Technique is something you do when you're too lazy to really act." This set off a mini debate among the cast members. "You need technique at least as a foundation to build upon," Marie insisted. John still held to his assertion that acting is something you do naturally. Pansity asked an interesting question: "Which school of acting did you all study?" "What school did I study at?" Karlen repeated. "The New York Academy of Dramatic Arts." Chris Pennock had studied at the Actors' Studio. "Danny DeVito was in my class," he recalled. "That was the little guy you used to talk about? We see too much of him on TV," Karlen joked. Nancy Barrett also studied in New York. David Selby studied in West Virginia. We didn't get to hear from everyone on the panel though because we were running out of time.

The panel ended and we were ushered out of the ballroom; some people went into the autograph line and others went to claim their banquet tickets. I snatched up my ticket, changed for dinner, and came back down to wait in the line to get back inside for the banquet. The schedule was pretty much on time this night and we didn't have to wait too long. At 7:15 we were seated (dinner had originally been scheduled for 7:00, so I call that good timing.) I was seated at table 34 in the back with JamesLady, Cassandra, Cassandra's daughter, CollinsportHussy, pansity, Lalinda, AngeliqueWins, adamsgirl/deckert, and QuentinsGal. We were served salad first and then the main course: chicken dumped on mashed potatoes and sprinkled with vegetables and some kind of tomato sauce. I can't say this was one of my favorite meals; of the four banquets I've attended, it's the one whose food I liked the least. Usually, the chicken is served with either rice or potato and vegetables, but everything is spread separately over the plate, not piled up one over the other. It looked sloppy, and because I have dairy allergies, I couldn't eat the mashed potatoes or the parts of the chicken that had been sitting in them. The chicken wasn't bad, however; in fact it was pretty juicy. I do wish it had been prepared differently though.

After dinner entertainment included a raffle. Nobody from our table won, but LdyAnne got a Dan Curtis book and Millicent's son won one of Chris Pennock's comic books. Diana Millay read her ghost story (I've recounted this originally in my 2003 Fest report but the gist of it is that while filming *NoDS*, Diana was trapped overnight at Lyndhurst during a bad storm and was either visited by ghosts or temporarily slipped through a rift in time) and then we saw some video presentations.

The first was of Jonathan Frid's appearance as Barnabas on the game show *Generation Gap*. Barnabas stalked through a cemetery set filled with fog and asked the host, "What is your blood type?" "Type O," the man replied. Frid snapped his fingers in a regretful 'Oh, rats' manner and then sidled off-stage. Next came Joan Bennett's episode of *The Dating Game*. The guy she picked (Bachelor #3) was a real loser (of the three, I would have chosen Bachelor 2.) We also saw Alex Stevens (the werewolf) on *What's My Line* in full costume and make-up. After his identity was revealed, he removed the werewolf trappings (furry wig, prosthetic nose, strips of fur on his cheeks, black eyeliner). He said it took about an hour to put on but it took him less than a minute to get it off. We also saw some clips of Alex's other stunt work (he even doubled for Frank Sinatra). In the clips we saw, he dressed as a woman and leapt from a moving car before rolling down a hill and also jumped off a tall building.

Relevant clips from the *King of Queens* and *Gilmore Girls* episodes pertaining to DS also aired; these were very cute to watch. We saw a deodorant commercial with Jerry Lacy as Bogart and Marie Wallace as a dame, and a brief romantic comedy sketch with Lara Parker and George C. Scott. Before the evening closed, Pierson made an announcement that a Polaroid camera had been found. This belonged to JamesLady. She'd been lamenting its loss all evening and was very glad to have it back at last.

Following the banquet, we went out to the lobby to take pictures and chat. EmeraldRose, Quentin'sGal, Mary, jimbo, EvanHanley and I were the last to leave circa 3 AM. I was so sad to see the evening end; it had been a wonderful weekend. Fortunately, I was able to stretch it out a bit the next morning by wishing friends farewell in the lobby. I can't wait to see everyone again in Brooklyn next August 25, 26, and 27.

2006 Dark Shadows 40th Anniversary Weekend (Brooklyn, NY)

Day 1: Friday, August 25, 2006

Friday started predictably enough with a long registration line. This time, for the first time in seven years, I was at the very front of the line along with Minja/Wicked_C. We'd originally been told registration would start at 3:00, but the materials (badges and programs) had not yet arrived and would not until 4:00. We were encouraged to get back in line later, but I preferred to wait at the front of a line rather than at the back since I was clearly going to have to wait either way. This year's program features Victoria Winters running away from Collinwood on the cover. On the inside back cover is a tribute to the late Dan Curtis with several photos of him. One page from the end is a collage of photos from the first episode and its rehearsals titled "The Beginning:1966".

Events began about fifteen minutes after the listed 6:00 PM start time. The first thing one noticed upon entering the ballroom was a lovely recreation of the Collinwood drawing room just to the right of the podium: in consisted of a portion of paneled wall, a fireplace, a portrait over the mantel (a Charles Delaware Tate, perhaps?), and a couch.[69] I was thrilled to see some set dressing this time around. The Festival stage usually looks so bare, with just a podium and occasionally a "Dark Shadows" banner. The set was built by Patrick deBlasi, who intends to add to it next year. (Wouldn't it be cool to have surprise Fest guests enter onstage via the secret panel?) After a greeting from emcee Richard Halpern, we settled in to watch the second episode of DS with original commercials (most of which were aimed at women, such as ads for laundry soap, shoe polish, and cleaning supplies, but also included spots for *The Dating Game* and *F-Troop*). The episode itself showed Carolyn and Joe dancing and fighting, respectively, at the Blue Whale, and Vicki alerting Roger that Burke Devlin is back in town.

Next, came the first guest, Marilyn Ross, whose name is associated with the famous DS paperback novels of the 1960s and 70s. She and Richard had a seat on the sofa while he interviewed her. First of all, Marilyn revealed that it was actually her husband Dan who had written the novels using her name ("He always wrote using a variation of his name") and that neither of them had actually seen the show at the time. "They needed someone who could turn out the novels quickly, once a month or more, and he was in the Guinness Book of Records for writing the most novels." (over 300!) Dan wrote and Marilyn edited. "I also coached him on some of the characterizations, mostly for the female characters. After a while, writing and reading so many books in such a short period of time, they all blend together."

Because the Rosses lived in Canada, they did not have the same access to DS as American viewers, and hence were not familiar with the setting or characters from TV. "The first book was really different from the show. It had Barnabas in London.[70] The publishers contacted us and said, 'You can't do that; we can't have a story where Barnabas is running around London because we can't bring in the other characters. You're going to have to put him back in Collinsport.' The books and the characters were always very different from the show. Some people actually liked the books better than the show."

Someone asked Marilyn if they had been given an outline or any kind of directions on what to write for the novelizations. "No, we were told about the main characters, Barnabas and Quentin, but that was it. Except for the movie novelization; I remember we got a copy of the script for that and we had to stick very closely to the script." "How much give and take did he have with the studio and the publisher?" Ross was asked. "Could he pretty much write anything he wanted?" "Yes," she responded. "Did he have a favorite DS novel?" another fan wanted to know. "Yes, *Barnabas, Quentin, and the Serpent*. He really enjoyed bringing in the sci-fi elements and being able to write a sci-fi novel."

"Why did he stop writing?" another fan asked. "He died! He was writing right up until the time he died. I guess if you're a writer you have to write, and if you're an actor, you have to act. It's a compulsion." Marilyn described how, after Dan died, she had attempted to clean out his closet and study. "I opened the door and all these manuscripts poured out and almost engulfed me. It scared me." One fan asked how much research Dan Ross had done in preparation for his books. "He did lots and lots of research. There was one novel (non-DS) he wrote about mummies and Egypt. An Egyptologist contacted him thinking that he was an authority on Egypt, but he only knew what he had read for his research." Halpern and Ross also showed off the painting of Victoria Winters that had graced the cover of the first paperback book (although they didn't make clear that this was what the painting had been used for, so unless you read the Fest's publicity materials, you might not know exactly what the painting signified).

The next panel was "DS: The First Year" with Kathryn Leigh Scott and ConARD (not ConRAD) "Connie" Fowkes, who played the family's lawyer and Vicki's beau, Frank Garner, during the Mathew Morgan and Laura Collins story lines. Immediately, Conard received several questions. "What happened to you? Where did you go so suddenly? Frank Garner opened up an office in Collinsport and it seemed like he was going to become a regular character and be more involved with Vicki. Did you have to leave the show for some reason?" Connie was hesitant to go into detail. "I don't want to spoil the mood of the event by stirring up bad memories. It had to do with studio politics. On December 23, I received a letter that my services were no longer needed. I spoke to Bob Costello, the producer and he said, 'Baloney! You're on the show; the executives are just shaking up the cast a little.' So, I went home and tried to relax; even though I didn't have a contract, I had his assurance that I was still going to be on the show. Then, my agent contacted me about appearing on *Edge of Night*; the salary was twice what I was making on DS. I had a family and three children to support, and it just made sense to take that job instead. But I always thought it was in poor taste to fire me right before Christmas." "Did they ever try to get you back on as another character, or to bring your character back?" No.

Someone asked Kathryn Leigh Scott what became of Josette's music box. "Do you have it or did Dan Curtis have it?" "No, it disappeared, and it's a shame because it was a really lovely music box," she recalled, "with a carved glass lid and it actually played music." (This is contrary to the recollections of various people who worked behind-the-scenes and claimed the 'music box' was just a drinking glass with the top and bottom fastened on with electrical tape.)

Another question was directed at Conard: "What did you think after DS started becoming so popular? Did you used to tell people that you had been on the show before Barnabas?" "Oh, I told them I had been on DS, but not that it was before Barnabas," he chuckled. "They were always very impressed. I remember that my kids loved to watch DS. Whenever they visited their grandfather, they would be right in front of that television set, even after I was no longer on the show." "Well, everyone who appeared on the show, however briefly, is part of the DS family," the fan assured him, "and you certainly made an impression. Thank you for coming to the Fest!"

Someone else asked Conard if he remembered the other DS actors that he worked with. "Mostly I was working with Alexandra Moltke, but I do remember Mitch...Miller? No, Mitch Ryan. And Joan Bennett, of course, and Louis Edmonds." How did the actors feel about being at a Festival 40 years later? Conard voiced his amazement and appreciation for the fans while Kathryn became more philosophical. "I think it's that Dan Curtis was able to tap into stories and ideas that are universal and resonate with audiences even years later—stories of love, betrayal, jealousy. In that way, he was much like Gene Roddenberry, who created *Star Trek*, another show that's turning 40 this year and has a large, dedicated following."

Conard was also asked what other serials he had been on, and he rattled off a list of names including *Kitty Foyle, Love of Life, Search for Tomorrow, As the World Turns, The Edge of Night, Secret Storm*. Someone asked Kathryn Leigh Scott if she knew what had been Thayer David's favorite character to play on DS. "His favorite character? Oh, my. I don't know if he had a favorite. He played so many characters—more characters than any other actor on the show. (He played eight in fact—Matthew Morgan, Ben Stokes, Prof. T.E. Stokes, Sandor, Count Petofi, Parallel Tim Stokes, Mordecai Grimes, Parallel Ben Stokes, and if you count *Night of DS*, Rev. Strack.) Was there a Professor Petofi?" People in the audience shouted back "Count Petofi" (though Kathryn may have meant Professor Stokes). "Yes, I think that was his favorite," Kathryn agreed. "Thank you! That's what I wanted to hear," the fan said.

Someone else asked Kathryn about Joel Crothers. "First of all, he was a child actor—did you all know that? He was also very intelligent. He was a Harvard man and a Dickens scholar. Joel and I were very close; he was like a big brother to me." She also shared the story, discussed in her *DS Memories* book, about how the two had gone to Italy together on a vacation during the run of the show. "I was going to visit my boyfriend and Joel was able to join me at the last minute. People who saw us thought that Joe and Maggie were running away together!" Conard also chimed in on this question, as he and Joel had worked together on *The Edge of Night* after each had left DS. He cited Crothers's major role in *Barefoot in the Park* on Broadway and mentioned a small part he'd had in the film *What's So Bad About Feeling Good*? (a psychedelic romp that Richard Halpern remembered fondly). "It was so strange to have seen Joel in such a big part in the play, and then in the movie playing such a tiny part," Fowkes recalled. "If you blinked, you would miss him."

"Did you feel that there was more depth to your character that should have been explored?" one fan inquired of Conard. "After all, there was a lot of tension between you and your father—he kept reminding you that Elizabeth was your client and not Vicki, but you still wanted to help Vicki." "No, I never got that impression," Conard said. "Frank Garner was pretty bland and one-dimensional—a potential love interest for Vicki. That was the only image the producers wanted." Regardless of whether or not Frank was one-dimensional, it didn't keep one fan from remarking, "I always thought that of all the men Vicki dated—Barnabas, Burke Devlin, Jeff Clark—Frank Garner was perfect for her. He was young and handsome, a lawyer!" Many in the audience cheered.

Lara Parker was up next to read from her latest book *The Salem Branch*. However, as I had already heard her read from the book at the past two Festivals, I decided to duck out and visit the dealers' room instead. Actually, the "Dealers' Room" (AKA the DS Marketplace) consisted of only two vendors—MPI and Shadowgram. The other sellers—including all of the actors who were selling books, Majestic Toys, CynD's jewelry, and people selling vintage photos of the DS actors, books, and videos—were scattered out in the hallways.

While I stopped at CynD's table, where I bought a bat charm, a man came up behind me. "What's this? *Dark Shadows* jewelry?" he asked. I explained to him how CynD made all the jewelry herself, including charms of the characters' faces and Barnabas-style rings. He then began to ask me several questions—Where was I from? Did I work in the entertainment industry? (lol!) Was this my first Festival? No? How many had I attended? And who were those people who just finished talking in the ballroom? I explained what parts Fowkes and Scott had played (and how Kathryn had multiple roles on the show). He seemed especially interested to learn that Kathryn had played Barnabas's fiancée, Josette. Finally, the gentleman revealed that he was a reporter, Gary Shapiro of the *New York Sun*, and introduced his assistant, Lauren.

He began to seriously interview me then, asking how many people usually come to the Fests (it varies depending on the coast: generally, in the high hundreds for the West Coast and a couple thousand for the East Coast). Where do people come from to attend the Fests? (From as far as England and all over the United States—Florida, Ohio, California, Illinois, Texas, New Jersey, New York). What was I most looking forward to at this Fest? (Seeing old friends, seeing fan-generated activities like the fan videos, skits, and Costume Gala, and hearing from the new Fest guests like Betsy Durkin, Conard Fowkes, and Donna McKechnie). Why did I think DS has such a strong following 40 years later? I thought that nostalgia played a large part in its longevity. The show came along at a time when there were lots of major changes, both in the fans' lives (as they grew older and entered their adolescent years—middle school and high school) and in the world (the Vietnam War, political turmoil) and probably served as an escape hatch from all the pressure. (Ultimately, that was what he latched onto, and it's the only part of my interview that made it into the article). I added that I thought KLS had made a good point about the stories having broad and enduring appeal. He then asked what drew me to DS, since I am not an original fan. I answered that I had always been interested in the supernatural, and that was the aspect that initially attracted me to the show. He also wanted to know if I had attended any other types of conventions, like *Star Trek*. Except for the *Lost* convention in Burbank last year, I said no, but that I was involved in a local fan club in Southern California,

Shadows in the Sun, and in Internet fandom. When asked what was the best DS site, I named www.dsboards.com (I am sorry the plugs didn't make it into the article). Then, Mr. Shapiro thanked me for my time, and that was the end of *my* Q&A session.

Just at that time, John Karlen came by and asked where the ballroom was. We fans pointed him in the right direction, and he hurried off. Figuring that there was bound to be some excitement when he crashed Lara's Q&A, I followed and found a seat in the ballroom. As Lara was telling the fans that she would write another book if *The Salem Branch* sold well,[71] Johnny edged up to the stage and came up behind her. Amid cheers from the audience, the two shared a long kiss. Then, Karlen addressed the fans. "Every year, we get the same old questions. This year, I want you all to ask some real, meaty questions, and Kathryn and I will—" Lara stared at him as he fudged her name and stormed to the opposite end of the stage in mock fury. Johnny laughed. "I'm sorry. Sorry, Lara. Lara and I will answer them for you."

Obligingly, the first person to the microphone asked, "Can you tell us some dirt about the cast?" "Oh, what a question," John waxed. "How to answer that question? Here's a little-known story about a guy named Lenny Spoleto. Most of you never heard of him; he wasn't with the show very long." "No, don't tell them about Lenny," Lara joined in. "You're not supposed to tell!" But Johnny continued. "Lenny came on the show, and right after, several ladies got pregnant. And that was the end of Lenny." (I'm sure the story is made up, but I thought it was cute that Lara helped John ad-lib it).

Lara was asked how she enjoyed making the new Big Finish audio dramas of DS. "It was terrific! And if you all buy the CDs, we'll be able to make more of them—in London! They'll fly us to London to record." John was asked to share his favorite DS memories. "My favorite part of DS was the Brittany. After taping the show, Dan Curtis would take us all to dinner at the Brittany (du Soir). How many native New Yorkers are in the audience? Then you know about the Brittany. It was terrific!" One bold young fan approached the mike and said to Lara, "I know you're like, 60 years old, but could you still do your Angelique laugh?" (With manners like that, he should be so lucky to live to 60.) She did so, and it drew great applause.

However, there was trouble with the microphone, and both John and Lara complained that they were having trouble understanding the questions. It took some time before they could finally understand what one man in particular was trying to ask. "In *Angelique's Descent*, it seemed really masochistic to make Angelique Josette's sister. Why did you choose to do that?" "You didn't like that? Well, I'm not sure I would call it masochistic," Lara defended. "I was trying to show how much Angelique had been abused as a child. Her father mistreated her, she was forced to act as a kind of living goddess on the plantation, and finally she was abandoned by Barnabas. All of those hardships show how she eventually became the person she was."

After their Q&A came the tribute to Dan Curtis. This consisted of a clip reel from Mr. Curtis's many works, including DS, *The Night Stalker, Dracula, Trilogy of Terror, Melvin Purvis—G-Man, the Last Ride of the Dalton Gang, When Every Day was the Fourth of July, Winds of War*, Curtis's Emmy acceptance speech for *WoW, War and Remembrance, Our Fathers*, and *Saving Milly*. (This was primarily an edited version of the clip reel that played at the Museum of TV & Radio's salute to Dan Curtis in 2004). The clips concluded with the caption, "In Memory of Our Fearless Leader." When the lights came back up, many of the DS actors went to the microphone to share their memories of Curtis. Kathryn Leigh Scott was up first. "Dan Curtis really shaped my career. I got my first acting job because of him. I got to go to London for the first time to work with Dan Curtis (in 1977's *The Turn of the Screw*). I started my publishing company because of DS and Dan Curtis. He had a very big impact on my life. I really want to thank Jim Pierson for fixing it so that I could see Dan again before he died. It was a good day for him, and he was cheerful and outgoing. That's how I want to remember him." Her voice cracked as she spoke, and it seemed that she might cry.

David Selby reminisced next about auditioning for Dan for the role of Quentin and first picking up all the golf balls that Curtis putted around his office. "A woman came up to me today and told me she'd just had a baby boy that she'd named Quentin. I imagine there have been a lot of babies named

Quentin, but that's more Dan's doing than mine." (A comment intended more to credit Curtis for the popularity of DS than to imply that he was naughty).

Marie Wallace talked about the last time she saw Curtis at the premiere of *Saving Milly*. "None of us knew he was sick. He may not have even been sick then. He was happy to see me and he told me, 'Marie, I always loved you.' That made me feel so good to know that! He meant what he said (in his Emmy speech) about loving actors. Dan really enjoyed actors." She also described her first time meeting Curtis. "I was auditioning for the part of Eve, and my agent warned me, 'You're probably not right for the part, so don't be offended if he turns you down.' I went to Dan's office expecting to be yelled at, and instead this very nice man introduced himself and hired me for the part."

John Karlen's tribute was more light-hearted. He mentioned how fond Dan had been of him. "He used me in almost all his movies after DS. How about the rest of you?" he teased the cast.

Jerry Lacy approached the podium. "I'm not very good at impromptu speeches," he apologized. He then told the story of how he was hired to work on DS. He had been in a play with David Ford (Sam Evans) at the time. "I knew that he was on this show called *Dark Shadows*, and I asked him how it was going. 'Everything was fine, but now they've brought a goddamned vampire on the show,' he grumbled." When the part of Tony Peterson came up, Ford recommended Lacy to Dan. "I went to his office for a meeting. David went in first and shut the door and I could hear loud voices, like they were arguing. I was beginning to think I wouldn't get the part. I knew David had a loud speaking voice, and I found out later that Dan did too. The door opened, Dan came out and asked, 'Are you Jerry?' I said I was. 'You're hired.' And that was that."

And that concluded the live events for Friday. As the autograph lines formed, I headed out to the lobby and lounge to spend time with my friends. We must have chatted until almost 3:00 in the morning before finally dispersing for bed. Saturday would bring a full twelve hours' worth of activities.

Day 2: Saturday, August 26, 2006

The day opened with one of my favorite events: Fan Videos. These generally include clips from the show set to relevant songs or taped skits of fans acting as the characters. First up was one of Guy Haines's music videos showing Barnabas and Julia's evolving relationship set to the Pet Shop Boys' "Always on My Mind." Next, Richard Halpern played his "Baby Dark Shadows[72]" in which he and his niece and nephews (who were 6six and under at the time) re-enact various storylines of DS in comedic ways. For instance, the 1897 video showed an over-the-top Rev. Trask (Halpern) harassing Jamison (nephew Damian) about having wire hangers in his closet while 1795 involved Natalie (Halpern again) and Josette (niece Angelique) using a Ouija board to foretell the future. Their exchange went something like this:

Natalie: "Should Josette stay away from Barnabas?" (Yes)

Josette: "You're moving it Aunt Natalie!"

Natalie: "No, I'm not!"

Josette: "Then let *me* ask: Should Aunt Natalie stay out of my business?" (Yes)

Natalie: "You're moving it, Josette!"

The *piece de resistance* was JVjr's Cheep Productions: Save Our Cemetery, a full-length (30 mins), professionally-made DS episode starring his impersonator brother Daryl in a dual role as Barnabas and Julia (and he's a dead ringer for each!). The episode featured recreations of the Old House and Eagle Hill Cemetery sets, costumes, and actual DS music. The story is that Eagle Hill Cemetery is about to be demolished (to make way for Petofi's Peep Show Palace), so to protect his incestors' (and ancestors') final resting place, Barnabas and Julia fight back against merciless Construction Worker Jonas. They get help from the ghosts of Dave Woodard (Mark Moyer), Sam Evans (Guy Haines), and Sarah Collins (a grown-up Sharon Smyth-Lenz). Each of these screened videos is classic, highly entertaining and humorous. I appreciated having the opportunity to see them again, but I couldn't help regretting that we weren't treated to any new offerings this year (DLA75 in particular had told me earlier about two new videos that he'd submitted, but which weren't played). At previous

Fests, fan videos were screened at least twice over the weekend, and I wish more time had been set aside to showcase more of them on this occasion. Fan creativity is really something splendid to behold, and since the fans are at least as important to DS as the stars, I think they deserve the spotlight more than once in a while too.

Marie Wallace was the first star to do a Q&A that day. She began by reading selections from her memoirs, *On Stage and in the Shadows*, published last year. The book chronicles Marie's work on and off Broadway and on TV (especially as a cast member on DS). She shared vignettes about entering a canoe race publicity event as part of the *Gypsy* chorus against chorus girls from *Flower Drum Song* (and deliberately tipping their own canoe in order to attract attention when it looked like the *Flower* girls were going to win), working with Bert Lahr in *The Beauty Part*, performing a comical burlesque to entertain Gwen Verdon on her birthday (Verdon fell off her chair laughing), and auditioning for the part of Eve on DS.Â Marie's stories are lively and entertaining; I have her book and enjoyed it very much.

After the reading, there was time for a few questions. "The Festivals must be a lot of fun for all of you actors because you get to see each other again. Who do you keep in touch with from the show during the year?" "I actually don't keep in touch with the other actors," Marie admitted. "Some do keep in touch with each other, but I don't. Most of the actors live on the West Coast. Diana Millay and Nancy Barrett are in New York, but we don't really socialize outside of the Fests." Later on, she corrected herself. "I did used to keep in touch with Louis Edmonds. He invited me out to his estate, the Rookery. I hadn't thought about him when the question first came up because he's passed away now. I also keep in touch with Jonathan Frid. He wrote the Foreword for my book, but again, he's somebody who doesn't come to Festivals anymore."

David Block asked a question that I was tempted to ask myself. "When you played Mad Jenny, did you do research for the part in order to portray someone with a mental illness?" (I've always thought that Jenny was a perfect example of someone with schizophrenia). "Yes, I try to research every role that I do, and I especially enjoyed Jenny. I told my agent, 'Find me another mad woman to play, and I'll return to acting.'" Someone else asked Marie if she was surprised that she was brought back to the show for multiple roles. "No, I wasn't surprised. I understood that was how the show worked. You died, and you were brought back as someone else." Would she have returned to the show after playing Megan Todd if she were invited? "I think they did try to get me back, but I was under contract on *Somerset* by then." Another lady asked Marie to repeat a story that she had evidently told before about how someone stopped her in the street once and told her she was the most beautiful woman in the world. "I actually don't remember that story. I wish I did; it sounds nice."

Betsy Durkin (the 2nd Victoria Winters) made her Festival debut after Marie's Q&A. We started out by watching a couple of clips from her time on the show, including the scene where she confronts Nicholas Blair about being a warlock and tells him not to marry Maggie, and the scene where Jeff Clark fades away into the past while Vicki desperately tries to call Prof. Stokes for help. When the video ended, Betsy stepped up to the podium, clearly emotional. "Oh, my god, I haven't seen those scenes in so long. I think I'm going to cry. Thank you so much for inviting me here to the Festival! It's so nice to meet all of you!"

Betsy told us how she'd learned about DS's continuing fandom. She had been at a book fair to promote her new book *Dressing the Man You Love.* "Craig Hamrick was there too, and he had his book *Barnabas & Company* on display. I walked over and picked up the book to see if I was mentioned. I wanted to talk to him, but he wasn't at the table then, so I got my business card and wrote on the back of it, 'I was here' and tucked it into the book. He contacted me later and encouraged me to come to the Festival." (Thank you, Craig!) Craig's revised edition of *Barnabas & Company* will include an interview with Durkin.[73]

Right away, someone asked Betsy why she was on for such a short period of time. "Craig told me that he thought the audience had grown so attached to Alexandra Moltke that it was hard for them to accept another actress in the role. I agree, and I think it would have worked better if, instead of recasting the part, I had come to Collinwood as Vicki's sister or some other new character that the audience could adjust to more easily. Anyway, they wrote out the character by sending her back in time. I went to Europe after that to do a play, but I got a call from the producers to play Victoria again. I asked if they were planning to write the character back into the show, and they said no, it was just for a couple of episodes. It wasn't worth it for me to go back to the States just for that, so they found somebody else to film those episodes." (That would be Carolyn Groves). She also shared that she had run into Alexandra Moltke by chance years later. "I told her that we had played the same role on DS, that I had taken over for her when she left. She was very surprised and we spent some time comparing our experiences on the show."

Later in the Q&A, Betsy was asked to elaborate on her DS memories. "Lela Swift, the director was very strict. I guess she had to be; she was one of the first—the first? the only? female television directors.[74] She must have had to prove herself. It was difficult to tape the show without stopping. You know, we filmed in order, from start to finish, and if you messed up, you couldn't go back to fix it. I remember one day that I was upset because I didn't think that I had done the scene as well as I could have. I was crying in my dressing room and Grayson Hall came by and heard me. She came over and asked, 'What's the matter, honey?' I told her that I thought I could have done better in the scene and she said, 'On this show, you're lucky if you get even one good scene in.'" "Were you ever invited back to play other characters on DS?" someone asked. "No," Betsy answered. "I wish they had asked me back. I think I was the only person that Jonathan Frid ever asked to marry him, but I turned him down. I went into the past with Roger Davis instead and I think I made a terrible mistake." Everyone in the audience hooted and applauded.

"Did you work on any other soap operas after DS?" someone else asked. "No, but I did a lot of commercials at the same time that DS was on—you might have seen me advertising Ivory soap or Irish Spring—" Here, Betsy broke into an Irish brogue to recite the soap slogan. "That was you!" the fan exclaimed. "I'm so glad I know that now. I loved that commercial!" Another fan commented on her work with Humbert Allen Astredo. "I heard that he was an acting teacher. Is that true?" "I don't know about that," Betsy admitted, "but he was a very good actor, so I'm sure he was a very good teacher."

Betsy was asked if she had any memories of the kids who hung around outside the studio doors. "There were two kids who ran my fan club. They would be outside the studio in the morning—they wouldn't go to school—and at night when we left. I used to worry about them being out in the cold and the dark. Around Christmas time, I gave them both boxes of candy and I snuck them into the studio. They weren't able to watch the show being taped, but they could see the sets. That was my Christmas gift to them. I often wonder about them—where they are now, how they are, what they grew up to be." She also told a very touching story (I can't remember the context in which it came up, but I think someone had asked Betsy if she was ever recognized as Victoria) about a situation in the town where her mother lived. "There was a little boy, about eight-years-old, who had been in a car accident, and he was left paralyzed. Someone from the hospital knew my mother and knew that I was on DS.Â She told her, 'This boy is a huge fan of DS—he watches it every day. Do you think your daughter would send him an autographed picture?' Well, I heard the story and I felt that I had to do more than that, so I went to all the other cast members—David Selby, Louis Edmonds, Nancy Barrett, Jonathan Frid—and got autographs and photos from them all to send to this boy. He was the star of his ward for a long time after that."

Betsy also talked about her book, explaining that it took her three years to research the information about various fabrics, styles, etc. and write it. Finally, the last person to speak at the microphone told Betsy, "I don't know what those producers were thinking when they let you go. They obviously didn't see what we saw in those clips. You're just as beautiful and talented as Alexandra Moltke or anyone else." "Thank you," Betsy said demurely. Betsy truly is a delightful lady, and I hope she attends more festivals in the future. As she left the stage, she received a standing ovation.

The first of the charity auctions came next. I chose to go get lunch instead of attending this, so I'm not sure exactly what was sold or for how much, but I did pass the table on my way out and I recall seeing these items: copies of the now-out-of-print DS novels *Angelique's Descent* and *Dreams of the Dark*, several Marilyn Ross paperbacks, programs from previous Festivals, Quentin and Barnabas figurines from Majestic Toys, bricks from the foundation of the Spratt House (used as the Old House exterior), a set of vampire fangs used by Stefan Gierasch (Prof. Woodard) on the 1991 DS series, several items belonging to Dan Curtis including an award from the Ann Radcliffe society, a leather jacket, his own copies of the books *Burnt Offerings and Tales of the Mysterious and Macabre* by Algernon Blackwood (I actually had a collection of Blackwood's stories up in my hotel room—I'd been reading it on the plane—and thought about bidding on this one, but didn't think it would fit in my suitcase), used as references for his movies, and the lovely painting of Victoria arriving at Collinwood that served as the cover of the first Marilyn Ross DS novel, donated by the real Marilyn. Proceeds went to UCLA Alzheimer's research, a poignant cause since Curtis's wife Norma suffered from Alzheimer's Disease.

Following the auction was a presentation from Big Finish Productions, which has just given us two new DS audio dramas, "The House of Despair" and "The Book of Temptation." The Q&A opened with the screening of a breathtaking trailer for the dramas that I believe is included on DVD Collection 26. Clips of David Selby musing about Quentin's return to a changed Collinwood, Lara Parker cackling, and John Karlen warning of danger play over images of an ominous house. The panel included Stuart Manning (who wrote "House"), Scott Handcock (who wrote "Book"), and Jason Haigh-Ellery (who produces the dramas). They introduced themselves and thanked the fans for being so supportive of their work (apparently, sales had been going very well so far that weekend). Many fans in return thanked Big Finish for bringing back DS and praised the company for its work on the *Dr. Who* audio plays. "I hope you won't be discouraged if sales start out slow at first," one fan voiced. "Please stick with it and keep making the dramas!" "Don't worry," Jason reassured, "we understand that it will take time to get the word out and make American audiences aware of what we do."

The panel was asked if the audio dramas fit the continuity of "Return to Collinwood." "The dramas have been authorized by Dan Curtis Productions," Stuart explained, "but they don't necessarily take place right after the show ends or right before "Return to Collinwood" begins. We've set the stories 'now'. We don't want to say, 'Well, this takes place in 1970, this is 1980.' We want to keep it current. I think it's good to have as many different visions of the show as possible—whether it's the movies, the

TV show, "Return to Collinwood," or our dramas." Another fan asked if the three men were all fans of the show when they came to the project. "Actually, Stuart is the only real fan among us," Scott revealed. "He showed us some episodes to give us a feel for the show. We hadn't seen it before; our access to it is different in the UK than in America." Someone else asked if there were plans to include characters other than Quentin, Maggie, Angelique, and Willie. Jason hinted that a future drama would include a surprise cameo from another original actor. "Yeah, I think Jim Pierson let that one out of the bag earlier," the fan commented, but no clues were given about the mystery guest's identity. It was also pointed out that original, recurring characters would be included in the dramas too. Lastly, one woman wanted to know how old Scott was (I think she was hoping to set him up with her granddaughter). "Young enough not to mind, but old enough to know better," Scott joked.

Big Finish was followed by the DS production and publicity panel, featuring publicist Jim Butler, publicity and promotions man Les Schecter, cameraman Stuart Goodman, and Henry Plimack, who had worked on sound on the show and was helping out with the audio for the Festival. (Associate Producer George DiCenzo was originally scheduled to be on the panel too, but it had been announced the previous day that he was unable to attend). The four told stories about the work they had done on or for the show.

Jim Butler told how it was his job to get information about the actors for various magazines. "At first, there wasn't a lot of interest in DS because it was just another soap opera, but when all the kids started getting hooked, there was a huge demand for information and stories. Did any of you read *Tiger Beat*? I wrote a monthly column about DS for that magazine."

Schecter told amusing anecdotes about the various publicity stunts he staged for the show. "Jonathan Frid was flying in to Washington D.C. to do publicity for the show, and I had this brilliant idea that we would hide Barnabas's fangs somewhere in the airport and have the kids in to hunt for them. Whoever found the fangs would get to have lunch with Jonathan Frid. I talked it over with him and he was game for it. It was crazy having all these kids running around the airport, but it was a huge success. After that, anytime Jonathan had to travel for an event, we would have a search for Barnabas's fangs. We'd put them in a pretty obvious place and they were always found right away. But after a while, Jonathan got tired of it. He didn't want to do interviews as Barnabas anymore; he wanted to do interviews as Jonathan."

Plimack told about his first day on the show. "First, they had me run the sound check to get the hang of the equipment, and then they said, 'Well, you know more about the equipment now, so you might as well do sound for the rehearsal.' So, I did, and then they said, 'Well, you already did the rehearsal; you might as well do the actual show.'"

Goodman discussed how difficult it was to work with the huge studio cameras in such a small set. "Most of the time I was sitting in Louis Edmonds's lap while I tried to film," he joked. He also made a reference to the unwanted 'dark shadows' of the boom microphones that can be seen in the show. The studio just wasn't big enough for appropriate lighting. Goodman also told us how Bob Costello had asked him one day in 1967 to stay late after taping and operate the camera for some screen tests for a new character. "There was one guy there, Jonathan Frid, who was really odd looking. After the screen test, Bob asked me, 'What did you think?' I told him, 'That Frid guy was creepy. He looked like a vampire or something. What part did you have planned for him?'" So, it appears we can thank Goodman in part for Frid's hiring.[75]

David Selby was scheduled to read from his new book next, but by then I was feeling the need to stretch my legs and get away from the air conditioning, so I instead wandered through the dealers' area, (where I discovered that MPI was already sold out of several items) visiting with Julia99, Dawn, and mscbryk. I was having so much fun, that I missed David's entire presentation, as well as the beginning of Donna McKechnie's. When I returned to my seat, she was just telling about her audition for the part of Amanda Harris.

"I had just come from *Promises, Promises*, where I'd fallen in love with Ken Howard (Thomas Jefferson in *1776*). But it didn't work out, and I was heartbroken. When I came to audition for *Dark Shadows*, I read a scene as a woman who is really a painting come to life. She has to convince her boyfriend, Quentin, that she's not actually a person and begs him not to leave her. (I was very surprised to learn that the writers had planned Amanda's story so far in advance; there were no hints about her true nature when the character first appeared). I was able to channel all of my sorrow and tears into the role of Amanda, so it worked for me."

McKechnie also discussed Amanda's death sequence, which came about because she had signed on to do the show *Company*. "It was very dramatic. I had to cross a bridge and was killed in a rockslide. Let me tell you what happened when they filmed that scene. For a long time, nobody believed me when I told this story; then I finally found a cameraman who said, 'Oh, yes, I remember how they left you.' In rehearsal, I was given a plastic bag to put over my head to shield me from the peat and Styrofoam rocks that they were going to drop on me. They only dropped a little bit of material on me then. But when we filmed the real thing, I didn't have any plastic. I was in full period costume with a huge 25-pound wig, trying to cross that rickety bridge. (Actually, the death scene was filmed in contemporary dress and McKechnie sported a short hairstyle, much like Julia's.) When the time came to kill me, they dumped a wave of rocks and peat on me, mounds and mounds. I was lying in a pile of debris with peat in my mouth, nose, hair, eyes. Then, the lights went down on me, and everybody ran to the next set to keep shooting, leaving me lying there. It's funny now, but at the time, I thought it was very mean." We then watched the clip that Donna had mentioned where the rockslide knocks Amanda/Olivia off the bridge.

Another fan asked Donna to share her memories of working on *Hullabaloo* (apparently, a clip of her dancing on that show had been played earlier). "I remember what great acts we had on the show: the Rolling Stones, Freddy and the Dreamers, the Animals. When the Animals performed, we stuck our heads through the wall like we were mounted animal heads and we were supposed to stay very still, but I kept bopping my head to the music slightly and I got yelled at for doing that." While on *Hullabaloo*, she had worked with Michael Bennett, who created *A Chorus Line*, the show for which McKechnie is best known. "Everyone could tell that he was going to be somebody famous and we all followed him around." She also remembered the friendly rivalry between the *Hullabaloo* cast and *American Bandstand*, which aired on the West Coast.

As Donna finished her Q&A, the other actors lined up to take their places for the cast reunion. Jim Pierson introduced each one by one. As he and Richard Halpern tried to seat everybody, Jim pulled out his cell phone. "Is this an appropriate time for a phone call?" Richard chided. Jim said, "Hello?" and the voice on the other end came booming over the loudspeakers. "Hello. This is Jonathan!" It was him all right—the voice sounded only slightly aged but the rich sound was the same as ever. "Who is this again?" Jim asked. "It's Jonathan Frid—or Barney. Barney Bas." It was so exciting to hear him again, live, over the phone. Many had speculated that he might appear at the Fest as one of the often-touted "surprise guests," and even though we all knew it was unrealistic, I think a lot of people were still holding out hope at the last minute. But next to a face-to-face appearance, the phone call was the best thing. Even though Jonathan couldn't be with us in person, it was touching to know that he still cared enough to check in with us.

The crowd went wild. People erupted in cheers, standing up and yelling, "We love you!" "Oh, my! It sounds like there are a thousand people there!" Frid marveled. Jim quickly named to Jonathan all of the other actors who were present. You could see that they were also delighted to hear from him again. "Tell us what you've been doing lately," Pierson encouraged. Jonathan told us how much fun he was having with his website and all the new technology. "I'm looking over my script for the reading (this confused me; I knew Frid had made a video greeting for the Fest, but the way he was talking made it sound like it was going to be a live video greeting; perhaps he was preparing to film a different take for his website?) You'll all get to see it later." He also mentioned how grateful he was to be able to converse with us. "I've been having trouble with Bell Canada over an unpaid bill. I knew they had been trying to get in touch with me, but I didn't realize it was because of a bill. I was afraid they were going to cut off my service. That would have been terrible if it had happened today and I had missed you, but at least I'm still able to receive calls."

Jonathan also marveled at the passage of time and that we were celebrating the 40th Anniversary. "Unfortunately, so many have left us now, but I'm sure they're happy where they are now. It's like *Gone with the Wind*. That movie became so popular and then almost immediately, the cast started to die off until, for a while, Olivia de Haviland was the only one left." "She's still around," Jim assured. "She is? Well, good." Jonathan also told us that he was doing well, "at 82, 83, however old I'm supposed to be now." Apparently, Jonathan was also willing to take questions from the audience (though I did not catch that remark), which would have been delightful, but time was limited. As Jim bid good-bye to Jonathan, the ballroom once again chorused, "We love you!" Frid's phone call was one of the highlights, not just of this Fest but of any. Many thanks to Nancy Kersey and Jim Pierson for encouraging his participation!

Finally, Jim turned his attention to the actors on-stage, asking them to update us on their recent activities. Most of the actors spoke about their books. Diana Millay reminded us about her *The Power of Halloween* ("It's all about my ancestors, who were witches in Salem") and told us she would have a new book out next year called *Create Success and Recreate Your Life*. She also mentioned that several people had asked her about the Diana Millay Travel Club, but that she would have to give more details about it the following day. Marie Wallace talked about her book of memoirs and her new career as a photographer. Betsy Durkin spoke about *Dressing the Man You Love* and how she was inspired to write it after finding that there was no real layperson's guide for women to buy clothes for the men in their lives. Donna McKechnie once more mentioned her autobiography, *Time Steps*, and a couple of upcoming local book signings (one of which was to be at the Lincoln Center Barnes & Noble; I can't remember the other location).

Kathryn commented on the recent phone call. "It was so good to hear Jonathan's voice again! I started to get teary-eyed when I heard him. And isn't it wonderful—all of us have written books this year. Well, all of us except Johnny. Maybe someday he will too." She, of course talked about her own book, *Murder in Prime Time*, a fictional mystery about an actress who has long played a detective on TV and uses her TV experience to solve a real murder. Lara also remarked on Jonathan's phone call. "As soon as I heard Jonathan's voice, it took me back to the studio, listening to Jonathan forgetting his lines. She told us about *The Salem Branch* and how it serves as both a sequel and a prequel to DS; not only does it pick up in 1971 when the show ends, it goes back to Salem in the 1600s when Miranda duVal was persecuted for witchcraft. "It took me six years to write it; Kathryn turns out a new book every year." "I think we need to get Jonathan a webcam," David Selby said, "so we can get a picture of him while he's talking and see him at home in his bathrobe and slippers." Selby's new book is called *A Better Place*. This year, he also has a new granddaughter, Brianna.

Chris Pennock took the mic and breathed into it Leviathan style, which drew applause. His new comic this year is not part of the *Fear and Loathing* series but something called *Buddhism for Wolves*. "If you buy it, I'll give you a personal mantra," he advertised. He also told us that his daughter Tara, "the real talent in the family," had recently auditioned for *American Idol* and would be singing the next day during his scheduled reading.

John Karlen was next. "What have I been doing lately? For 51 weeks out of the year, I do nothing but wait and wait for this moment now." (So do I, Johnny). Since he was the first person with nothing to peddle, he instead reminisced about his life and career. But when he paused for breath, Jim went on to the next person in the line, Lisa Richards, who was present only for this segment. John seemed to resent this: "Did I just get cut off?" However, Lisa tried to soothe him. "You're the greatest, John. I remember when you and I appeared together on-stage in *Marat/Sade*. He was Marat and I was Charlotte Cordier (Cordier, a servant, assassinated Marat, one of the masterminds of the Reign of Terror, while he was bathing). He jumped out of the bathtub, waving a knife, and ran around the stage. I think somebody got an arm broken."[76] Echoing Chris Pennock's pride in his daughter's achievements, Richards told us that her son's band, I'm a Robot, had just released a new CD. These brief interviews essentially formed the cast reunion. I was disappointed that the audience wasn't able to ask questions of the panel as we've always had the chance to do in previous years. Although most of the cast did individual Q&A's during the weekend, (e.g. Marie Wallace, Kathryn Leigh Scott) others did not (e.g. Lisa Richards, Chris Pennock).

Nancy Barrett's cabaret came after the reunion. This time, we were allowed to remain in the ballroom while the sound system, microphones, dance floor, etc. were set up. Nancy's cabaret show, variations of which she has performed in the past, focused on her search for her true identity and her experiences as an actress. After a couple of false starts, she launched into several staple songs, including a Carolyn Stoddard-centric version of "Girls Just Wanna Have Fun," "So Beyond," "Razzle Dazzle," "I am Who I am," "I'm Tired," and two of my favorites, "The Bus from Amarillo" and "Look What Happened to Mabel." The songs from her performance are now available on CD, which I was unable to pick up at the Fest and which I hope will be available on her website.

When the show concluded, the autograph lines formed. Those of us who were in the Costume Gala (e.g. my roommate, victoriawinters, and myself) adjourned to our rooms to warm up. We were supposed to meet to turn in our entrance forms and receive our numbers about an hour before the event was to begin, but by this time, events were running at least two hours behind. While we waited to be put in order and clarified who needed microphones, tables, chairs, etc. for their acts, we had to miss the screening of the 2004 DS pilot (which many people ducked out to catch) and Jonathan Frid's video greeting. We were quite dismayed when we learned that the latter had already played, but were assured that it would be repeated the following morning and at the banquet. Finally, all 30 of us trooped downstairs (cramming into the elevators a few at a time). We walked into the ballroom just as the Collinsport Players' skit was beginning.

The premise of "Golden Shadows" was that the Golden Girls—Dorothy (John Schaefer), Sophia (Peter Mac), Blanche (Diane Eckert), and Rose (Dennis Petragnani)—are vacationing in New England and become stranded in Collinsport when their car breaks down. Roger Collins (Jay Keaveny) directs the ladies to the Old House where Barnabas (Richard Halpern) becomes infatuated with Rose, who reminds him of his beloved, dim-witted Josette and Vicki. Meanwhile, Willie (Walter Down) is quite taken with Blanche. Barnabas attempts to put Rose under his spell, but when the other ladies discover his secret, they intervene. The skit was uproarious with numerous jokes pertaining to both DS and GG, and the actors played their roles to the hilt. The skit concluded shortly before 10:00, and the Gala began.

Many people had entered the Gala this year. Unfortunately, because there was such a large turnout and because we were running so far behind, many people were forced to abridge their acts (for instance, I had planned to sing two song parodies this year in honor of the 40th Anniversary; I had to choose only one, so the other will have to wait until the 45th Anniversary).[77] Nevertheless, the participants turned in stellar performances. Costumes ranged from Josette after her fall, Judith Collins Trask, and a skit with a quartet of women in lovely 1795 period outfits (Josette, Angelique, Naomi, and Abigail Collins). Performers included Michael Culhane and his classic Nicholas Blair/music cues routine, VAM as a "Bad to the Bone" Count Petofi, David Block as Gabriel and Daniel Collins in a pivotal confrontation sequence, an elegant singing vampire, Charles Ellis as Charnak the Magnificent (a DS version of Johnny Carson's Karnak act) assisted by the lovely MaineGirl, Jenny Collins and Magda singing Patsy Cline's "Crazy," a couple waltzing to "I Wanna Dance with You," Lalinda's nostalgic poetic tribute to DS, Alice Faye Landis dancing Polynesian style, a "Creeque Alley" parody about the summer of 1970 hauntings, several original songs, and more. victoriawinters stole the show with a parody of "Memory" about running home from school to catch DS. Peter Mac as Miranda duVal promoted *The Salem Branch* and sang the Bette Middler version of "I Put a Spell on You" from the movie *Hocus Pocus*.

The grand finale was an epic poem by Angelique_Wins[78] (performed by her and adamsgirl/deckert[79]) called "A Pirate's Maine Treasure" that explains how Naomi and Joshua got together and reveals the details behind one of the show's intriguing, neglected subplots (that Naomi was given valuable jewels by a pirate admirer). During the skit and the Gala, both Lara Parker and Chris Pennock watched from the audience.

During the Gala, I was also fortunate to meet the charming and very talented PennyDreadful (thanks to CyrusL for making the introductions)! As you may know, Penny hosts *Shilling Shockers*,[80] a local program in New England that plays classic horror films like *The Terror* interspersed with skits starring the witch Penny, her husband Garou the werewolf, and a monster hunter called Dr. Manfred VonBulow. Occasional DS-references have been slipped into the show. Penny had brought with her DVD copies of one such episode as well as a CD compilation of DS-related music, both of which she was generous and kind enough to give me—for free! Just for being a fellow DS fan! Wow! Thanks, Penny![81] They're terrific, and the "Drunk Shadows" episode is particularly hilarious! It's a motherlode of inside jokes for DS fans to enjoy. For more information on *Shilling Shockers*, visit http://www.shillingshockers.com.

Once the Gala ended, everyone scattered—some going to eat a late dinner, others going to the lounge/bar to relax. I stayed up visiting with friends until about 3:00 in the morning, trying to make the most of the weekend. We had only one day left.

Day 3: Sunday, August 27, 2006

Sunday's first event was the fan panel with Marcy Robin, which I usually attend. However, this time I was having so much fun standing in the lobby gabbing with my friends QueenKitty, Laraine, Ghost_of_Sarah_Collins, and Donna_Friedlander that I missed both the panel and the Frid video. I would have one more chance to view the video at the banquet that night, but I don't know what was discussed at the panel (e.g. if there was any news about the recent ShadowGram surveys, or a new DS, or the Halloween in Hollywood event).[82]

Diana Millay was scheduled to talk next. In previous years, Diana has read her Lyndhurst ghost story, but this year she opened her Q&A by reading a lyrical piece about the phoenix rising from the ashes and fulfilling its destiny, which she dedicated to the late Dan Curtis. Then, she began to talk about her books. "You've bought all my books already; I don't have a new one yet. My latest was *The Power of Halloween*. I'm working on a new one now called *Create Success, Recreate Your Life*. It's about—but wait, it's not even out yet. I'll tell you more about it next year. In the meantime, does anyone have any questions?"

One woman asked Diana extensively about how to deal with negativity around her, both in her workplace and in the veterans' hospital where she volunteers with those returning from Iraq. Diana advised her to stay cheerful, to not worry about trying to change others but to focus on herself and changing her own attitude, and to stop by her table if she had any other questions. A man asked Diana to share her memories of David Henesy, "the boy who played your son twice on the show." She seemed to have trouble remembering. "The boy who played my son twice. . ? Well, he was a very good actor. He knew his lines as well as an adult."

Since there were no other questions, Diana was finally able to share with us the information about her travel club. "As many of you know, I have a knack for finding exciting places to travel to—cheaply. You think you need lots of money to travel? You don't. Last year I took a group to Romania (I thought the Romania trip was in 2003, unless she went again). But now, I'm turning over the reins to this gentleman." She gestured to a bearded man in the front row, who then came onstage with her. This year's destination, he explained, was Tibet (which does sound like a fascinating place, but I don't like to travel). "I have brochures if you're interested. Please stop by the table and let Diana and me know about places you'd like to visit." People from the audience began suggesting places to go. "Are you planning any trips to China or Brazil?" "I've been to Brazil before," Diana answered. "I'd love to go back. What interests you about Brazil?" The soccer. "Well, that's a good reason. However, I'm not planning any trips to China right now. It's something to suggest though." She highly recommends the experience of travel for all of us.

Next, Chris Pennock treated us to a reading from his most recent *Fear & Loathing* comic. As always, his reading was wild and exuberant, and as promised, he paused mid-way so that his daughter, Tara, could sing for us. She performed "Defying Gravity" from the musical *Wicked* and received much applause.

At last, it was time for the final auction at which the portrait of Barnabas from *House of DS* would be auctioned. The portrait had been on display throughout the weekend (at times, propped on an easel on-stage in the 'drawing room') and I'd had a chance to see it and photograph it. Alas, it hasn't aged very well; the left side is very faded (I guess someone must have left it in the sun too long) but it certainly is the portrait. I believe this must be the highest-profile item ever auctioned. Again, I ran out during the first half to get lunch, but I hurried back to catch the tail-end of the auction. At that time, Jim Pierson auctioned off a poster replica of the portrait (which went for close to $100). Another big item was the pair of red contact lenses that Stefan Gierasch had used in the DS Revival series (apparently Rebecca Staab's lenses and fangs had sold the previous day). "And if you win these, you'll get a copy of *DS Resurrected* to go with it. Just go out and tell Kathryn Leigh Scott that I said to give you a copy, free." He paused. "To give the one winner a copy for free." We chuckled.

Then came the portrait. For the first time, bidding was also open to people who were not present, who had registered their bids online or were phoning them in. Marcy Robin and Helen Samaras stood behind Jim at the foot of the stage on their cell phones to keep in contact with the absentee bidders. The bids quickly climbed to over $1,000. Earlier in the week, we had speculated how much the portrait would bring (and whether Midnite would be tempted to add it to her growing museum of collectibles): Bobubas guessed $3,000, I guessed $5,000, Teresalita/Springsteena guessed $10,000. It went even higher than that. Soon, even the absentee bidders were knocked out. Finally, bidding came down to a showdown between a woman in the front row and a man who was sitting right behind me; he went as high as $10,500. The final sale price was $13,000! Jim conversed with the woman who won and explained, "She was saving to buy a new car, but decided she wanted this instead."

After the auction was the highly-anticipated Remembering Grayson Hall panel with R.J. Jamison, AKA Julia99, the author of the new biography *Grayson Hall: A Hard Act to Follow*. Nancy Barrett, a dear friend of Grayson's, was also on-stage to help answer questions about Grayson. R.J. began by introducing herself, explaining a bit about the book and how Sam and Matthew Hall had been so supportive and helpful in providing information and rare photos for the book, and showing a clip roll of Grayson's various works, including an appearance on the TV show *Lights Out*, a 'lost film' *The Parisienne and the Prudes, Night of the Iguana, That Darn Cat*, a French film called *Qui Etes Vous, Polly Magoo, End of the Road, Adam at 6 AM*, "Kojak," and *The Man from UNCLE*.

Next, Nancy read a selection from the biography, "The Birth of Grayson Hall." "Can you imagine Grayson being born?" she asked. The reading was actually about how Grayson, born Shirley Grossman, took her stage name. For a time, she was calling herself Shirley Grayson and had considered taking the name Liz. "Grayson as Liz?" Nancy didn't seem to think it fit. But Sam always called his wife Grayson, "like an old army buddy," and when she was performing in Jean Genet's *Le Balcon* (with Sylvia Miles, Salome Jens, and a young Barbra Streisand), he told his secretary to "draw up a contract for Grayson Hall" even though Genet was friends with the Halls and knew her real name.

After the reading, R.J. took a few moments to dispel some of the myths surrounding Grayson's time on DS. First of all, the story that Julia Hoffman was born from a secretary's typo is false. "They always intended for Dr. Hoffman to be a woman to add sexual tension with the vampire." Secondly, the story that Sam was writing for the show first and Dan Curtis met Grayson at a party and decided to put her on the show was false. "There was another actress who was cast as Dr. Hoffman first, but she backed out at the last minute for reasons unknown. Her name is lost to history." Grayson's agent contacted her about the opening on DS at a time when Sam and Grayson (who were struggling financially) were preparing to leave New York and move back to Ohio. Grayson got the part, Sam became a writer for DS about a month after, and the Halls were able to stay. Nancy fondly recalled that throughout the run of DS, Grayson and Sam were "Mom and Pop" to the cast members.

Then, the audience was invited to ask questions. One of the first questions to come up was whether Grayson had been disappointed that she didn't do more in her career. "Why didn't she become a big movie star?" "I have my own ideas about that, but I'll let Nancy answer first," R.J. deferred. "It depends on what you mean by 'more,'" Nancy explained. "What else could she have done? She could have gone to Hollywood, but I don't think that was what she wanted. She loved New York, she loved being on stage, and she did a lot of stage work in her lifetime." R.J. added that Grayson had lived in Hollywood for a time with her first husband, actor Ted Brooks, and hadn't enjoyed the ruthlessness of the town. "Also, it was the 1950s, McCarthyism was targeting a lot of Hollywood actors, and Grayson fit the profile of a communist. She was a Russian Jew, she was leftist in her politics. In fact, her family kept a picture of Eugene Debs over their mantel. If she had stayed in Hollywood and pursued a film career, she might eventually have been blacklisted. But a lot of people expected her to go Hollywood after *Night of the Iguana*. Her mother even moved to Los Angeles expecting Grayson to follow."

Another fan wanted to know why Grayson's first marriage was never mentioned publicly. "Was it kept secret for some reason?" R.J. explained that Sam Hall's parents were upright Ohio Protestants and when Sam and Grayson decided to get married, he told her, "We can either tell them that you're Jewish or that you're divorced." They decided to stick with Jewish because divorcee could be considered a character flaw and Grayson wasn't especially devoutly Jewish anyway. R.J. also talked a bit about Sam and Grayson's courtship: they had actually gone on a date just before Grayson had married Ted, and it was a disaster. But, after Grayson divorced and came back to New York from California, they went on a second date, and really hit it off. "Their date ended at the Algonquin Hotel. They got married soon after."

Someone else asked if Grayson had had any medical training. "No, but she was always fascinated by medicine," Nancy shared. "I think she was a little frustrated with Sam because he couldn't go into detail in the dialogue about the procedures she did on the show as Julia." Another fan wanted to know if there were plans to put the book on audio for the blind. "I have considered that," R.J. said. "In that clip we saw, Grayson was speaking French. Did she know French, and is that why the character of Countess Natalie DuPres was written for her?" asked another fan. "It's possible," Nancy admitted. "Sam was writing by that time." R.J. told us that Grayson had studied French in school and all her life afterward and was fluent. "I have her school records. She was a good student with a very high IQ, but she missed a lot of classes to go on auditions in New York."

Though several people were still in line at the microphone, there was no more time to ask questions. "Mr. Lacy is here now," R.J. explained, "and we have to wrap this up." I really enjoyed her presentation, for it gave us a chance to hear a lot of new stories about a beloved DS star and gave fans the opportunity to ask more detailed questions of people who would actually know the answers. I hope that R.J. (and Jim) will consider doing another Grayson-oriented Q&A at the next West Coast Fest. I purchased R.J.'s book at the Festival;[83] it is a very thorough account of Grayson's career and also reveals a number of personal details about her childhood and adult life.

Mr. Lacy had been absent on Saturday because he'd gone to see his daughter, a drama student in NYC, perform in a play. Fortunately, he was able to join us this day. We started by watching various clips of Jerry as Tony Peterson trying to talk to a hysterical Julia, Barnabas bricking up the Rev. Trask, and a possessed Charity Trask scandalizing her father Gregory by singing and bumping him. Then it was time for questions and answers.

"To what extent did your resemblance to Humphrey Bogart help or hurt your career?" "It was a help in getting me certain parts, like in *Play it Again*, Sam and in a few commercials. I even did a Right Guard commercial with Marie Wallace. But in other ways, it hurt me. After a while, the casting directors couldn't see me as anything other than Humphrey Bogart. They didn't look at how I would play the part as an actor." The next question was, "When you played Rev. Trask, your voice sounded different than when you were Tony Peterson. Did you do something special to your voice?" Jerry admitted that he had tried to make Trask's voice sound rougher and more 'fanatical'. One fan asked Jerry about his experiences working in *Play it Again*, Sam. "It was my first—and it turned out to be only—Broadway show. Woody Allen is just as neurotic in real life as he is on film." The fan then asked Jerry to do his Bogart impression for us. "I haven't done it in a while.[84] I don't know if I can." He hesitated and then gave us, "Of all the gin joints in all the world, she had to walk into mine." Everyone applauded.

"Whatever happened to Tony Peterson?" one fan asked. "I'm not sure. I think Adam may have scared him away." "Did Rev. Trask ever accept that he was wrong about anything?" someone else asked. "No, he never did. He believed that he was doing the right thing by hunting for a witch, and he believed he had found the right witch in Victoria. I mean, she came running out of the house screaming that there was a fire. What else was he supposed to think?" Jerry went on to tell us a bit of trivia about that scene. "You couldn't see it, but as we were struggling, Alexandra walked into my cape, and as we were trying to walk off-stage, we kept walking further into the cape and getting tangled in it." As for *Night of DS*, one fan mentioned, "Thayer David played Rev. Strack, which was another psychosexual reverend witch-hunter role. Why weren't you cast in the movie?" Lacy said he didn't know.

Kathryn Leigh Scott gave the weekend's last Q&A session. She started by marveling over what forty years of DS had brought. "It amazes me how much my likeness has been used; my picture's been on the packaging for the music box. I've been on books, trading cards, I'm a bobblehead, and next year I'll be an action figure." (That sounds promising for fans who've been hoping for a second line of Majestic action figures). Kathryn also mentioned that she had just filmed an episode of *Huff.* "Did any of you see it?" A number of hands went up. "I was going to suggest to Jim Pierson that he show it, but I think it's X-rated. That's Showtime for you."

Then she talked about her new book, *Murder in Prime Time* and her detective character Jinx Fogarty. "Many of you have been at my table already. How many have read the book?" A number of hands shot up. "Did you like it?" The responses were affirmative. "I tried to write what I know—about my background working in television. I'm not going to write any more DS books.[85] From now on, I'm going to stick to fiction. I plan to write more Jinx Fogarty novels.[86]" Kathryn invited fans to give her feedback on the book and suggestions for future novels.

She also talked about a previous book, which she erroneously introduced as "My Scrapbook Memories of the Bunny Years." When she caught her mistake, Kathryn laughed. "One of the actors, Roger Davis, who's not here this weekend, always joked that he was going to write a book called *Kathryn Leigh Scott: The Girl Scout Years.*" She repeated her story about working as a Playboy bunny while simultaneously working on DS for the first few weeks of the show. "We didn't know how long the show was going to last, and I figured it was better not to give up my other job. But then one day, a group of ladies came in, recognized me, and wanted to know why Maggie Evans was working as a Playboy bunny. That's when I decided to hang up my bunny ears for good." She also introduced one of her friends and former fellow bunnies who was seated in the audience. "Stand up and show them how beautiful you are," she encouraged.

Next it was time for questions. One woman asked Kathryn about her role in *Police Squad,* ("The one where I'm wearing all the wigs," KLS said knowingly) "What was it like to work with Leslie Nielsen? He seems like such a funny man." "He is! He used to carry around a whoopee cushion and make funny noises behind people's backs." Richard Halpern corroborated this. "I worked with him in *Repossessed* (the Leslie Nielsen/Linda Blair *Exorcist* parody) I had a small part in that. He used that whoopee cushion on the CEO of Paramount Studios. We couldn't believe it." Kathryn also told us about her audition. "I read the script and thought it was hilarious, but when I went to read for the part, they wanted me to be serious. 'Read it like you're Gene Tierney,' they told me. So I did, and they were cracking up. Then, when we were filming it, I was supposed to have braces, but the make-up man had forgotten to get me some. So I took foil and tied it on my teeth with dental floss to look like braces. (Ingenious!) I played the part of 'The Big Blonde' and I was a brunette. It was a lot of fun."

Another fan asked Kathryn about her work on *The Great Gatsby*. "I love that movie, and I've watched it so many times, but just this last time I finally realized, 'That's Kathryn Leigh Scott!' Did you like playing Catherine, Karen Black's sister?" "Oh, yes, it was wonderful to work with Karen Black, Robert Redford, and Scott Wilson."

One man went up to the microphone gleefully. "Kathryn I've got a question for you that I guarantee you've never heard before in all the twenty years of the Festivals." We all leaned forward in anticipation. "How did they get that car inside the studio for your last scene?" We laughed, knowing how hard it would be to get a car inside the notoriously tiny studio (funny, but that never occurred to me; it was a good question). "It was actually half a car," Kathryn explained. 'They cut off half of it and set it up inside the studio. It was a convertible, so they turned fans on me to make it look like wind blowing." She then explained to the audience what scene the guy was talking about. "For those of you who haven't seen the entire show, the character Sebastian Shaw was taking Maggie to Windcliff, the insane asylum. I was without a contract at the time and I had told Dan I wanted to leave the show to go to Paris and marry my boyfriend. He told me, 'You're crazy! You'll never work again!' I was a young actress and my career was just getting started. So, because he thought I was crazy, he sent me to the mental hospital. It was his little joke."

The last question was, "If Maggie had continued on the show, what would you have liked to see happen to the character?" "I would have liked to see Maggie become a stronger character again after all that she'd been through, and be able to stand on her own two feet."

Once Kathryn's Q&A concluded, it was time for the actors to recreate the first and last episodes of the show. I have to admit that I wasn't that excited about the recreations when I first heard about them, but some of the casting choices intrigued me (John Karlen as Burke Devlin? David Selby as Brutus Collins?) and I did attend the performance. I sat in the back with mscbryk during the first episode and with Minja/Wicked_C during the second. Diana Millay sat in the row just in front of us. Later in the evening, we would see a feature on the making of "Return to Collinwood" in which a number of actors commented on "the power of voice." I have to say that the power of voice was very powerful in these performances!

The first episode cast included Kathryn Leigh Scott reprising her role as Maggie Evans (she was the only original role/original actor in this episode), Karlen as Devlin, Lara Parker as Victoria Winters, David Selby as Roger Collins, Marie Wallace as Elizabeth Stoddard, Jerry Lacy as Mr. Wells, Chris Pennock as the private investigator Strack, Nancy Barrett as Sandy, Vicki's friend from the orphanage, and Donna Wandrey in a dual role as Mrs. Mitchell, the chatty lady on the train and Ms. Hopewell, the orphanage matron. The script for the first episode must have come from the writer's first draft because the introduction that Lara Parker read was not the same one Alexandra Moltke recites for the first episode. Marie Wallace was amazing as Liz; she adopted Joan Bennett's mid-Atlantic drawl perfectly. Donna Wandrey was able to create distinct characters even when her two characters had consecutive lines. She would just turn in a circle when shifting roles and it would be as though she was someone new. I have to say that Donna is a very strong actress (I still remember Mrs. Franklin, her "RTC" character, fondly) and I'm glad that she was able to participate in this show. I was delighted with Jerry Lacy's innkeeper; he actually attempted a Maine accent, and even though it was a small part, he was terrific in it. I thought Parker was quite good as Victoria. She was able to convey innocence and naivety without seeming forced or too much of a caricature, which I felt Catherine Harridge was. Karlen was much gruffer as

Burke than either Mitchell Ryan or Anthony George; it took some getting used to, but I guess it fit the character since Burke was a bitter and vengeful man when he first returned to Collinsport.

One of the funniest moments (albeit unintentionally) came when Vicki (Lara), seeking a taxi to take her to Collinwood, asked how people get from place to place in Collinsport. "Broomsticks" Burke responded. Though it would have drawn a chuckle anyway as a harmless joke, because the line was now addressed to Lara Parker, so famous for playing the witch Angelique, it seemed especially ironic. Another crowd-pleaser was when Maggie told (and spelled) to Vicki that she was a jerk.

When the first episode recreation concluded, the final episode immediately began, with the cast additions of Richard Halpern (who turned in one of the best Thayer David imitations I've heard yet) as Ben Stokes and Jim Pierson as the 2nd footman. Unfortunately, performing the first and last episodes back-to-back really highlighted how far the quality of writing had fallen by the end of the series. We went from memorable stingers (Elizabeth to Roger: "The only problem I've invited is standing before me right now") to repetitive wailing ("Bramwell!" "Catherine!" "Oh, Bramwell! I'm afraid." "Oh, Catherine!"). That said, the final episode was still a lot of fun. Nancy, John, and Lara resumed their original roles of Melanie, Kendrick, and Catherine, respectively. Jerry played Bramwell very stoically and at times even sounded like Jonathan Frid. David Selby, with the aid of sound effects, gave a chilling and much-applauded reading as the ghost of Brutus Collins. Meanwhile, Chris Pennock was having a high old time as a wildly insane Morgan Collins. Marie was matriarch Flora, and Donna took the Aunt Julia role. By this point, the actors were starting to block parts of the show, which was very action-packed (Morgan abducts Catherine, Morgan fights with Kendrick and Bramwell). When Bramwell was supposed to fall after being shot, Jerry actually dropped to his knees. Nancy and John really did kiss when Kendrick and Melanie were reunited. Everyone was really getting into their parts, pretending to fight, fall, screaming, etc. They also started to break up in laughter.

As with the first performance, the final episode followed the writers' original intentions rather than what we ultimately saw on tape. I was hoping for Halpern to read the closing narration in his Thayer voice, but instead the last line "If I didn't know better. . .") and narration were given to Bramwell/Lacy. The actors received a standing ovation and much applause for their performance. Then, people began to filter out of the ballroom to get into autograph lines or to get their banquet tickets and change for the dinner.

The banquet started roughly on time (we'd all feared another 3-hour wait like we'd had in 2003, the last time the Fest came to Brooklyn). But in fact, not only were we on-time, we were early as far as the kitchen was concerned. "For the first time in twenty years," Pierson told us, "we're ready and the chicken's not." However, our bread and salads were already at the tables when we sat down. I sat at Table 39 with Minja/Wicked_C, EmeraldRose, JVjr, his cousins Donna and Cindy, DSFAN1970, and Springsteena. To fill the time while we waited for our main course, Pierson started the door prize raffle. Most of the prizes were current products—MPI's *Trilogy of Terror*, DS Volume 26, a Josette's Music Box, various T-shirts, a copy of *The Salem Branch* (which VAM won). To our regret (but not to our surprise), none of the back tables won anything. Kathryn Leigh Scott also spoke to thank everyone for attending this weekend and added that she looked forward to seeing us next year (although no definite announcements were made about whether or where a 2007 Fest would be held).

The food arrived and consisted of pasta for the vegetarians and chicken, rice, and vegetables for the rest of us. Dessert was cheesecake. For some reason, the waiters only served half of our table before wandering away, and poor Minja and EmeraldRose had to wait even longer for their food.

Finally, while we were all eating, we saw another video presentation: a public service announcement about Alzheimer's Disease that Dan Curtis had directed (probably his last work). There were multiple versions of the ad—a 30-second spot, a 60-second spot, and one that was almost 2 minutes long. The ad features an elderly couple walking on the beach. They stare at a dance floor half-buried in the sand and we see flashbacks of their courtship in the late 1950s/early 1960s on that same beach, at a bowling alley, at a diner, their wedding, their children, moving into their first home, etc. while Barbra Streisand's "The Way We Were" plays in the background. At the end of the flashback sequence, the couple dances together on the beach.

Peter Falk reads the closing announcement. We also watched Jonathan Frid's video (though with waiters moving about and the sound of clinking silverware and plates and conversation, it was very hard to hear what he was saying).

Lastly, we saw some of the extra features that appear on either the *Bloopers and Treasures* or Volume 26 DVD (I'm really not sure which). One was a tribute to Joan Bennett where the actors and at least one fan shared their memories of her. The other was a behind-the-scenes look at "Return to Collinwood." Even though the performance was recorded live at the 2003 Fest, it was impossible to use that recording for a marketable release because of all the applause, cheers, and other noise from the fans in the background. So, the actors had to record the play again in a studio. Half of it was filmed in New York and the other half in LA; the parts were then spliced together. The actors spoke about how exciting it was to recreate their roles and to hear the familiar voices of the characters live again.

While these videos were screening, droves of people were scurrying back and forth from the tables to the back of the room in order to collect their annual banquet collectible—an original episode negative. Now, when I first heard what we were supposed to receive at the Fest, I pictured that we'd walk into the ballroom and find a tiny square of film on our chairs: I'd pictured the 'original negative' as a separate frame snipped off a larger reel. Imagine my surprise (and dismay) when I learned that the negative was in fact an entire reel of 16 mm film in a canister that must have weighed at least 7-10 lbs packaged in a cardboard container the size of a large pizza box. *How am I ever going to get that home?* I wondered. I had taken great pains to fit everything I would need into a carry-on bag so I wouldn't have to check my luggage, and I knew that even if I took the canister out of the box, it would never fit in my suitcase. We were given the option of foregoing the negatives and choosing an outdated calendar or a program from a past Festival instead. But, as difficult as it would be to get it home, I did want a negative, even if I had to check it. I ended up with Episode #3 (I wonder who, if anyone, got Episode #1? Maybe they're saving that one for next year's auction.)

When the videos ended and the negatives were distributed, people began to filter out of the ballroom. Some stayed behind to have their photos taken on the drawing room set. I hurried up to my room to drop off the negative and then rushed back down to meet my friends in the lounge for the last time.

JVjr and his cousins had brought with them an actual DS board game that they had won on E-bay, and invited other fans to play. I watched them play for the first round and then joined in the second round. I played against EmeraldRose, Roger K., and Phil M. When the game was over, I hurried up to my room to pack because I knew there would be no time to do so in the morning with my early flight. I came back down, planning to again spend the time until the wee hours with my friends, but security drove us all out of the lounge at 1:30. Who knew Brooklyn closed up? I thought New York was the City that Never Sleeps. Reluctantly, we said good-bye and went our separate ways. Although I did feel cheated of the additional time I'd hoped to spend with my friends, I am grateful for the time that we were able to spend together. Again, it's the people who keep me coming back to the Fest each year and who make it so worthwhile. Thanks again to everyone for a wonderful time!

October 26, 2006 - Dark Shadows Haunted Halloween Party (Vista Theatre, Los Feliz, CA)

In September 2006, ShadowGram newsletter started to advertise a one-night special DS Halloween event whose programming would include a Barnabas costume contest, appearances by Karen Black, Barbara Steele, and various named DS actors, a tribute to the late Dan Curtis, and a musical performance. Initially, the advertisement referred to a "live DS music concert onstage with composer Robert Cobert conducting;" shortly before the event, another newsletter changed this description to, "A half-hour concert of Robert Cobert's original music from DS with Robert Cobert in attendance." The reality of the event differed somewhat from what was promoted. Several of the DS actors who were advertised did not actually appear, citing other commitments. Further, the musical performance turned out to be a woman with a synthesizer who accompanied a CD of DS music while clips from the show were projected onscreen. Black and Steele were both there and did put their handprints in cement.

I was quite disappointed in the event. I understand the organizers cannot be held responsible for the actors not appearing, since they are subject to prior commitment, but so much else was falsely advertised.

This morning, I went back and re-read the announcement on collinwood.net and on the postcard sent by ShadowGram: the collinwood.net announcement plainly states, "Composer Robert Cobert will be conducting the first-ever concert of his infamous *Dark Shadows* soundtrack music" while the postcard is more coy, referring to a "live music performance conducted by Robert Cobert." I don't consider accompaniment by a synthesizer and keyboard to be a "live music performance," let alone a "concert," and if the pre-recorded music was conducted by Cobert, we weren't told about it. He sat in the audience during the entire show and did no apparent conducting whatsoever.

The sound quality of the music was pretty bad, too; it sounded screechy, and after the first, watery, broken song, the recording had to be started over (with only slight improvements). I don't know where the videos came from, if these are the "DS music videos" released by MPI or if they were newly developed for the event. Some of them were fun, like the "Back at the Blue Whale" and "I Wanna Dance with You" montages, but others were questionable (scenes of the cemetery and mausoleum set to "No. 1 at the Blue Whale"?) I knew no videotaping was allowed, but I smuggled a tape recorder into my purse and left it running throughout the musical segment (I haven't yet checked the playback quality.)[87]

However, Selby's dramatic recitation [of "Shadows of the Night"] (standing beside a gramophone) was one of the high points of the night. He looked stunning in his Quentin sideburns, and the fact that he emerged from backstage in a cloud of mist enhanced the eerie, romantic effect.

Last night was also Cobert's birthday, and Jim Pierson surprised (and embarrassed him) by making Cobert stand up while we all sang "Happy Birthday" to him. In honor of Cobert's birthday, we were all given a complimentary CD of Cobert's big band, jazz, and disco compositions.

The Barnabas costume contest didn't turn out as I'd thought it would either. The winner was chosen through a less-than-precise method: the five entrants lined up, and whoever received the most applause won—not the *DS: The Beginning* DVDs as mentioned in the original collinwood.net announcement, but a copy of *Trilogy of Terror*, DS Collection 26, a *DS: The First Yea*r book, and some other vampire movie I'd never heard of (*Orgy of Blood*?) (The SG postcard simply says to enter to contest "for a prize," so I guess that covers this.) Wally Wingert (spelling?) won the contest with an impressive present-day Barnabas costume and a snippet of the monologue about Josette's death.

The event was beset by traditional delays: it started late and ran later (the autographs didn't even begin until after 11:00, the stated end-time). What bothered me more though was the physical organization. It was impossible to see the handprints in cement ceremony unless you were at the very front of the line, like Midnite, or unless you ran up and squeezed through the crowd. The line of people waiting to get in wrapped all the way around the building and around the block. You wouldn't even know the ceremony was going on unless someone came to the back and told you. I was at the *Night of DS* event in 2001, and as I recall, there were two lines on either side of the door so that all attendees could gather around and observe the ceremony.

I was also disappointed with the program itself. It consisted largely of videos rather than the actors speaking. But instead of the "rare footage" that we had been promised, they were things that are either commercially available or that we've seen time and again, like the blooper tape (half an hour could have been shaved off if they hadn't played the entire thing) or the trailers for the DS movies.

The Dan Curtis tribute was the same video that played at the Brooklyn Fest (which was itself an edited version of the tape that played at the MT&R salute to Curtis in 2004). For me it was repetitive, but of course I realize that this was a treat for people who didn't attend the Fest or the earlier event.

I did enjoy listening to Karen Black. She talked poignantly about her last meeting with Dan Curtis, who by then could not talk because of his brain tumor. Still, he managed to communicate by stroking her hair (extensions), squeezing her hand, and grumbling when she teased him. She also talked about *Trilogy of Terror*—the making of it and its impact on her life. Apparently, the special effects team was inexperienced (and a bit clueless), so she and Dan had to figure out for them how to pull off certain tricks (e.g. how to make blood appear on Karen's finger after the doll stabbed her, how to film the doll running without it crashing into the camera or losing its limbs). She mentioned how everybody recognizes her as the Zuni doll woman and often imitates the doll. She gave three different amusing impersonations based on her own categorizations: the "EEE EEE!"s, the "AY AY!"s and the "YAYAYA!"s.

A charity auction was also held at which Ben Cross's Barnabas cane commanded $1,250. Other items were a bound copy of both *Night Stalker* movie scripts signed by Richard Matheson, an Adam & Eve episode on kinescope, and an award given to Bob Cobert certifying that "Quentin's Theme" was a #1 hit.

It's always a pleasure to meet up with DS friends, and I enjoyed seeing many whom I haven't talked to since August or even since the previous Festival! And as I mentioned above, there were several high points, but on the whole, I don't think the Halloween celebration was all that it was cracked up to be. I sincerely wonder about some of the changes (Did MPI think the original contest prize was too expensive? Was there no room in the theater for an orchestra for Cobert?) I was looking forward to much more and feel let down.

2008 Dark Shadows Resurrected Event (Burbank, CA)

Day 1: Friday, July 18, 2008

Robert Rodan was unable to make it to the Adam and Eve reunion because of traffic. We were told that he would be present later in the weekend. In the meantime, Marie Wallace watched all the video clips herself and commented on them, gushing over Humbert Allen Astredo as Nicholas Blair. (The first act in Saturday's Costume Gala was Michael Culhane as Nicholas Blair, who led the audience in a salute commemorating the 40th anniversary of Astredo's first appearance on DS. Apparently, Jim Pierson was going to send Astredo the video.) All of the actors' panels featured extremely lengthy video clips. Usually, a 2-3 min clip is played to highlight one or two characters or to generate some conversation, but these were entire scenes, each at least 5-10 mins long, and there were 4-5 of them per panel. Personally, I would rather watch fewer videos and have extra time for Q&As.

"Willie Remembers" came next. While on-stage, Karlen wore sunglasses almost the entire time, looking quite cool and reminding me of Jack Nicholson. In between video clips, Johnny joked a lot about his role as Willie and how he had to drain cows for Barnabas ("Not one, not two, but three or four cows a night! Do you know how hard it is to sneak up behind a cow? Do you know what they do? They don't say 'Moo'"). He praised Dennis Patrick and reminisced about all the fun and laughter they shared. After seeing a clip of Willie talking with the Eagle Hill Cemetery caretaker, he also asked for a minute of silence to honor "Whatever his name was" (Daniel Keyes).

One of my favorite questions for Johnny came from a woman in a wheelchair. She recalled the Las Vegas convention ten years earlier. "You were kind enough to push me all the way down that long hallway at the MGM Grand to get to the ballroom," she said. "Oh, good. I thought you were going to tell me that I pushed you into the pool." Karlen laughed. He said the Vegas Fest was his favorite. Another lady asked him "a burning question that we ladies have wanted to know for the past 40 years." Since

Willie had to help Barnabas find a new wardrobe for the 20th Century after releasing him, she wanted to know, "Does Barnabas wear boxers or briefs?" Karlen chuckled before reporting to the amusement of all, "He doesn't wear anything." Another fan complimented him on all the weight he'd lost and how good he looked. "The secret is to get rid of all the junk food," he explained. "You've got to have the willpower to just throw it out. Don't worry about the people in Shanghai and Thailand; they aren't going to be able to get it, so just get rid of it." I thought he was hilarious!

I missed Lara and Kathryn's Q&A because I had to get ready for the Collinsport Players' skit. Thank you to everyone who attended our performance of "Curtains"![88] I know it was very late and you were probably hungry, chilled, and tired from so much sitting already, but I appreciate that you came and supported us anyway!

Day 2: Saturday, July 19, 2008

Marcy Robin was delayed, so her opening talk was cut short (mainly she reviewed how all of the actors died). Pierson spoke for five minutes about the Depp movie, and then we watched an episode of the comedy series *JJ and the Governor* guest-starring Joan Bennet (in her yellow tent dress from *House of DS*) as a madam trying to make a political donation to the title character. This show was a lot funnier than I'd expected it to be, and Joan was terrific.

Stuart Manning took the stage for the Big Finish panel and revealed that we will soon be hearing a new audio drama (maybe two) from [*Dreams of the Dark* co-author] Mark Rainey! Stuart said that the next season of audio dramas has already gone into production and should be available by the end of the year.

I was in and out of the room for Sy Thomashoff's talk.

Bob Cobert was another laugh-a-minute guest. He came onstage dancing to the DS soundtrack and pretending to conduct the music. Throughout the panel, he'd whistle and sing the songs (e.g. "Bee bee be bop be bee be bee"). He even came up with some lyrics for Josette's music box ("Hello, Jo. This is your music box...") Cobert retold the story of how he became a composer: "I was supposed to be 'My Son, the Doctor.' I did several years of medical school, but I just hated it. I'd always loved music and finally, I told my parents that I wanted to be a composer. Well, naturally they were thrilled. Now instead of 'My Son, the Doctor,' I was going to be 'My Son, the Unemployed Composer.'" Cobert admitted that he's always been a lousy pianist and hated practicing piano. "I finally begged my parents, 'Get me a clarinet or a saxophone, anything but a piano!' So, they gave me a clarinet, and I couldn't put it down. They'd say, 'Son, don't you want to eat?' I just kept playing."

He also told a funny story of how his kids, who were DS fans, were completely unaware that he wrote the music for it until a classmate pointed it out. "They asked me, 'Dad, are you Robert Cobert?' I said, 'Yes, that's my name.'

'Do you write the music for *Dark Shadows*?'

'Yes, *Dark Shadows* puts food on our table, puts clothes on your back, sends you through school.'

"Oh, OK.'"

He also mentioned what a thrill it was to take the kids Christmas shopping at Macy's and, upon visiting the record department, to learn that "Dark Shadows by Robert Cobert" was the Number 1 album. We learned that all the DS music, except for the theme song, was recorded in London because it was cheaper.

Cobert told another amusing story of how he came up with the DS theme (the paycheck and the need to eat are always his inspiration, he says) and how Curtis mucked around with the bass during the initial recording of the song. Curtis was sure the song would sound better without the bass. Cobert tried to discourage him, pointing out that the experiment would waste both time and money, but he insisted. Upon hearing the bassless tune, Curtis asked, "What happened?" After that he never interfered with Cobert again.

We also learned (it was news to me anyway) that Cobert was commissioned by MGM to co-write the score for the wedding of Grace Kelly and Prince Rainier of Monaco. (They had asked a friend to write the main theme, but the studio, to whom Cobert was contracted, needed a

B-side song so they could release a record of the music. So, he wrote "The Mediterranean Waltz").

Lastly, Cobert flirted with a young woman who asked a question (which I can't remember now) at the mic. "We'll talk later," he promised her. "I'll give you my phone number," she offered. Members of the audience whistled. "Just don't expect too much of me," Cobert warned, "I'm 83 years old. But I am a very good kisser. At least that's what I tell myself."

Frid's first panel was called "The Growth of Barnabas" where he screened clips of his favorite scenes from the show. This event opened with John Karlen as Willie opening a large coffin placed in the middle of the stage, releasing Frid just as he had so many years ago. I thought the entrance from the coffin was the most exciting part of the weekend. After spending so many years trying to downplay his role as Barnabas, to be willing to get into a coffin and play the vampire again for his fans. . .what a tremendously good sport Jonathan Frid is! I was standing in the back of the ballroom when Karlen first came out, and though I realized what was happening, I couldn't see any of it once the people in front rows jumped up to get their photos (I screamed and cheered along with the crowd anyway). In retrospect, I realize Jonathan could have really gotten hurt with the way this was set up. It was amazing that the casket did not fall off the flimsy stand it was on.[89] I'm afraid the possibility of a safety hazard didn't occur to me at the time, and I'm glad there were no problems with the stunt.

The selected clips included Barnabas meeting David at the Old House, Barnabas and Burke having their 'duel' conversation at the Blue Whale, Barnabas hearing Sarah's voice singing for the first time in over a century, Barnabas learning Josette and Jeremiah were married. Frid discussed how mortified he was during this last scene because he forgot a line. He managed to persuade the editor to let him back into the studio after hours in exchange for a publicity favor in order to fix the scene and cover up the gaffe.

Frid also mentioned what a wonderful actor Thayer David was and how much he admired him and enjoyed working with him. He played three clips of Thayer's characters (Ben, Sandor, and Prof. Stokes). The last scene was of Stokes conducting a seance to communicate with Pierre Cordier, the ghostly lover of Danielle Roget.

After the clips, Frid took a few questions from the audience, including a question about working with Grayson Hall, whether he would accept a cameo role in the new movie (no),[90] and what he thought of Johnny Depp playing the part of Barnabas. Frid confessed that he does not know who Depp is. "I have not been to a movie theater in years. I think the last film I saw was *Titanic*. . .maybe one other. However, I'm told that he's a very good actor."

The cast reunion followed, featuring David Selby, Chris Pennock, John Karlen, Lara Parker, Jerry Lacy, KLS, Roger Davis, Marie Wallace and Robert Rodan. I had hoped Frid would participate in this event too, but perhaps he was too tired. It's always a treat to see the actors interacting and teasing each other. At one point in the Q&A, a fan asked Pennock if he was still selling his comic books and Karlen exclaimed, "He's a shill! Pennock planted him!"

Pennock was asked about his death scene as Gabriel in 1841 parallel time and whether he intentionally gave the middle finger to the camera (because that's what it sure looks like if you pause the scene) "Oh, I was very angry to be killed off," Pennock admitted. "I was not ready to leave. But no, I wasn't crazy enough to do that. I don't remember that at all." Pennock also said that he would be appearing in a comedic play in Idyllwild and another short film in which he plays a sociopath ("It's a stretch, I know.") who sells drugs to teenagers.

Lara Parker gushed about her new grandson Wesley, the light of her life. "After he was born, I went online to visit different Bad Mother-in-Law websites and read the advice. 'Don't ever criticize your daughter-in-law or question her. Don't tell her what to do with the baby.' She wants him to develop at his own pace so she tells us not to play with him or challenge him. When she leaves him with me, I listen to all of her instructions and say, 'OK'. Then I wait for her to leave and I wait about ten more minutes in case she comes back—sometimes she does. Then, I take him out of the playpen and say, "Come on, Wesley! Let's play!" Her enthusiasm was adorable. Lara also mentioned that she is writing a new DS novel set in the 1920s where

Elizabeth is a flapper who falls in love with Quentin. "Of course, he doesn't age, but she does." Her description of the book sounded fascinating. I've always like the Roaring 20s as a setting for DS. I simply wasn't sure if Elizabeth's age on the series fit the timeline (would she be old enough to be a flapper?).

Someone asked Karlen about working with Tyne Daly on *Cagney & Lacey*. He said they still keep in touch and had had dinner together recently. "In all the years we worked together, we never once had to exchange notes on our scenes. That's remarkable for an actor." Karlen also started reciting Shakespeare at one point. He was pretty passionate. He confessed that he misses acting ("I stopped doing it because I just got lazy") but that he is considering getting back into the business. I was thrilled to hear this. I think Johnny's work on the DS audio dramas is spectacular and I would absolutely love to see him on TV again, or the stage.

The biggest surprise of the panel was from Roger Davis, returning to the Fest for the first time since 2003. He told us that his brother had recently died of a heart problem, and it inspired him to get a cardiogram of his own. "The doctor told me, 'You have a blockage. In another 90 days, you'll be dead.' It was the same thing that killed Tim Russert. I had a bypass and I've been on a special diet ever since." He talked about attending events for *Alias, Smith & Jones* with Ben Murphy. "Murphy told me, 'I would have been nicer to you if I had known this was going to be the high point of my career."

The cast was asked if they ever attended conventions for their other shows besides DS (e.g. *Falcon Crest, Alias, Smith & Jones, Cagney & Lacey*.) Nearly everyone said no. "We only love *you*!" John Karlen declared. The cast was also asked about their most memorable moments on DS. Selby remembered the studio catching fire and the fire department coming to put it out. Karlen remembered everyone going out for drinks to the Brittany du Soir after taping. Roger Davis recalled that when he played vampire Dirk, he rushed at Joan Bennet and she fell over. "That's because you pushed her," KLS scolded. "I didn't mean to," he argued back. "I just get so caught up in my roles." The panel talked at length and were very interesting. I think a lot of people from the audience missed this event though because they had gone to get food.

I missed Darren Gross's *Night of DS* panel because I was getting ready for the Costume Gala. A couple of people told me the next day that there were technical difficulties and Darren was not able to show the special restored scene after all! This clip did play at the banquet (the one good thing about the event). It's a scene where Angelique (in the past) is playing Quentin's Theme and tells Charles that it reminds her of him when he's away. They flirt—right in front of Charles's wife Laura, who accuses Angelique of bewitching her husband.[91] It was a splendid scene, one that really helps to round out the characters. The only downside is that Diana Millay's voice sounds so much rougher and older than she did in 1971, so it's not a seamless redo.

I missed the first half of the Collinsport Players' skit, but what I did see was quite funny. The Costume Gala was another high point of the weekend. This year's group of performers seemed to have all been professionally trained. They all sounded beautiful. A gentleman dressed as a vampire sang a jazzy tune that I didn't recognize. AngeliqueWins sang a charming parody of "Beauty School Drop-Out" about Angelique (*a capella*!), then she and deckert/adamsgirl performed a duet of the Collinsport chant. Afterward, deckert/adamsgirl herself sang a solo, "I Dreamed a Dream" from *Les Miserables* to illustrate Angelique's thoughts about Barnabas marrying Josette. victoriawinters sang her own parody as Victoria after being bitten by Barnabas (instead of "I Could Have Danced All Night" from *My Fair Lady*, it was "I Could Have Bled All Night"). A woman dressed like Pansy Faye sang, "I'm Tired" from *Blazing Saddles*. My Fest roommate from 2006, Julie, sang a DS medley. Peter Mac wrapped up the show by dressing as Angelique and singing in character as Lara Parker, venting her frustration because her character has just been killed off. This song was a riot!

Several friends reenacted a drawing room scene of Carolyn, Vicki, Elizabeth, and Mrs. Johnson discussing Barnabas's arrival.[92] Another woman dressed in a poodle skirt performed the twist (or in Rev. Trask's book, 'devil dancing'). Among the costumes were a luscious Eve, two lovely Josettes, a historically accurate Naomi and Joshua, borgosi in his elegant suit and cape, and "Sam the Umbrella Man," a peculiar figure from Jonathan Frid's earlier presentation.

Day 3: Sunday, July 20, 2008

The first event of the day was a presentation by author Frank Borzellieri about *The Physics of Dark Shadows*, a newly-published book that analyzes how modern theories about time travel, multiverses, etc. relate to story lines from DS. Frank stressed that time travel does not violate the laws of physics and that the only reason it has not happened yet is because of our limited technology. He opened his talk by discussing inventions that we now take for granted but were considered fantastical at the time (*e.g.* an airplane that would take you from New York to Tokyo in one day). He used examples from *Dark Shadows* to illustrate Einstein's ideas about relativity and the twin paradox. His slideshow contained photos of DS characters who were associated with a particular time paradox (Willie for Barnabas not being in the coffin to be released after 1897 and 1840, Roxanne for having become a vampire in the original history despite the lack of Barnabas in 1840), as well as pictures of famous physicists like Heisenberg, Hawking, and Einstein. We also saw diagrams of warp speed and wormholes. The presentation flowed along at a rapid clip and was peppered with good-natured jokes—some of them impromptu and at the expense of Chris Pennock, whose arrival interrupted the presentation.

Unfortunately, there was no time for questions and answers from the audience. Perhaps Frank will be able to give another lecture at the next Festival, especially if it's in New York and in the presence of a new audience.

I found Pennock's presentation to be very uplifting. Instead of reading from his comic books, he had brought a DVD of a short film called "Cardboard Signs" in which Pennock plays a homeless man struggling to maintain his dignity and his long-term relationship. It's a much more mature role than Jeb Hawkes. Apparently, the director was only 17 at the time this movie was made. At first, the DVD would not play; it kept freezing. The organizers tried three times to clean the player, and then to change the disc. In the interim, Chris's daughter Tara performed the song

"Defying Gravity" from the musical *Wicked* (she sounded nervous, but she does have a lovely voice). A Q&A line also formed, but only one person got to ask a question before the movie was up and running again. I thought it was a beautiful movie, and I'm glad that we were able to watch it after all.[93]

After Frank's lecture and Chris's video, KLS spoke. She complimented his short film as a compassionate study of homeless life, explaining that she knows a lot of people in show business who have fallen on hard times and are now living out of their cars. Kathryn volunteers with the homeless through her church during the weekends. She is working on three different novels right now, including two mysteries, and has also just filmed a commercial for Actonel (Osteoporosis medication). "Apparently at my age," she joked, "the only commercials you get to make anymore feature body parts that don't work anymore or are falling off."

She spent the bulk of her Q&A outlining her vision for Maggie's character in the new movie. Her ideal Maggie is tough, akin to pre-Barnabas Maggie, and as the primary caregiver to her itinerant, alcoholic, artist father, who is now going blind, she feels stifled and trapped in Collinsport. In this version, Maggie and Joe are already a couple, but he really has eyes for the rich girl who lives in the house on the hill. While Maggie dreams of a life and a career beyond the small fishing village, she conscientiously attends to the diner and bakes her own pies. When Barnabas visits the diner late one night, when Maggie is dog-tired after an especially long day, she is charmed by his (other)worldliness and they immediately connect. This time, when asked who was her pick of an actress to be Maggie, KLS cited, "Someone edgy, someone like Evan Rachel Wood."

Jerry Lacy watched clips of all of his performances as Trask (but not Tony Peterson). Asked what was 1795 Rev. Trasks's first name, he christened him Orville, then admitted the character had never been given a first name. Lacy was also asked if he'd ever received hate mail because his characters were so evil. "If I did, nobody ever gave them to me."

I missed Lara Parker's Q&A, the auction, and the first part of the "lost script" [an Adam and Eve-era episode that was never filmed]. Roger Davis,

Lara Parker, Robert Rodan, and Marie Wallace performed in the style of a staged reading, though Roger soon broke away from the mic to wander the stage and perform his own blocking. I thought the performance of "the lost script" was a big disappointment. The script just wasn't very good! It was heavy on dialogue with no real action, and nothing happened to advance the story arc. According to Roger Davis, Dan Curtis's own notes on the script say, "Lose this!" Roger's performance seemed listless to me, though this may be because he wasn't speaking directly into the microphone and was hard to hear. I was more impressed with Robert Rodan: his voice is still deep and resonant, and he read Adam's lines with the character's typical befuddlement and impatience.

I had enjoyed Frid's Saturday video presentation, but I was somewhat underwhelmed by his Sunday appearance. I was under the impression that he would be performing all of his readings (from *Washington Square, Richard III*, and "Yma Dream") live. Instead, he only read for *Washington Square* and part of (I believe) *A Midsummer Night's Dream*. The other performances were all on video, and these were more lively and energetic than the live readings. Frid's video performances were dynamic and delightful; he has an excellent voice. The last video was of Frid performing "The Cask of Amontillado" in Spanish. My Spanish skills are lousy so I could only pick out one or two words, but the cadence and the rich sound of Frid's delivery were still fun.

While Frid's Saturday appearance was packed wall to wall, the back half of the auditorium was nearly empty for most of his Sunday panel. I saw lots of people leaving in droves as the videos played. I don't know if these people were bored with watching videos, if they were desperately hungry for something to eat, or if they wanted to get ready for the banquet early. It was just something that surprised me and made me a little sad. Nevertheless, I'm very grateful that Frid was willing to attend a second Festival in a row and made the long trip to Burbank for the benefit of the West Coast.

By far, the lowest point of the Festival was the banquet. I've attended the banquets since 2002, and the main course has always been chicken. Imagine my dismay when this year, the wait staff plopped a plate of goo in front of us. It was lasagna. I'm allergic to cheese and have been since I was a baby, so I could not eat the dinner. I couldn't even eat the vegetables because they were also drizzled with cheese. There were two other people at my table who had similar dietary problems (one could not eat dairy and one could not eat pasta). I asked for an alternate meal, but was told there was none. (I've heard conflicting reports about this: someone told me that people at another table were able to order chicken, and KLS mentioned that she had asked for a non-vegetarian meal, but when my friend Jeff asked Jim Pierson about this, he was told that Kathryn had only been kidding). Jeff, who played Barnabas in the Friday night skit, requested that the waiters bring us each a plate of steamed vegetables. This was supposed to take only five minutes, but it was more like twenty. In the meantime, we parceled out the last two rolls of bread amongst ourselves. When the waiter did return, he had only brought vegetables for Jeff, not for myself or the lactose-intolerant lady. Our seatmates were eating dessert before we got served.

I ended up going to the Daily Grill (in-house restaurant) and splitting a chicken dinner with Jeff after the banquet. I was pretty angry about this. I talked to a number of other people in the Daily Grill who said they had been unable to eat the banquet meal either. Apparently, the lasagna was served because it was a cheaper alternative to the chicken, but it seems to me that much of the food was wasted on those of us who could not eat it. You can't please everybody, but chicken (with an alternative for the vegetarian fans) is a relatively inoffensive choice (I've never heard of anyone allergic to chicken). I was tempted to ask Pierson for a partial refund to cover the second dinner that we ended up having to purchase, but ultimately decided that nothing would come of it. I enjoy attending the banquet as a final closing celebration with my friends; I sure hope that next year's menu is an improvement over this year's, otherwise I may have to discontinue that tradition. $50 is too much to spend on just bread and salad.

Each night of the Festival, I stayed up until the wee hours socializing with other fans, both old and new friends, and had a blast! On Saturday night, we even had a little birthday celebration for Minja and sheenasma in the corridor between the West Wing tower elevators and the Daily Grill.

The friendships and camaraderie are always the highlight of these events in my book. I already can't wait for next year.

2009 Dark Shadows Festival (Elizabeth, NJ)

Day 1: Friday, August 14, 2009

The weather in New Jersey was absolutely gorgeous: lots of sunshine and temperatures in the high 80s all weekend long. On all but one of my five trips East, the weather has always been overcast, gloomy, humid, and usually rainy, so this was a delightful surprise. I understand that I just missed thundershowers on Thursday night. I didn't venture out of the hotel except to hike up the highway in search of food on Friday afternoon, but it would have been a perfect time to be out and about. I had a lovely time at the Festival catching up with old friends and meeting two Internet friends for the first time.

Most of the programming during the Fest consisted of videos from the vault or from fans (including two Cheep Productions videos and two of DLA75's music videos). I missed the two panels on Friday night because I went to the airport to meet a friend.

Day 2: Saturday, August 15, 2009

On Saturday morning, the Fest opened with a screening of Cheep Productions' "Save Our Cemetery," co-starring Sharon Smyth. The people all around me seemed to love Daryl Schaffer's imitations of Barnabas and Julia. Kate Jackson's appearance on the final episode of *Password* came next.

The first live event of the day was a reprise of Frank Borzellieri's presentation on time travel. Frank used the same structure and slides as last year, introducing new jokes and repartee with the audience. This year, there was time for fans to ask questions at the end of the talk. One man asked whether the discrepancy between the original history that Barnabas first told Julia (that Josette came from France to marry his middle-aged uncle Jeremiah) and the events we actually saw transpire in 1795 could have been due to the creation of a parallel timeline. "I think the real answer is that the writers changed course on that one," Frank explained. Another fan asked for clarification on how the concept of parallel time is connected to the notion of traveling back and forth in time. "Parallel time is an explanation for how to solve the grandfather paradox of traveling to the past. If you go back in time and kill your grandfather, you wouldn't exist to be able to travel backward. But suppose your actions created a separate timeline, one where you had never been born, as well as the one where you still existed." One of the other points mentioned in the presentation against the likelihood of time travel is that nobody has ever met a traveler from the future. "What about UFOs?" one gentleman countered. "What if they're time travelers from the future?" "It's possible," Frank remarked. Frank also addressed the issue of whether a catastrophe was necessary to create a parallel timeline; theoretically, a parallel universe could be created each time we make a choice, with the alternative choice occurring in the other world.

I did not stay to watch the entire charity auction, although I was present when the big-ticket item, Jonathan Frid's original contract for *House of Dark Shadows*, was sold for $600.00. There was a pretty fierce duel for it between two particular audience members. I heard that the final bidder never did show up to claim the item. Does anyone know if this is true? Did the runner-up finally get the prize instead?

Jeff Thompson took the stage next to discuss his book *The Television Horrors of Dan Curtis*. Jeff explained that the book had grown out of an invitation to contribute an article about Dan Curtis to one of the entertainment magazines (I can't recall which) upon the director's passing. At the time, Thompson was also preparing his doctoral dissertation in the field of media studies, and decided to write his thesis about the work of Dan Curtis. The book is based on this thesis. He's currently working on a new book about Curtis's mystery movies.[94] I was a bit disappointed that Jeff didn't talk more specifically about Curtis's work or the ideas discussed in his book (I guess he wants everybody to buy and read it).

The majority of his presentation consisted of rapidly-edited clips from various Curtis productions (*Dracula, Scream of the Wolf, Dead of Night, The Picture of Dorian Gray, The Night Stalker, Trilogy of Terror*, the two DS movies). At first, there were technical difficulties with getting the video to play, so Jeff took some questions from the audience. One fan wanted to know what input (if any) Curtis had in the new *Night Stalker* show that aired on ABC a couple of years ago. Jeff said that Curtis had a producer's credit but not much influence over the show at all. Someone else wanted to know what Curtis's last production had been before he died. "That would have been the pilot for the new WB *Dark Shadows* TV series, which was not picked up," Jeff explained. The pilot had been screened Friday night and would be again on Sunday. He also shared an anecdote from one of Dan Curtis's interviews (I believe this is an extra on the DVD of the *Night Stalker* movie) wherein Dan complained about how the television business had changed over the years. "In the old days, all he had to do was go into the studio and say, 'I've got a great idea for a TV movie!' and he would get a green light to make the movie. Later, making movies became more about who you knew in the business. Movies had to be about relevant issues rather than pure entertainment value."

Thompson also corrected himself about something he had put in his book; he'd claimed that *The Great Ice Rip-Off*, which featured Grayson Hall, had never been released on video or DVD. "In fact, it was released on VHS, but only in Canada." As proof, he held up the cassette box. Business was very good to Jeff at the Fest; he warned us that he had already sold out of all but three copies of his book and advised anyone who wanted the book to hurry to the dealer's room once his talk was finished. I did manage to get a copy, and I look forward to reading and reviewing it soon.

At last, it was time for Jonathan Frid. He began by introducing two former studio kids, ladies who became his friends during the time DS was on the air and have remained in touch with him all these years. Unfortunately, I don't remember the ladies' names. Hopefully they'll be named in ShadowGram, or somebody who took notes can pitch in.

The first woman who spoke described her first visit to the studio. "I was lucky to have parents who allowed me to take two trains and a subway by myself to the studio. The first time I went, I had no idea who I would see. We waited until taping ended, and then Joel Crothers came out dressed as Nathan Forbes, followed by Jonathan Frid in 1795 Barnabas's costume. They were very nice to us, and after that, I went to the studio every day after school. During the summer and school breaks, I'd be there all day." Here, Jonathan showed his mischievous side. "Usually, it was hard to get out through the front door because the fans were outside mobbing it. They'd throw themselves right against the glass (he mimicked crazed kids). So, we would try to sneak out the back way. But one day, I decided to turn the tables on them; when they jumped at the glass, I lunged forward at them. Everyone scattered. . .right into the street. Fortunately, no one was hurt."

The other lady discussed a fan mail party where fans helped Frid respond to all of his letters. "The party started in the studio and then spilled over into the Hotel Edison in Times Square (I thought that was a neat tidbit; I have some DS friends who often stay at that hotel during their trips into NYC, but I never knew it had a DS connection before). There were boxes and boxes of mail piled up to the ceiling. I remember Jonathan yelled at us because we kept trying to read the letters. He said, 'Put that back!'" Jonathan recollected the first time he ever received fan mail. "Dan Curtis came over to me with a tray that had some envelopes on it. I thought, 'Here it comes! I'm getting my pink slip.' I asked, 'What are these?' and he said, 'They're letters. For you. You've got fan mail.' And I was so astonished by that." The women ended their time onstage by presenting Frid with a pair of shorts trimmed with bells, with his name embroidered on them. This was a replica of a gift they had given him once before; the shorts had been immortalized in a magazine photo where they were displayed on the wall in the background. "Well, bless your heart!" Frid praised as he accepted the gift. "Now what am I going to do with these?" (I wonder how much they would draw in an auction.)

This year, Frid assumed the role of Quentin by getting fans to take part in "The Game." Fans were invited to vote on their favorite Barnabas scene on Frid's website. Frid explained that he would be screening the top ten vote-getters for us at the Fest. He warned us that the clips were not going to be aired in the order of popularity, but that the order would be announced afterward. He also said that if the Game proved popular enough, it might become a regular feature at future Festivals. (That would seem to indicate that he plans to keep attending Fests, though he gave no hint as to whether he would be present in Burbank next year). It really was eye-opening to see what appealed the voting audience. The only thing that would have made the presentation more enjoyable for me would be if Frid had commented about the scenes as they were played (*e.g.* talked about whether he remembered filming it, what he personally liked about each clip).

The top three scenes all favored Grayson Hall more than Frid. The confrontation [where Julia tells him she knows what he is] was voted Number 1, which shocked me because it must have been all of 45 seconds long. Second place was the scene when Willie goads Barnabas into admitting that he cares more deeply for Julia than he'd like to admit after she's disappeared to meet Tom Jennings. Third place was the scene from 1995 where Julia admits that she is under Gerard's spell and begs Barnabas to return to 1970 alone. He refuses, vowing, "Never without you!"

A majority of the scenes were from Barnabas's first year on the show. Not only did none of the clips feature KLS, but there were no scenes of Barnabas with Quentin either, which I found to be surprising since he's one of the "main" characters on the show.

Frid played each clip in chronological order and ended by replaying them in a countdown format from 10 to 1 to show us where each scene had placed with the voters. We saw Barnabas's first meeting with David at the Old House and heard him address the portrait of Josette. We watched Barnabas recount to Vicki and Carolyn the story of Josette's death on a stormy night (knowing what an iconic scene this is considered to be, I was sure it would be named Number 1 or 2; instead, I think it made the list at 5 or 6). We saw the scene where Barnabas shoots Angelique and is cursed, as well as Barnabas's final scene with Angelique in 1840. The scene where Julia returns to Collinwood after getting her hair cut and Barnabas pleads with her to help him find out what Vicki remembers from 1795 also placed on the list, though I don't recall exactly where. The countdown recap also included the "duel" discussion between Barnabas and Anthony George's Burke Devlin; however, this scene was not played during the introductory screening.

After the screening, Jonathan took a number of questions from the audience. I was actually surprised by how many people were allowed to go up to the microphone. I recall that last year, only a handful of fans were able to get their comments in. Most people wanted to thank Jonathan for coming to the Festival and to tell him how much they enjoyed his work on the show. One very excited lady asked Jonathan to wave hello to her mother in the audience. "It's a dream come true for her to see you!" Another gentleman asked if he could present Jonathan with a portrait of him that he had painted. Once more, Frid was very touched. "Bless your heart!" he thanked the man. Frid was asked what part of Canada he was from. "Ontario," he replied. "Living in Canada isn't really all that different from living in the United States, though I do prefer it. I'm a bit of a royalist at heart and also. . .I think it's better to able to just sit back and observe what happens in America without the pressure to be loyal all the time."

One man asked Jonathan what advice he would give about acting. He seemed flustered by the scope of the question, and advised the man to get to really know the characters he was playing first. Another man asked Jonathan if he'd ever made any recordings for the blind and also if he could share memories of working with Jean Stapleton in *Arsenic and Old Lace*. He only answered the first question. "I know I must have worked for the blind because I can remember doing so. You have to be very careful when you talk to them; they're very sensitive to what you say. They have very sensitive hearing." A lady asked Jonathan if actors, in general, like it when fans come backstage to see them after a performance. He revealed that he actually didn't like it all of the time. "Sometimes you're tired and you just want to get out of there and go home." Another fan asked Frid to recite a bit of Shakespeare for us, but while Frid was trying to decide between a line from *Hamlet* or *Richard III*, Jim Pierson admonished us that it wasn't fair to ask Jonathan to perform for us. "He'll be on-stage tomorrow doing dramatic readings."

To my surprise and delight, Jonathan remained on-stage for the cast reunion this time. When Lara Parker took the stage, she sat in his lap briefly. John Karlen gave him a big hug. Jonathan did not receive the majority of audience questions either; they were pretty evenly distributed among the cast members. Although, I noticed there seemed to be unspoken agreement among the cast in certain cases where only one or two people would give a response instead of each person contributing to the answer.

"I know that John Karlen had a reputation for being a prankster," one man began, "but apart from him, who else in the cast liked to play practical jokes?" "That's it, you've got him," Jerry said. "No, I wasn't really so bad," Karlen demurred. "What sort of things did he do?" the fan asked. "He'd put rude notes in drawers so when you opened them up, you'd get flustered and forget your lines," Kathryn recalled.

"One of my favorite episodes was when Willie kidnapped Maggie and took you to the mausoleum to save you from the experiment," the next fan addressed KLS. "If you were really locked up together for a month, how would you and John Karlen get along?" "You mean our characters or us?" Johnny asked. "Oh, I adore John Karlen. I've always liked working with him," Kathryn gushed. "Better than being cooped up with Roger Davis, eh?" the fan teased. Kathryn seemed embarrassed by this. "Some of you may have read comments from my diary that I included in the *DS Movie Book* about Roger." She tried to downplay the idea of any animosity toward him, diplomatic as ever.

Someone asked the cast which other characters they would have liked to play, other than their own. "I wanted to be Josette," Lara said. "I wanted to be the heroine, but when I finally got my chance (in 1841) it wasn't as much fun as being the heavy." "I would have liked to be Pansy Faye," KLS confided. "I wanted to be Maggie Evans," John, chuckled. "How do your relatives react to seeing you on the show?" another fan asked. "What do they think of your work?" "My kids have never even seen DS," Jerry Lacy revealed. "My daughter Caity used to come to the Festivals with me, but she's bored by it now," Lara said. "My two sons are grown now, but they watched the show when it was on. They were embarrassed by it and they refused to ever let me come near their school. Their friends used to ask them why their mother was so mean and did such horrible things to everybody," she explained ruefully.

One fan complimented Jonathan on his performance in *Arsenic and Old Lace* and asked if he had any blooper stories to share from that show. "It was a complicated show; there was a lot of potential for things to go wrong," he admitted, but didn't name any specific mishaps. "I remember that we saw you in that up in San Francisco," Kathryn remarked. "We went back to the stage door to meet you." (I hope that was a night when he was in the mood to receive visitors).

The next question was for the ladies in the panel: "It seemed to me that your male co-stars always did everything they possibly could to touch your hair and mess it up. Did that bother you?" "It didn't bother me, but it bothered the hairdresser," Kathryn replied. "She had to readjust the hairpieces at the end of the day." "We had to wear such elaborate wigs all the time," Lara agreed. "I think I wore three different pieces as Josette," KLS reminisced. "Lucky you," Lara teased.

Someone asked John Karlen to share his memories of making the film *Daughters of Darkness*. "It was great. I loved the hotel in Belgium where they put us up. It used to be Gestapo headquarters during the war, so you know it was a nice place. The food was delicious, too. I remember we went on a picnic. The interesting thing about that movie is that I wasn't supposed to know that my character, who had just married a woman, was also having an affair with an older man. That was very cutting-edge back at that time, in 1970. The director filmed me having a phone conversation with my 'mother' and I wasn't supposed to know that 'Mother' was really a man while I was playing the scene. He was a guy about Jonathan's age and I was in my twenties. But I had a friend in the production and he told me the secret."

"How do those of you who have worked on the audio dramas like it so far?" another fan asked. "I think it's wonderful," Lara gushed. "It's a very special format, where the stories take place all in your imagination. You can hear our voices, and we sound the same as we did back then, and in your mind, we look the same." The cast was asked whether anyone had saved any props or costumes from the show. "I used to have my vampire fangs," Lara shared, "but they went up for auction years ago." "I wish I had my music box," Kathryn lamented. Someone asked about Humbert Allen Astredo. "I still write to him and e-mail him," Lara shared. "He lives on a boat in New Hampshire. I keep trying to get him to come to a Festival. I think he will one of these days." Marie was more circumspect. "I keep in touch with him too, and I've told him how much fun these conventions are. He did attend a convention once years ago before it became the Festival. But he's told me that, as much as he likes all of us (cast members), it's not something he's interested in doing."

One of the highlights of the cast reunion for me was when a fan asked the actors to share their memories of Thayer David. Instantly, shouts and applause rose from the audience. "My character would often order Thayer's character around," Lara recalled. "I'd send him into the woods to get me a spider web so I could cast horrible spells on Josette. He was a big hulk of a man, and I'd remember he would sort of glare down at me when I'd give him these orders. But he was such a sweet man. Very erudite. Extremely intelligent. He was a speed reader and he read more than any person I knew." "Every time he'd pass me in the hall," Karlen remembered, "he'd say, 'Pray for me, Johnny. Pray for me.'" "He was probably the nicest man I ever knew," Jonathan Frid said. "Such a kind and gentle, extremely gentle, man. There was something he used to do to warm up for his scenes. . .I can't quite remember what it was now. It's such a shame that he...well, he's in a safer place now." "He would always try to correct my pronunciation of words," Kathryn said. "I came from Minnesota, so I had a different way of talking. For instance, I would say, 'hoh-ver" instead of 'huh-ver.' He kept trying over and over to get me to say the word properly. I remember running into him once in Greenwich Village. He wanted some pastries. So, we went to a French bakery and bought a box of pastries, and then went back to my place to talk. He ended up eating the entire box of pastries!" I was very touched by the reverence that everybody in the cast obviously felt for Thayer.

Someone asked, "Which contemporary actor would you like to see playing you if DS were re-cast?" "It will be for the movie," Lara laughed. She named Charlize Theron as her pick. Kathryn wants Keira Knightley to play Maggie. I don't think Jonathan Frid really follows current actors; he seemed to not know how to answer. Kathryn suggested Johnny Depp to him. "Right! Johnny Depp," he asserted. Jerry Lacy chose Alan Rickman (he would have been my pick too, and considering that he's worked with Tim Burton on his latest movies, it's not a long shot). Marie, liked Jonathan, seemed to be making up her mind. "How about Britney Spears?" someone in the audience shouted. "All right, Britney Spears," she acquiesced, drawing a laugh. John Karlen bested her though. "Woody Allen! He'd make a great Willie Loomis."

Another fan asked the cast to share their memories of working with Grayson Hall, again to shouts and cheers from the audience. To my surprise, there was some hesitation among the cast. Lara was the first to speak, and she told a story that I'd never heard before. "When I first came on the show, Grayson was very cold to me. She had another actress in mind that she wanted to play Angelique and because her husband was a writer for the show, she thought she had an in. When I showed up, she wasn't pleased.

But eventually we became close. We even tried to get our two pugs to marry and have puppies, but they wouldn't cooperate."

Kathryn told a story about being asked to care for Grayson's finches, Lord and Lady Finch, when she and Sam went on vacation. One of the birds died, and Kathryn panicked. She shared some of the wild advice she got from others about how to cover up the death, but ultimately came clean. Grayson didn't make an issue of it. She also added that Grayson gave them pointers when they were filming the movie because she had done films before. "She told us to stay absolutely still, because when your face is projected on a giant screen, every expression is magnified." Jonathan spoke of working with Grayson. "When you forgot your lines, you were supposed to refer to teleprompter and I think I was much better at it (checking the prompter) than she was. I remember she would get flustered when she forgot a line. I told her, 'Just look at the teleprompter,' but she insisted that she had to know her lines."

Jonathan Frid was asked to share his memories of working with Katharine Hepburn. "She was a lovely person, and she was another person who knew I had trouble with lines. She told me, 'If you ever go up on a line, just look up at me. I know the entire show; I can cover you.'" The cast was asked if they had a favorite blooper. "There was a scene with Roger Davis where he came to the door of my cottage, and when I answered it, the sash of the window fell down," Lara recalled. "I just looked at it, thinking, 'Oh, the sash fell down,' and then I kept going with the scene. (I think she's actually misremembering a scene between Charles Delaware Tate and Pansy Faye).

"Of the cast members who are no longer with us, who do you think would enjoy these conventions the most?" another fan asked. The panel quickly began naming people who used to attend Fests before they died: Joan Bennett, Dennis Patrick, Michael Stroka. "Joel Crothers would have enjoyed it," Kathryn said. "And Grayson!" Kathryn and Lara began reminiscing about Joan Bennett. "I remember the first day of taping," Kathryn said. "She wasn't a quick study and she had poor eyesight so she couldn't see the teleprompter. You could tell she was absolutely terrified of going out on camera, but she did it anyway. I thought she was the bravest person I'd ever known. She was an inspiration to me." Lara confirmed Joan's stage fright and professionalism. "She knew her Hollywood friends were at home watching the show and she wanted to do a good job for them." Jonathan Frid told us how Joan Bennett used to invite him over to her home to run lines with her. "She had trouble learning her lines too, and she was very patient. She was always willing to help you out and run lines with you."

"What would you, as actors, say are things that a director should never do?" another fan asked (I think it was the same guy who wanted general advice on acting from Jonathan Frid). "Don't tell the actors how to do the scene. Bigger, softer, louder, angrier," Kathryn ticked off. "Don't say things like that; it's too vague." Jonathan Frid talked about his experience directing *The Lion in Winter*. "I had the cast read through the script one time, and then we all sat down and I asked them to explain what it was their characters were saying. I tried to get them to really know their characters and their motivations. I don't know if that was a good strategy." "It was," Marie (who played Eleanor of Aquitaine) assured him. "I had a wonderful time in that show."

Lara Parker mentioned how Harry Kaplan used to come into the dressing rooms at the end of taping and give the cast grades. "He'd open my door and yell, 'B minus!' And he always told us, 'If I don't see anything happening on your face, you won't get your close-up.' He really wanted us to show it in our faces whenever our character discovered something startling or distressing. We had to show that transition" "That's right. He'd always yell, 'Transish! Transish!'" Kathryn recalled. "Grayson was a master of Transish." At this point, Johnny Karlen jumped in. "Harry Kaplan was a freak! A horrible human being! What he did to poor Lamar (Lara's real name) was inexcusable! He used to bully the ladies. But he'd only do it to people if he thought he could get away with it. He never talked that way to Jonathan Frid. What's the name of that big guy who usually comes to these things?" "Robert Rodan," the audience called out. "No, not him...Pennock! Chris Pennock. He beat the shit out of him one day. Harry Kaplan had no business directing. I don't know why Dan Curtis hired him. He must have been willing to work really cheap." (I get the feeling that Johnny doesn't much like directors. He famously punched out Harry Kumel during the *Daughters of Darkness* filming, again because the director was being cruel to the female co-star, Danielle Ouimet. Also, I talked briefly with Karlen on Monday while I was waiting to go to the airport. During the past year, I followed the *Murder, She Wrote* re-runs on Hallmark Channel and saw several episodes where Karlen guest-starred; I asked him about his experiences on the show. He said Angela Lansbury was very professional and wonderful to work with, but that her son, who directed a couple of Johnny's episodes, "only had half a brain.") The cast and audience were quiet for a moment after this display. Jeff Thompson asked if anybody had memories of Lela Swift, who directed more episodes than anybody else. "I remember she always dressed in leather," Johnny said. Shortly after that, the panel broke up for the autograph sessions. All in all, I thought it was a lively and revealing time.

The Collinsport Players' *Bewitched* skit was adorable. The premise was that Angelique was being summoned to the witches' council to be stripped of her powers because of her incompetence in witchcraft ("You can't even keep a flame lit long enough to finish casting your spell!") and her love for a (gasp!) human. Along the way, Angelique is counseled by Endora, Uncle Arthur, and various other recurring characters. I didn't watch the show often enough as a child to be able to remember Aunt Clara, Uncle Arthur, or Dr. Bombay, but the characterizations that I saw on-stage were amusing. Lara Parker was spot-on, knowing all of her lines and cues, and seemed to be having a blast with her part.

The Gala may have run long (about half-way through the performances, a rush of late-comers appeared, doubling the number of entrants) but the performances were well worth the time, IMO. One of the highlights of the night was a performance by Angelique and the Supremes (played by Cassandra, her daughter, and Mary) of "Stop in the Name of Lust!" We were also treated to an ambitious musical retelling of Jason Maguire and Liz Stoddard's aborted wedding; this performance featured Bobubas, EvanHanley, josette_by_candlelight, nightshadows342, and her mother and sister. The same group had previously presented a drawing room skit where Vicki, Carolyn, Elizabeth, and Mrs. Johnson muse about Cousin Barnabas's eccentricities and strange resemblance to his portrait (which was painted by Mama nightshadows342). Charles_Ellis was present as Charnak the Magnificent, reciting the punchlines of jokes and then opening a sealed envelope to determine what the question was (*"Twilight, True Blood*, and *The Vampire Diaries*: What are three shows that rip off *Dark Shadows*?"*) CrazyJenny brought her baby daughter onstage dressed as Little Sarah (the costume was the same one Jenny herself wore when she was little). There was another young girl dressed as Sarah later in the program. She and her father got the audience to sing one verse of "London Bridge." borgosi dressed in an elegant costume and came on-stage with his video camera to ask the Fest guests to join him in singing "Happy Birthday" to his niece, a major DS/vampires fan. I thought that was a great moment, and a very creative idea. Peter Mac closed the show by singing "What Happened to My Part?" in character as Lara Parker lamenting that Angelique was dead and her role on DS was abruptly finished.

Day 3: Sunday, August 16, 2009

Sunday was mostly a video day again, especially since Donna Wandrey had to drop out of the Fest because of an illness. Events had to be rescheduled to compensate for her panel. The presentation by Big Finish productions was bumped back from noon to 2:00, so there were no live events in the morning. I did come in for the tail-end of the auction. More papers of Jonathan Frid's were sold off, including the rental agreement for the apartment he occupied in New York during his time on DS. "You're very lucky that Jonathan has kept all of these," Jim Pierson admonished. "Most people would just throw them out." The bidding wasn't as high as for his contract the previous day; I don't even remember what the final price was. They also auctioned a copy of KLS's *My Scrapbook Memories of Dark Shadows*. That one tempted me since it's the only Pomegranate Press book that I don't have; it went for $40.

The postponed Big Finish presentation began after the auction, with Stuart Manning and Jason Haigh-Ellery representing the company. Jason opened by asking for a show of hands of how many people have listened to the audio dramas and how many have not. Quite a number of Big Finish fans were in attendance. When the mic was opened for questions, more than one person mentioned how much they enjoyed old-time radio broadcasts and how they appreciated the DS audio dramas for following in that tradition. We were told that the next series of dramas, which will pick up from "The Rage Beneath," is due to be recorded in December. This next set of dramas will be an exciting 4-part epic story.

Someone asked how long it takes to record one of the dramas (about a day). One gentleman inquired whether Big Finish planned to include any other cast members from either the original series or the 1991 remake in the dramas. "We would love to include as many people from the Dark Shadows family as we can," Stuart assured him. 'We've been wanting to get Marie Wallace involved for a long time, but it was difficult to find a place for her." (Seeing as all of her characters died on the show). He explained that the company is only licensed to release dramas based on the original series, but he did say that Lysette Anthony, who has done work for Big Finish's *Dr. Who* series of dramas, has been approached for DS. He also pointed out that Alec Newman, who would have been Barnabas for the WB, has lent his voice to "Clothes of Sand" and "The Ghost Watcher." Another fan wondered if there were any plans to record Lara Parker's other novels (*Salem Branch* and the book she's now writing) as audio books. "We were just discussing that with Lara earlier, actually," Stuart admitted. "The difficulty is that *Angelique's Descent* was already out of print when we recorded it while *The Salem Branch* is still owned by Tor Books." (Which is also considering a reprint of AD, apparently) Somebody else wanted to know about the possibility of hiring Robert Cobert to write new music for the audio dramas. "He's in his eighties and he's retired, so it's not a very realistic option."

At this point, Lara Parker joined the gentlemen on-stage. She repeated some of the points she'd brought up the previous day. One fascinating bit of news was that her friend Debbie Smith has written an audio drama that will include "a real knock-down, drag-out catfight between Angelique and Josette. It's about time sweet little Josette got back at Angelique for everything she did to her." Someone asked Lara if there would be a catfight between Angelique and Victoria Winters too. "There's not as much reason for one. Angelique didn't do much to Vicki." (Framing her for witchcraft in 1795 doesn't count?) She also praised Stuart for condensing her 500+ page *Angelique's Descent* so that it fit onto two CDs. "It was a tremendous feat!" Lara also admitted to having some trouble trying to do voices for her characters during her reading. "Whenever I attempted a Caribbean accent for my character Thierry, it came out sounding like an Irish accent."

After Lara, Jerry Lacy took the stage. He was asked if it was easy for him to get back into character as Trask for the audio dramas. "Not really," Jerry confessed. "It took me a couple of tries to get the voice right. I kept referring to a fan who was there, who would let me know when I was on the right track." A young boy asked Jerry for a Bogart impression, and he obliged ("It's nice to see ya again, kid.") Finally, Jerry read a brief introduction for "Kingdom of the Dead," complete with eerie background music and sound effects. It was quite affecting. The tale is about a race of superhuman beings once entrusted with ruling the Earth before man ascended and banished them to another realm. But the ancient creatures lust for vengeance . . .

Next, Brian Kellow, author of *The Bennetts: an Acting Family* returned to the Fest to talk about Joan Bennett's life history. He discussed her family's pedigree, beginning with famed stage actor Richard Bennett, and moving on to her sisters, Constance Bennett, the first big family movie star, and Barbara Bennett, a talented dancer and the mother of Morton Downey Jr. (apparently Joan was embarrassed by her nephew and tried to hide the fact that she was related to him. Kellow related that when he brought it up during his interview with Joan, she sharply replied, "Must we talk about him?" putting an end to the topic.)

Joan grew up feeling very insecure. She married young to a millionaire, but the marriage broke up because of her husband's alcoholism. Joan finally turned to her father for help in getting a job. He got her a small role in one of his plays and drilled her endlessly each day on improving her acting technique. Sure enough, Joan received rave reviews for her small part. She performed in a series of movies, but her career didn't really take off until she dyed her hair brunette for a part in *Trade Winds*. From then on, her popularity soared and she was featured in several films noir, the best of which were directed by Fritz Lang.

Kellow touched briefly on the major scandal in Joan's life; her husband, Walter Wanger, caught her sitting in a car with her agent, with whom Joan had been having an affair, and he shot his rival in the groin. DS was really Joan's big comeback after that. Initially, she hated being on the show because of the grueling shooting schedule and the fact that she had trouble learning new lines each day. But eventually, Joan began to enjoy her work on the series and developed a maternal bond with her fellow cast members.

Kellow emphasized how motherly Joan was and stated that she was always protective of her own children and shielded them from the media. She mothered other Hollywood children too, including Loretta Young's daughter. He recounted comments Joan Bennett had made about a visit to Joan Crawford's house. At the end of the dinner party, Joan C. insisted that all her guests come and watch her children say their nightly prayers. Joan B. remarked, "That was the strangest thing I've ever seen. Why would anybody do something like that?"

The opportunity for questions came up. A couple of fans praised Kellow's delivery style during his presentation. One person said he should have been a professor. Charles Ellis asked if Kellow thought that the reason why Joan was never nominated for an Oscar despite her many wonderful performances was because her husband, Walter Wanger, was head of the Academy. "No, I think it was more because she wasn't contracted to a major studio, so the funding and publicity weren't there." Another fan wanted to know what it was like to be a biographer. "How do you go about getting interviews with these people and their family and friends? Do you just call up out of the blue and say, 'Hi, I'm writing book about you'?" "You need a lot of luck," Kellow admitted, "first in tracking them down and then in hoping that they'll speak to you." Kellow was asked to weigh in on whether it was true that Joan Bennett would have had the role of Scarlett O'Hara in *Gone with the Wind* "if Larry Olivier hadn't shown up with Vivien at the last minute." "That's how Joan always told the story," Kellow admitted, "but in truth, she was a longshot for the role. In fact, until Vivien Leigh tried out, Paulette Goddard was the front-runner. When Joan was invited to come in for the screen test, she was reluctant to do so because she didn't see the point. If you've seen her screen test, you know that she did a good job, but she just wasn't the right sort of person for the role. Of course, we can say that with hindsight now knowing what Vivien Leigh did with the role." He explained that he had wanted to show Joan's screen test at the Fest but could not because of copyright laws and prohibitions against public display of the material for financial gain.

Kellow ended his presentation by bringing Kathryn Leigh Scott on-stage to share her memories of Joan. They talked about Joan's "second career." "She thought she could have been an AD (assistant director?) because she was such a facilitator," Kathryn explained. "She was always bringing everyone together." She recalled a visit that Fritz Lang had made to the studio when the crew was trying to figure out a lighting problem for an upcoming scene. "He watched for a minute and finally suggested, 'Put a light on top of the camera.' I watched him place the light there myself. Joan had that light from then on."

She also re-told a couple of favorite anecdotes about filming *House of DS*. There was a plumbing problem at Lyndhurst, and the plumber who came to fix it recognized Joan. "I had the make-up table next to hers. I saw him do a double take and he asked her, 'Aren't you Joan Bennett?' She said, 'I used to be.'" KLS also mentioned that the cast was picked up on their first day of shooting by limos. "We were so excited because we thought we were finally big stars, getting to ride in a limo. Well, those limos were only hired for the funeral scene, and when shooting was done, they left. We had to ride back in a rattle-trap station wagon, sitting on each other's laps."

Kathryn had another purpose in joining Brian Kellow; he was the editor for her article "Fatal Attraction: The Star and the Stalker," which recently appeared in *Opera* magazine. "My working title for this was 'In Search of Nell.' Nell Theobald spent the last years of her life stalking the great Swedish opera singer Birgitte Nilsson. My inspiration for this article came when I opened up the *New York Times* one day and saw a story about her. I went to high school with this girl. We were Playboy bunnies together. I'd lost track of her after that. As I read the article, I kept thinking, 'That's not all there is to her.' I wanted to write a fuller picture of what Nell was like." Referring back to the difficulties in tracking down a subject's friends and relatives, Kathryn acknowledged a debt of gratitude to Charles Ellis, who was able to direct her to most of the people she needed to see through his workplace. "He just happened to answer the phone when I called up to ask for information and he recognized Maggie Evans's voice!" Kellow had copies of Kathryn's article at his dealers' table (I understand that he sold out of books, too, over the weekend). I recall that it's also available online; it sure sounds like an intriguing read.

I didn't stay for Jonathan Frid's dramatic readings, instead taking the opportunity to wander through the dealer's room one last time and spend a few minutes socializing with friends. The readings ended on time, leading to a mad scramble to get ready and lined up for the banquet.

By 6:00, a long line was wrapped from the ballroom doors down the hall to the elevators (the banquet began at 7:00; Lara Parker walked by and seemed amazed by all of the people who were already queued up). Because there was an overflow of people wanting to attend the dinner, there were two classes of attendees; those with a dark green ticket would actually get to sit inside the ballroom, but the people with a light green ticket would be seated just outside in the corridor in front of the dealer's room. The overflow crowd was brought inside for the video screenings and door prize give-away though.

This year's banquet was a tremendous improvement over last year's! In fact, the food was some of the best I can remember having at any DS banquet. At every place setting was a glass of iced tea in addition to a glass of water (we've never been given beverages before; usually anyone who wants a cocktail or something stronger than H2O has to go out to the bar to buy it). The main course this year was chicken instead of lasagna; it was not rubbery, and it was covered in some kind of sauce (not teriyaki, but tasty just the same). The meat was served with crisp green beans and mashed potatoes. For dessert, we were given a piece of chocolate cake with a strawberry on top instead of the customary cheesecake or fruit tart. I was thrilled with the selection; because of my dairy allergies, I've never been able to eat the mostly cream-based desserts of the past. This was the first time I was actually able to have the dessert, and it hit the spot.

Lara and Marie conducted the raffle, and a number of people that I knew won door prizes. Lara Parker's table was also called, and the winning seat number turned out to be her own! However, she gave her prize to another man, Jimmy, who was having a birthday. Everybody at the banquet serenaded him with the birthday song. In another first, my table was actually called during the raffle; it was the first time in my seven years of coming to banquets that that's happened! We were the last ones to be named. Mary won a DS T-shirt from MPI. The odd thing was that I'd had a feeling all along that one of us would get a door prize that night, though my seatmate didn't believe it.

Our video presentation consisted of a couple of public television commercials by Kathryn Leigh Scott and David Selby (who howled like a werewolf during his segment), followed by a film of Lara Parker's tour of Salem. The evening concluded with two music videos set to novelty songs about DS: "Barnabas Collins, Love Bandit" and "Barnabas" (sung as "Barrrney-Buss" in the chorus). The company at my table—including Pansity, darkshadowsrick, Cassandra, Quentin'sGal, jimbo, EvanHanley, Mary, and josette_by_candle_light—was great fun and really livened up the night. It was a lovely end to a lovely weekend and I hope to see everyone again next year.

2011 Dark Shadows Festival (Brooklyn, NY)

Day 1: August 19, 2011

I had a wonderful time at the Festival, but I have to admit that I felt a bit underwhelmed. The event seemed too low-key for the 45th Anniversary. For one thing, there was a smaller turn-out of actors relative to past Festivals. For another, the panels (at least for the first day and a half) did not include Q&As. Instead, the actors watched a series of clips from DS and then commented on them or spoke generally about their time on the show. I thought that was strange. Personally, I missed the fan interaction and thought the panels were duller for the lack of questions. Even though most people ask the same things year after year, you never know what will come up. A couple of times, Jim Pierson (with Richard Halpern and Jeff Thompson both out this year, there was no proper emcee for the Festival) would ask the actors questions to draw them out. During Lara Parker and Jerry Lacy's time onstage, he asked if Lacy did anything to prepare for his role as Trask. Lacy's response was hilarious: "Oh, I took a couple of girls out to the woods." The audience laughed and Pierson looked uncomfortable. "Well, what else was I supposed to do?" Lacy asked innocently.

Day 2: Saturday, August 20, 2011

When David Selby took the stage Saturday afternoon, he did take questions from the audience, but for some reason, nobody was using the microphone in the center aisle. Instead, people shouted their questions from wherever they sat. I couldn't understand what was being asked from where I sat toward the back of the ballroom and I don't know how Selby was able to decipher the questions. Somebody must have asked if he ever gets recognized in his daily life because he told us how a traffic officer stopped him from crossing a street by calling, "Hold on, Quentin!" He also related something that had occurred earlier in the week when his son-in-law and grandson were flying home from a trip. Selby's grandson sat in the middle of the row with his father on one side and a stranger with a laptop on the other. At one point, the little boy started calling out, "Pappy! Pappy!" "My son-in-law tried to quiet him down," Selby explained, "then he looked over and saw that the other guy was watching *The Social Network*." Selby also praised Abraham Lincoln and spoke fondly of shooting a guest spot on *Mad Men*.

The cast reunion (sans Frid) came next, and Roger Davis immediately began to hog the show. After the other actors had provided a quick recap of their recent news, Davis launched into a lengthy ramble about the housing market and all of the money he's made and lost on his building ventures. This went on for many minutes when, suddenly, his spiel was interrupted by a loud pop! "Did someone cut my mic?" Roger squawked. "We'll save the real estate seminar for next year," Pierson replied drily. Davis's co-stars were also weary of his talk. "I feel much more cheerful now after listening to that," Kathryn remarked in a rare show of sarcasm. "Don't you, Lara?" "Oh, yes," Parker agreed. "Don't you feel entertained by that, Marie?" At this point, Roger seemed to realize that he had spoken out of turn and apologized, but instead of giving up the mic to someone else, he inexplicably launched into a monologue from *Treasure Island*, speaking in an Irish accent. It was the most bizarre thing I've ever seen him do (and that's saying quite a bit). The audience was clearly confused and disquieted, and as Davis went on and on, KLS got up from her seat in the middle of the stage (Davis was seated at the far right) and began tugging at the cord of his microphone as if to pull it out of his hands! Finally, Davis gave up and the panel was allowed to progress.

The actors were asked about doing voice work for *Night of DS,* and Jim acknowledged that the restored film will be released next year;[95] at this point, they need to find an impersonator to record Grayson Hall's lines. "What? You mean there are people who imitate dead actors' voices?" Jerry joked.

Chris Pennock talked about his soap opera work after DS and how panicked he became when he learned, after landing a role on *Guiding Light*, that the show did not use teleprompters. Someone asked the actors who had appeared in the 1795 story line after playing present-day characters if the roles from the past had been written specifically for them. Kathryn acknowledged that she had been assigned to play Josette because of her prior work as Josette's ghost, but Lacy claimed it was just by chance that he was given the Trask character to play. "That was the part they needed to fill when I returned to the show. I could just as easily have ended up as Angelique."[96] Lara mentioned that she and Kathryn are very good friends and sometimes even finish each other's sentences. Sharon Smyth was asked to sing "London Bridge" (she said possibly the next day) and Jerry Lacy was asked to do a Bogart impersonation ("Of all the gin joints in all the world, you people had to walk into mine.")

A fan asked about the new movie. KLS mentioned how she, Selby, Parker, and Frid had flown to London to film a cameo. "Do you remember a children's book called *Where's Waldo*?" Selby asked. "That's what our cameo is going to be like." Lara chimed in, "I know people will tell me, 'I watched that movie 75 times and I didn't see you at all.'" Hearing that was disappointing. I had thought that the actors' cameos would at least be speaking roles. It sounds as if they're going to be part of a group scene as just faces in a crowd. What a waste! Why would Burton & Co. bring them all the way to London just to make them part of the scenery?

I missed most of this year's screening of *The Crucible*, though I have seen it before (more than once) at the Museum of Television and Radio.[97] The DS actors all appear in the first act of the teleplay, but by the time I reached the ballroom, Elizabeth Proctor was begging John to go to town and expose Abigail. The performance was compelling and I didn't want to leave to line up for the Costume Gala. I hope this program is shown again at future Fests. It really is well-made, and the set pieces and videotaped look combine to give one the sense of watching a DS episode. I was surprised to later read reports online about people walking out during Kathy Cody's introduction, although I witnessed something similar happen on Friday night when Lara Parker and Jerry Lacy ceded the stage to Marie Wallace and Chris Pennock. So many people streamed out of the ballroom that, at first, I thought the room was being cleared for some reason.

Day 3: Sunday, August 21, 2011

I missed most of Sunday's events, with the exception of the panel between Sharon Smyth and Kathy Cody. Smyth explained that she has not been to a Festival for many years because the NY event always falls during her son's birthday. "I thought it was important that I be there for his birthday, so we didn't have to hire a therapist. But today he turned 18, and he told me, 'Bye, Mom.'" Cody missed conventions because she was either caring for her elderly mother or sick herself. "I kept meaning to attend a Festival, and last year I finally did. I felt so loved and so appreciated. I had a blast, and now I'm going to be back every year."

Both Sharon and Kathy had a similar career background, having worked in modeling ("You wear heavy coats in summer and freeze your little tushy off in a swimsuit for winter," Kathy recalled) and commercials prior to acting in DS. Also, each had to overcome their regional accents. One fan asked Sharon why she sometimes attempted an English accent. "I don't think I was trying to speak with an English accent; I was just trying not to talk with a Philly accent," laughed Sharon. "How about a New Yawk accent?" Kathy joined in. "When I went to Hollywood, the director would have to stop tape and say, 'No, Kathy, it's not an Ah-range, it's an Oh-range.'" Both had positive things to say about David Henesy. ("He was very generous. Did you see how he was helping me with my lines?" Sharon recalled, referring to a clip of David and Sarah that had just played). When asked whether either had brought home any props or costumes from their time on the show, Sharon revealed that she had picked up the remnants of Barnabas's old man face and saved them until they disintegrated years later. (Wouldn't that have been a cool prop to auction?) "I still have my letter from Dan Curtis saying my services are no longer needed. Maybe I'll bring that next year and auction it off."

I had been looking forward to hearing Lara Parker's preview of her new novel, which is supposed to involve a romance between werewolf Quentin and flapper Elizabeth in the Roaring 20s. Even though the timing does not align with canon, I'm fascinated by the 20s and was curious to hear more about the book. However, when I found out that it will be a continuation of *The Salem Branch*, with the Quentin/Liz story interwoven with the Barnabas/Antoinette romance, I lost interest and didn't stay for the reading. I wandered off, and by the time I came back to the ballroom, it was nearing the end of the dramatic reading between Lara Parker and Jerry Lacy. Originally, this was supposed to be a performance between Lacy and Nancy Barrett. I don't know what the original play was to be, but this reading sounded like a retread of "Vengeance at Collinwood" from 2005 with Lacy in a dual role as Tony Peterson possessed by his distant ancestor, Reverend Trask. Trask is determined to kill the witch, Angelique, but Tony resists his urgings.

The banquet was very well attended, with dual lines wrapping around the hotel lobby. The "awards ceremony" involved a series of trumped-up prizes, mainly His and Hers titles (e.g. "Favorite Non-human Male and Female" for Chris Pennock and Donna Wandrey; Favorite Reincarnated Female and Male for Marie Wallace and Roger Davis) to ensure that every actor was acknowledged. Lara Parker was the Favorite Female Villain and Jerry Lacy was the Favorite Male Villain. I believe KLS won Favorite Female Lead. Barbara Woronko won a DS Hall of Fame award. Nancy Barrett was awarded Favorite Character Actress in absentia and Jonathan Frid's nephew Don accepted his award for Favorite Vampire. The actors accepted their awards with tongue-in-cheek grace and the banquet wrapped up with a slideshow of the deceased actors and personnel and selected highlights from the show. It was all over much too soon.

Nothing has been officially announced about the next Fest, but KLS and Marcy Robin repeatedly made references to "next year in Burbank" so one can hope.[98]

The banquet gift bag included a 2008 Fest program, a DS checkbook cover, a Big Finish catalog, and a DVD labeled "DS 45th Anniversary." I was hoping the DVD would feature some new cast interviews or other footage, but to my disappointment, it was merely a copy of the awards intros, In Memoriam slideshow, and clip show played during the dinner.

March 13, 2012 – Preview Screening of Dark Shadows (Burbank, CA)

Living in the greater LA area, I've sometimes had the opportunity to attend preview screenings of movies before they officially debuted. The purpose of these screenings is to gather feedback to help the studios understand how to better market the films (e.g., audiences may be asked to name other movies that they've seen and enjoyed that were similar to the target, or to name their favorite scenes or performances, which will probably feature in the trailers). In rare instances, if an audience signals that something about the movie really isn't working, the studio may re-shoot or edit parts of the film.

In March of 2012, I was given the opportunity to attend a preview screening of Tim Burton's Dark Shadows movie. Another DS fan friend of mine, who frequently attended movie previews, had four free passes and couldn't use them because the test audience was age-restricted, such that no original fan would have been able to get in. (Typical screening guidelines are that one must be aged 16-50; sometimes older adults are able to attend family films if they accompany a child). I'd initially had no desire or intention of seeing this remake, but I saw my chance to both represent the original series fandom and be the first among my friends, many of whom had spent years actively speculating about this movie, to actually see the darn thing. (As it happened, the first film trailer was released on the day of the screening, which deprived me of any edge because it effectively covered the movie in a nutshell).

What follows is my initial attempt to review the movie without actually saying anything about it, due to the non-disclosure agreement I had to sign.

I went to the preview screening tonight even though [pre-registration] was full, figuring that if I got in line early enough with my ticket, I just might get in.

And I did.[99]

We all had to sign non-disclosure agreements, however, so I cannot comment on the comedic aspects of the film in any way. Instead, I will link to random YouTube clips that are completely unrelated to DS.[100]

I suppose it's OK to discuss what I heard other people saying about the movie, if not the movie itself. The gentleman who introduced the picture referred to it as, "A Gothic, humorous, off-beat film." Many people laughed frequently throughout the movie. As people left the theater, I heard some complaining that they were confused about the story and disappointed with the film overall. The audience didn't seem to know what to make of it.

For my own part, I thoroughly enjoyed the first 20 minutes, but became progressively disillusioned as the movie went on and left feeling very discouraged. It's a very good-looking movie with several terrific performances (though not necessarily from the stars you might have expected). However, it is definitely not DS as we know it. Granted, this was an early cut of the film, but I don't know how it will be received by a mainstream audience, let alone the fan base.

April 22, 2012 – Los Angeles Times Festival of Books with Seth Grahame-Smith

I attended my first *Los Angeles Times* Festival of Books yesterday. One of the biggest draws for me was the "Bump in the Night" supernatural fiction panel at 11:30 featuring Seth Grahame-Smith, Richard Kadrey, Deborah Harkness, and Melissa de la Cruz. I even reserved my ticket in advance online, expecting the panel to sell out. The audience was large, but by no means was the panel standing room only. Paul Tremblay, who was brought out from Boston specifically to moderate the panel, mostly addressed the authors individually with specific questions about their work rather than inviting them to discuss the genre or the writing process in general. Personally, I found that approach less accessible, since I'd never read any of the panelists' books and couldn't fully follow the details of the discussion. However, I'm sure the authors appreciated the opportunity to discuss—and pitch—their particular works.

SGS got the most panel time. The moderator introduced him as the author of *Pride and Prejudice and Zombies, Abraham Lincoln: Vampire Hunter, Unholy Night,* "and the script for Tim Burton's new movie, *Dark Shadows.*" At this point, there was a brief hush, followed by whistling and a smattering of applause from the audience (I don't know if this was on behalf of DS or Tim Burton). Behind me, a young woman said, "I want to see that!" So, there is some positive anticipation for the film.

Tremblay then began describing the plot of SGS's new book, *Unholy Night.*[101] "You decided it wasn't enough to piss of Jane Austen fans. Now you've made the Bible gritty. . .Will you have to go into hiding like Salman Rushdie?" Grahame-Smith laughed and spoke of his surprise at how accepting the reading public is of his work. "Jane Austen fans have a sense of humor. I even got a call from Doris Kearns Goodwin telling me she loved *Abraham Lincoln: Vampire Hunter.*" He explained the rules he established for himself with *Unholy Night*: 1) The name "Jesus" is never mentioned. 2) The Jesus character is only two weeks old in the novel and never says anything, obviating the problem of putting words in Christ's mouth, and 3) Whenever Mary and Joseph appear, they are paragons of virtue. The story is primarily about Balthazar's journey from doubt to faith, and not an attempt to mock the Bible.

Fellow panelist, Richard Kadrey, joked, "I think Seth is going to make the most money of any of us; they can't return your books to the store once they've burned them!" "But will I be alive to get the royalties?" Seth wondered.

Grahame-Smith acknowledged that his works have a "somewhat absurd premise, but the more absurd your premise, the more grounded your execution has to be. What really pulls you through the narrative is character. You have to give them an emotional landscape that feels real. You don't give Lincoln the Mel Brooks treatment." He explained his inspiration for *Abraham Lincoln: Vampire Hunter*: "I was doing a tour in the summer of 2009, the Centennial of Lincoln's birthday, and in every bookstore I went to, the biggest displays up front were biographies of Lincoln and vampire novels. I thought, 'If you could find some way to combine the two, you'd have a license to print money!'"

When asked about the experience of screenwriting, particularly adapting his own novel for the screen , SGS made some comments that I thought were very revealing. "When you're an author, you're God. You get to do whatever you want and you don't have to explain yourself to anybody—except maybe arguing with your editor a little. But when you're a screenwriter, you really have to service the vision of the director, *even on your own book*." (My emphasis) Even though he was speaking of his experience with ALVH, I suspect the same was true of DS.

When the moderator opened the floor for the audience's Q&As, one of the first questions asked was why horror continues to be so appealing to people. SGS shared his theory about why we love scary things. "Thousands of years ago, our ancestors faced constant danger. hey had to go out and kill their food. Today, in our modern world of creature comforts, we lack scares but we still have a physical need for them. Horror fills that need. It's an affirmation of life." He added that supernatural creatures also appeal to our specific psychological needs. Vampires have an aspirational quality. They don't have to die. What would you do with all of that time? We wonder about having the powers of angels and witches. What would we do with them?"

All of the panelists agreed that human beings are often the scariest creatures in their works. "The monsters may want to kill you, but they aren't responsible for wanting to kill you," SGS explained. "Look at one of the earliest horror stories: Mary Shelley's *Frankenstein*. The monster was happily resting in his coffin—a brain over here, a skull over there. He didn't ask to be created; it was the scientist's fault. Man creates the monsters. We did this to ourselves."

A young girl who is a student in the creative writing program and enjoys reading and writing genre stories complained about how the more serious writers look down on her. "It's like if you can't quote Kafka and Proust, you're not worth anything. Do you have that problem with your work?" The authors counseled her not to let people put her in a box. "People are always trying to label me. I'm 'the mash-up guy,'" SGS observed. "In academia, you get looked down on, but not by the general public. Look at all the popular movies that have magic, the supernatural, or superheroes in them."

The panelists were also asked how long it takes them to research their works. SGS explained that he does a lot of research prior to writing. "I try to really know my history before I destroy it."

From the lengthy interview with SGS that was reposted [on dsboards.com] a couple of weeks ago, I had anticipated a big personality, someone loud and outspoken. On the contrary, on this Sunday morning, Mr. Grahame-Smith seemed the most reserved of anyone on the panel. He was always the first to respond to questions addressed to the panel, but when he wasn't speaking, he leaned back in his chair, arms crossed and a neutral expression on his face, instead of smiling expectantly into the microphone like Deborah Harkness and Maria de la Cruz. Maybe he was tired, or he's not much of a morning person? I thought he was a good speaker, both witty and self-deprecating. He knows his success is unlikely and appreciates it for that very reason.

When the panel concluded, the authors headed outside to covered tents to sign their books. A dealer's table was set up in the lobby of the building where the panel had been held, and audience members quickly lined up to start buying books. I was reluctant to buy anything myself, but I did want to meet SGS, so after hemming and hawing and seeing that only one copy of *Abraham Lincoln: Vampire Hunter* was left (the other titles had all sold out), I took it as a sign and bought the book. (If it was good for Doris Kearns Goodwin, it's good enough for me).

SGS had the longest line of all—in fact, the other four authors had long since departed by the time I got into line—and he continued signing for a full hour after the panel ended. He was an excellent sport; although we were supposed to limit ourselves to three items, several people had entire stacks of books with them (one woman had multiple editions of *Pride & Prejudice & Zombies* in addition to hard- and paperback versions of *Abraham Lincoln: Vampire Hunter*) and he signed them all. He also posed for pictures and chatted leisurely with the fans.

When I finally reached the front of the line, SGS greeted me warmly and thanked me for standing so long in line. He seemed much more animated than when he'd spoken on the panel (maybe SGS is more comfortable in one-on-one interactions than in speaking to a huge audience?) I told him I was pleasantly surprised to see him, considering how busy he is these days. "You've got to do the Festival of Books. You can't miss it!" he enthused. "You get to meet so many people. It's a real ego booster." I asked him how much of DS he had seen for research purposes before working on the script. "I had a couple of the boxed sets, the compilation discs, and the compendiums. (Kathy Resch's Concordances?) It wasn't possible to watch the entire series." I remarked that I had seen one of the movie preview screenings and could tell that he'd done his homework from the number of more obscure series references in the film. "We're just finishing the final cut of the film now," he confirmed. The ending has been finalized and "it is very dark." "I'm so excited for you that you'll get to see the final product in just a couple more weeks!" He was so genial, I didn't have the heart to admit that I wasn't crazy about his movie. We shook hands and I wished him luck with all of his projects before heading to my next panel on the other side of campus.

I came away with a positive impression of the author. I think Grahame-Smith is very sincere about his work (even if he often uses a goofy premise as a jumping-off point) and tries to put his subjects in a positive light. I believe he tried to do right by the DS fans and, while I'm not happy about the tone and direction of the movie, I don't think he was deliberately irreverent with the material.

2012 Dark Shadows Weekend (Tarrytown, NY)

This event took place from Saturday, July 28, 2012 – Sunday, July 29, 2012. Day 1 consisted of traditional Festival programming (e.g., actor Q&As, video presentations) staged inside a tent on the grounds of Lyndhurst. Day 2 consisted of a luncheon only, with video programming, at the nearby Double Tree Hotel.

It was a thrill to see *Back From the Grave to Haunt Me*[102] played on the big Festival screen. This was my third time getting to see the film, and I notice new nuances to the performances every time. I know how much work everybody put into this project, and I was gratified by the audience's positive reaction to it (and especially to the twist ending). The film was shot on location at Seaview Terrace with the participation of the owner, Denise Carey, and so it includes a number of inside jokes geared toward people who have been to Seaview. However, I was glad to see that a general audience was able to relate to the movie and appreciate its humor too.

I only attended three of the star panels: Sharon Smyth's, Marie Wallace's, and Jerry Lacy's. Sharon was a delightful speaker, very down-to-earth and friendly. She recognized several people in the audience as her Facebook friends and greeted them by name. She was also the first person to address the "controversy" of the movie,[103] even polling the audience as to who did and did not like it (the split was about 50-50). Sharon herself seemed to lean toward the latter camp, admitting that she thought certain scenes in the movie didn't need to be there and extolling Jonathan Frid as the one and only Barnabas. However, she expressed her dismay over the polarization of the fandom in the wake of the film and did not try to fan the flames between the camps.

Sharon also shared a funny anecdote about working with David Henesy, remarking that she naively trusted him because of his experience on the show, and sometimes allowed him to get her into trouble. For instance, he once persuaded her to get inside Barnabas's coffin, then sat on the lid, trapping her inside and causing her to miss her cue! She explained that she didn't have many friends her own age because of her odd work schedule (commuting to NYC during the week and returning to Philadelphia over the weekend) and didn't mingle with the much older adult cast members, so it was a real thrill to work opposite someone her own age. She also freely confessed that her acting career came to an end because she became cocky and uncooperative as she entered her teens. Finally, when her exasperated mother confronted her about whether she wanted to continue acting or not, Sharon declared she wanted to quit. However, she didn't seem to think the move was a great loss, and joked that she got the role of Sarah more because of a superficial resemblance to Jonathan Frid than because of her talent.

Marie Wallace was very gracious, thanking the loyal fans from around the country who have turned out to see her recent stage performances in the New York area. She shared her memories of performing in *Gypsy*, especially of participating in the legendary "Christmas Tree number," which has never been replicated since the original run due to prohibitive costs. She also described an art show that the cast put together, as many of the actresses had taken up painting as a hobby during the show's run. Ethel Merman purchased two of Marie's paintings to gift to relatives.

Jerry Lacy spoke about working with Woody Allen on *Play It Again, Sam*, saying that Allen's even more neurotic than the characters he plays. He also revealed that the Trask-bricking scenes were accomplished using a three-sided wall. I asked about his work on *Doctor Mabuse*. Citing the original film and emphasizing that this movie is a new incarnation, Lacy described his role as that of an evil hypnotist who wants to enslave the world and rule over the ashes. The movie will likely not be ready for release until December at the earliest.[104] Evidently, the director[105] is some kind of prodigy, a man in his early 20s with some twenty films already under his belt.

I missed Lara and Kathryn's panels (and the *Mabuse* teaser) because I took that time to walk through Lyndhurst and its greenhouse/rose garden. Unfortunately, I made a wrong turn on my way back and ended up trudging through the woods on the River Walk path (aptly named because the walkway turns into a river during a heavy downpour) just as the rain started to come down in earnest. After carefully retracing my steps along the slippery road back to the Fest tent, I was completely soaked and more interested in getting back to the hotel to dry off and change clothes than in sticking around to watch videos or hear the Frid tribute.[106]

2013 – Friends of 1991 Dark Shadows[107] Cast Reunion (Tarrytown, NY)

Saturday, July 13, 2013 – Sunday, July 14, 2013

I was fortunate to attend the event last weekend and I had a wonderful time. As has been mentioned, a number of the guests dropped out at the last minute, albeit for perfectly understandable reasons.[108] This was unfortunate, and I really felt for the organizers, who had put so much effort into cultivating these contacts and then had to rearrange the schedule and format on short notice. However, the absences made me appreciate the guests who did show up—Nick Besink, Henry Plimack, Sharon Smyth, Chip Coffey, Joanne Dorian and Donna Wandrey—all the more. My goal in attending DS events is to see my friends anyhow, and I was able to spend long periods of time sitting around and chatting informally between activities. Everybody that I talked to seemed to be having fun.

Each day featured one Q&A session and one raffle. The grand prize was a private tour of the tower room at Lyndhurst, which is not open to the public. On Sunday, a secondary raffle awarded six people the opportunity to tour the pool house, which is also generally closed. Lyndhurst was also open for tours, and visitors were allowed to take non-flash photos. However, free tours were only available between 10-12, a fact that had not been widely-publicized and that irritated several attendees who were asked to pay when they tried to get into the house in the afternoon. Apparently, the Facebook page for the event listed the free tour times, but I would hope that in the future, such details would also be included in the e-mail updates and/or listed on the program for the benefit of people who do not visit Facebook.

Autograph sessions at this event were very orderly. Every attendee had a number written on their badge, and groups of numbers (e.g. 1-50) were called up at a time. Some guests charged a nominal fee ($2) as a donation to Lyndhurst. Sharon Smyth had a large get-well card at her autograph table for people to sign for John Karlen.[109] The absent guests had also provided autographed photos for purchase or auction.

The guests told some fun stories that I had never heard before. The soundmen, Nick Besink and Henry Plimack, were talking when I arrived, telling a story about how the producers had tried to introduce portable microphones "about the size of a pack of cigarettes" as a replacement for the boom mics. The devices (the name of which I don't recall) could be clipped onto an actor's clothing. Grayson Hall ("Bless her!") was one of the first guinea pigs with the new device clipped under her jacket. She began her scene by coughing and thumping her chest—which caused terrible feedback, dissuaded the producers from continuing to rely on these mics, and ultimately saved the boom men their jobs.

Chip Coffey,[110] who was a child actor in the 60s, recalled his enthusiasm when he was tapped to fill in for David Henesy for a day after the actor broke his leg. Chip was a fan of DS already and looked forward to the role, but at the last minute, the gig fell through when the decision was made to give David a broken leg as part of the story. Coffey had another brush with DS when he played a guest at the costume party in *HoDS*, but sadly, his appearance has been cut from the final version of the film.

Donna Wandrey told how she talked her way into the role of Roxanne Drew by telling the casting director, "I deserve the role because I have short red hair and there aren't any actresses with short red hair on TV." (Her competitors had long blonde and long dark hair, respectively.) "I hoped that my acting talents were reason enough for me to get the part, but luckily Dan Curtis agreed about my hair." She spoke fondly of working with Virginia Vestoff, who died much too soon. "She was so talented; she was appearing in *1776* while she was on DS. I always try to catch the movie when it comes on TV just to see her again and say hello." Donna also shared some lovely memories of Thayer David, whom she called "My true love. He was the sweetest, kindest, gentlest man. . .who could scare the crap out of me. In one scene, he was supposed to hit me in the head and knock me down. He told me, 'Don't worry, I won't hurt you.'" She also told how Thayer would carry a briefcase full of candy bars to the studio every morning, line them up, and start eating his way down the line as rehearsals progressed. "We all teased him about trying to keep his girlish figure."

Sharon also recalled working with Thayer David in one scene where Thayer had to carry little Sarah. "He had a bad back, and I felt bad that he might get hurt because of me, but he told me, 'Don't worry; I've got this." Jonathan Frid was also very kind and "brotherly" toward her. She also had a specific memory of working with John Karlen. "We were standing behind some scenery, getting ready to go out for our scene. He asked me, 'Are you starstruck by all of this?' I was pretty naïve and I didn't understand a lot of what he said to me, but I acted like I knew. I said, 'Oh, no, I'm not starstruck.'"

Sharon laughed over how people often ask her whether she, as a child, was frightened by the coffins and other spooky accoutrements of the set. "You have to remember, I didn't see the same things you did. I saw broken Styrofoam everywhere. If you rolled up the spider webs, you could make a super ball. I saw people out of make-up, standing around drinking coffee and smoking. " She recalled getting scolded when she tried to collect the waxy run-off of the candles, not realizing the drips were intentional to achieve an effect.

Both Sharon and Donna talked about giving autographs during the show's heyday. Sharon never participated in giving autographs at the studio door and knew nothing about the following the show had. "I guess my mother was sheltering me from all of that." Kids back home in Philadelphia did recognize her. "They would say, 'You're that girl!' and I'd say, 'No, I'm not!' 'Yes you are!' 'Oh, OK, I am.' Then they'd say, 'No you're not.'" Donna did participate in giving autographs to the studio kids, and though she wasn't quite as in demand as Jonathan, David Selby, or Lara Parker, at least one overzealous fan once tried to follow her home. "I learned that the thing to do is to sign the autograph and just keep walking. If you needed to leave right away after work, if you had another audition to get to, you could slip out the back door and avoid the crowd. For some reason, nobody ever waited by the back door. I guess they all expected us to come out the front." She recalled that, "Jonathan was always so polite to everyone. He was a true professional."

The latest Spencer Productions feature, *Curse of the Full Moon*, which co-stars Sharon Smyth and Chip Coffey, played on Sunday afternoon following the Q&A with Donna Wandrey and Sharon Smyth. The film drew many laughs.

Rumors circulated on the last day of the gathering that a similar event will be held next year at Greystone. I sure hope that's the case! It has been far too long since CA had a proper DS event.[111]

2014 Dark Shadows Weekend (Tarrytown, NY)[112]

Day 1: Saturday, June 28, 2014

In my opinion, the programming on Saturday was nothing special. Essentially, it was only a half-day at Lyndhurst. Lyndhurst remained open to the public for guided tours until 2:00. From then until closing, the mansion was open to fans, who could walk freely through the rooms and take non-flash photographs. Vendors (primarily MPI) and autographing actors gathered inside the barn. The main activities took place inside a large tent.

Marcy Robin spoke for the first hour, answering fan questions and reciting the litany of the dead. Afterward, Marie Wallace and Jim Pierson performed a staged reading of a deleted scene from *House of DS*. She was to have played Nancy Hodiak, a customer of Jeff Clark's, who commissioned a portrait and was murdered by Barnabas while returning with it to her car. Although the performers struggled at times to decipher Dan Curtis's handwritten notes, Marie was very emotive and even screamed when Barnabas attacked her. She seemed to regret that the piece had not been filmed. "I could have been immortalized in a portrait," she lamented. "Maybe they could have even made two portraits—one for Barnabas to destroy and one that I could have kept." The scene also revealed that Maggie had given notice, unable to cope with David's pranks and Roger's vicious attitude.

According to the schedule, the next events were the charity auction to benefit Lyndhurst (the grand prize was a tour of the tower room with the actors; it went for $900) and an informational appearance by Big Finish about the audio dramas. I was not in the tent during this time and returned only during the last half of David Selby's musical poetry slam.

Accompanied by his wife, Chip, on piano and by Jim Storm on guitar, Selby performed/sang some of his poems to a country-esque beat. Some of the pieces related to DS. Others had political overtones. Selby performed this same show at the April luncheon in Coronado last year,[113] so if you were there for *Doctor Mabuse*, you heard it.

Finally, the cast reunited to take questions from the audience and sign more autographs. Both films were supposed to be shown too, but I did not stay to see them. The last event I attended was back at the Double Tree Hotel in the gazebo outside the hotel. After hours (around 10:00 PM), Sharon Smyth-Lentz regaled a healthy crowd of fans with ghost stories (some that she had experienced first-hand, and others that had been related to her by others). She also invited audience members to share their own tales. Unfortunately, Ms. Smyth-Lentz was not provided with any lighting nor even a microphone during her talk. Although I had been looking forward to this event, I ended up not staying long because it was too difficult to hear anything.

Day 2: Sunday, June 29, 2014

The luncheon on Sunday featured several delightful performances by the actors. Marie Wallace, Lara Parker, and KLS performed their own rendition of "Friendship" with DS-themed touches, prefaced by some mock backstage cattiness. The act got off to a slow start due to some technical difficulties with the music, but the ladies remained in good spirits and kept on with the show. Next, James Storm played some classic country songs and dedicated a performance of "Will the Circle Be Unbroken" to Jonathan Frid. He recalled the last Festival where he had seen Frid (2010 in Burbank) and that, even though it had been the first time in 40 years that the two had been together, Frid still recognized him and vividly remembered details about Storm and his family. Finally, Chris Pennock gave a lively and funny reading of his 2002 semi-autobiographical comic, *Fear of Losing Dark Shadows*. The luncheon closed with another charity auction and more opportunities for autographs.

There were no fan-centric activities (*e.g.,* skits, trivia games, videos) this year, which saddens me because these activities have given me the greatest enjoyment at DS events through the years. I always loved to see the creativity of the other fans, to feel like I was part of a big inside joke, to share my own songs and skits, and to partake in our common culture, so to speak. Personally, I wish there was a larger participatory element at the Fests/conventions/DS Weekends. Here's hoping that 2016 will see a return to the traditional 3-day format with a variety of activities on schedule!

2016 Dark Shadows Festival (Tarrytown, NY)

Day 1: Friday, June 24, 2016

The 50th Anniversary Fest opened with the traditional registration line, autograph line, and entry line, all snaking around the lobby of the Double Tree and reaching back toward the hotel restaurant. Registration opened at 4:00 and the first event was not until 6:00. Those two hours were needed to assist all of the people. For a smaller venue with capped attendance, lots and lots of folks were present. I was thrilled to see old friends for the first time in years, but sadly, registration was the only opportunity we had to see each other.

Sharon Smyth opened the Festivities by greeting the fans and offering a surprisingly serious tribute to some who have passed away in recent years, including Ken Friedman, Judy Caswell, and Diane Eckert. These are fans whom Sharon got to know personally and befriended in recent years. As they were also my friends, I was very pleased that she acknowledged them publicly. I saw Sharon's tribute as a wonderful example of how the DS actors are just as happy to meet us as we are to meet them.

The first true event was a screening of the final episode of DS (Morgan, Catherine, and the lottery) with the original commercials, including dish soap and a Rankin & Bass holiday special, *Here Comes Peter Cottontail* with Danny Kaye. Later in the convention, Nick Besink would talk about salvaging the master for Episode 1245. I'm glad he did recover it, because I enjoyed the vintage viewing.

The next item on the program was an interview with Jonathan Frid from the *Dick Cavett Show*. What we weren't told was that this interview was audio-only; the recording was set to still-frame images of Frid as Barnabas, much like the "lost" episode. I didn't find the recreated interview to be particularly interesting so I wandered away to the dealer's area and returned after the first Q&A was in progress.

The format for Q&A panels on Friday night consisted of pairs of DS actors screening clips of their work on the show and talking about their memories (or lack thereof) of working on the show. Occasionally, the floor was thrown open for questions, but for the most part, Richard Halpern kept the events running right along. The Fest stayed pretty close to the printed schedule for that first night. Nancy Barrett and Kathryn Leigh Scott were the first speakers. Their talk was already in progress when I returned to the ballroom. We saw Carolyn's first scene with Vicki, Maggie visiting Collinwood in her best suit to confront Roger, a clip of insane Carolyn from 1995 (Nancy couldn't recall this character or story line) and Josette discovering Barnabas 'alive' in the mausoleum. The sound went out during this last clip, so though we couldn't hear Josette pleading with Barnabas to come back to her, we could clearly see her gesturing and following him around. "Is that really us?" Nancy marveled. KLS recalled how DS was her very first acting job. "So many of us got our start on DS," she explained. Nancy listed a few examples: "Alexandra, Kathryn, Lara." There was no time for questions for this first pair, but before they left, Richard announced that Nancy had donated her fangs from *House of DS* for the auction. "And she'll throw in a photo of her wearing them to prove that they were in her mouth!"

Chris Pennock and Marie Wallace came up next. Chris squirmed as he took his seat, explaining that he has hip replacement surgery pending. He also lamented that he forgot to bring copies of his *Fear and Loathing* on Facebook comic for sale. The first clip selected was of Jeb and Megan opening up Paul Stoddard's grave to find a grinning Dennis Patrick. "Do you remember filming that scene?" Richard Halpern asked. "Was Dennis Patrick just lying there the whole time?" Chris said that he was (however, it's been established elsewhere that Patrick was already off the show by then and that scene was filmed with one of Patrick's head shots).

We also saw a scene of Chris Pennock as John Yeager in Parallel Time. Chris talked about the false nose he initially had to wear. "I didn't want to wear the nose, but Dan Curtis said it made me look like Jack Palance. Under the hot lights, the make-up ran and the nose kept sliding around. It was a big mess. So, finally, they said I could stop wearing the nose." He also revealed a secret about his acting technique. "Do you know who Cyrus Longworth really was? Do you know who I was doing?" He imitated the shrinking, stammering scientist. "David Niven! Lela Swift complained that my Cyrus was too much like Jeb, so I went back to my dressing room in a panic, thinking, 'How can I come up with a different character? How am I going to make him different?' And finally, it hit me to do David Niven. That's how I did all my characters. I imitated other actors—badly."

Marie's clip was of crazy Jenny Collins threatening Judith in the attic. It was a truncated variation. Displaying a sharper memory than most of her colleagues, Marie said, "I thought that scene went on longer. I remember I had a line: 'Sometimes you wear my green dress!'" Marie revealed that Jenny's crazy hair was her very own hair, not a wig. "Lots of people assume I was wearing a wig, but I would put up part of my hair in curlers and then tease out the rest of it so it would be in different lengths." When asked by an audience member about her favorite character, Marie claimed that her favorite role was always the one she was currently working on at the time, but that she had a soft spot for Jenny. Chris's favorite was wheelchair-bound Gabriel Collins.

Jerry Lacy and James Storm took the stage next. When told they would be looking at show clips, Storm turned to Lacy and asked, "Did we ever do any scenes together?" Indeed, they did in 1840, and their joint clip featured Gerard and Lamar discovering a certain skeleton in Barnabas's basement. We also saw a scene of Gerard's ghost menacing Quentin and unleashing his pirate zombie team on Collinwood, and a 1968 clip of Tony Peterson advising a hysterical Julia. Both actors talked about their current projects. In addition to his music, Jim Storm has taken up photography and spent time traveling around the country to take his pictures. Meanwhile, Jerry has written a comedy called *A Reunion of Sorts* that will be performed next month by the Town and Country Players in Bucks County, PA.

Many of the questions were directed at Jerry. He was asked to do his famous Humphrey Bogart imitation. He demurred, claiming his voice has changed with time, but after repeated encouragement, he finally gave us, "Of all the gin joints in all the world, she walks into mine" to much applause. He was also asked how soon after he was cast as Tony Peterson did he become aware that he would be playing Rev. Trask. Jerry recalled that he was told about the new character almost immediately after he started working. He also fielded a question about the relationship of one of his audio drama characters to the Reverends Trask.

The final panel featured Roger David and Lara Parker. Roger was texting on his cell phone as he came onstage, and continued to fiddle with his phone during the Q& A session. "I'm talking with my contractor," he explained. "It's Friday, and I have to pay my workers." (He does a lot of building in the LA area). Lara was in high spirits, asking how many fans were attending for the first time (nearly two-thirds of the room raised their hands) and giving a shout-out to the Orlando DS fan club.[114] She also spoke about her forthcoming Vicki-centric DS novel, *Heiress of Collinwood*, due out in November. In her clip, she played vampire Angelique attacking Peter Bradford. Roger portrayed a vampire in his own clip, in which Dirk Wilkins menaced Rachel Drummond. Roger spoke about his voice-over acting career and mentioned how his agent, in one of their last meetings, commented that they had never been able to find someone with as nice a voice as his. ("Not even Peter Fonda?" Lara cracked). She also ribbed Roger about roughhousing his co-actresses, including Joan Bennett. The teasing continued in the next day's cast reunion. I got a real kick out of Lara at this year's Fest.

The night closed with a screening of *House of Dark Shadows*, *Night of DS*, and fan film *Curse of the Full Moon*.

Day 2: Saturday, June 25, 2016

Saturday's events opened at 11:00 AM. Although registration started at 10, no one was allowed near the ballroom or into the dealer area until after 11. Fan videos (one of my favorite Fest features!) opened the day. We were treated to Richard Halpern and his niece and nephews reprising the roles of Barnabas, Elizabeth, Sarah, Burke, and Willie in "Baby Dark Shadows" as well as another fan's student film from his USC days, called "The Creepybopper." This adorable short film, shot in B&W and set to popular tunes of the era, center on a prototypical DS fan, the proud owner of fake fangs, DS models, and *Famous Monsters* magazines. The plot thickens as the boy flips through a series of poorly-scored spelling tests and is swiftly punished with no DS for a week unless he can improve his grades. Sadly, the picture went out midway through the film, so we never got to see if the boy was able to charm his mother into letting him see his favorite show again. (Fortunately, the video is available on YouTube).

I wandered away to the dealer area just before Marcy Robin began a panel on DS news and fan questions, so I missed all the excitement when a smoker triggered the fire alarm and nearly precipitated an evacuation of the ballroom! I heard plenty of people talking about this incident throughout the day, however. I'm glad it wasn't a real emergency—particularly as I never heard any alarm going off even though I was just in the hallway on the other side of the ballroom!

The next event I attended was a panel called The Collinsport Historical Society, hosted by Wallace McBride and Patrick McCray. Apparently, this is a website or a page on Facebook (I'd never heard of it before) whose moderator collects information about the history and fandom of the show. He described the first item to inspire his curating: a drinking mug stamped "Blue Whale, Collinsport, Maine." "It was obviously something a fan had made, but it looked like something you would really find in Collinsport." (It sounds to me like CynD's work). He also spoke about a semi-hoax that earned notoriety for his site. The Collinsport Historical Society had held a contest to write the story for a hypothetical third DS movie. The winning entry, *Child of Dark Shadows,* sounded fascinating:

A failed televangelist called Trask (Jerry Lacy) acquires Collinwood and converts it into a boarding school. One of the students is Victoria Winters (Alexandra Moltke). Vicki swiftly becomes the target of poltergeist and other supernatural activity. After she discovers an old portrait of an accused witch that looks just like her, she is catapulted back in time. Meanwhile, a psychic/Satanist, the brother of ill-fated Tracy Collins (played by Chris Pennock), arrives at the school to investigate the haunting. He realizes that the ghost is actually Vicki herself, trapped and condemned in the past and trying to prevent her modern self from making the same poor choices. (Kind of like *The Twilight Zone*'s "Spur of the Moment"). The audience loved this story outline. Many called out to McBride that he should film it himself. Evidently, at the time he posted this outline on the Historical Society website, he failed to make clear the tongue-in-cheek nature of the post. "Many fans started circulating the story that there was another, lost DS movie out there somewhere. When they found out it was a joke, they got mad and accused our site of having lost its credibility."

The next speaker was Patrick McCray presenting The Collins Chronicles (another website, I'm guessing). His conceit was that David Collins had returned to Collinsport after an absence of many years to find the great estate abandoned, save for a box of letters and journals left for him by Cousin Barnabas. McCray read sample entries, all written in a flowery imitation-18th Century style, rather like Ichabod Crane's monologues on the *Sleepy Hollow* TV show. In Barnabas's own words, he retold incidents from the show, such as discovering Angelique was a witch or meeting Julia Hoffman, and shared insights about Ben Stokes, Willie Loomis, and Julia. This segment was not my cup of tea. The readings were essentially fan fiction that did not enhance my understanding or enjoyment of the show. It seems to me his readings would have been better suited to the Costume Gala.

At last, it was time for the much-anticipated presentation of "The House." None of the Fest staff had seemed entirely certain of what "The House" would be, though it was hinted that we would be watching a rediscovered TV broadcast. Indeed, we were able to see a half-hour episode from the 1950's thriller anthology *The Web* (complete with creepy Theremin music for the opening title) that had originally aired in 1954. In 2006, the DS actors gave a live reading of an Art Wallace teleplay called "The House" that had served as the foundation for "Shadows on the Wall," the original DS story bible. That script differed in specific detail from the show we saw, though the basic outlines remained the same.

The show opens with a wayfarer stopping by the local bar (a set very similar to the Blue Whale) to inquire about old friends in the area. He is told that Liz Stover still lives in the old house on the outskirts of town and that she has seldom left the house ever since her husband deserted her nearly 20 years ago. The stranger gets a cunning gleam in his eye as the scene cuts to Liz (in a drawing room that looks much like Collinwood's), awaiting her daughter's return from a date.

The girl (whose name escapes me) has big news: her long-time beau, Joe, a successful fisherman, has finally proposed! However, she is reluctant to accept the offer because she would have to leave her mother behind in the crumbling old house that she seemingly can't afford to repair. Over the next several scenes, the young woman negotiates with her mother and her fiancé, finally devising a plan that she and Joe will marry and move into the house with Mother. As the family prepares to celebrate, they hear a knock at the door. Joe admits the stranger from the bar, who introduces himself as Walt Cummins, an old friend of the family. Liz is visibly shocked to see him and sends the others out of the room so she can deliver her 'You said you would never come back!' speech. It is clear that she and Walt have an unsavory history, and he uses the threat of revealing her secret to persuade Liz to put him up in the house until he can get back on his feet.

Her daughter is thrilled to have Walt visiting; she's decided he must be her long-lost father returned at last. In fact, through further arguments between Liz and Walt, the audience learns that Liz accidentally killed her husband when she caught him trying to abscond with her jewelry. Walt helped her dispose of the body and she paid him off with the jewels. Anxious to keep her daughter from learning the truth, Liz acquiesces to Walt's escalating demands, including the young bride's insistence that he attend her wedding, but when he starts to hint that they ought to get married themselves, Liz reaches her limit.

As a surprise for his mother-in-law to be, Joe hires a handyman to make basic repairs to the house. Liz initially is angry and demands that they leave, but she finally loses her temper with Walt and escorts the handyman to a spot in the basement where she tells him to dig. Then, she comes clean with the whole sordid truth. However, when the handyman returns without uncovering a body, Walt reveals that Liz's husband was only stunned by her attack, and that the two of them split the loot and ran off to sea, leaving her to wallow in her guilt. The no-good husband died at sea ten years earlier. Joe offers to commit Walt to the constable for extortion, but Liz doesn't want to press any charges. Walt's confession has freed her and she declares, "Now I can finally leave the house!"

This version of "The House" condensed the major points of the Jason Maguire blackmail plot into a significantly shorter running time while yet maintaining a sense of suspense and scandal. The resemblance of certain characters and sets to their later DS counterparts made "The House" even more entertaining to watch. I don't know the background of how this show was uncovered, but I'm glad that it was made available. It was a lovely treat for the Festival.

Following the screening, a panel of behind-the-scenes personnel (Henry Plimack – sound, Nick Besink – cameraman, Daniel Morgan - stage manager) assembled. Those behind the camera had a much different experience than the actors, and hearing their perspective was fresh and exciting.

Besink recalled his first day at the studio. It was his habit to take candid photos, and he snapped some of KLS in her robe doing a read-through. "She didn't like that, and she asked the director to tell me not to take any more pictures. Later, she apologized to me. She didn't know I was working on the show; she thought I was a fan who had somehow got backstage."

Plimack reminisced about the giant records with the sound cues that the team, including Sybil Weinberg, had to use. Some of these records were on the table to be auctioned off, and Plimack showed one off with Richard Halpern's assistance. "You had to line up the needle with the groove and find the right cue. We were always trying to time the cue exactly right. You couldn't have the music come in too early or too late. Later, we had all the cues on tape cartridges and you just had to push a button to play one."

The crew also talked about a new portable microphone Dan Curtis had tried to implement (as opposed to the boom mics and mics on fishing poles)—one that would have required no personnel to operate. However, after Grayson Hall repeatedly knocked the mic offline with her effusive gesturing, Curtis gave up on the idea, and everyone's job was safe.

One fan asked about the infamous studio fire that broke out during the Phoenix story line. "Not only do I remember that, I was there," Besink declared. "It was contained within the fireplace—we used a real fireplace. When I told Lela Swift we had to stop tape, she said, 'What for?' and I told her, 'Because the studio is on fire.'" Another fan wanted to know what was up with all the blue candles. "They were probably cheap to buy," Morgan mused. "Or, nobody bothered to change the candles after the show went to color."

The first charity auction of the weekend followed. I didn't stay for the auction itself, but did observe some of the items up for grabs: copies of *Angelique's Descent* and *Dreams of the Dark*, scripts, a 4-CD set of DS soundtrack music, and a lovely afghan blanket.

When I next came back to the ballroom, it was during the tail-end of Will McKinley's presentation on Jonathan Frid's post-DS stage performances, including his one-man shows and *Arsenic and Old Lace*. While a student, McKinley had been an assistant to Jonathan in many of his productions. He was joined by another of Frid's assistants, (she was uncredited in the program, but according to ShadowGram she was Mary O'Leary), who had worked with Frid on *Arsenic and Old Lace*. She revealed that there had been talk of changing Jonathan Brewster's famous line, "He said I looked like Boris Karloff!" to "He said I looked like Barnabas Collins!" However, Frid firmly vetoed this idea. "It was probably for the best," she admitted. "Changing the lines might have led to issues with the copyright."

McKinley also shared a charming anecdote of Frid's involvement in a telethon for the New Jersey Network. Frid had wanted McKinley to accompany him, but McKinley begged off, citing his big Spanish final for the next day. Fortunately, Frid had a degree in Spanish. "He said, 'We can study in the car' and he spent the two-hour limo ride drilling me. He even mentioned helping my prep for my exam during the telethon, and after that, people kept asking me how I did." We in the audience called out, "So how did you do?" McKinley grinned. "I did better on that Spanish test than on any before it." (What an awesome experience, to have Jonathan Frid as a tutor!) The presentation closed with a slideshow, set to "Best Day of My Life" by American Authors, with photographs of Frid posing before the marquees at various theaters around the country where he had performed.

And then it was time for the cast reunion!

One at a time, the actors filed in to cheers and applause: Sharon Smyth, Roger Davis, Donna Wandrey, Marie Wallace, Chris Pennock, James Storm, Lara Parker, Jerry Lacy, John Karlen, David Selby, and Kathryn Leigh Scott took their seats on the stage, which was quickly swarmed by photographers. Each offered a short greeting. Lara Parker, still in a joking mood, kidded, "I wasn't born yet when DS first started. My grandmother introduced me to the show. And when I found out about this Festival, I was so excited, because I got to come meet my favorite actor of all time,

John Karlen!" KLS was the last to appear, bringing with her a bottle of champagne with which she led a toast for the 50th Anniversary of DS. Richard Halpern then invited fans to bring their questions to a microphone in the center of the ballroom. A long line quickly formed. Though the Q&A session ran for over an hour, the line nevertheless had to be cut before it was more than half-way through.

Many of the questions prompted lengthy responses from everybody on the panel. For example, the actors were asked what other part on DS they would have liked to play, if given the chance. "I always wanted to play Little Sarah," Karlen said mischievously. "Johnny, you can borrow my bonnet anytime," Sharon promised. Chris Pennock and James Storm each said they wanted to play Grayson Hall. That prompted the cast to share memories of her. "She had the best apartment ever!" Karlen said (I thought he was going to reminisce about her cooking). Lara talked about how Grayson would go swimming in the morning before work and then come to the studio with wet hair. She also repeated a story from the *DS Companion*. "Grayson had a pug named Thing and I had a pug named Rosie. We had big plans for them. We were going to go into a partnership raising pugs." But unfortunately, they never got any puppies. Jerry Lacy's choice was Nicholas Blair. "Humbert Allen Astredo played him as so suave and so evil. It was a great role and he was a very talented actor." Lara said that she wanted to play Josette. David wanted to play Angelique. "I would have liked to be Elizabeth," Kathryn said. "I always felt like Dan Curtis had a great story in mind for her, with her husband's disappearance and her staying in the house all those years, and just never got around to telling it." (Evidently, she didn't watch "The House," or the Jason Maguire episodes.)

A young lady just starting in the acting business asked if the cast could share any advice or techniques. "Know your lines. Don't bump into the props or the scenery," Roger told her. "I imitate other actors," Chris shared, repeating his revelation from the previous evening. "I based John Yeager on a movie that James Earl Jones did. He acted like a joyful, murderous gorilla, and that's exactly what John Yeager was: a joyful, murderous gorilla." (Has anyone any idea what film Chris was referencing? I would be curious to see it.) James Storm took the microphone next. "I imitate other actors," he deadpanned, with a glance at Chris. John Karlen told the young actress,

"No matter what role you're playing, always remember, that's you. No matter who you're pretending to be, you're still you. Understand?"

Another question that drew insightful responses was what the cast members would have liked to do if they had not gone into acting. "In addition to being an actress, I also got to be a mother, and I did a pretty good job!" Sharon declared. Roger Davis has a background in architecture and restored a historically important hotel in his native Louisville.[115] Marie has found a passion for photography and also dabbled in painting when she was a chorus girl on Broadway. She even submitted some of her paintings to an art show and attracted the attention of Ethel Merman. (She discusses this at length in her memoir *On Stage and in the Shadows*). Chris Pennock also revealed that he had an artistic background, having always loved to draw. As a child, he entered a statewide art contest sponsored by Crayola with America as its theme. Western movies inspired his material. "I drew a picture of a cowboy killing an Indian with a spear. I said, 'Yeah! That's what America is about!' And I won! The local paper wrote, 'Christopher Pennock is the winner with his drawing of a man digging.' I said, 'But...but...That's not a shovel, it's a spear!'" James Storm mentioned his love of photography. Lara was drawn to all of the performing arts. "When I was a little girl, I wanted to dance, but I wasn't a very good dancer. So then I decided I wanted to be a singer, but my mother told me, 'You can't carry a tune.' So I said, 'I'll be an actress! Then I won't have to do anything.'" Since then, she has raised three children, written four novels and taught both high school and college English and creative writing. David Selby initially went into teaching when he moved to NYC. "But my wife, Chip, told me, 'That's not the reason we came here. You need to follow your dream of being an actor.'" David also told a story of how the FBI tried to recruit him to do reconnaissance[116] at the local ham and eggs joint, "But I turned them down because I was afraid some friends of mine might be involved."

Other questions were directed to specific actors. One of the first women to take the mic asked David Selby for a dance and began to serenade him with a beautiful rendition of "I Wanna Dance With you." David did pitch in on a couple of the lyrics. He was also asked by another fan if he could perform "Shadows of the Night." "If you'll hum the tune for me, I'll try it," he accepted. "Does anyone have the words?" Someone handed him a copy of the record album, which had the lyrics printed. The ballroom buzzed with the strains of Cobert's music while Selby recited the words.

A middle-aged man had a question for John Karlen. "Have you noticed that David Selby has all these beautiful women asking him questions and I get the old guys? Is it me?" Johnny teased. The fan asked if Karlen was influence by the other actor who had played Willie Loomis before him. Richard Halpern jumped in. "That was James Hall! He lives in Santa Monica and is on Facebook. He's written about DS. I'm friends with him. Maybe we should have a reunion with the two Willie Loomises in LA." Karlen didn't look too enthusiastic about the prospect. Kathryn revealed that Hall had been a student in her acting class. "It was awkward working with him on his last couple of episodes because we all knew he was on his way out the door. He was a nice guy. . .did he do any acting afterward?" (According to Halpern, yes).

Roger was asked about *Alias, Smith and Jones*. "Putting aside how you got the role,[117] would you have preferred to be cast as a new character instead of being put in Pete Duel's role?" Roger told how he had been good friends with Pete and that they had worked together on a pilot for a Western called *The Young Country*, but that the producers hadn't thought he had the right look for the show.

CyrusL asked the cast to share their memories of Virginia Vestoff and Thayer David. "Virginia was lovely," Donna Wandrey said. "She played my sister—or rather, I was her sister. But my favorite actor to work with was Thayer David. He was the sweetest, gentlest man in the world—except when he would come up to you and say, 'I'm going to push you into the coffin now, but don't worry; I'll be right here waiting for you. Sometimes they forget to let you out, you know.'" "He had the most voluptuous wife," Selby remarked, "Valerie French." "He was a speed reader." Lara imitated Thayer flipping through pages. "I'd ask him 'How do you do that?' and he'd say, 'Oh, it's easy.'" Everyone recalled how he would binge on sodas and candy bars at rehearsal.

One of the fans whose mother started watching DS because of Joan Bennett asked if the actors had ever met her sisters Constance or Barbara. Roger started to answer, but Lara cut him off (as he has so often done to others.) It was a very funny moment.

The Q&A session was brought to a close with many disappointed fans still at the mic. Most glumly turned back to their seats, but one ardent lady seized the mic as the actors prepared to leave the stage. "We need to acknowledge the person who is responsible for DS's success: Lara Parker! Without Angelique, the show would have been nothing."

At some point during that evening, Lara Parker and Chris Pennock each read from their new books, and Sharon Smyth read a ghost story. However, I don't know when this happened because none of these events were listed in the schedule. Following the cast reunion, I left to prepare for the Costume Gala. I do know that in the interim, the 2004 WB pilot was shown.

The Costume Gala went on around 8:00 with a modest number of entrants (around 20). This year's set of performers included several men dressed as Barnabas, Leviathan rappers, a Barnabas proclaiming his love to a dead Angelique, Pansy Faye singing and dancing with Quentin, Pansy Faye getting attacked by vampire Roxanne Drew, the future Mr. and Mrs. Buzz Hackett, Victoria Winters and Judge Braithwaite, both from 1795. Charles Ellis performed his famous Charnak the Great routine, assisted by Suzanne ("Where's the remote? What do DS fans say when a certain Tim Burton film comes on TV—where's the remote! The Hunger Games? What happens when Willie Loomis teases Adam with chicken—the Hunger Games!") The stand-out performer of the night, IMO, was a gentleman named Michael, who traditionally sings beautiful tributes in memoriam to DS personnel who have passed on. Part-way through his song, the CD began to skip and then went out altogether. Undeterred, Michael dashed off-stage to get a different CD and went back up to sing a new song. He acted like a true pro (in the same position, I would have panicked).

For this year, widely expected to be the last Festival, I wanted to present two song parodies. Having learned my lesson from 2006, however, I knew I would only be allowed to sing one of them. So, rather than choose, I performed one song solo ("Gone Around the Bend," a Windcliff-centric song, while in costume as a psychiatric nurse) and recruited friends to help me sing the second (a celebration of DS fandom at the height of the show's popularity in 1969 to the tune of "Summer of 69"); technically, performing together, we were a different act. I had envisioned that each person would sing a different verse, as if different fans were taking turns sharing their memories. We hadn't been able to thoroughly rehearse the song though, and my friends asked me to sing along with them and keep them in tune. So, I got to sing the whole thing anyway. I was thrilled to be able to share both songs after all. Many thanks to Bobubas, Janice, and Phil!

During the final bow, Kathryn and Lara came onstage in beautiful costumes of their own, designed by the same costumer who outfitted the new *Cabaret* cast. Lara looked just like her 1897 self in a green brocade dress, while KLS imitated Josette's film apparel in an ivory gown with ruffled sleeves, a lace-trimmed skirt, and a fashionable bonnet. KLS's dress was new, but Lara had previously worn hers on the cruise.[118] "During the cruise, I wore my grandmother's 1910 wedding dress," Kathryn said. "It seemed perfect for Josette." The ladies posed at length for photos with the other Gala participants.

Then, the Collinsport Players took the stage. "Séance Fiction"[119] retells the events of 1967 that led up to the 1795 flashback ("a séance that will send the Collins family back in time—and triple our costume budget!") with a twist. Barnabas anxiously tries to prevent Elizabeth from holding a séance to contact Sarah Collins, clashes with a histrionic Julia, and flirts with a besotted Carolyn (Nancy Barrett herself). Sarah does briefly appear to Barnabas, cautioning him to clean up his act, but Barnabas refuses to heed her warnings. He succeeds in changing the location of the séance from Collinwood to the Blue Whale, where the family encounters Buffie Harrington, a waitress transplanted from the 1970 PT story, and must submit to a 2-drink minimum. After they chant "Eenie meenie chili beanie" and call upon Sarah to speak to them, Carolyn dramatically pretends to be possessed by the small ghost. However, it's Vicki who is truly touched by the spirits. With a dramatic scream, she vanishes behind the stage to be replaced by 18th Century governess Phyllis Wick. "Aw man," Buffie gripes. "I thought you were holding a séance. Manifestations mean you have to order the hot wings." And on that cliffhanger, the skit concluded to loud applause and I adjourned to get some dinner.

Day 3: Sunday, June 26, 2016

Sunday's luncheon consisted of salad, rolls, chicken in sauce, mashed sweet potatoes, carrots and broccolini, and a red velvet cake dessert that, unusually, was already on the table when we sat down. The Fest vendors were generous with the door prizes, providing a DVD 2-pack of *The Haunting of Collinwood* and *The Vampire Curse*, a copy of the book *Produced and Directed by Dan Curtis*, and a reprint of Gold Key Comics' "Interrupted Voyage" story.

Unfortunately, the ballroom was not really large enough to accommodate all of the tables (I think there were around 50). Some tables spilled into the erstwhile hallway where vendor tables had previously been set up; these tables were set behind a wall and a coffee service station that blocked some attendees' view of the stage where the performances and films took place. The first event was the door prize drawing. There were fewer prizes this year than in the past, but the range of tables selected was wide. Nancy Barrett nearly ended up with a prize. (In fact, I think Table 2 got two prizes.) The giveaways included the new Big Finish CD "Blood and Fire" and MPI's commemorative 50th anniversary T-shirt.

Next, Nancy Barrett and David Selby took the stage to sing "I Wanna Dance with You." David also gave another rendition of "Shadows of the Night." "I had so much fun yesterday with all of you humming along," he explained. Once again, the audience obliged with the background music.

The performances were followed by KLS's charity auction to benefit Progressive Supranuclear Palsy[120] research. I can't help but imagine KLS has a vault at home with compartments earmarked for each milestone Festival. (IIRC, at the 40th Anniversary Fest, she auctioned off some of Jonathan Frid's hair). This time, she auctioned off several impressive items of memorabilia from her own collection, including one of Maggie Evans's falls, her own script from Episode 1 (which was so rough, some of the parts were written in pencil rather than typed), the script from her last episode in 1970, and most impressive of all, waitress Maggie's original short blond wig, head band, and saddle shoes (size 8 ½) with a replica of Maggie's coffee shop uniform. All of the items sold for over $500. The winner of the waitress ensemble was seated at the table ahead of mine; throughout the rest of the event, people kept stopping by to admire it.

James Storm also held an auction for a photograph of a landmark tree he had taken while on a road trip to the heartland. Nancy Barrett gave the highest bid. Storm performed three country-style songs. I didn't recognize the first two (one was about Sampson), but the third was the spiritual "Will the Circle Be Unbroken?" "In my travels, I learned that the Native Americans don't have a word for "Good-bye," he explained by way of introduction. "Their equivalent is 'See you later,' and 'later' could be tomorrow or in the afterlife." He has shared this song in the past to commemorate the deceased cast and crew members and performed it again as a means of saying 'see you later' to those who have gone on ahead of us.

The Fest also had an In Memoriam slideshow featuring stars, day players, and behind the scenes personnel. Next, they played three short films by Ansel Faraj that featured several of the DS stars (Karlen, Pennock, Parker, Scott, Lacy, and Richards) as well as references to the show. I won't go into the details of "The Interview," "Dark Reunions in a Strange Paradise," or "Madame Le Soeur" as I understand Faraj has plans to make the films available. They were very entertaining, and in the first two cases, very funny.

The luncheon concluded with another auction of general memorabilia (e.g., comics, autographed photos) while the actors engaged in a final autograph session. I understand that Nancy Barrett's fangs from *House of DS,* the expected big-ticket item, were not actually offered due to low attendance at the auction. At least this way, we can be guaranteed that another DS event will be in the works.

April 23, 2017 – Los Angeles Times Festival of Books with Lara Parker

Today, Lara Parker attended the *Los Angeles Times*'s Festival of Books on the campus of USC. She participated on a panel called "From Page to Screen to Page" alongside Brian McGreevy (creator of the supernatural show *Hemlock Grove)*, Tod Goldberg, and Pamela Ribon. The other panelists had all written works that were later adapted for film or TV; Lara came from the other direction, beginning in television and turning to write novels. "So, it's all over for me," she joked.

The discussion got off to a slow start. Moderator Richard Rayner talked extensively and somehow managed to turn his introductions of the panelists around so he ended up talking about himself. When introducing Lara, he erroneously said she came from Texas (she's from Memphis, TN). McGreevy, who's lived in Texas, interjected, "If you want to figure out whether someone is from Texas or Tennessee, ask them how they do barbecue."

Lara didn't speak until almost the end of the session, and then she went into detail about her journey from screen to page. She began taking screenwriting courses through UCLA's extension program because she was tired of the terrible lines she had to read in the scripts she was given. (The worst was, "There'll always be a candle in the window for you, Steve!" from *The Six Million-Dollar Man*.) "When you do screenwriting, you do everything from scratch, so all the years I spent as an actress didn't help me at all," she recalled ruefully.

Around this time, Harper Collins decided to launch a series of novels based on DS, and someone from the company contacted Lara, knowing she was doing screenwriting. "I told them, I don't know anything about writing a novel. And they said, 'Well, we really want to use your name, so just write something. We'll bring in a real writer to fix it up later.' And I thought, 'I'm going to spend a year, maybe two years, writing this and some smartass is going to change it all? No, I'm going to do the best I can.' So, I had all these models—DS borrowed from all the great horror stories in literature—but I had no idea how to begin. I spent about a year and a half just reading, looking at structure, dialogue, story, trying to find a model. I think I finally settled on Daphne Du Maurier."

Rayner stepped in. "That's where your acting experience came in handy! All the scripts you've read must have given you an idea of story."

Lara shook her head. "No. All you do is learn your lines and show up, hit your mark. What did help was that as an actor, you create a character. You come up with a backstory in your head for them. My first book was about my character, the witch, and how she became a witch. I spent about three years writing it and when I got to 575 pages, my editor said, 'You need to stop.' 'But I'm not finished,' I said. She told me, 'Save it for the next one.'"

Later, she reflected on the Burton film. "It's too bad Tim Burton didn't contact me to help him write his script for the Johnny Depp movie. I could have fixed it for him, and we would have had several movies by now and my books would be selling better. But he didn't want to have anything to with the old guard. Isn't it always that way? No one ever cares about learning what worked in the previous version. Tim Burton, bless him, is a brilliant man but he doesn't care much about story. The show was all about story. We kept people on the edge of their seats, tuning in every day for five years. His movie was a series of set-pieces, one after the other, all of them good-looking, but you just didn't care about anything that was happening. He was off the mark with it. The TV show was very serious, but he made fun of it. Our vampire never would have hung upside-down from a chandelier!" (I thought that was a very good analysis.)

She did say that she has a feeling a new film, "a real version of DS," is likely to happen someday, given the perennial interest in remaking DS. "And I have a contract that says I get a percentage if they choose to film any of my books!"

Several DS fans were in the audience (as were Jim Storm, Jim Pierson, and Ansel Faraj). One man asked if Lara was concerned about the possibility of running out of material: given that DS had covered so many themes and stories already, how many more books or audio dramas can continue? Lara laughed. "That's right, we did run out of ideas, didn't we? And then we started to repeat ourselves." But she has no such fears for herself. "As a writer, you have a platform to communicate with your readers about themes that are important to you. I put into my books (*Angelique's*

Descent and *The Salem Branch*) my hatred of hypocrisy and of people in power abusing the people below them. But I never came right out and said any of that. I was just telling a story. You can riff on any number of themes when you have a platform." Another woman said that she was one of the kids who ran home from school to see DS. She remembered Angelique's top-knot hairstyle and frilly blouse (the 1795 costume), and she expressed sadness on learning Jonathan Frid had died. It was an interesting discussion and I'm glad Lara got to participate and share her experiences.

October 20, 2018 – Master of Dark Shadows Screening (Los Angeles, CA)

I attended the *Master of Dark Shadows* event. Bob Cobert, Mitch Ryan, Robert Rodan and Nancy Barrett were no shows. Jim Pierson announced Cobert had had a fall ("but he's OK"), Mitch Ryan had a health-related conflict ("but he's OK"), Rodan is relocating to Oregon and had to move earlier than expected, and Nancy Barrett was in an accident that totaled her car ("but she's OK.") John Karlen and Chris Pennock attended the screening but left before the Q&A, and Jerry Lacy had to leave partway through the Q&A.

An unexpected attendee was David Selby; I had read an announcement a few weeks ago that he would not be attending, but perhaps that only referred to the daytime Hollywood Show. Major kudos are due Lara Parker, who was attending a major, eight-months-in-the-planning wedding in Topanga Canyon earlier today but left the reception even before dinner was served in order to be with us.

The theater opened on time at 5:30 and the event launched practically on time at 6:00. Unfortunately, when the video began to play, it had no sound. For the next 10-15 minutes, a group of people worked (in the dark) to get the laptop hooked up properly, check the speakers, and deliver a functioning presentation. Jim claimed everything had worked during an earlier sound check. I had been nervous when I saw the laptop in the middle of the room (as opposed to a projector or a proper DVD player) and throughout the multiple computer reboots, I wondered what would happen if nobody could get the big documentary to play. Would they refund our money? Would they cut straight to the reunion/interview segment?

In the interim, Pennock led us in a meditation session and made shadow puppets on the big screen. Karlen recited Shakespeare. At last, the team got the volume to a level where most people could hear it (though we continued to have microphone feedback for a while) and the show began.

We had a few teasers prior to the doc itself. The first bit was a commercial for DS airing on the Decades Channel beginning October

29th. Next, we saw a music video featuring Kathryn Leigh Scott. "Dark Shadows" by Kyle Motsinger featured the male singer attempting to seduce Barnabas ("I'll be your willing, eager slave/I may not be your first love/ but Josette's dead and in her grave.") It is filled with DS references. The opening, in which Motsinger releases Barnabas from his coffin, looks like it was filmed at Sleepy Hollow Cemetery in the Collins family vault. Next, it cuts to the image of waves crashing on the rocks and the video title superimposed over an image of Seaview Terrace. The rest of the piece shows Barnabas's introduction to the Collins family (Scott plays Elizabeth). I thought it was an innovative approach to the material and I appreciated the tribute to the original show, but it wasn't Selby's cup of tea. Third was a trailer for Ansel Faraj's latest film, *Loon Lake*, starring Selby and Scott. It looks like it has to do with a witch trial and came across as very atmospheric. Shot on location in southern Minnesota, the movie will be out in 2019.

Finally, the main attraction began. Narrated by Ian McShane, *Master of Dark Shadows* has been alternately billed as a 50th Anniversary DS documentary and a documentary about Dan Curtis. It is definitely more DS-centric, discussing the creative development of the show, its wild popularity, various incarnations, and the post-DS careers of Frid and Curtis. In addition to the original actors Parker, Selby, Scott, Pennock, Storm, Karlen, Lacy, Barrett, and Davis, revival actors Ben Cross and Barbara Steele, and unaired pilot star Alec Newman, the film includes interviews with Curtis's daughters, Tracy and Cathy (who looks just like her dad), Curtis's secretary, Rita Fein, Frid's manager Mary O'Leary, celebrity fans Whoopi Goldberg and Alan Ball, Paley Center TV experts, writers Malcolm Marmorstein and William F. Nolan, as well as vintage interviews with Frid, ABC executives, and Curtis himself.

The doc opens with a personality sketch (William Nolan started reading off a list of descriptors: impatient, commanding, pragmatic, intimidating. . .) and brief biography of Curtis's early years. His daughters revealed that Dan's life was shaped by the early trauma of his mother's death, as she was driving and conversing with him, when he was only 13. After that, he was sent to boarding school. He married Norma at a young age and attempted to forge a path in television on his own, since he didn't like having to answer to a boss. His first success came from *CBS Match Play Golf Classic.*

Curtis told the story of how the plot of DS came to him in a dream. But the detail I hadn't heard before was that when he woke up, he decided the idea was stupid. It was Norma who told him it was a great idea and talked him into pitching the show.[121] Curtis wanted it to be a nighttime drama, but grudgingly agreed to make it a soap opera when ABC finally showed some interest. Even so, he tried to energize the show by speeding up the traditionally glacial soap opera pace. When it looked like DS would be canceled at the end of its first 13 weeks, Curtis bargained for an additional 13 weeks on condition that he could "take the lid off" and "make it scary" like his daughters wanted.

Malcolm Marmorstein claimed he introduced the first spook, Laura the Phoenix, and that Curtis was skeptical of the idea, but was happy when the new plot bought the show some additional weeks. Next up was the vampire, which Marmorstein conceived as a young, blond guy, the antithesis of Bela Lugosi. Yet, Ron Sproat cast his fellow Yale alumnus—middle-aged, dark, Jonathan Frid (I'd heard it was Bob Costello who picked Frid)—who inexplicably became a major sex symbol, attracting the attention of housewives and teens alike. Another detail that diverged from what I'd previously understood was that the character Barnabas was always intended to be sympathetic. (What I've read and heard is that Curtis wanted Barnabas to be a bloodsucking monster, but when Frid started to imbue the character with vulnerability, he made Barnabas reluctant and sympathetic in order to keep the audience's attention).

The Paley experts weighed in on how DS was revolutionary, both because it shook up the horror genre by creating a likable antihero vampire for the screen, and because it captivated the youth market. We saw the onslaught of toys and other products, clips of Frid's various TV and personal appearances, and the actors' reminiscences about the piles of fan mail and crowds of fans outside the studio. Storm remembered "it was a problem" when some of the fans found out where he lived. Frid drew so much attention that he had to move out of his apartment and into a more secure building with a doorman. Pennock's experience was more colorful:

he remarked that DS was popular with prostitutes and drug addicts. "Who else is going to be home at 4:00 to watch it?" He recalled walking home after taping and, "The hookers would call out, "Hi, Jeb!"

After the first movie, both Curtis and Frid felt burned out. Frid refused to do *Night of DS* and complained that playing a vampire was hurting his career. "How about playing an unemployed actor?" Curtis retorted. But Curtis himself was chafing creatively, too. He felt horror was limiting him. Even though his secretary would bring him back horror story books from the London bookshops on her annual vacations, he felt he'd run out of material. Curtis wasn't enthused about later plots like the Leviathans and was glad when the show ended in 1971.

Even then, both he and Frid found themselves typecast. Frid was cast in *The Devil's Daughter* and *Seizure*; Curtis made a series of horror novel adaptations for primetime, as well as *Trilogy of Terror*, the two *Night Stalker* movies, and the theatrical feature *Burnt Offerings*. Eventually, Frid took a break from acting, and Curtis got funding to adapt Herman Wouk's *Winds of War*.

Both it and the follow-up, *War and Remembrance* (which almost didn't get made; Steele revealed that shortly after she and Curtis began to plan the second mini-series, the network announced they were canceling the project. Curtis convinced executive Barry Diller to pick it up again) were critically acclaimed, but *Remembrance* wasn't a ratings-buster like its predecessor. Curtis knew he would never reach those heights again; the funding and the network support would never be available again.

Getting the call to revive DS as a primetime show for NBC felt like a major step down. Curtis "didn't want to go back to that world" and only agreed to do the show if he could reuse the original's plots. The cast was great and the show was well-made, but the first Gulf War knocked it off the schedule. We saw footage of fans protesting to save DS (maybe the future members of the CFDS Fan Club?), albeit to no avail.

DS next became a pilot for the WB in 2004. Mark Verheiden remembered the WB executives told him his script was the best pilot they had read for 2004. Alec Newman said he'd been assured the show was bound to be picked up and was stunned to get the call that the show wasn't happening. Verheiden faulted director PJ Hogan, who'd been brought in at the last minute to replace Rob Bowman, who'd been seduced away to make the movie *Electra*. Hogan was an accomplished director, but his vision was at odds with the material. He was enamored of Dario Argento, and the red-saturated look he created for DS didn't look very Gothic.

But the fans keep DS alive! We got to see brief clips from the 2016 Festival. I recognized some of my friends in the background.

After the documentary ended, Jim Pierson announced it would be available in a few weeks (In what context? Airing on TV? For purchase on DVD? He didn't elaborate.) Then he called up the remaining DS guests (Davis, Storm, Scott, Parker, Selby, Marmorstein, and Lacy) to join in the Q&A. He asked each to briefly introduce themselves, but that format was soon derailed.

Jerry went first. When Pierson asked if he'd learned anything he hadn't known before about DS, he admitted that he had trouble hearing the film because he was seated in the back. Instead, he shared that a fan once thanked him for his portrayal of Rev. Trask because "it showed religion for what it really is."

Malcolm Marmorstein came next. The man can out-talk Roger Davis! He kept the microphone for an unexpectedly long time, mostly repeating anecdotes that had already been discussed in the film, and continued to break into the Q&A when other actors were talking to tell his own anecdotes. His original prompt was whether he'd used his experiences on DS in any of his other jobs. Marmorstein remembered telling Bette Davis he had worked with Dan Curtis (this would have been during *Return from Witch Mountain*). "You should have heard what she had to say about him. She hated Dan Curtis!" Later, he told a story about having his latest birthday party at a local Mexican restaurant. One of the cakes was decorated with a picture of Barnabas. "They (the restaurant staff) all went crazy when they saw it." Pierson said DS had been aired in Latin and South America and was very popular there during its run.

Jim asked David Selby if he'd ever thought of doing a rap version of "Quentin's Theme." David laughed the idea away.

Lara Parker spoke of how intimidated Curtis made her feel. "I was afraid he'd fire me...I just tried to stay out of his way." Selby countered that he'd never experienced any of Curtis's gruffness as described in the doc.

He had a warm relationship with the director and they saw each other off and on after both had relocated to LA. Selby remembered when Curtis was making the '91 DS, but that he was too busy at the time to get involved in it. A few weeks into filming, however, Curtis called Selby and asked him to come to the studio and talk to Jean Simmons. "She's afraid of me." So, Selby went to Warner Studios, sat next to her, and told her that while Curtis had a lot of passion, "He had the accompaniment to that, which is compassion. I told her she was safe, he wouldn't eat her up." Selby also talked about visiting Curtis at UCLA during his last illness. As they talked over old times, Curtis sighed and said, "I can't believe this (that he'd reached the end of his life)." Finally, seeing the emotional toll on Selby, "He told me, 'Go home.'"

KLS also spent time with Dan about 10 days before his death. "He was in the garden. It was the first day in a long time that he'd been able to go out. And he couldn't talk. One of my DS books was nearby, so I put it in his lap. He couldn't turn the pages, so I turned the pages and I'd point to a photo and tell him a story about the photo. He couldn't talk but he'd nod and I could see he understood what I was saying." She got choked up as she related this. "Dan was a Leo, a lion, but he was a pussycat at heart. I was never intimidated by him." She acknowledged, however, that Curtis was forceful. During the filming of *House of DS*, he became exasperated that the families coming to the cemetery to bury their dead kept interrupting his shots, and stared them down. "Remember when you were reciting the 23rd Psalm?" she asked Jerry. "Dan thought it was taking too long and the assistant director said, 'Oh, God! Now he's editing God!'"

Jim Storm told how Curtis was a huge help to him after he came out to California, immediately casting him in *Trilogy of Terror* and ordering the casting director to "find him an agent, this kid is a great actor" and help him get his union card. "I was forever grateful to him. I owed him a lot." Eventually, Storm was cast on *The Bold and the Beautiful*, right about the same time Curtis was making *Winds of War*. "He called me up and said, 'I've got a part for you; you're on a ship out at sea...' I said, 'OK, that's great, but I just got cast on a soap opera—' 'OK, never mind. Thanks anyway.' And he hung up." He felt a bond with Dan because they shared the same birthday.

Roger Davis said he always got along with Curtis. "You may have seen the video of someone asking, 'Why did Roger Davis keep coming back on the show?' Well, Dan really liked me. He kept bringing me back, even though I sometimes did things my co-stars found offensive." (He later proved them right by telling the story of Don Briscoe's bad trip, apropos of nothing at all). He confessed, "I'd never seen DS when I was offered the chance to do the show. I was told I was going to be playing the love interest, and I thought that sounded boring. In a horror movie, no one pays attention to the love interest. Even my wife of 20 years, who I met at a DS Festival, told me, 'I never watched you. You weren't a vampire.' Well, I did get to be a vampire, once." Dan insisted on bringing Roger back to play Maggie's love interest in *House of DS*. By that point, Davis had gone to California and signed a contract with Universal. Curtis got in touch with the higher-ups and Universal and either talked or bullied them into letting Davis be in his picture.

Pierson opened the floor for questions. One woman asked the cast if they had ever seen the entire show on DVD. "All twelve hundred twenty-five episodes?" KLS asked. The woman told them they were missing out. "The acting is really good."

The next question: "What did you think of the Tim Burton movie?" KLS grimaced "I think we're contractually obligated to not say." Selby either hadn't signed the same contract or hadn't any qualms. "The first five or ten minutes were really good. I remember thinking, 'We're going on a nice, great journey.' After that....Someone will get it right one day." Toward the end, Lara also shared her in-depth opinion. "We all had high hopes for it. We thought it would be the next *Pirates of the Caribbean* and they would just go on making more and more movies. There were so many stories to tell." Instead, "The opening was great, the music was great. Then we saw Barnabas hanging upside-down." The biggest problem was that the movie had no story. "It was just one set-piece after another. There was nothing to hold on to. You didn't wonder what was going to happen next. Our show had so many stories and conflict in every scene. It kept you coming back every day." Like Selby, she believes DS will rise again one day.

Kathryn spoke a little about the music video. She had just met the artist recently at an event and he asked her to play the Elizabeth Stoddard role.

"I thought, 'This will be the perfect time for me to wear the ball gown Joan Bennett gave me before she died.'" She appreciated the video's homage to DS. She also praised Faraj, in the audience, for keeping DS alive by casting the actors in his films. His first movie was made shortly after he turned 20; for his birthday, his parents had offered him auto insurance or a film budget. He picked the movie. "You can imagine what our budget was like. But it's gotten better since then." She and Selby both enjoyed filming with him in Minnesota. "All of us on this stage are committed to keeping DS going," she emphasized. "So, if there's something you want to do, send us your ideas."

Finally, a man in the audience announced he wanted to recognize Lara's birthday a week from now. He went up to the stage to give her a card and a gift (and passed out reusable bags to everyone else on the stage) and invited us all to join in singing her "Happy Birthday."

The night concluded in a haphazard manner. Although autograph tables were set up in the lobby, there were no formal autograph sessions (I suppose because the event had run long). People who had purchased photo ops with the actors earlier in the day were called up again to take pictures now that the composition of available stars had changed. As some attendees filtered out, others rushed the stage to get their own photos and/or autographs. Kathryn announced she and Lara will be back at the Collector's show tomorrow at 11:00.

Apart from the technical difficulties and disorganized dissolution, it was a fun event. A number of people had come dressed in DS costumes, offering a festive atmosphere. The documentary was technically well-made and offered some details that were new to me. I appreciated the breadth of perspectives beyond the usual interviewees. I'm very glad LA got to host the premiere (since we haven't been given the chance to host a Festival in eight years) and I look forward to the general release Jim was talking about.

2024 Dark Shadows Remembrance Weekend (Burbank, CA)

Day 1: Friday, July 5, 2024

It was the best of times; it was the worst of times. The Dark Shadows Remembrance Weekend was the first official DS event in over five years, first convention-like gathering in eight years, and the first convention-like gathering in California in fourteen years. Surely cause for celebration, no? And yet, the purpose of the gathering was to commemorate the passing of a cherished member of the DS family: Lara Parker. While the second day of the gathering was intended to celebrate the life and career if Jonathan Frid, that prospect also had elegiac overtones since Frid has passed away twelve years earlier. Hence, the tone of the event was somewhat confused, though certainly everybody that I saw was enjoying the opportunity to gather again.

At this event, I acted as a volunteer for the first time. I'd been contacted several months earlier by Mary O'Leary, one of the co-organizers, who was looking for locals to assist. (I was then living in Los Angeles but have since relocated). At the time, she envisioned the remembrance gathering as a small event for people in the LA area. In fact, the event sold out with a number of people traveling in from other states over the busy Fourth of July holiday weekend. Tickets were only required for Saturday, the Jonathan Frid celebration. The memorial for Lara on Friday was open to the public. (Her family had held a private memorial gathering in Topanga Canyon earlier in the year. Some of the speakers at Friday's event alluded to this).

While at least fifty people were traipsing around the grounds of Greystone Manor the heat of Friday afternoon, I worked in a small conference room with seven other ladies on an assembly line, stuffing gift bags that would be at each place setting during Saturday's luncheon. Festival banquets always included some kind of door prize: a magnet, a bookmark, a signed photo, and once, memorably, an episode of the show on an old film canister reel. This event featured the most generous gifts. Each bag included a DVD of the documentary *Dark Shows and Beyond: The Jonathan Frid Story*, a copy of *Dark Passages* by KLS (or a nonfiction manual about writing fiction from Pomegranate Press), the photobook *Produced and Directed* by Dan Curtis, a headshot of Lara (various poses from different points in her career were available), a Big Finish audio drama or Marilyn Ross/KLS audiobook, either *My Mother's Autumn* or *Lincoln's Better Angel* by David Selby, a 2015 DS calendar, postcards to advertise Lara's novel *The Salem Branch*, and a QR code for *The Great Nick D*). Periodically, Jim Pearson would pop into the room to check on us, announcing himself by saying, "This is a raid! Everybody, hands up!" We prepared 350 gift bags in about three hours. By the time we finished, we could barely walk around the room because the floor was covered with black bags. I enjoyed being able to help out in this regard and felt that the work went fairly quickly with so many people pitching in.

Later that evening, I also assisted by distributing programs for the memorial at the ballroom entrance. Again, I struggled with the dual nature of the event in trying to decide how to comport myself. Should I smile and greet people as they entered? It's the first DS event in years! Should I be solemn? It's a memorial service! Was I supposed to be a hostess or a funeral director? Further, what should I say to Lara's family when they arrived? "I'm sorry for your loss"? "Thank you for sharing your mother with us"?

As it happened, my interactions were brief as people poured into the ballroom. All I really did was ask, "Would you like a program?" Occasionally, someone tried to show me a QR code and I explained that wasn't necessary tonight. Some people also asked me if certain actors would be signing autographs later. I explained that the autographs would be taking place on Saturday; Friday was reserved for the memorial. Some of Lara's novels were available for sale on Friday, with proceeds going to her favorite charity, Peace4Kids, but otherwise there was no merchandising that night either.

A handful of Lara's relatives did attend the event, including her daughter, whom I had seen onstage acting with her mother in the Collinsport Players' sketch "The Spy Who Bit Me" when I attended my first Festival back in 2000.[122] All I did was shake hands with her and tell her my name. Once everyone in her party had finished parking and assembled, they took their seats in a designated area near the stage. None of the family members spoke at the memorial, but some of the speakers did address the family when sharing an anecdote.

The memorial opened with a slideshow of photos from Lara's time on DS set to "Ode to Angelique." Next came a short reel of clips from her film and TV work, including *Save the Tiger*, *The Night Stalker*: "The Trevi Collection," *Race with the Devil, Washington Behind Closed Doors, Foxfire Light, Remington Steele,* and several other programs I didn't recognize. After the videos, a series of speakers, including original *Dark Shadows* actors and several fans who had been close to Lara, took turns at the podium to share their memories and experiences with her.

Jim Pierson spoke first, offering a description that many would echo of a Lara who was beautiful inside and out, fiercely curious, wickedly funny, and kind. He noted her varied interests in art, animals, nature, acting, writing, and teaching, and said that he was proud of assisting her in her research for her novels. "Lara wanted everything in her books to be as accurate as possible. For *The Salem Branch*, she insisted on going up to Boston in the winter when it was freezing cold and attending a Saturday night witches' coven. They were good witches, so everything was aboveboard."

Then Jim Pierson introduced Jim Storm, who launched the memorial with a musical number called "Red Light, Green Light," a song that Lara liked. Storm described it as a song about children in turn of the century Chicago singing to notify hookers when the police were coming. James described how he had been practicing the three-finger picking guitar playing technique one day when "a beautiful woman in an evening gown, hair piled high, and the most compelling eyes" approached him and told him, "I'm from the South. I like that type of music: country, folk." She introduced herself as Lara Parker and talked to him about his technique and his music. (I wasn't clear if "Red Light, Green Light" was the song he'd been practicing when they met or if it was merely a song in the same style). Later, they ended up working together on DS. James said Lara was always inquisitive about everything, but it was authentic. He described her as a beautiful, kind woman and a good friend whom he'd miss very much.

Next up was Roy Isbell, a long-time fan who'd been close to Lara Parker. He had been fascinated by her portrayal of Angelique on DS and was thrilled to see her picture appearing on the covers of no less than three magazines soon after she joined the show. In later years, he came to know Lara after he critiqued something she had written (he didn't specify what it was). Lara read his review and contacted him to ask if he would take a look at something she was writing. It turned out to be the manuscript for *Angelique's Descent*. "I don't know why she contacted me. I was just a fan, but something I said in my review must have seemed cogent to her." He said that Lara struggled to understand Barnabas's motivation and get into his head. "She wanted me to give her more feedback on the plot, characters, and theme, but I was more focused on fixing the grammatical errors and typos. When a reader sees something like that, it takes them out of the story." He said that Lara's favorite of her books was *The Salem Branch* because it turned out. the closest to how she had imagined. Roy said he and Lara had many long, deep conversations about a variety of topics. He also said she had a wonderful sense of humor. "I would set her up as a straight man and she would come back with amazing, wickedly funny comebacks." He wrapped up his talk by discussing a personal experience, a medical episode that caused him to have an out of body experience. "It felt like it went on for half an hour, but it was only fifteen minutes. I could look down and see the doctors working on me. A voice told me that my family members would be joining me in about 90 seconds, but the doctors woke me up before that happened." The experience was profound, and when he'd discussed it with Lara, "she asked 'Did it feel real?' I said 'No, it felt more real than this *(i.e.,* real life). This feels syrupy. Everything moves more slowly. I have no doubt that Lara is in a better place now because I've been there. I've seen it."

Afterward, Kathryn Leigh Scott spoke. She said that one of the last times she had seen Lara in person was for a series of interviews. (I understand the mutual interviews will appear in the second volume of *Daytime Gothic* due out later this year.) "Stuart Manning suggested that Lara and I each interview each other. It was our opportunity to ask each other anything. 'Anything?' Lara asked. 'Like, if you were a tree, what kind of tree would you be?' Kathryn picked silver birch; Lara chose native oak. "It was also an opportunity to explore in depth a 56 year long friendship. We recorded the interviews, of course. There's no way that two writers and actors will interview each other and *not* record it. I went over to Lara's house in Topanga Canyon on two Sundays. She always greeted me eagerly at the door and tried to get me to stay for supper. She'd want to talk long into the night about everything. Two women couldn't be more different, and yet we were such good friends." Kathryn remembered meeting Lara in November of 1967 when they shot the first scene of Josette and her ladies' maid Angelique "wearing 18th century frocks and babbling in incomprehensible French. It was Lara's contention, and I disagreed, that our first encounter on the show set the tone of our friendship. I was the rich girl and she was my maid, when actually it was the opposite. I told Lara 'You were the debutante. You went to Vassar.' With Jane Fonda as her roommate!" Lara had a deep passion for learning about everything. It sounded like she had a deep passion for life. "On that last Sunday, as I was leaving, she gave me a tight hug and said 'Aren't we lucky? We get to write and act. That's what we've always wanted to do. I've had a wonderful life. I don't want to leave, but if I do have to leave, I have no complaints. I've had a wonderful life. I have a wonderful family.' Family meant everything to Lara." Kathryn expressed how greatly she missed her dear friend.

Next, Lee Rosenbloom, a fan whom I recognized as having assisted Lara at various Festivals, spoke. He had been fascinated by her portrayal of Angelique when he watched the series as a youngster. Once the series started to air on PBS, Lee recorded the episodes on his Betamax. Eventually, he learned about the Shadowcons (precursors to DS Festivals) and contacted the person in charge, a woman named Barbara. (I'm not familiar with her). "She asked me if I could make a bloopers reel for the show. That hadn't been done before. She said, 'If you do it, I'll introduce you to Lara Parker.' I needed to use two Betamax machines but I made the blooper reel, and I focused a lot of it on Lara. I watched her expression as it played and she was laughing. She seemed to enjoy it." They became friends from that point and spent a lot of time together during the conventions.

Lee said spending that time with Lara was the highlight of the Festivals and that he might not have gone to so many had it not been for her. "She would ask me, 'Don't you want to visit with your friends?' and I'd say 'No.'" At the 1997 Festival at the Marriott Marquis in New York, a convention that had record attendance and about which I've heard friends speak (the Costume Gala was over two hours long because of the number of participants), Lara began to feel uncomfortable because of the number of people pressing around her. "Jim Pierson noticed this and he asked me to sit with Lara. He said, 'Your job is to take care of her,' and that's what I did for the next 41 years."

His devotion to Lara even surpassed concern for his own health. "At the 2001 Festival at the World Trade Center, I went into the city to get some pizza for dinner, only I ended up having salmon instead. I got food poisoning from the salmon. Sitting at Lara's table in the autograph line, I couldn't stop shivering. On my break, I went into a department store [inside the hotel] and bought the biggest, puffiest jacket I could find to wear. When Lara realized why I was wearing it, she grew concerned and asked, 'Why don't you go to your room and lie down?' but I didn't want to leave her. Afterward, we joked about it."

Lee recalled that when he would phone Lara, she'd answer with her laugh. She could always tell it was him by looking at the caller ID because he was the only person she knew with that area code. Like others before him, Lee cited her great sense of humor and how much he misses Lara.

Krista Knicker, another friend of Lara's, talked about her first reaction to seeing Lara as Angelique when she was a small child. "She took my breath away with her stunning beauty. She became such an inspiration to me as a woman. Years later, I told her this and Lara said, 'But I don't understand how. You're not an actress.' I had been a shy, introverted child, too afraid even to raise my hand in class. Seeing her [as an assertive woman] inspired me to join the drama club and take public speaking classes that prepared me for a career in politics and finance." Krista was further inspired by seeing Lara adopt a second career as a writer in late adulthood. She revealed that Lara had plans for another book unrelated to DS about the experience of being a woman in the entertainment industry and dealing with sexism and sexual harassment. She envisioned it as a book of fiction, a series of stories about women encountering various adverse such experiences. "Lara told me she'd even chosen a photo for the cover. She had so many plans for the book, it wasn't to be. She ran out of time." It sounds like it would have been a fascinating work to read. Perhaps somewhere in parallel time, Lara is on tour for it now.

Next, Alexis Knicker read a poem from *Bugs and Other Critters I Have Known*, a beloved book from her childhood. The poetry was written by Lara's mother, illustrated by her aunt, and published by Lara herself as a tribute to her mother through a small press Lara started specifically for the purpose of issuing this book. The poem Alexis chose, called "The Mayfly" was about the first and last day of the titular creature's life and contrasted her experiences with that of an industrious ant politician and a grumpy stink bug. It was a beautifully written poem, inspiring, and well-suited to a celebration of life, and Alexis read it well, avoiding the tendency to slip into sing-song rhymes as many people who recite poetry do.

Ansel Faraj, director of the independent films *Loon Lake* and *The Great Nick D,* talked about his experiences directing and getting to know Lara as a young fan. He first watched *Night of Dark Shadows* as a six-year-old child. "I saw Lara Parker as Angelique in diaphanous blue dress floating down the hallway and it terrified me. I was sure that I would see her floating down the hallway at night for real. And then, fourteen years later, Lara Parker really was walking down my hallway to sign my poster of *Night of Dark Shadows*."

As an ambitious 20-year-old, Ansel made his own version of Fritz Lang's Expressionist crime film *Doctor Mabuse* with Jerry Lacy in the title role and Kathryn Leigh Scott as one of a pair of witchy sisters. Kathryn introduced him to Lara as he was hoping to include her in the cast, too. "She never said yes and she never said no. She just looked at me with those luminous eyes and asked, 'Do you have lights?' I said, 'Yes, we have plenty of lights.' That night when I went home, I ran to my parents and said, 'Lights! We have to get lights!'"

Of course, Lara did end up joining the production as Madame Carrozza (though the photo in the program credited her as Madame Von Harbou), and her English teacher self, as well as her actor self, emerged in full force. "She critiqued the grammar and marked up the script, as she should." One day during filming, Kathryn, who had finished shooting a scene, was in another room while Ansel was filming Lara. "She grilled me about directing and writing, asking question after question. When we finally went out, Katherine asked, 'How did it go?' And Lara said, 'Ohh, he made me do take after take after take!'" which of course wasn't true. Lara took a great interest in the script and in her character. In one scene, she was supposed to spread out some tarot cards. "Lara asked, 'How do you want me to do it? There are different ways to arrange the cards.'" He also recalled a scene with Jerry Lacy when she had used her signature Angelique laugh. "Jerry looked up at her and said, 'Boy, you can turn that on like a faucet!'"

Ansel marveled at his unlikely good fortune as a young fan becoming friends with the actors. "I thought it would be fun to watch *Night of Dark Shadows* with Lara so I convinced Darren Gross to come over to her house in Topanga and bring his footage (scenes cut from the film that Darren has been working diligently to restore). We watched it in Lara's bedroom. She told me, 'Here, sit on my bed'! We asked her questions about how they did certain effects. She said, 'I have no idea. I wasn't paying attention.'" She was also evidently surprised by the plot of the film. "She said, ' I was married to Chris?!'"

He discussed filming a short called "The Job Interview," a very funny and charming little film that was previously shown at the 2016 Festival banquet. John Karlen, Chris Pennock, and Lara were part of the shoot. When the cameras weren't rolling, they did quite a bit of cutting up. "John would start it and then Lara would finish it. She was so funny. She wasn't like Angelique at all." He recalled a time at the Festival, when after several hours of signing autographs, "She turned to me and said, 'I'm exhausted; take me to bed.' I told her, 'You might want to rethink that.' She looked at me for a moment and said, 'Hmm.' Lara's final film appearance was in Ansel's latest release, *The Great Nick D.* "Lara was very frail at the time, but acting rejuvenated her. She just blossomed with inspiration once the cameras were rolling. But she still critiqued the script and asked (lead actor) Nathan Wilson, 'What's the through line?' At least we had plenty of lights." Ansel spoke of how all the actors and the fans are like a big family. "They've always been part of a family, ever since the show was on. That's why this fandom has endured so long, because we're a family."

Lisa Richards spoke briefly about how wonderful it was to see all the people whom Lara had inspired but she didn't share any of their personal interactions.

When David Selby took the stage, he read one of his poems called "Angelique," a tribute to Lara's physical beauty. It seemed to me that he was writing in Quentin's voice, lamenting a relationship that never was and unrequited admiration. The poem included the refrain: "Your beauty like a star/I loved you from afar/It never seemed naughty/Admiring your perfect body/The God's above did sigh/Oh my, Oh my/And so did I/So did I." Personally, I thought it was an unusual choice to focus so on Lara's physical attributes.

Janet Meehan, a fan artist who, among other fine works, illustrated scenes from *Angelique's Descent* and *The Salem Branch* (these illustrations were auctioned for charity the following day, and they were impressive), started by asking for a moment of silence for both Lara and Marcy Robin, a fixture at Festivals who had passed away just a couple of months after Lara. She then described how, as a child, she had fallen in love with a weird daytime soap opera. "No, not *Dark Shadows*, the one that came on before it." But when that show eventually went off the air, she started watching DS and decided that it was all right. It took some time to grow on her because the early episodes moved a bit slowly. When Lara joined the series, it became more interesting. Janet said that she had written to Lara to praise her performances and Lara would reply demurely, denying she was a celebrity. "It frustrated me. She was such a marvelous talent." After Lara wrote *Angelique's Descent,* Janet wrote a review of the book to which Lara replied enthusiastically and "more quickly than I'd ever heard from her before. She wrote back within one week. 'You *got it*. I feel so validated.' Having that validation was very important to Lara." Janet ended by saying, "Spirit doesn't die. Lara is still with us. Say a prayer for her if you want. She'll hear it."

Finally, Roger Davis took the stage in what was the most surprising and emotional speech of the evening. He began by saying that Lamar (he was the only person that evening who called Lara by her given name) was the coolest, sexiest girl he ever knew. Later, he emphasized that remark by reminding us that he had once been married to Jaclyn Smith. He said he could relate to David Selby's poem about admiring Lara. As he spoke, he got choked up and frequently had to pause. I hadn't seen Roger like this before.

However, he soon switched to more familiar form by speaking about his real estate ventures. He told how he had invested all of his savings in developing an apartment complex and hotel in his hometown of Louisville,

KY. He spent over a year trying to get an investor to close the deal. When the investor finally agreed, he told Roger, "There's good news and bad news. The good news is we're going to do this deal. The bad news is we're going to do this deal. This hotel should be at 5th and 59th streets in New York. It'll do all right around the Derby, but the rest of the year it will be empty. Within five years, you'll be begging me to take it off your hands." Roger confirmed that almost five years to the day after that meeting, he was indeed begging the investor to buy the hotel from him.

Having lost all of his money in the venture, Roger returned to Santa Monica feeling adrift and unsure of what to do next. The first person he called when he came back was Lara. "She said, 'Come stay with me and Jim (Hawkins).' So, I moved in with them, into their home in Topanga Canyon. She made a safe space for me. a nest where I could get my thoughts in order and decide what to do next. I've always been grateful to her and to Jim for doing that for me." He gestured to the audience to where Lara's widowed husband was sitting. Roger stressed how warm and generous Lara was in contrast to the villains she so often played on DS.

James Storm concluded the memorial by leading the audience in a singalong of "Will The Circle be Unbroken," a song he's also performed in honor of Jonathan Frid at past Festivals. While he played, another sideshow of Lara photos from her childhood through adulthood ran in the background. When the song ended, the audience dispersed for a scheduled break before the screening of *Night of Dark Shadows*. I had hoped this might include some of Lara's cut scenes, but since there was nothing in the program or said by the speakers to indicate such was the case, I opted not to watch the movie.

Instead, I lounged in the lobby and chatted with friends, some of whom I hadn't seen in years—in some cases, not since the last Festival, or even the last California Festival held in the same hotel in 2010. Again, the atmosphere was odd. On the one hand, we were delighted to be back together again, but on the other, we were cognizant of the solemn reason for why we'd been brought back together. I came away from the event feeling that I knew more about Lara, the person off-camera, than I had before. She sounds like a fascinating lady and a wonderful friend. I'm happy for everyone who had the chance to get to know the woman behind Angelique's beautiful face and bewitching eyes.

Day 2: Saturday, July 6, 2024

The second day looked and felt more like a Festival. For me, it started with a return to the storage room to put the finishing touches on the gift bags and transport them to the banquet room to place them on all the chairs. A couple of friends who weren't even scheduled to work kindly volunteered their time and their strength to help us move the heavy luggage carts and the boxes of bags and memorabilia that would be up for sale in the day's auctions. We started at 8:00 and finished shortly before the posted time of 10:00 for when activities would begin.

KLS and James Storm each had tables in the lobby for selling their respective books and photographs and signing some preliminary autographs before the ballroom doors opened for the luncheon. MPI also had a table of merchandise for sale that included Big Finish audio dramas, reprints of Marilyn Ross's novels, Barnabas rings, and sweatshirts with the DS logo. One fan had brought in a replica of Quentin's gramophone and fans posed for photos with it. Later, during the actual autograph session, the gramophone was placed at David's table.

Tickets for the luncheon started to be distributed a little bit after 11:00 instead of at 10:30. Despite long lines of attendees that coiled outside the ballroom and around the tables of the hotel's patio restaurant, everyone was seated and the program was ready to start shortly before noon. Again, the volunteers had prepared 350 gift bags, and despite being told of about a dozen cancellations, it looked to me like every table had full seating.

I had the good fortune to share Table 4 with Valerie and Jim Storm, Danielle "Penny Dreadful: Galehrter, John Logan, two old friends, Amy and Michael, and two new friends, Flo and Ed. I had listened to Logan's interview on *Terror at Collinwood* and was astonished to hear he'd watched DS as a child in San Pedro, CA, where I spent my own early years. San Pedro (pronounced "Pee-dro") is a fly-speck coastal town in Southern California[123] and obscure enough that when I hear somebody else mention it, it's noteworthy. Upon further discussion, we discovered we had also attended the same elementary school, albeit a few years apart. What a neat coincidence!

Attendees had two options for the banquet meal: chicken with mashed potatoes and carrots or risotto with mashed potatoes and asparagus. Dessert was a tasty, very rich chocolate tart or cheesecake. The meal was filling and the servers were efficient—perhaps too efficient. A couple of people at our table weren't seated until after the salad course had already been delivered and didn't get theirs. Instead, they went straight to the main entree.

Jim Pierson briefly opened the event with another slideshow, this one without music, to highlight the actors and prominent fans whom we've lost in recent years. First, he showed a picture of a young Marcy Robin and Ann Wilson (Festival founders and long-time volunteers) clowning around, with Ann menacing Marcy with a Barnabas cane. He then showed a still from *Night of Dark Shadows* of Chris Pennock and Thayer David, followed by individual pictures of Robert Cobert, Robert Rodan, Diana Millay, Denise Nickerson, and John Karlen.

Next, Jim announced the luncheon raffle. In addition to receiving a gift bag containing fabulous merchandise, one person at each table had the chance to take home the table centerpiece, a special bottle of wine dressed in a Dracula cape donated by Vampire Vineyards (Vampire Vineyards also donated the T-shirts worn by the Festival volunteers). The winner had a card taped under their seat. This set off a flurry of people twisting and fumbling under their chairs in search of the golden ticket. Some mistakenly tore off the chair manufacturer's label; I later saw several labels scattered over the floor. When the excitement subsided, Pierson offered the first auction items for sale.

The morning's auction consisted of various items that had belonged to Lara. Proceeds were to benefit Peace4Kids. A second auction much later in the afternoon would consist of more traditional DS collectibles and books as well as some items that had belonged to Dan Curtis. Lara's auction included Advance Reader Copies (ARCs) of some of her books, the first draft manuscript of *The Salem Branch* with editorial notes written in the margins, copies of *Angelique's Descent* that Lara had personalized to each of Jonathan Frid and to her father (sadly, Jonathan died before he received his copy), a photo album of Lara assembled by the president of her fan club, a script from a TV show she had made with George Peppard (*Doctors Hospital*), and promotional materials from her book tours. That auction went quickly. Many items were grouped together in lots instead of being parceled out one at a time, which is what happened in the afternoon auction. To my surprise, the lots went for only $200.00 or less. I had thought that the uniqueness of the items having belonged to Lara personally would add value to them, but as one friend pointed out, the fact that the auction would only accept payment via cash or check might have deterred many people who have become accustomed to paying electronically.

The end of the auction signaled the beginning of the celebration of Jonathan Frid's life and career. This day was billed as the 100th anniversary of Jonathan's birth, although he was actually born in December. (His birth year was 1924). Mary O'Leary welcomed us to the event and gave us a brief overview of Jonathan's career. At one time, he embarked on a program to teach English teachers how to present Shakespeare in the classroom. A former alum of that program, a woman named Cindy, was at the banquet. Mary invited her to stand, and Cindy waved to everyone. It would have been nice to have her speak at the event, too. She would have been able to share an original perspective about Jonathan.

Kathryn took the stage first and spoke about the first time she met Jonathan when he came to the studio for hair and makeup tests. His arrival drew little attention at the time, probably, she joked, because the refreshments for the day had just been delivered. She remembered him appearing fully formed as Barnabas, posing in costume with his cape, cane, and styled bangs. He had a regal presence. She said her favorite scene with Jonathan was when Maggie meets Barnabas as he arrives at the diner when she's locking up. Kathryn said she felt like they had a lot of chemistry in that scene and thought the writers must have noticed, because they later cast her as Josette, Barnabas's eternal love interest. She said that Jonathan was the linchpin of the series. Even though it was an ensemble show, when he joined the cast, it felt as though he became the captain, guiding them along. "Jonathan saved our show. Because of him, we went from the brink of cancellation to having 20 million viewers. More than that, Jonathan affirmed our position as the show that celebrated the Other, the outcast, the outsider." Children who ran home from school to watch DS put aside whatever had happened during the day or in the classroom to sit briefly in the safety of Collinwood where they could watch monsters striving for acceptance. Kids who didn't feel like they fit in could relate to Barnabas. "Many people don't just tell me that they ran home from school to watch, they say that DS got them through their childhood." She cited a number of people then in attendance who had gone on to do creative work in television or film and had cited DS as a source of inspiration.

Next, Kathryn introduced the video interviews. Promotional materials for the event had teased a video interview with a surprise guest. Speculation focused on either David Henesy or Alexander Moltke. Indeed, it was Henesy, who has also worked with the cast in a YouTube dramatic reading of *A Christmas Carol*. Kathryn also said that she is still in touch with Alexandra, who sends her best wishes, and with Nancy Barrett, who was devastated that she wasn't able to attend the event as originally planned.

David greeted Kathryn as "Katie" because, "That's what I used to call you." "You still can," she encouraged him. Asked about his memories of Jonathan, David recalled that the show didn't feature any supernatural elements originally, but instead was a Gothic series about the tormented and dysfunctional Collins family. "When we first heard there was a going to be a vampire on the series, we said, 'Ohh OK, that works. This is a quirky family. He'll fit right in.' He recalled Jonathan as an elegant man with a formal presence and a dry sense of humor. His most vivid memories were of Jonathan in makeup, walking around with tissues stuffed under the collar of his shirt. He also spoke generally of his time on DS, how everyone always treated him like an adult ("which caused problems for me later in life"), and what the studio was like: the metal folding chairs that served as the coffin, the old coffee machine, and the old Xerox machine. "I wonder if David Selby ever paid ABC back for all the copies of his dissertation that he made on that machine." As David and Kathryn stared into the camera, scolding, Selby, who was seated at the table next to mine, doubled over laughing. The interview was brief and looked like it had been edited, possibly because the connection was choppy.[124] It was nice of Henesy to join us in spirit.

Kathryn also played two other videos, from Marie Wallace and Donna Wandrey, respectively. I was especially happy to see Marie, as she's long been a favorite of mine. She looked radiant on the screen and spoke with warmth and verve about Jonathan. She first met him as Eve, a woman that Julia created out of old bones from the family mausoleum, but though she interacted with Jonathan during the series, she wasn't particularly close to him. After two years and three roles, her time on the show ended. "I thought, 'Well, that was fun, but it's over now.' But it wasn't. A few years later, the Dark Shadows Festivals began, and that's when I really got to know Jonathan." Frid would bring dramatic material to perform at the conventions, and Marie enjoyed watching his shows. After one such performance, Jonathan and a producer named George Moore invited her out for dinner and pitched to her the prospect of appearing as Eleanor of Aquitaine in a production of *The Lion in Winter* at Georgia College. Marie eagerly agreed, anticipating that Jonathan would play her King Henry. But no, Jonathan was going to direct. "I don't know if you know this, but he got a degree in directing from Yale. However, he had never directed anything before." Marie and Jonathan stayed at the Governor's Mansion in Milledgeville on the top floor. While the students were in class during the day, he rehearsed scenes with her. Marie shared with us Jonathan's favorite of Eleanor's monologues (I've taken the text from imdb.com), reciting it for us with feeling:

> *Of course he has a knife, he always has a knife, we all have knives! It's 1183 and we're barbarians! How clear we make it. Oh, my piglets, we are the origins of war: not history's forces, nor the times, nor justice, nor the lack of it, nor causes, nor religions, nor ideas, nor kinds of government, nor any other thing. We are the killers. We breed wars. We carry it like syphilis inside. Dead bodies rot in field and stream because the living ones are rotten. For the love of God, can't we love one another just a little - that's how peace begins. We have so much to love each other for. We have such possibilities, my children. We could change the world.*

"I wondered why he loved that monologue so much, and then I realize it's because it's a speech about love. Jonathan was all about love. He loved all of you. As you go about your day, think about that love and your love for him, and be kind to one another." I thought that was an uplifting note and a lovely way to honor Jonathan's spirit and memory.

A taped piece from Donna Wandrey followed. She also emphasized Jonathan's warmth and kindness. Donna recalled how anxious she'd been as a young actress joining the cast of long-running principles. "Every day, one of the directors—whom I won't name[125]—would make a comment to me that just tore me down. Jonathan noticed this, and one day he called me to his dressing room. I was panicking. I thought, 'Oh no! The director hates me, and now the star does too.' But Jonathan told me, 'Don't pay any attention to him.' I said, 'I have to pay attention to the director.' 'Yes, pay attention to where he tells you to go, how many steps he tells you to take, when he wants you to enter, but as for the rest of it, forget it. As soon as someone new joins the cast, he'll start picking on him or her and he'll leave you alone.'" And indeed, that's what happened. Virginia Vestoff, who was then starring in *1776*, became the target of the director's aspersions. "Virginia didn't let anyone push her around. I learned a lot from her and from Jonathan."

Donna also shared tragicomic memories of a public appearance she and Jonathan had made. "I had never been on tour before. I had never flown first class before. To Minneapolis. For the Auto Show. Where the other guests were Tiny Tim, Miss Vicki, and Arnold the Pig. Kathryn was kind enough to make me a jumpsuit covered with sequins. I thought I would look so sharp. I ended up sitting on the hood of a car as it drove in circles again and again, all day. Finally, I stopped and waited for Jonathan's line to finish. They ended up cutting Jonathan's line because the line for Arnold the Pig was longer. Then, Tiny Tim and Miss Vicki invited us out to eat. That's what we called them: Tiny Tim and Miss Vicky. They were the most unusual people I had ever met. They acted like they were holding court. They sat at table above us; Jonathan and I sat on cushions on the floor. Jonathan managed to extricate us from that dinner fairly quickly with his wit and good humor and got us back to the studio in one piece." Donna's wry facial expressions and euphemistic descriptions made the anecdote especially amusing. She said the most important lesson she learned from Jonathan was kindness. It's a lesson she's carried with her always. Donna closed by saying, "I'm sure Jonathan is looking down on us now, along with. Grayson, Thayer, Lara, and so many others".

We had one more video greeting to watch, this time from the Director of the Lawrence and Lee Theatre Research Institute in Columbus, OH. Mary explained that she had arranged to donate all of Jonathan's paper to the Institute. In her greeting, the Director explained that she herself had been a fan who ran home from school to watch Jonathan. She discussed the history of the school, which is named after the authors of *Auntie Mame* and *Inherit the Wind* (one of my favorite movies, though I've yet to see the play), while stock footage of the campus played in the background. The Research Institute is open to the public. She invited everyone to come to Columbus to peruse John's papers. No date was given as to when they might be become available. Mary explained that she's still in the process of putting the collection together for transfer.

The next person invited to speak was James Storm. He seems surprised to be called up, though he was listed in the program. He certainly had delightful memories to share. Jim spoke of the first time he saw Jonathan when he attended a Shakespeare Festival to see Jon Voight perform in *The Tempest*. The actor who really impressed him, however, was the one who played Caliban. "I saw this creature moving from upstage left across the stage. It was such a powerful transformation. He was able to be so sympathetic. I'd never seen the role performed that way before. Years later, when I walked onto the set of DS, I saw Jonathan and thought, 'Ah, it's him! Caliban!'" Storm also talked about his last meeting with Jonathan during Fred's final Festival. "I'd just finished singing and had moved off-stage, down the stairs, and into the hallway. I saw Jonathan approaching with some other people. He looked up at me and said, 'Oh, it's Jimmy Storm!' Right away, he picked up the last conversation we'd had when we bumped into each other in New York on 4th Street and Lexington. He asked, 'How is Jonathan?'—my oldest son, who had just been born at that time. He remembered my son's name, my wife's name, and he was fully alert." Jim was clearly touched at being so well-remembered.

Lisa Richards spoke next, acknowledged that she hadn't interacted very much with Jonathan. "I was in love with the werewolf, Chris. Then he went back to Tennessee, and I fell in love with Chris Pennock. I was his lab assistant. Then, Dan invited me to join the cast of *House of Dark Shadows*. I was thrilled—until I saw the script. I died on the first page! Still, I did my best to get into the Method. I thought about being dead and how it would feel to die. The make-up man painted some marks on my neck. I screamed and then lay down in the driveway and died. You could say it was love at first bite between me and Jonathan."

Rounding out the cast, Roger Davis spoke. He claimed not to have interacted much with Jonathan either, though they certainly did share many scenes. "I mostly saw him in hair and makeup. Vinnie Loscalzo was always trimming his bangs." He pointed to Kathryn in the audience. "Didn't you take some of his hair once?[126] Of course, we worked together in *House of Dark Shadows*. What was I doing in that movie? I hadn't been on the show in years. At the time, I was under contract to Universal for a pilot with Pete Duel, which later became the series *Alias, Smith and Jones*, but Dan lured me back. He told me, 'You'll be the hero who destroys the vampire. You'll have a great romance with Kathryn.' But it was a bait and switch. Most of the romance got cut out of the movie. It didn't advance the plot."

The scene he most remembered was Jeff's climactic confrontation with Barnabas. "The atmosphere was very thick that day. Some people will tell you that atmosphere doesn't matter, but that isn't true. I picked up the crossbow, aimed it at him, and then he turned." Roger pointed his finger onto the audience and bellowed, "Claaark!" in an effort to emulate Frid, though, he confessed that his voice wasn't as powerful. "He locked eyes with me, and then—" Roger motioned with his hand, as though directing somebody to move down. "—he started guiding me. I followed him all the way down the stairs. He said, 'Every wedding must have a witness, and you shall witness this one.' Then, we took a short break to set up the prosthetics, the fake blood for the staking scene."

"Dan Curtis took me aside. He said, 'When you hit Jonathan, I want you to give it all you've got.' I said, 'No, you can't do that to Jonathan.' But

Dan ordered me, 'Just do it.' It's very dangerous to give me permission [to push someone around]. You remember what happened when I pushed Joan Bennett [during a scene in 1897]. She fell over, and a little flask rolled out of her pocket. She was feeling around onstage for the flask. She never spoke to me again after that. Dan yelled, 'Action!' I stepped forward and punched my fist into Jonathan's back as hard as I could. I had to push with all my might. Jonathan was a big guy. He wasn't tall, but he was very broad. He arched his back, and all the blood spurted everywhere. We did it all in one take. As an actor, you strive for that one perfect take. It doesn't happen very often, but that time it did. When the scene was finished, Jonathan turned to me slowly." Roger adopted a hulking stance, made a steely expression with his lips twitching into a snarl, and spoke slowly and menacingly. "He said, 'You really pushed me hard and it hurt.' I was panicking, expecting him to punch me out. Then he said, 'Thank you.'" To my surprise, Pierson announced *HoDS* would screen later that night; it wasn't listed in the program.

The highlight of the tribute to Jonathan was brought to us by the combined forces of Mary O'Leary and David Selby. Instead of reminiscing about his friendship with Jonathan, David read selections from Jonathan's personal letters to his mother back in Hamilton, Ontario. "Telephone calls were expensive in those days," Mary reminded us, "so Jonathan wrote letters. He was a wonderful, witty writer. We've really lost the art of letter writing." She explained that she had edited down the letters to the sections that focused primarily on DS. Mary further explained that David would be reading the letters from a music stand because that was how Jonathan read his scripts when he did his one-man shows. She indicated the music stand onstage and told us it had once belonged to Robert Cobert. We were also told that Jonathan had a deep sense of gratitude to his parents for supporting him emotionally and financially in his drive to become an actor. Sadly, his father passed away in September of 1966, so he never got to see Jonathan's rise to fame as Barnabas. The letters to his mother documented the character's growth, both in art and in popularity, as well as Jonathan's own excitement and insecurity about being able to maintain the momentum of the character, and above all, to deliver truly good performances. Jonathan was indeed a brilliant letter writer, and David's readings were amusing and entertaining. I can only do my best to paraphrase the content.

Jonathan's first letter was about successfully completing his first paid television appearance. His character recited three pages of Old Testament scripture. Jonathan confessed that memorizing the lines was a challenge and said he would decide whether doing television work was a good thing or not after he saw how the broadcast turned out. Another early letter foreshadowed DS when Jonathan described some recent dental work. "I now have a pair of very white, very even, temporary fangs." He wasn't entirely happy with them, as the short-term model wasn't a good fit, and expressed his hope that the permanent product would be more comfortable.

In early 1967, he wrote about completing the screen test for his new role as a vampire member of a rich family with a lineage long enough to include a vampiric ancestor. Jonathan explained that Barnabas's true origins and motives would become apparent only with time. He discussed the design of his character. "I've been fitted for two Mod, six-button suits from Ohrbach's and they're making an Inverness cape for me. I'm supposed to look vaguely Edwardian or Regency. I shall carry a furled umbrella instead of a cane because that would draw too much attention." Jonathan complained about the challenge of crossing the stage and trying to hit his mark, which was about the size of a cigarette butt, without looking at the ground to see where the mark was. He added that he had investigated whether any ABC affiliates near Hamilton, ON carried the show so his mother might be able to watch it. "It's playing in Rochester and Cleveland, but not in Buffalo."

Jonathan wrote about watching his first episode air. He was nervous about seeing how his performance had turned out and had hoped to be able to absorb it in private. His housekeeper usually left by noon, but that day she lingered. "'You're on in ten minutes,' she reminded me, proving that she knew exactly what was going on. I told her, 'All right, you can stay, but sit in the back and please don't say anything.'" His housekeeper proved to be an asset because she fielded a number of congratulatory calls for Jonathan that came in during the viewing. Despite this acclaim, Frid wasn't entirely satisfied with his work.

Another letter described a fire at the studio during taping. (I knew the set had caught fire during the Phoenix storyline, but wasn't aware that it happened multiple times). "I could see smoke rising over the shoulder of my lady love and flames reflected in the glass. The fire appeared to be near the main exit. I heard a loud clattering and commotion as people attempted to put the fire out, but the person in the control booth didn't yell to us to cut. I continued with my scene, but I'm afraid I fumbled my dialogue because I was distracted by thinking of other ways to exit the studio. I was not about to die in service of DS. Unfortunately, they decided to keep that take instead of reshooting it. The budget really is that tight."

More mishaps occurred in a later episode where Barnabas menaced his sleeping victim-to-be, showing his fangs and revealing his vampirism for the first time. During the dress rehearsal, an assistant had passed him his fake fangs as he entered, and Jonathan easily snapped them into place. However, when it came time to film the actual episode, the fangs simply would not fit. Jonathan described the nerve-wracking process of trying to get the fangs into place in time to deliver his sinister smile. The script required that he pause for the camera to show a telltale close-up of his distinctive wolf's head walking stick (that furled umbrella went by the wayside), and Jonathan tried to strategically stall just long enough to get his fangs in order. Nothing worked. Finally, Jonathan confessed he shoved them in the back of his mouth and bared his own canines as fiercely as he could.

Jonathan also described his growing popularity, from "I'm being told I've received fan mail" to "The PR man tells me that I've received more fan mail than anyone else in the cast, including Joan Bennett. Some of the letters are of a sexual nature. The most passionate ones are written by married women." And finally, "My new assistant has come up with a brilliant strategy. She says we should pull out the letters written by married women and not respond to them because they were probably written behind their husbands' backs."

In his letters, Jonathan frequently cited the unslacking pace and the frequency with which Barnabas appeared in the episodes. He remarked that he at first worried that the writers would pull back on his part. "Now I'm irritated that they're not." His missives described his dedication to developing Barnabas's character and to giving his best possible performance.

He was especially proud of his work on a series of episodes set to air from July 17th to the 21st, in which Barnabas throws a costume party for his family. The second episode of the costume party dealing with the results of the seance, which would air July 24th, was so worthwhile to Frid that he urged his mother to come to Rochester and stay in a hotel so she could watch it. He provided detailed instructions about how to contact the ABC affiliate in Rochester to confirm which episode would be airing on that day and if it would be the same episode that aired in NYC. He also advised her to contact the hotel to confirm that it could get a clear broadcast. "There's no point in making the trip if you can't see the show."

Of course, playing a popular character didn't hurt. Another letter reported, "The director's 13-year-old daughter has a crush on Barnabas. Linda Curtis visited the studio today and followed me around all day. Maybe I should ask for a raise. . ."

Yet, Frid also presented as a realist, uncertain of how long his good fortune could last. "I was told we are soon going to begin a sequence in which the actors will play ancestral members of the family. This will explore the origins of how Barnabas became a vampire. That should give me at least four or five more weeks of work. We'll see what the ratings are like." Jonathan seemed ambivalent about the 1795 flashback once it began. "Now that the focus is on Barnabas as a love interest, I look ridiculous calling Joan Bennett 'Mother.'"

One of the final letters described Frid embarking on his first publicity tour to lobby ABC affiliates who were reluctant to change the time slot of the show from 3:30 to 4:00 so that more children, and not merely the fastest runners, could enjoy watching it after school. David received rousing applause for his wonderful interpretation of Jonathan's journey through DS. It was fascinating to hear Jonathan's naive perspective on his character and unexpected fame as events were unfolding. I'm grateful to Mary for gifting us that peek into his life and to David for presenting it to us.

The next event shifted focus slightly, as it was the presentation of a Saturn Award to Mary for her work on *Beyond Dark Shadows: The*

Jonathan Frid Story. Eric Wallace, producer and DS fan, provided a short biography of Mary and named her many achievements in daytime television. With every mention of another soap opera—*Guiding Light, Another World, One Life to Live, The Young and the Restless*—another batch of devoted fans applauded. He told of how Mary had contacted Jonathan after watching one of his one-man performances to ask if he needed an assistant. Jonathan swiftly replied in the affirmative, launching what would be an eight-year partnership and friendship. When Mary took the stage to accept her award, she recalled that the last time she had seen Jonathan had been in the Burbank Marriott Hotel at the 2008 Festival when they went out to dine together. He had thanked her for all the help she'd given him over the years. She appreciated hearing that form him in person.

We had a short break before the Q&A session with the actors. Lisa, Roger, David, Kathryn, and James took the stage with Jim Pierson moderating. He asked each person to give an update on what they've recently been working on. Lisa talked about the other TV series she's worked on after DS and about her children. Currently, she's teaching at the Actors' Studio.

Roger began by commenting on how the number of chairs onstage had shrunk, alluding to the many regular attendees who have recently passed away. In particular, he mentioned John Karlen. "You never knew what was going to come out of his mouth. One minute, John would tell you how much he loved you, the next minute he'd tell you how much he hated you." He then spent an excessive period of time discussing all his business ventures. "Do you remember years ago when I was selling T-shirts and tote bags? My company was the Original Fruit Crate Company. I only had that company for five years, then I sold it for $15 million. One of the T-shirt designs we sold had the slogan 'Baseball Forever' on it. Kevin Costner wore one when he did an interview for *Field of Dreams*. That shirt became so popular that Columbia Sportswear bought my company." Roger added that he had brought a few shirts and bags to sell during the autograph session, then he went on discussing his real estate ventures, which he had previously brought up the night before in relation to Lara Parker.

He then grew serious and discussed a major health scare. Roger explained that he had a brother who had died of a heart condition. (It wasn't clear to me if he said his brother died in 1968 or his brother died at age 68). Consequently, Roger was concerned about his own health and got examined, but his doctor assured him he didn't have the same condition. Then, one morning around 5:00 or 5:30, he received a call from the doctor. "He was in tears. He said, 'I made a mistake. You do have the same condition. You might die within the next 30 minutes if we don't get you into surgery right away. You have a major blockage.'" Filled with concern, Roger rushed to the hospital. "I woke up about 20 hours later. I was cracked open and the doctors were working over me." He imitated someone pulling on a rope or a line. "I heard someone say, 'We've got to get him back into surgery!' and another doctor replied, 'He won't survive another surgery. We've got to clear these lines now.' Then I slipped back into unconsciousness." It sounded like a harrowing experience. During his story, many people in the ballroom, called out in support, 'We love you, Roger!" Others signaled with a show of hands that they, too, had undergone bypass surgeries. Roger said, "I consider myself very lucky to be here at the age of 85, especially when so many others are not." He quoted *The Shawshank Redemption*: "Get busy living or get busy dying."

At various times during Roger's monologue, Pierson dropped heavy hints that it was time to give someone else a chance to speak, but Roger, evidently oblivious, kept going. At one point, he paused for breath and KLS turned to Selby and said, "David, what are you working on these days?" But Roger quickly picked up the thread of his own story.

"Is it a line from *The Love Song of J. Alfred Prufrock*? 'Was it her dress that made me so digress?' That's what I do. I digress all the time. I had a terrible upbringing. My father was a serial womanizer." Roger took care of his father in his old age. "I always dressed him in Brooks Brothers suits. He looked sharp. We went to a funeral for a neighbor. During the funeral, he became very upset and begged me to take him home. I didn't understand. We didn't really know [the deceased] very well. He told me, 'I just couldn't stay there and face all those old ladies. I had affairs with all of them, all those friends of your mother's.' I said, 'Dad, you say some disgusting shit.'" It seemed to me Roger was blaming his hyperactivity and tendency to digress on his father's bad behavior. I thought the story was in poor taste. Poor Kathryn looked mortified as he was telling it. I shared her pain.

Selby finally did get to speak and joked about how much time had passed while Roger was speaking. "Are you all hungry again by now?" He also shared the update that he's working on another project with Kathryn. On her turn, she elaborated that they are filming additional episodes of *Smartphone Theater*, working with Susan Sullivan and Granville Van Dusen. She also said she's working on another project with Ansel Faraj but didn't go into detail about it. James told us he's married to a beautiful photographer and they're planning another road trip later in the year to Montana, Wyoming, and possibly the Dakotas. He recalled his post-DS career and how nervous he was about calling up Dan Curtis when he got to California. "Dan said, 'Where the fuck are you? I'm down at the Playboy building. Get over here right now!' When I got there, he told [the other staff members], 'This is the best young actor. Get him an agent! Get him some work!'" Storm was grateful for Curtis helping to launch his broader career.

Finally, the floor was open to questions. One of the first came from a young fan who praised David for his portrayal of Count Petofi during the brief body switching of 1897. She asked if he had any memories to share from that time period of working with Thayer David. Selby merely said Thayer was wonderful and had a strong presence, but didn't speak about that particular story line.

Another fan complimented David for his portrayal of Ebenezer Scrooge in the actors' online performance of *A Christmas Carol* three years ago. "What was the impetus that brought that about, and is that program going to be available anywhere for home viewing?" "They should show that every year," David agreed. Kathryn said that Dan Curtis had always wanted to do *A Christmas Carol*, and that someone named Todd (she didn't mention his last name) had finally brought everybody together to do it. As for whether it would ever be released on a DVD or Blu-ray, nobody said. (It currently can be streamed on YouTube).

Another fan asked the cast members who had played multiple roles on the show which was their favorite. Lisa said she liked being the girlfriend of the werewolf best. Eventually, Selby said he liked the original Quentin, Kathryn said she liked Maggie because she was ambitious and always had her eye on the next thing, and James said he only got to play one character.

(Actually, he played a parallel time version of Gerard in one episode). He was being fitted for costumes for a new character when it was announced that the series would go off the air. Before the latter three could speak, however, Roger commandeered the microphone again.

He told a story about his work on *The Twilight Zone* prior to DS. "I was playing an alcoholic in an episode with Diana Hyland. I was supposed to walk drunkenly across the room and say something like, 'How ya doin'?' But the night before, I was at a party with Jack Nicholson. I know it sounds like I'm name dropping; I don't mean to. He knew that I'd been working on a Long John Silver piece and said, 'Why don't you do that?' So, when I came through the door—" Roger stood and slipped into a pirate accent, delivering a short monologue from *Treasure Island*. "Diana sat up and said, 'What in the world was that?' But the director said, 'I don't know, I kind of like it. Let's pick up and keep going.' I remember it was raining that day. When I got to the studio, I saw a man wearing a raincoat and a hat, but I didn't pay too much attention to him. I asked him to run lines with me, and he did. He told me, 'Good luck. You don't know your lines.' After my episode aired, I got a call from MGM studios. I was surprised and wondered, *How did MGM studios get my number? What do they want?* I called back and was connected to the man who had been trying to reach me. It was the guy in the raincoat.

I said, 'What do you have to do with MGM Studios?'

He said, 'I produce *The Twilight Zone*.'

I said, 'Rod Serling produces *The Twilight Zone*.'

'That's right.'

'You're Rod Serling?'

'That's right.' Serling asked Roger how he had managed to pull off his scene. "'I saw the episode. You did well, and you didn't know your lines before.'"

Roger concurred. He said, "Something happens to me when the cameras come on. It's risibility." I love *The Twilight Zone* and Rod Serling, so I thought that was an interesting story. However, it had nothing to do with the original question. Roger eventually named Dirk Wilkins as his favorite role because vampires had the most fun.

Other people called out questions. One person asked Selby if he liked working with Kate Jackson as Daphne. This prompted Roger to remind us that he had been married to Jaclyn Smith. "Do you know who bought the house next door to us? Kate Jackson. Jaclyn went over there one day. She came back and said, 'We've got to have Kate over to our house all the time!' Do you know how many times she came to visit us? None. Why do you think that was?" (I'm thinking she didn't want to get trapped into listening to Roger's obnoxious stories for hours).

James got to tell his own Kate Jackson story in response to a question about whether anything spooky had ever happened on the set. "Yeah, I got knocked out." He explained that during the 1840 story line, he had a scene that required him to throw Kate on the bed, which he did. "She hit her head on the bedpost. That brought down the censors. They said we couldn't throw a woman on the bed; it was too sexual.[127] So, the writers came up with a scene where Kate would hit me in the head with a breakaway bottle. Now, she was a new actress. This was her first role on a soap opera, and she was very nervous about hurting me. Our director that day was Harry Kaplan, who had zero sympathy. He said, 'Darling just hit him with the bottle.' 'But what about—' 'Just do it!' So, she hit me—with the solid, spun glass bottom of the bottle. I went down and woke up in the emergency room with eight stitches. Kate feels terrible about this day."

Pierson finally had to cut off the questions so that people could line up for the autograph sessions By then, it was almost 4:00, nearly two hours past the time the Q&A should have ended, though that isn't unusual for DS events. I took a short walk outside in what was unusually warm, balmy weather and a pleasant respite from the air-conditioned ballroom, then chatted with various other fans in the lobby. I popped back into the ballroom around 5:15 during what was to have been the start of the Frid documentary but, due to the time lag, was the beginning of the second auction.

Most items were DS memorabilia, including CDs of Bob Cobert's music, out-of-print or limited-edition books like *Dark Shadows: The First Year*, or the Hermes Press collection of comic strips, Angelique and Quentin action figures, a prototype for the talking Barnabas bobblehead (it recites his monologue to the portrait of Josette from after he's released from his coffin). However, a few items were unique. Jim offered up the copy of the *Dark Shadows Almanac* that Kathryn had gifted to Lara with a personalized inscription. Some of Dan Curtis's property was also available, including an artistic, close-up photographic portrait (Jim asked for a starting bid of $50.00 for this; initially, nobody bid, but I did see someone carrying it through the lobby later, so it seems to have found a buyer), a 35mm print of Episode 208, and another of the *Dead of Night* pilot "A Darkness at Blaisedon." (That would have been really cool to own, but I've no way to play 35mm films). Also up for bid was a large, floppy, dark green hat that Curtis was fond of wearing. "It's a large size, for people who have big thoughts," Jim claimed. I anticipated that this item would fetch a large amount, but when people noted that Ansel Faraj had joined the bidding, they backed down and let him have it. I thought that was a poignant passing of the hat, rather than the torch, from the director of DS to an up-and-coming director who works with DS actors.

I was particularly interested to see what amount a set of scripts that had belonged to Curtis would bring. However, it was then past 6:30 and I was starting to feel restless and hungry. I saw one binder of 1971 scripts sell for $350.00. (Pierson said they had used them for research for the 1991 series, though I don't see how; that reboot had nothing to do with parallel time). At least, that was the last bid I heard. It was a challenge to keep up with what people were calling out from the various corners of the auditorium given the acoustics. I stepped out for a bite, then spent time catching up with an old friend I hadn't seen in many years. I finally drifted back into the ballroom just as the documentary was winding down and Mary was taking the stage to answer questions about it.

By that point in the night, the audience had dwindled from a full ballroom to only a few rows. Still, the audience was very appreciative of the film. I was unable to hear the questions because I was sitting in the back and no one in the audience had access to a microphone. I had to infer them from Mary's responses.

One of the first questions pertained to how long it had taken to make the film. Mary said MPI had given her a small budget, mainly for cameramen. She began collecting interviews in autumn 2019 and interviewed two people per day, moving up through the Midwest and into Canada. Then, in March 2020, the world shut down for COVID, and it became much more difficult to arrange meetings. With the interruptions of COVID, it took about three years to finish the film.

Another person asked if it was possible to watch Jonathan's early television performances, such as the one he'd referenced in his letter to his mother. Mary said that most of that material hasn't survived. Jonathan had been contracted to appear in a television adaptation of *The Picture of Dorian Gray* in a sizable role, but, "It was very hard to summarize the entire story in one hour, and Jonathan's part was severely cut back. He was still under contract though, so they had to use him. There is one brief scene where some men are talking in the background. You hear one man reciting Shakespeare and see a blur move in front of the camera. That's Jonathan. It didn't make sense to use that clip, though, without giving it context." One of Jonathan's Shakespearean performances (I believe she said *Henry IV*) was videotaped. Jonathan had believed it was a live show, but Mary discovered a recording in the UCLA archives. "You can never be certain if what you request is actually what they're going to give you. Some things get mislabeled. Sometimes film is damaged. You have to fill out a request and pay for the film to be pulled from the archives and transferred to DVD." Luckily for her, and for all Jonathan's fans, the label was accurate and the film was in good condition, so it could be included.

Someone asked if the movie was available on DVD. Mary reminded us that copies were in all the gift bags. (I thought this was very generous of MPI).

Another question seemed to focus on Jonathan's family. Mary mentioned that Frid had a brother, Ken, who had served in the war, been traumatized by service, and become an alcoholic. She then talked about a woman who had married into the family. (I didn't catch whether this was Jonathan's sister-in-law or someone who had married his nephew) When Mary interviewed this woman, she had talked of how intimidating it was to be among so many new people and learn the family's dynamic. Jonathan was the easiest person to talk to. He was very welcoming and an excellent listener. Mary confirmed Jonathan's good listening skills from personal experience. She also mentioned a niece, Susan, who had been depicted in the film in a picture where she's sitting with Jonathan and he's reading a book to her. "That was Susan's clearest memory of Uncle Jonathan."

The question must have also had a component about whether or not Jonathan had a significant other because Mary added that Jonathan didn't want a committed relationship. "Unlike many people, he was comfortable being alone. It's like when some people have children and other people don't want them. It's a preference. Jonathan had the opportunity, he just liked being alone."

I didn't stay in the ballroom to see if *HoDS* was actually going to be screened. I returned to the lobby to search for friends with whom to chat. Periodically, I could hear music that I recognize from *HoDS* drifting from the ballroom (then again, it could have been somebody's ringtone).

The second half of the day was much more muted and less active than the first part. That felt odd. Traditional Festivals always had a packed schedule, though of course, this was not intended to be a Festival. Day Two of the weekend did feel most like a traditional convention.

Much speculation abounded among the attendees as to whether this was a final hurrah as far as DS events are concerned or if we would see more scaled-down events down the road. I didn't hear anything official one way or the other, though I didn't spend the entire time in the ballroom and could have missed hearing an announcement.[128] Given that Saturday's attendance sold out, and judging by the enthusiastic reactions of the audience members to the actors and presentations, I believe DS is still popular and can still command a dedicated attendance. I know many people who had wanted to attend the Remembrance Weekend but either couldn't afford the exorbitant costs to travel over a holiday weekend or had already made other arrangements for the holiday prior to the event announcement. Under slightly different circumstances, I think we would have seen an even bigger crowd. Personally, I hope that bodes well for more activities, especially with the 60th anniversary only two years away.

Appendix I: Costume Gala Song Lyrics

The Dream Curse (2002)
(To the tune of "All I Have to Do is Dream" by the Everly Brothers)
Dream, dream, dream, dream
Dream, dream, dream, dream
When you've been cursed by Angelique
You fear the worst, your future's bleak
By morning you will weep because once you fall asleep
You will dream the dream
The dream, dream, dream curse
Will force you to tell the next in line
You can't resist the spell, as you will find
If you try to break the chain, your fear will drive you insane
Oh, the dream!
The dream, dream, dream curse, dream curse.
A knocking at your door like so many times before
But your visitor on this particular night
Will lead you to your doom in a mist-filled room
Where you're in for a terrible fright
Ahead a blazing light does burn
And one door leads to the point of return
Through trial and error, sight, sound, and faceless terror
It's the dream
The dream, dream, dream curse, dream curse
It consumes your every thought, ties your stomach in a knot
And with each night that passes by
The terror will increase, you will never have peace
For the next time you dream, you could die
If cobwebs, wolves, bats, your own tombstone, a guillotine
A headless body, a skeletal bride, and a skull glowing green
Really drive you up the wall, give Professor Stokes a call
To stop the dream
The dream, dream, dream curse, dream
The dream, dream, dream curse

Ode to Collinsport (2003)

(To the tune of "Octopus's Garden" by the Beatles)
I'd like to be in a house by the sea
In a town called Collinsport, up in Maine
It would be the norm if every night there was a storm
With thunder and lightning but no rain
Secret rooms and passageways abound
Explore with caution or you'll never be found
I'd like to be in a house by the sea
With a view of Widows Hill - what a thrill!
In the dead of night when the moon is bright
And the werewolf's roaming through the woods again
You've no need to fear if silver is near
In the form of a bullet, pentagram, or cane
It would be a fairly common sight to see
Your incestors—ancestors—rising from their graves
I'd like to be in a house by the sea
With a view of Widows' Hill and the waves
Which ghost will speak at the seance this week?
Seems like they have one nearly every night
Supernatural foes can cause plenty of woes
But a sedative will make everything all right
When you hear all the dogs howling
You know a vampire must be prowling
I'd like to be in a house by the sea
In a house called Collinwood; wouldn't you?
In a house called Collinwood, yes, it's true
In a house called Collinwood; wouldn't that be good?

Bad to the Bone (2003 and 2006)[129]
(To the Tune of "Bad to the Bone" by George Thorogood)
In the forest of Ashden, just a century ago
When I lost my hand, the gypsies gained a deadly foe
When it comes to vendettas, I'm worse than Don Corleone
I will get my revenge 'cause I'm bad to the bone
Bad to the bone
Bad to the bone
B-b-b-b-b-b-b-bad
B-b-b-b-b-b-b-bad
B-b-b-b-b-b-b-bad
Bad to the bone
I killed lots of gypsies before I came to town
And I'll kill many more if I see them around
King Johnny Romano had better leave me alone
'Cause I fight *mano a mano* and I'm bad to the bone
Bad to the bone
Bad to the bone
B-b-b-b-b-b-b-bad
B-b-b-b-b-b-b-bad
B-b-b-b-b-b-b-bad
Bad to the bone
I'll make Charity a slattern and Beth Chavez a slave
I'll make Edward a servant and send Julianka to her grave
Destruction's a hobby few people condone
Unless you're like me and you're bad to the bone
Bad to the bone
Bad to the bone
B-b-b-b-b-b-b-bad
B-b-b-b-b-b-b-bad
B-b-b-b-b-b-b-bad
Bad to the bone

1897 is starting to look rather bland
Collinsport is already in the palm of my hand
So I'll pull a switch to make Quentin's body my own
And show folks in the future that I'm bad to the bone
Bad to the bone
Bad to the bone
B-b-b-b-b-b-b-bad
B-b-b-b-b-b-b-bad
B-b-b-b-b-b-b-bad
Bad to the bone

Vicki (2004)
(To the tune of "Mickey" by Toni Basil)
Oh, Vicki, you're so blind
Can't you ever use your mind?
Hey, Vicki! Hey, Vicki!
Oh, Vicki, don't be dense
Please use your common sense
Hey, Vicki! Hey, Vicki!
Vicki, you are so naïve
It's almost too much to believe
Hey, Vicki!
Hey, Vicki!
He's only out at night, you never see him in the day
Both Burke and Willie have told you to stay away
Now, isn't that enough to set off a warning light, Vicki?
Ever since he came to town, the local livestock bleeds and dies
But when he talks about the past, you just sit there mesmerized
You could be the next victim of his gruesome appetite, Vicki
Oh, Vicki, what a pity you don't understand
The real reason Barnabas can never get a tan
Oh, Vicki, it's a shame you just don't understand
You're such an ingenue, Vicki
The things you do, Vicki, ooh Vicki
Can't you get a clue, Vicki?
Hey, Vicki
Now, when you travel back in time, it would be kind of dumb
To tell everyone you meet that the future's where you're from
Unless you want to hang, you better keep your profile low, Vicki
'Cause Reverend Trask and Abigail need someone to blame
And Angelique's decided it's you she wants to frame
Now if they ask if you hold seances, say it isn't so Vicki
Poor Vicki, it's too late, you just don't understand
Peter never should have put you on the witness stand
Oh, Vicki, it's too late, you'll never understand
You're just an ingenue, Vicki

The things you do, Vicki, ooh, Vicki
Get yourself a clue, Vicki
Oh, Vicki, you're so blind
Can't you ever use your mind?
Hey, Vicki! Hey, Vicki!
Oh, Vicki, don't be dense
Please use your common sense
Hey, Vicki! Hey, Vicki!
Vicki, you are so naïve
It's almost too much to believe
Hey, Vicki!
Oh, Vicki, you don't realize the mess you're in
David is a menace and should be on Ritalin
Oh, Vicki, it's too bad, you'll never understand
You're such an ingenue, Vicki
The things you do, Vicki, ooh, Vicki
Better get a clue, Vicki
Oh, Vicki, what a pity you don't understand
Wy the search for your family didn't work out like you planned
Your identity's a mystery you'll never understand
You're just an ingenue, Vicki
The things you do, Vicki, ooh, Vicki
Please get a clue, Vicki
Oh, Vicki, what a pity you don't understand
You would be much better off without this kooky Collins clan
Oh, Vicki, it's a pity you just don't understand
You're the ingenue, Vicki
The things you do, Vicki, ooh, Vicki
Just a clue, Vicki!

He's Possessed (2005)
(To the tune of "Be Our Guest" from Beauty and the Beast)
He's possessed, he's possessed
By a spirit that won't rest
David and Amy went exploring
In a wing known as the West
They found a room
Quentin's tomb
And it brought David to his doom
Things all started as a game
Now life will never be the same
David threatens, tries to kill
He's controlled by Quentin's will
If you want proof, take a look at how he's dressed
Nineteenth century clothes? Why else would he wear those?
He's possessed!
See? Possessed!
He's possessed!
With the ghost
He conspires
Amy helps them string trip wires
With a smile, the devil child
Will see to it that you expire
Roger's tumble down the stairs
And Madame Finley's fatal scare
Were all part of his terrorizing
Now it's time for exercising
Maggie took his phone away, but Mr. Juggins made her pay
When he came to life and tried to wring her neck
Now Professor Stokes prays
But the gramophone still plays
And we're distressed
Now we're homeless
And the boy is still possessed
He's possessed, still possessed, he's possessed

Growing up is scary
When you always must be wary
Of vampires, Phoenix fires, and other spooks
David's life was never very easy
After all, his family's full of kooks
For twelve years he's been lonely
Because he was the only
Kid in Collinsport, at least till Amy came
It's natural that he should want a friend or two
But consorting with the dead
Can cause unintended bloodshed
Now he's possessed, again possessed
Well, he always was a pest
But now the kid's downright demonic
And I'm afraid this could be chronic
Every year, David is host
To another unfriendly ghost
If not Quentin, then it's Tad
Or else it's someone really bad
Like Count Petofi or Gerard
Or some other dead blackguard
To defeat them, we will surely do our best
So, you better pray to God
And get your dowsing rod
'Cause he's possessed
He's possessed
He's possessed
This kid's possessed

Who Put the Bite? (2006)
(To the tune of "Who Put the Bomp?" by Barry Mann)
I'd like to thank the guy
Who starred in the show
That gave me so many happy memories.
Who put the bite on the ladies of the night?
Who shot the witch shortly after they were hitched?
Who broke down and cried when his sister Sarah died?
Who took Maggie away to recreate Josette Du Pres?
Who was the man
Who saved the show from getting canned?
And helped Dark Shadows run for four more years
When Dan Curtis chose
To bring a vampire onto the show
He planned to drive a stake right through his heart.
But when the fan mail rolled in
That's when inspiration told him.
That Frid was meant to be a star.
So
Who sleeps all day and makes the hounds bay?
Who's got his own room hidden in the family tomb?
Who put the bricks around Trask the fanatic?
And carries around a wolf-head walking stick?
Who's got pointy bangs ?
And even pointier fangs?
He helped Dark Shadows thrive for five full years.
Everyone ran home from school
To catch the adventures of their favorite ghoul
With faithful Julia Hoffman at his side
He explored the future and the past
With a cliffhanger in every broadcast.
You must admit it was one amazing ride
Now tell me - Who seeks a cure for a curse he can't endure?
Who taught Ben to read and punished Nathan Forbes's greed?
Who gave Adam life and created him a wife?

Who saves his family by changing history?
Who was the man
Who made me a lifelong fan
And helped Dark Shadows survive for 40 years?

Needles and Pins (2008)
(To the tune of "Needles and Pins" by the Searchers)
I saw her today, I saw the face
Of the girl Barnabas loves, and I knew
I had to run away
Make a voodoo doll out of some clay
To get her out of the way
And now I'll begin
To use my needles and pins
To be Barnabas's bride
Would give me so much pride
Well, I thought it was fate, we were soul mates
And we would never part, but now I see
He loves her more than me
But maybe if she's dead, he'll turn to me instead
And married we will be
Together for eternity
We could be so happy
That's why I must do her in
I'll use a needle and a pin
To hurt her, I'll hurt her
I never stop
To wonder if it's wrong
To want her gone
I just can't wait
To tell his new sweetheart so long
You know I saw her today, I saw the face
Of the girl Barnabas loves, and I knew
I had to run away
Make this voodoo doll out of some clay
Get her out of my way
Barnabas will never win her
Because I'll needle and pin her
You can call it homicide
But my wrath I will not hide

Oh, needle and pins
I'll use my needles and pins
Needles and pins

Lost (2009)
(To the tune of "Lost in Your Eyes" by Debbie Gibson)
I get lost in your eyes
One look and I'm hypnotized
I forget my own name
And start to believe I'm this Josette dame
Music plays, puts me in a trance
Tell me is this what you call romance?
You're obsessed with long ago
Won't somebody save me from this weirdo?
Now I don't like the aching in my neck at all
You've put me at your beck and call
I feel I'm being pulled
Between two different lives
When I look in your eyes
The sun descends, dark shadows loom
While I sit, imprisoned in this room
Hoping to be rescued
From another night as vampire food
And if I can't get away
I'll never again see the light of day
For I'll be bound
And I'll be locked in endless night
Oh, I don't like knowing
What this coffin's for
Soon I'll belong to you forevermore
It's like being trapped in a nightmare and I can't arise
When I look in your eyes
I get weak from one nip
I lose my will with every sip
Soon night will fall
And I'll be lost in your eyes

324

Hey, Judah (2010)
(To "Hey, Jude" by the Beatles)
Hey Judah, don't look so grim
You may be dead but things will get better
The minute you practice using your head
You can begin to fulfill your vendetta
Hey Judah, you ladies' man
In Daphne's dreams you'll manipulate her
Add her to your harem with Edith and Sam
Before Quentin learns that you're a traitor
Just take Gerard's form for your own
And when you're made flesh and bone
You'll be able to make all your enemies cower
Kiss up to Daniel and don't delay
Where there's a will, there's a way
Of seizing the Collinses' wealth and power
Hey Judah. draw your followers near
Have Dawson plant some phony evidence
Get Mordecai and Lamar to cry warlock
So you can start to take your vengeance
Just frame him for the death of Lorna Bell
And if all goes well
Quentin's head will soon be parted from his shoulders
Don't worry about Miranda DuVal
The Mask of Baal
Will help you to keep her from getting any older
Hey Judah, now the trial begins
Once the judges declare a double beheader
Both Quentin and Desmond will be history
And you'll at last have achieved your vendetta
You'll feel better
When they're dead and gone
Na na na na na na na
Na na na na
Hey, Judah

In the Year. . . (2011)
(To the tune of "In the Year 2525 (Exordium and Terminus)" by Zager and Evans)
In the year 1966
Everyone watched TV transfixed
To see Dark Shadows make its debut
Starring Joan Bennett and Alex Moltke too, Whoa, whoa
In the year 1795
Barnabas makes Angelique his wife
Josette jumps off a cliff, Vicki is hanged
And the ladies of the night get fanged
In the year 1968
Barnabas didn't treat Adam all that great
Angelique vamps, Nicholas goes up in flames
David and Amy play Quentin's games
In the year 1897
Reverend Trask, Count Petofi, and Evan
Are just a few of the villains to beware
And Quentin Collins when he's covered with hair, whoa, whoa
In the year parallel time 1970
Cyrus Longworth has a split personality
Quentin's first wife returns from the dead
And sends her sister to the tomb instead, Whoa, whoa
In the year nineteen hundred ninety-five
Quentin and Carolyn are the only family left alive
Everybody has gone insane
And Collinwood what is haunted once again
In the year 18 Four-Zero
Angelique becomes a hero
She saves Quentin from Judah Zachary's head
But then Lamar Trask shoots her dead, Whoa, whoa
In the year 1841 PT
The Collins family holds another lottery
Bramwell and Kathryn survive a cursed night
And Melanie suffers from a strange neck bite, Whoa, whoa

Now it's been 45 years
Of suspense, romance, laughter, and tears
This show has brought us joy
Since we were young girls and boys
The years may fly by, but Dark Shadows will never die
And though Sci-Fi took it away
We hope it will return some day
(Reprise)

1969 (2016)
(To the tune of "Summer of 69" by Bryan Adams)
I got my own Barnabas Ring
Bought it at the Five and Dime
I had the record and the horror heads
It was the summer of 69
I ran home every day from school
I had to see what would happen next
Like when Quentin prematurely got buried
And later on when he was gypsy-hexed
The werewolf and Leviathans
Used to keep me lying awake with terror
I just knew that Count Petofi's hand
Would grab me if I went into the cellar
That was the best show of all time
The Vietnam War was raging
America went on a moon trip
Barnabas partied at the White House
And got his own cartoon strip
Standing at the studio door
I was prepared to wait forever
And when the actors shook my hand
I knew that I'd always remember
These as the best days of my life
Yeah, those were troubled times
The world was restless, and some said in decline
Oh, but the show just kept on getting better and better
Now I'm older but my love hasn't changed
Though I laugh when I used to feel scared
Sometimes when I read my old *Sixteens*
I smile and think about the fun we shared
Singing *Shadows of the Night*
The board game always took forever
Trying to get the models right
The joke book used to seem so clever

That was the best year of my life
Oh, yeah!
It was the year 1969
Oh, yeah
Being a Shadows fan in '69
All through the spring and the summer and the fall and the winter of
'69

Gone Around the Bend (The Windcliff Anthem) (2016)
(To the tune of "Up Around the Bend" by Credence Clearwater Revival)

There's a place where we send all our characters
When their stories hit a plateau
It's a place that's got bars on the winders
And the sedatives freely flow
Windcliff is where we send
Everyone who goes 'round the bend
The asylum sits outside of town now
About a hundred miles away
But somehow everybody who breaks out
Can just walk home in half a day
Joe Haskell's gone 'round the bend
And Willie Loomis has gone 'round the bend
Ooh!
Our director's perpetual devotion
To a vampire could be certified
Monster making, transfusions, hypnosis
Are the services she'll provide
Liz Stoddard's gone 'round the bend
And Maggie Evans has gone 'round the bend
Twice!
Take a room at the end of the hallway
Wear a jacket that straps behind
Have a kook or a spook for a roommate
Then sit back and lose your mind
Windcliff is where we'll send
You when you've gone around the band
Yeah!

Appendix II: Collinsport Players Skits

As of this writing, several of the skits performed at the Festivals I've covered in this book are available to watch on YouTube. The current links are as follows:

Curtains (2008): https://www.youtube.com/watch?app=desktop&v=W69M6xrbQt8&t=42s&fbclid=IwZXh0bgNhZW0CM

The Shadow Zone (2010):

Part 1: https://www.youtube.com/watch?v=L4A0-iODGZM&t=204s[1]

Part 2: https://www.youtube.com/watch?v=I6aIsHmTq2Q[2]

Tim Burton's Dark Shadows (2011):

Part 1: https://www.youtube.com/watch?v=ATYJcmVOLqA

Part 2: https://www.youtube.com/watch?v=EolRyANcXck

Part 3: https://www.youtube.com/watch?v=E8T3Mqqsm8Y

Dark Shadows Bloopers (2011):

Part 1: https://www.youtube.com/watch?v=XHNyiN91pzs&t=286s

Part 2: https://www.youtube.com/watch?v=MU4v8mmhL0c

Part 3: https://www.youtube.com/watch?v=v-TpX896_f8

---

1. https://www.youtube.com/watch?v=L4A0-iODGZM&t=204s&fbclid=IwZXh0bgNhZW0CMTAAAR3yfHEPR8wyl0OfrcoOHCuS2N-BFT9d0Z95oW3nidV9DBkZ9o2wQiN39vM_aem_AQP8j3a_2BMP2KCojGDD3OY1LGJgzcFYtJLYbqdNqbNAU-_LUNlZX1w-loHsu9aUEVOVoCemRK5snWblVpBi_vFV

2. https://www.youtube.com/watch?v=I6aIsHmTq2Q&fbclid=IwZXh0bgNhZW0CMTAAAR0KSUwoTNTb5uTe0_Y8qQ4NomvFFLumowqDcL0KvpcVVPTjltMTQGjK1Dg_aem_AQMZ0kNwugX9SRsW4MIjSWPH55hJigIMjxPNNIL_SQ7ruCiIIgToyVhlKeyRoCzYLfULmEwuKNndoN4C4fBtDeDE

Séance Fiction (2016):
    https://www.youtube.com/watch?v=b9-uGy2Y9gQ

[1] The Dark Shadows Festivals were official, annual conventions partially sponsored by Dan Curtis Productions/MPI and organized by a committee whose prominent members included Jim Pierson, Marcy Robin, Kathleen Resch, and Ann Wilson.

[2] It was customary, at the time, for the Festival to alternate coasts every year. The Fest was in New York in 1999, 2001, and 2003, in Las Vegas in 1998, and in LA in 2000 and 2002.

[3] My only notes refer to the Banquet entertainment: "We saw a short video [from Friday afternoon] of Frid putting his hands in cement at the Vista Theatre and the many fans crowding around (I was surprised someone had been able to edit a video together so quickly), the Depp/Burton interview on a British TV program (which kept freezing), and a reel of clips and trailers from movies in which the stars had appeared (e.g., *Race with the Devil, The Girl in Blue*)."

[4] See 2002 Dark Shadows Festival, Day 3 for a discussion of the unaired "Sciography" documentary.

[5] As seen in the Dark Shadows Reunion 35th Anniversary DVD

[6] Kathryn Leigh Scott

[7] *House of Dark Shadows*

[8] *Night of Dark Shadows*

[9] At this time, Sci-Fi Channel was running the pre-Barnabas Phoenix episodes.

[10] Peter Mac of the "Dark Shad-Bros" podcast

[11] Eileen Lynch-Ferrar of the Collinsport Players

[12] See 2001; Day 3 for a detailed description

[13] A number of my online friends responded to this comment to rave about what a wonderful show *The Prisoner* was. I hastened to Hollywood Video to check it out for myself and was suitably impressed.

[14] A man who appeared to have a developmental disability stood up in the audience and started calling Kathryn a liar. She seemed to recognize him and to view this behavior as out-of-character. Other fans quickly moved to block him from the stage, and he was removed from the ballroom.

[15] See 2001; Day 1 for more details

[16] See Appendix

[17] "Sciography" = a Biography-style documentary about popular sci-fi shows. At the time, I didn't write a detailed description of the program; it seemed best not to publicize it. I had watched the *Quantum Leap* Sciography when it aired in August 2000 and loved it. (The only other episode that aired treated *Battlestar Galactica*). I thought it was a

respectful and affectionate treatment of the series and actors, and was thrilled to read that DS would also be profiled. Unfortunately, network personnel changes between the taping of the QL and the DS episodes let to a shift in tone and focus that brought the latter more in line with an *E! True Hollywood* exposé . While the DS Sciography did include some legitimate segments, including an interview with long-term fan Michael Miozza at Seaview Terrace and film historian Darren Gross, it emphasized sensationalized aspects, such as one actor's alleged drug use. After the screening, KLS and Marie Wallace took the stage to denounce the program for its sleazy depiction of the show and the cast and to complain that it had been shown at all. Karlen had walked out when the screening began. We learned that Robert Cobert had revoked permission for Sciography to use the DS theme music, and that ultimately was what had prevented it from airing.

[18] And which conflicted with her ability to appear at the Anaheim Festival three months earlier.

[19] See 2002, Day 3

[20] Be careful what you wish for.

[21] Sadly, this tree was toppled by a storm in October 2024 and subsequently removed.

[22] As of this writing, the Cheep Productions videos are not available in any venue, but some of the parties involved can be seen on YouTube in other works; search for "Dark Shadows the Lost Episode" and "Spencer Productions Back from the Grave to Haunt Me"

[23] Unfortunately, this turned out to be the final COLLINS Association event. Though a Halloweenathon was advertised for 2003, organizer Ed Lambese canceled the plans in order to travel to Romania with Diana Millay and thus far has never organized another DS event.

[24] Patrick had died in a house fire the previous October. Initial news reports said "A *Dallas* actor" had been killed, but I wasn't familiar with *Dallas* and had no idea the actor was anyone from DS. That night, the Dark Shadows Forums was hosting its first (and last; the technical logistics proved too overwhelming) live chatroom. In the early days of the Internet, the ability to interact with one another in real time was a thrilling novelty. At first, participants spent the time introducing themselves, familiarizing themselves with how the chat feature worked, and gushing about the Angels' surprise win in the World Series. After a time, one of the moderators announced that he had sad news to share: the deceased actor had just been confirmed as Dennis Patrick. The tone of the chat swiftly turned funereal. We were shocked. At least one person left the room to grieve. If you're going to get bad news about DS, at least getting it in the company of other DS fans makes the news easier to digest.

[25] This same video had played at the public memorial for Dennis Patrick in December 2002. I attended with other members of the Los Angeles fan club, Shadows in the Sun. John Karlen sat in front of us and cried quietly throughout the montage.

[26] This was the year California held a special election to recall then-governor Gray Davis. It was my first opportunity to vote. (I did not vote for Arnold).

[27] Much good that did! On Saturday morning, when we went to make sure that Salon I would be open in time for our rehearsal, not only did we find the doors locked, but we could hear voices coming from inside. It was Marcy Robin answering fans' questions. We realized that the Festival was just on the other side of the doors, but how could this be? The night before, we had been in an entirely separate space located far from the ballroom, but now our rehearsal room appeared to have vanished, much like David and Hallie's playroom. We were in the right place; this *was* Salon I. We soon realized that the Festival ballroom actually spanned Salons A – I, and on Friday night, the last several rooms had been partitioned off because the crowd wasn't as large. Because Saturday was a peak day, these partitions had since been taken down, causing Salon I to be reabsorbed into the main ballroom. Once the mystery was solved, we made arrangements to meet and rehearse elsewhere.

[28] This was huge news because the 2003 Festival was widely advertised to be the "Final Festival." It later emerged that the organizers had wanted to move away from the "Festival" brand to do a lower-key event, though it would be another ten years before the format actually changed. The 2004 event would, in fact, span three days, as was customary, and would occur in Tarrytown, NY.

[29] The Shadows in the Sun LA fan club attended the show at the Actors' Studio that December. It was great fun, and Chris was terrific opposite Salome Jens's Martha. Afterward, he hung out with our group and took pictures. During this time, we also discovered a member of his stage crew had previously worked with Grayson Hall in *Marco Polo Sings a Solo*, holding her cue cards. Small world.

[30] A version of George Thorogood's "Bad to the Bone" she had commissioned me to write.

[31] The first edition of *Barnabas & Company*

[32] This actually sounds like Marj Dusay's scene from the *Dead of Night* "A Darkness at Blaisedon" pilot that would have aired in 1969, a year after Beth Chavez debuted on DS. Interesting if that script was already available in 1967-68.

[33] See 2005, Day 2

[34] See 2002 Dark Shadows Halloweenathon, Day 3

[35] A pilot episode, directed by PJ Hogan, produced by Mark Verheiden, and starring Alec Newman and Marley Shelton, was filmed but ultimately shelved. It has played at several DS events over the years, and occasionally pirated recordings have appeared on YouTube.

[36] Recently, I learned there was a pitch in the late 1980s to make a "next generation" type show under the working title *Darker Shadows*. Original cast members and

scriptwriters were associated with the project, but it never came to fruition. In 2022, a story bible with a treatment and character descriptions became available through Amazon.com, but as of this writing, *Darker Shadows* appears to be out of print

[37] This seems like a throwaway remark on the surface, but it actually reflects a moment in the zeitgeist. In 2003, as the new Iraq War was unfolding, France did not offer its wholehearted support. As a result, some Americans developed ill feelings against France. A member of the House of Representatives even directed that the cafeterias in Congress should change their menus to rename French fries "freedom fries" in symbolic protest.

[38] See "2004 Daughters of Darkness Screening (Vista Theatre, Hollywood, CA) to find out if anyone did get punched.

[39] *Dark Shadows: The Salem Branch* (2006)

[40] See 2002 Dark Shadows Halloweenathon, Day 3 for a description

[41] See 2005 Dark Shadows Hollywood Weekend, Day 2

[42] See also 2003 Dark Shadows Festival, Day 3

[43] At the time I penned my 2004 Festival report, I hadn't yet seen Corman's *The Haunted Palace* (1964), clearly a source of inspiration for Night of DS.

[44] Frid's refusal to participate in the second film inadvertently doomed DS. As revealed in *Dark Shadows and Beyond: The Jonathan Frid Story* and the 9/5/24 *Terror at Collinwood* podcast, Dan Curtis was so angered that he fired Frid. Upon being reminded that the actor was still under contract, he amended his dictum to ordering that Frid could no longer play Barnabas (thus the parallel time character of Bramwell was created so he could finish out his term). Soon after, Curtis decided to end the series altogether.

[45] See 2002 Dark Shadows Festival, Day 1

[46] On a slippery lobby floor

[47] Matt Czuchry

[48] The Museum of Television and Radio in Beverly Hills, CA held a celebration of Curtis's 40 years in the entertainment industry on April 22, 2004 called "A Conversation with Dan Curtis" First, a 40-minute series of clips of Curtis's work was shown (*CBS Golf Classics, DS, The Last Ride of the Dalton Gang, When Every Day was the Fourth of July, Trilogy of Terror, Melvin Purvis, G-Man, The Night Stalker, The Love Letter, Winds of War, War and Remembrance*) followed by the moderator asking Curtis questions about his various projects, casting, how he became a director, whether he had a romantic streak, etc. Only three questions were taken from the audience. Lastly, KLS and Jim Pierson presented Curits with a copy of their new book *Produced and Directed by Dan Curtis*. The evening ended with a reception in the museum's lobby.

[49] This appears to be a typographical error in my original report. Pennock's credits on imdb don't list anything resembling this title.

[50] Sadly, Rich died unexpectedly in June 2023. He was a kind man and a generous friend whom we didn't get to see often enough in his final years.

[51] LdyAnne was active in the Central Florida Dark Shadows Fan Club. In addition to DS, she was a fan of musical theater and all things Disney. She tragically passed away from surgical complications in 2022.

[52] Actually, I won; the 2005 Festival was held in Hollywood, CA.

[53] Spoiler; I did both.

[54] See 2004 Dark Shadows Weekend, Day 1

[55] A historic, Old Hollywood restaurant that opened in 1927 and closed in 2021 in the wake of Covid.

[56] Coordinated suicide bombings in London on July 7, 2005

[57] Per Darren Gross (in a post on Dark Shadows Forums), photo stills of this scene do exist, so evidently it was shot.

[58] See August 27, 2004 - *Daughters of Darkness* Screening (Egyptian Theater, Hollywood, CA)

[59] Noted photographer Ben Martin

[60] Though this detail has frequently been repeated at conventions and in print, Gross has disputed it. *Night of DS* was a modest success for MGM, particularly when taking into consideration its comparative lack of promotion vis-a-vis *House of DS* and the revenue from later home video rentals.

[61] I don't remember if the club did go. I didn't see this show myself, so possibly I was out of town or had another conflict.

[62] Published in 2006 as *Grayson Hall: A Hard Act to Follow*

[63] If Wikipedia is correct, she was actually closer to 18.

[64] See 2004 Dark Shadows Weekend, Day 3

[65] Though this screening was treated as a once in a lifetime opportunity, the pilot also aired at the 2006 Anniversary Weekend, the 2013 Dark Shadows Island Weekend, and the 2016 Festival. From time to time, a bootleg copy will show up on YouTube.

[66] Alice Faye was a Festival Gala regular known for her beautiful costumes and eclectic presentations that combined her recreational activities (e.g., hula dancing, clog dancing, belly dancing) with her love of DS and other media, such as *Gone with the Wind*. The lady had nerve! Not only did she perform onstage before a live audience, she took the Greyhound bus across the country to the Festival, by herself, every year. She passed away from cancer shortly after attending the 2010 Festival. I don't think anyone knew she had been ill.

[67] Mine too. At times when I'm nervous or indecisive about an upcoming action, I'll play this song, an anthem about regret over opportunities not pursued, to motivate myself to go for it.

[68] Mor recently, he wrote the comedy play *A Reunion of Sorts*; it was staged in August 2016 by the Town and Country Players in Buckingham, PA.

[69] This set made a reappearance in 2011 at the 45th Anniversary gathering. It now resides at Seaview Terrace in Newport, RI, TV's "Collinwood."

[70] Actually, Barnabas isn't in the first five books. Instead, Vicki is the focus.

[71] Before she passed away in October 2023, Lara also wrote *Wolf Moon Rising* and *Heiress of Collinwood*.

[72] As of this writing, all four episodes of "Baby Dark Shadows" are on YouTube. Search using the key words "Baby Dark Shadows."

[73] Sadly, Hamrick passed away just a month after the Festival. Grayson Hall biographer R.J. Jamison completed the update, and the second edition of *Barnabas & Company* was released in 2012.

[74] Ida Lupino directed at least one episode of *Thriller* (1961).

[75] Various personnel over the years have claimed or implied credit for hiring Frid to play Barnabas. Dan Curtis always acted as if it was his own idea. Producer Bob Costello claimed Curtis instructed him to offer the role to future gameshow host Bert Convey before leaving on vacation, and that he took advantage of the boss's absence to hire Frid instead. At the Master of *Dark Shadows* screening in 2018, screenwriter Malcolm Marmorstein said fellow writer Ron Sproat had cast Frid because they attended Yale together.

[76] See 2003 Dark Shadows Festival, Day 2 for more details

[77] And so it did keep.

[78] A wonderful lady, taken too soon by cancer, who loved hummingbirds, pirates, DS, and especially Angelique.

[79] She also passed away of cancer, just two years after her co-star.

[80] These days, she hosts the fabulous DS-centric podcast *Terror at Collinwood*.

[81] We actually reminisced about our meeting and this CD during my appearance on *Terror at Collinwood* in 2023 to discuss the 1840 story line.

[82] See October 16, 2006 – Dark Shadows Haunted Halloween Party (Vista Theatre, Los Feliz, CA)

[83] And read it on the plane trip home instead of Mr. Blackwood.

[84] Not since the 2005 convention, at least.

[85] Except for *Dark Shadows: Return to Collinwood* (2012) and the DS-inspired novel *Dark Passages* (2011)

[86] *Jinxed* was released in 2020

[87] The recording must have been worthless because I no longer have it and didn't even remember that I had made it.

[88] This was a reprise of a skit Jeff Thompson had originally written in 1997 to celebrate the centennial of *Dracula*. The Count and Barnabas fight for Victoria in what, to my knowledge, is the only dramatic skit of the Collinsport Players. The skit can be viewed on YouTube: search for "Dark Shadows Skit Collinsport Players Curtains (2008).

[89] Frid did accidentally fall off a stool and off the stage during his presentation on Sunday, an incident that was much discussed on the Internet at the time. Luckily, he was fine, picked himself up, and continued with his dramatic presentation.

[90] In fact, Frid did fly to London to film a cameo with David Selby, Lara Parker, and Kathryn Leigh Scott.

[91] See 2005 Dark Shadows Hollywood Weekend, Day 2 for further discussion of this scene.

[92] Search "2008 Dark Shadows Festival Gala" to view this on YouTube.

[93] At the time of the Festival, the film was available to view on YouTube, but I'm now unable to find it by searching with obvious key words.

[94] *House of Dan Curtis* was released in 2019.

[95] If only! As of this writing, the restored film has still never been released.

[96] At the 2016 Festival, Lacy would indicate that the plan for him to play Trask was already in place when he was hired as Tony.

[97] It was released to DVD in 2020.

[98] Alas, the 2012 event, now in a 2-day format, returned to the East Coast.

[99] All along, I had joked that my paper invitation to the screening was a "golden ticket," like the invitations to the chocolate factory in the *Willy Wonka* movie. As we were screened and admitted one-by-one into the theater, staff exchanged our paper invitations for tickets printed on yellow cardstock—so I really did end up with a golden ticket!

[100] The original links are now defunct. The scenes I originally shared were, respectively, a clip from *Dracula: Dead and Loving It* of Dracula trying to hypnotize Renfield and accidentally putting him to sleep, a clip from *Hocus Pocus* of the witches mistaking an asphalt-paved street for a "black river," and a scene from *Abbott & Costello Meet Frankenstein* where Chick and Wilbur try to barricade themselves in a room without realizing the door opens out.

[101] A revisionist story about the Three Wise Men

[102] A fan film made by Spencer Productions. As of this writing, the film is available on YouTube.

[103] Sharon may have had more leeway to speak candidly about the movie because she didn't appear in it. At the *Master of Dark Shadows* screening and the LA Times Festival of Books, Kathryn Leigh Scott and Parker, who did have cameos, separately alluded to some type of contract or NDA governing what they were allowed to say.

[104] The film premiered April 27, 2013 at the Coronado Village Theatre on Coronado Island, CA as part of the Dark Shadows Island Weekend.

[105] Ansel Faraj; See imdb.com for his full credits.

[106] Jonathan's nephew Don Frid was scheduled to be present and to share his memories.

[107] This fan-run event ostensibly focused on the neglected 1991 revival, but openly embraced all cast and crew members from all iterations of DS, including the original series and the 2004 WB pilot.

[108] From what I remember, Jim Fyfe was hired at the last minute for a project in France and recorded a video greeting for us; Roy Thinnes was injured in a fall.

[109] He was then hospitalized with complications from diabetes.

[110] Coffey, primarily known for his work as a medium, appeared opposite Kathy Cody in Spencer Productions' fan film *Curse of the Full Moon*. As of this writing, the full film is not available on YouTube, but an extended trailer is.

[111] The Friends of the 1991 Dark Shadows held one more event at Lyndhurst in 2015, and was fundraising to hold a Los Angeles-based event in 2020, prior to the Covid lockdown. As of this writing, the group no longer appears to be active.

[112] This event followed the same format as the 2012 Dark Shadows Weekend

[113] As part of the 2013 Dark Shadows Island Weekend on Coronado Island, CA

[114] The Central Florida Dark Shadows Fan Club has been active since 1991 and has an active Facebook page as of this writing.

[115] That would be the Seelbach Hotel. I visited with a friend in 2020 and was treated to a tour by one of the staff members, who did mention Davis. Not only did he work on the restoration, he was also a part-owner of the hotel at one time.

[116] Sounds like he was referring to COINTELPRO

[117] His predecessor, Duel, had committed suicide.

[118] In 2013, the Dark Shadows Festival sponsored a Caribbean cruise for Halloween, including a stop at the storied Martinique.

[119] The skit is available to view on YouTube: use keywords "Dark Shadow Festival 2016 Skit "Séance Fiction" with Nancy Barrett"

[120] Her husband, Geoff, had recently died of this disease.

[121] This reminded me of how Tabitha King dug the manuscript of *Carrie* out of the trash after Stephen decided it was awful and persuaded him to rework and submit it to a publisher.

[122] See also 2001 Dark Shadows Festival, Day 2

[123] It was the filming location for Collinsport in the 1991 series.

[124] Subsequent to the event, KLS posted a 20-minute version of the interview on Facebook that comprised additional, fascinating details, including Henesy's memories of other cast members and even of receiving geography tutoring from Fritz Lang when he came to the set to visit Joan Bennett.

[125] I wonder if it was the same director John Karlen mentioned at the 2009 Festival during the cast reunion. See 2009 Dark Shadows Festival, Day 2

[126] See 2001 Dark Shadows Festival, Day 3 and 2016 Dark Shadows Festival, Day 3

[127] That scene is in the series, so the censors must have objected to it after it aired.

[128] A few days after the event, the organizers sent out an email thanking attendees that concluded promisingly with, "We hope to see you all again at some point in the future. DS lives on!")

[129] Performed both times by Vera A. Marano

9 798822 740893